Praise for
THE BEST *of the* MARSHALL MEMO
BOOK TWO

"In my 49-year career, I have never met a more voracious reader of education-related literature than Kim Marshall. Since he launched the Marshall Memo almost 17 years ago, Kim has devoured numerous periodicals every week searching for salient articles to summarize and synthesize. Kim's many years of experience as a teacher, principal, district-level administrator and educational consultant undergirds his capacity to spot the most useful, thought-provoking, and timely articles, and enables him to capture their "big ideas" for efficient consumption by busy educational leaders. This book, with coauthor Jenn David-Lang, offers the second compilation of "greatest hits" and deserves a prominent spot on your nightstand or desktop for ready reading and reference."
—Jay McTighe, Author and Consultant, Coauthor with Grant Wiggins of *Understanding by Design*

"Professional reading not a high priority just yet? Think again. School-based leaders and practitioners require relevant, reliable, and contemporaneous information at our fingertips now more than ever; particularly, as we negotiate global health crises and embrace authentic anti-racist strategies in the service of truly realizing the American dream for all. The formidable collection of articles and resources that comprise *The Best of the Marshall Memo: Book Two* fits the bill nicely. Marshall and David-Lang have performed an incredible service on our profession's collective behalf. Now, let's get to reading. There's not a second to waste."
—David J Vazquez, Founder and Master Principal, Bronx Academy for Multi-Media/New York, NY

"The Marshall Memo has been a part of my personal leadership journey since the first publication in 2003. As deputy superintendent and superintendent in the Chelsea Public Schools in Massachusetts for 17 years, the Marshall Memo was my constant companion and go-to source. It was the place for me to learn, reflect, improve, and understand how to lead deep transformational organizational change on behalf of students and families. In 2012, we purchased a district-wide subscription, and the result was immediate and long-lasting. We began to have deeper and richer conversations at every level, and the Memo inspired the entrepreneurial educators in each school with the latest thinking and research from their chosen profession. Thanks to the Marshall Memo, we were able to build and support a transformational culture among our educators. And now Kim Marshall and Jenn David-Lang have compiled the very best of the Marshall Memo in two volumes, with professional learning suggestions for each topic. It feels too good to be true!"
—Mary M. Bourque, former Superintendent, Chelsea Public Schools/Chelsea, MA; 2017 Massachusetts Superintendent of the Year; Director of Governmental Affairs, Massachusetts Association of School Superintendents/Bedford, MA

"If you would like to move discussions of educational practice and policy in your schools from tradition, opinion, and prejudgment to solid research and facts, then ask your faculty, leadership team, parents, and policy makers to study this book. Curated from more than a decade's work by some of the world's leading researchers and practitioners, *The Best of the Marshall Memo: Book Two* is not the place to look for easy answers to complex questions. Rather, it will challenge conventional wisdom, offer divergent perspectives, and provide practical insights that can be applied immediately to some of the most vexing challenges in schools. The chapters could not be more timely, including a thoughtful series of articles about race in schools. Each chapter includes activities for practical application and reflection for a deeply engaging professional learning opportunity. As readers around the globe know, if you haven't read the Marshall Memo, you haven't done your homework."

—Douglas B. Reeves, Author/Consultant, and Founder, Equity and Excellence Institute

"Within the complex and busy schedule of a superintendent and principal, time is precious. The Marshall Memo allows leaders to make research-informed decisions to transform practices within their learning communities. District 4 in New York City was fortunate to have the opportunity to preview Kim Marshall and Jenn David-Lang's book during our monthly principals' book club. These discussions sparked deep conversations and brought to life new ways of tackling current areas of improvement. This morphed into deeper discussion and actions that improved our schools. I look forward to using *The Best of the Marshall Memo: Book Two* in my new learning community, the Norwalk Public Schools, to ignite thought-provoking discussions with my cabinet and school leaders. This book is a must-have for all educational leaders and pedagogues."

—Alexandra Estrella, formerly Community Superintendent, District 4/New York, NY; now Superintendent, Norwalk Public Schools/Norwalk, CT

"The Marshall Memo is a wonderful resource for educators. Every week, it brings together and summarizes the best of education-related writing from a wide array of sources. I always find something of interest in each issue. In this second volume of *The Best of the Marshall Memo,* Kim Marshall and Jenn David-Lang share the best of the best, organized by topics. For example, in a chapter titled "Race and the Education of American Students," there are nineteen article summaries on topics ranging from handling discussions of race in the classroom to helping black males succeed, to culturally responsive teaching. Each summary is well-written and gets right to the core of the issues and effective responses to real problems. The Marshall Memo itself, and the book based on it, put readers into real-life classrooms with real kids. You can almost smell the broccoli cooking in the cafeteria and hear the busses pulling up outside as you read these insightful, inspiring, and pragmatic discussions of issues faced by teachers, principals, and other educators."

—Robert Slavin, Director of the Center for Research and Reform in Education, Johns Hopkins University–School of Education/Baltimore, MD

"There is SO much out there regarding education, especially with current COVID-19 concerns! How do educators know what is the best research-based information on which we can make important and quick decisions? Kim Marshall and Jenn David-Lang succinctly share the most relevant ideas and insights to guide our actions in education. They do the research for us!"

—Kelly Hastings, Principal, Strike Middle School–Little Elm ISD/Little Elm, TX

"Since the beginning of the Marshall Memo, Kim's summaries have always kept me current on the best thinking about good teaching and successful leadership—an invaluable resource. His first book with co-author Jenn David-Lang proved an excellent resource when looking for innovative ideas and the most persuasive studies on current issues. With their new *Book Two*, I have lightning access to the finest minds in our field."

—Jon Saphier, Founder, Research for Better Teaching/Acton, MA

"The Marshall Memo is the holy grail for education. Each week, readers can drink from the unending well of research, analysis, and guidance contained in its pages, offering a pathway on how we can achieve a more equitable educational system. In *The Best of the Marshall Memo: Book Two*, you will find quotes, article summaries, and professional development strategies to answer a range of questions, from assessment and absenteeism to writing and work/life balance. As a subscriber since 2007, I encourage you to quench your thirst this week with this excellent compilation of resources."

—Shahara C. Jackson, Founding Principal, Summit Academy/Brooklyn, NY; currently: doctoral student, Harvard Graduate School of Education–Doctor of Education Leadership program/Cambridge, MA

"I've been a subscriber to Jenn David-Lang's The Main Idea book summaries for years. Her book summaries are salient, insightful, and ready for practical application. More recently, I have added the Marshall Memo to my professional reading and have found its article summaries equally helpful. *The Best of the Marshall Memo: Book One* and *Book Two* allow me to see and digest school leadership best practices with a wide-lens focus. Given the constant demands for educators' time, these books are a practitioner's best friend: efficient and useful."

—Roland Shaw, Principal, Career Education Center Early College/Denver, CO

"As an educator for the last 18 years, I have long appreciated the summaries created by Jenn David-Lang and Kim Marshall. It is crucial to keep up with the latest educational research, but it is impossible for one person to sort through the countless articles, research literature, and books released each year. Their summaries help me to get an overview of a larger variety of resources than I could read on my own and then focus in on those that are most aligned with my work. Having their resources readily available alongside suggestions for professional development in *The Best of the Marshall Memo: Book Two* makes it even easier to find the targeted resources that will help support learning and growth in my unique school community."

—Kimberly Swanson, Principal, Life Sciences Secondary School/New York, NY

"Kim Marshall and Jenn David-Lang have done the heavy lifting for educators by creating a curated guide to the best articles in the field with easy-to-read summaries, links to the original text, and connected professional development activities that are easy to use and share with staff and school communities. Combining Kim's work on the weekly Marshall Memo with Jenn's The Main Idea, a summary of the best books for educators with professional development tools, creates a remarkably valuable synergy—a resource that great educators can use each day."

—Mark Shellinger, Director, National SAM Innovation Project/Louisville, KY

"Daily, the overwhelming amount of information that I receive as an educational leader can make me feel as though I am drinking from a firehose! But on the mornings Kim Marshall's the Marshall Memo or Jenn David-Lang's The Main Idea book summary arrive, the resources in my inbox feel manageable with these two gems. I feel more like I'm slurping from a garden hose! Now, in *The Best of the Marshall Memo: Book Two*, Marshall and David-Lang have taken the best of the last 17 years of Marshall Memos and organized them into three broad areas: mindsets, effective pedagogy, and continuous improvement. With this go-to professional learning resource (along with *The Best of the Marshall Memo: Book One*, of course!), they have once again managed to curate an unwieldy amount of available information into smaller, digestible gems from trusted sources."

—Dawn G. Bentley, Assistant Superintendent for Diversity, Equity, and Inclusion–Acton-Boxborough Regional School District/Acton, MA

"Kim Marshall and Jenn David-Lang have created a resource that is invaluable! As an educator with 29-plus years, the information I have gleaned from *The Best of the Marshall Memo: Book Two* is a must-have, go-to resource for all educators in all fields! Educators will gain a deeper understanding of issues that are at the forefront of today's educational world. Kim and Jenn have done the work and research for you and compiled it into a user-friendly

book! This is a resource that is excellent for professional development and a way to gain deeper understanding surrounding your biggest questions. Without a doubt, this book needs to be on your shelf—or rather, right by your working desk!"
 —Kim Doepker, Principal, Garrison Middle School–Walla Walla Public Schools/Walla Walla, WA

"Every week Kim Marshall provides an invaluable service to educators across the country. He wades through and masterfully distills scores of educational articles that upend antiquated assumptions, deepen understanding, spark debates, and provide concrete, actionable guidance for promoting students' learning and development. His writing is clear, engaging, and vibrant. This book, his second anthology of articles, covers a vast and vital territory, including effective pedagogy, developing teachers' racial and cultural proficiency, and cultivating strong school leadership teams. Take this tour with Mr. Marshall and his coauthor Jenn David-Lang. Their knowledge of learning, teaching, leadership, and schools is remarkably wide and deep, and their hearts are in exactly the right place."
 —Rick Weissbourd, Senior Lecturer, Harvard Graduate School of Education/Cambridge, MA

"Any educator can conduct a Google search and find multiple articles on almost any topic. So, why do we need the Marshall Memo? I'll tell you why. The Internet provides us with *information*, from reliable to ridiculous. That's where the Marshall Memo found its niche. My go-to for educational perspectives and research on most any topic is the Marshall Memo. Why? Because the content has been read, reviewed, and vetted for credibility. I don't have to second-guess the credibility of the research, and Marshall provides a brief, impactful summary of each article. It's designed to inform efficiently. I don't know how they do it, but they do it and do it well. *The Best of the Marshall Memo: Book Two*, written with Jenn David-Lang, is an extension of this mission and should be on the bookshelf of every educator—dogeared, tattered, worn, and highlighted."
 —Ken Williams, Educator/Author/Consultant, Unfold The Soul/Sharpsburg, GA

"Among the jewels in *The Best of Marshall Memo: Book Two* is a chapter entitled "Beliefs About Intelligence and Ability." This collection of research regarding teacher and student mindsets disputes the notion that a student's mental acuity is determined at birth. Instead, it sheds light on the malleability of intelligence, and how parents, teachers and children can train the brain like a muscle to build the self-efficacy a child needs to believe they can excel and have the individual agency to succeed through their own efforts. This chapter, along with the others in *The Best of the Marshall Memo, Book Two*, are a must-read for anyone interested in helping children reach and exceed their potential."
 —Ian Rowe, Resident Fellow, American Enterprise Institute/Washington, DC;
 former CEO, Public Preparatory Network/New York, NY

"The history of American education is littered with examples of silly fads spreading far and wide while common sense and evidence-based practices remain stuck within the four walls of a classroom. The Marshall Memo breaks this tradition by giving educational leaders and their teams the best advice and analysis from around the nation and around the world. And in *The Best of the Marshall Memo: Book Two*, Kim Marshall and Jenn David-Lang give us the very best ideas and research from the Memo's seventeen years."
 —Michael J. Petrilli, President, Thomas B. Fordham Institute/Washington, DC

THE BEST
of the
MARSHALL MEMO

— BOOK TWO —

Ideas and Action Steps to Energize Leadership, Teaching, and Learning

Kim Marshall & Jenn David-Lang

EPIGRAPH BOOKS
RHINEBECK, NEW YORK

The Best of the Marshall Memo: Book Two: Ideas and Action Steps to Energize Leadership, Teaching, and Learning © 2020 by Kim Marshall and Jenn David-Lang

All rights reserved. No part of this book may be used or reproduced in any manner without written permission from the authors except in critical articles or reviews. Contact the publisher for information.

Paperback ISBN: 978-1-951937-58-4
Hardcover ISBN: 978-1-951937-59-1
eBook ISBN: 978-1-951937-60-7

Library of Congress Control Number: 2020916427

Book design by Colin Rolfe

Epigraph Books
22 East Market Street, Suite 304
Rhinebeck, New York 12572
(845) 876-4861
epigraphps.com

This book is dedicated to front-line educators who work every day to bring caring, inclusive, and effective schooling to all students.

Acknowledgments

Kim and Jenn want to thank those who supported and improved this book (and Book One) from earliest conception to last-minute suggestions: Justin Baeder, Paul Bambrick-Santoyo, Joanne Bragalone, Lee Bromberg, Andrew Bundy, Rudd Crawford, Mike Doughty, Karen Drezner, Alex Estrella, Sarah Fiarman, Kate Gagnon, Amelia Gorman, Tom Guskey, Linda Hartzer, Bill Henderson, Jeff Howard, Elizabeth Imende-Cooney, Shahara Jackson, Barry Jentz, the Jewish Education Project Study Group, Mike Lupinacci, Nick Marinacci, Maisie McAdoo, Jay McTighe, Mary Nash, the New York City District 4 Principals' Study Group, Mary Grassa O'Neill, Rob Ramsdell, Doug Reeves, Douglas Rife, Josh Roth, Kate Roth, Jon Saphier, Mike Schmoker, Mark Shellinger, Sue Szachowicz, Nick Tishuk, Betsey Useem, David Vazquez, David Ward, Bob Weintraub, Dylan Wiliam, and Sara Zrike.

The professional learning suggestions following each chapter were written by Jenn David-Lang, except for Chapter Three, which were written by Elizabeth Imende-Cooney; Chapter Seven was largely compiled by Kate Roth.

Kim gives special thanks to Jon Saphier and Jon Schnur, who played a key role launching the Marshall Memo in 2003; to Lillie Marshall, David Marshall, and Colin Turner, who have helped shape the Memo in innumerable ways; and to Rhoda Schneider, who works with me to polish the Memo every week and provides the love, support, brilliance, and common sense that make all things possible.

Jenn is deeply grateful to her family: To my parents, Patricia and Simeon David, who are thoughtful, gracious, and loving leaders in so many aspects of their lives. To my daughters, Zoe and Alexa—each day I am deeply moved by your warm and giving souls—my relationship with each of you is precious. And most definitely to my husband, Tim, who is my lodestar and, at the same time, my best friend.

Contents

Introduction   xiii

A. MINDSETS THAT SUPPORT LEARNING   1

Chapter One: **Beliefs About Intelligence and Ability** 3
Chapter Two: **Students' Social-Emotional Development** 46
Chapter Three: **Race and the Education of American Students** 84
Chapter Four: **Partnering with Families** 134

B. EFFECTIVE PEDAGOGY   171

Chapter Five: **The Five Key Elements of Good Pedagogy** 173
Chapter Six: **What Makes Learning Stick** 203
Chapter Seven: **Proficiency in Reading, Writing, and Oral Language** 233
Chapter Eight: **Differentiation and Personalization** 272

C. EDUCATORS CONTINUOUSLY IMPROVING   311

Chapter Nine: **Results-Focused Teacher Teams** 313
Chapter Ten: **Professional Learning That Works** 352
Chapter Eleven: **Teacher Leadership** 388

Appendix A: Marshall Memo Article-Summaries for "Live" All-Faculty Discussions   423
Appendix B: The Years from Which Marshall Memo Summaries Were Drawn   426
Index   428
About the Authors   435

Introduction

Both of us (Kim Marshall and Jenn David-Lang) have devoted our professional lives to making schools a force for learning, collegiality, and social justice. After a combined total of forty-eight years of classroom teaching and school leadership, we are now coaching principals, consulting with schools and districts, and spreading the word about what works in two online publications. Kim's weekly Marshall Memo, www.marshallmemo.com, summarizes the best articles from more than sixty publications. In The Main Idea, www.themainidea.net, Jenn writes a detailed synopsis of a carefully selected education book each month, accompanied by professional development suggestions. We're "designated readers," curating ideas and research for busy front-line educators.

The Best of the Marshall Memo, Book One and *Book Two*, are the resources we both wish we'd had throughout our careers: a collection of the very best insights on teaching, leadership, and learning. To write these books, our first step was deciding on twenty-two topics that are top-of-mind for PreK–12 educators. It quickly became clear that there was too much material for one book, so we divided them into two groupings of eleven topics. We then scoured the eight thousand-plus article summaries in the Marshall Memo archive, asking which would be the most thought-provoking and helpful for principals, leadership teams, teachers, instructional coaches, consultants, district leaders, and those who train and support educators. We looked for articles that had:

- practical and solution-oriented ideas with convincing evidence of impact;
- vivid stories and quotes from successful classrooms and schools;
- key insights from thought leaders;
- cautionary notes about ineffective practices.

Having chosen the best Memo summaries for each chapter, we sorted them into logical subgroups, found a powerful lead-off quote, posed some questions for reflection, and added a set of professional development suggestions to help readers make immediate use of each chapter's ideas. The big idea of these books: closing the "knowing-doing gap" we've all heard so much about.

The chapters in Book Two fall into three sections. *Mindsets That Support Learning* examines educators' and parents' beliefs about intelligence and ability, students' social-emotional development, race and the education of American students, and partnering with families. The second section, *Effective Pedagogy*, covers key elements of good teaching; what makes learning stick; proficiency in reading, writing, and oral language; and differentiation and personalization. The third section, *Educators Continuously Improving*, looks at results-oriented teacher teams, professional learning that works, and teacher leadership.

Book Two complements Book One, which is also organized in three sections. *The Leader's Toolkit* presents the foundational knowledge any school leadership team needs for strategic planning, making the best use of limited time, and managing emotions and interpersonal relationships. The second section, *More Good Teaching in More Classrooms More of the Time*, covers interviewing and hiring, effective coaching of teachers, conducting difficult conversations, providing effective feedback, and key issues with teacher evaluation. The third section, *Structures for Student Success*, covers positive classroom discipline, planning curriculum units and lessons, effective use of assessments, and new thinking on grading student work.

What are the best ways to use Book Two? You may read it from cover to cover, but it's more likely that you'll zero in on certain chapters when you face an issue on which you'd like more ideas, research, and recommendations. Some examples:

- A school grappling with the issue of race and cultural proficiency;
- A study group looking at teacher leadership;
- Teachers looking for ways to make their team meetings more effective;
- A staff curious about the research on memory and retention of information;
- Parents interested in how they can most effectively improve student learning;
- A committee charged with rethinking differentiation;
- A school leader who wants to improve the quality of professional learning time;
- An external consultant giving administrators insights on emotional intelligence;
- A superintendent determined to improve reading and writing achievement;
- A school board determined to inject social-emotional learning into the curriculum;
- A professional development retreat focused on improving teaching and learning;
- A graduate course preparing aspiring school leaders.

INTRODUCTION

You may also want to share individual article-summaries with colleagues, have teacher teams read and think through articles or a whole chapter, and ask the leadership team or the entire faculty to read article-summaries "live," use a protocol for small-group discussion, and then plan action steps. Or you may want to use the PD ideas at the end of a chapter to structure discussions, reflection, collaborative activities, and overall professional learning opportunities for you and your colleagues.

Each chapter of this book is like a theme issue of an educational journal, but with four important advantages: (a) we were able to cast a much wider net, choosing from almost two decades of articles in numerous publications; (b) Marshall Memo summaries are usually much shorter than the original articles, making it possible to read the key ideas from ten articles in under an hour; (c) tailor-made PD suggestions at the end of each chapter help put the ideas into action; and (d) the book has eleven themes under one cover, putting at your fingertips an extraordinary amount of useful information—visionary and practical, provocative and hands-on, and readily accessible as you and your colleagues wrestle with the myriad challenges of running a good school.

We hope this book, along with Book One, will help foster reflection on your school's purpose and goals, lead you to rethink old assumptions, spark productive debates, elevate the level of discourse, and lead to action steps that improve what students experience in classrooms every day. We're curious to know how you decide to use these chapters, and would be delighted to help in any way we can – or hear your ideas and suggestions. Kim can be reached at kim.marshall48@gmail.com, Jenn at Jenn@TheMainIdea.net.

Kim Marshall and Jenn David-Lang, August 2020

A. MINDSETS THAT SUPPORT LEARNING

Chapter One: **Beliefs About Intelligence and Ability**

Beliefs About Intelligence and Ability   5
How Measures of Intelligence Are Used   13
Developing Efficacy and Wisdom   20
Changing Students' Trajectories   28
Professional Learning Suggestions   33

Chapter Two: **Students' Social-Emotional Development**

Character and Moral Education   48
Worries About Social-Emotional Learning   55
Curriculum Content   60
Programs That Make a Difference   70
Professional Learning Suggestions   78

Chapter Three: **Race and the Education of American Students**

Implicit Bias and Microaggressions   87
Discussing the Undiscussable   96
Challenges for Children of Color   103
Stereotype Threat   109
Cultural Proficiency   114
Professional Learning Suggestions   122

Chapter Four: **Partnering with Families**

Parenting for School Success   136
Home-School Communication   143
Parent-Teacher Conferences   149
Homework and At-Home Activities   154
Professional Learning Suggestions   162

Chapter One: Beliefs About Intelligence and Ability

All those involved in the institution of schooling help to shape who we think we are,
who others think we are, and who we think we can become.
—Beth Hatt

The way people think about intelligence and ability has always played a major role in classrooms. Recent research is pushing our thinking in new directions, but change in schools is slow. The articles in this chapter explore four areas: beliefs about intelligence; how measures of intelligence are used; developing efficacy and wisdom in students; and changing life trajectories.

Beliefs About Intelligence and Ability – Beth Hatt describes a kindergarten class where outside-of-school factors become proxies for how "smart" students are. Carol Dweck describes the impact of a fixed versus a growth mindset on students' academic performance—and the effect of teachers' mindsets on their students. Kathy Liu Sun says that well-intentioned teachers can unconsciously convey fixed-mindset messages about mathematics achievement and explains how they can be changed.

How Measures of Intelligence Are Used – Robert Sternberg refutes outmoded rationales for IQ tests and suggests better ways to describe students' ability, predict how they'll do, and place them in programs. Claude Steele says tests are often used to triage students, with low scorers receiving an inferior education, and suggests better ways to measure and encourage performance. Seana Moran, Mindy Kornhaber, and Howard Gardner say the point of multiple intelligence theory is to teach with students' intelligence profiles in mind. Ben Levin says that, although poverty and other environmental factors are strongly correlated with school failure, many people who grow up with disadvantages do just fine—suggesting that we should never prejudge the potential of any child.

Developing Efficacy and Wisdom – Ellen Usher and Frank Pajares say that a sense of efficacy—a belief in one's own capabilities—is a key factor in students' success. Elaine Allensworth and six colleagues suggest how schools can get students to embrace four learning mindsets: I belong here; I can succeed; I improve through my efforts; and I value the work I'm doing. David Yeager and Gregory Walton describe a simple intervention that had a seemingly magical impact on students' beliefs and performance.

Changing Students' Trajectories – John Hattie provides an update on how and when mindset thinking is most useful in students' and teachers' lives. Daniel Willingham suggests six ways educators can turn around the life pathways of underachieving students. And David Brooks pokes holes in the widely believed "divine spark" theory of genius, proposing instead that brilliant writers and performers start with slightly above-average ability and achieve greatness through effective effort and skillful mentoring.

Questions to Consider

- What is the role of innate ability in children's lives?
- How do beliefs about ability and intelligence affect classroom interactions?
- Is it possible to change educators', students', and families' beliefs about intelligence?

Beliefs About Intelligence and Ability

1 Learning to Be "Smart" in Kindergarten

"All those involved in the institution of schooling help to shape who we think we are, who others think we are, and who we think we can become," says Beth Hatt (Illinois State University) in this *American Educational Research Journal* article. Hatt describes what she learned in a one-year ethnographic study of a kindergarten classroom in a semirural school district in southeastern US with a mix of twenty-five middle- and working-class white, African-American, and Latino children. She spent a total of 865 hours observing the classroom; interviewing teachers, children, and parents; following the students to lunch, recess, and specials; and examining classroom artifacts such as school assessments and report cards.

Right away, Hatt noticed that the teacher, Mrs. Rayburn (all names are pseudonyms), a white middle-class woman, had her own sense of which children were "smart." For example, the child with the highest entering pre-K assessment score was a white boy from a very poor family who had a mild speech impediment. Rayburn openly expressed her low opinion of this boy's intelligence, and by winter break referred him for tutoring. "Here the teacher's implicit theory of smartness trumped her explicit knowledge of intelligence evidenced by pre-K assessment scores," says Hatt. By Christmas in his kindergarten year, the boy had begun to actively dislike school.

Hatt describes two classroom artifacts that were central to student and teacher interpretations of smartness, The Stoplight and the Shoe Tyer's and Phone Number Club:

• *The Stoplight* – On a large poster of a traffic light, each child had a car with his or her name on it. At the beginning of the day, all cars were on green, and children's cars stayed there if they behaved well. If children disobeyed rules, Rayburn or her assistant, Mrs. Daniels, would tell them to move their car to yellow, which meant *You'd better slow down,* or red, which meant *Stop what you're doing and think about what you're doing*. "The student then typically walked to the stoplight with his or her head down, moved the car either to yellow or red (depending on where the car was originally), and most often began to cry," says Hatt. "When I interviewed students, I discovered *every* child defined being smart as 'not having to move your car.' For the children, being smart had come to be closely connected to the stoplight."

Rayburn and Daniels reinforced this by telling misbehaving children that if they made "good choices" and started being smart, they could move their cars back to green. They also chose students for special jobs based on whose cars were on green. Children were keenly aware of everyone's status on the stoplight. Parents reported that the first thing children talked about when they got home was who moved his or her car that day. When Hatt asked, every student was able to immediately identify Natalie, a middle-class white girl, as the child who never had to move her car—and Jackson, an African-American boy, as the one who had to move his car almost every day. On the very first day of the school year, Jackson moved his car to yellow for making "mouth noises." When he cried loudly, he was told to "shut it off" and "cry quietly." "You're in big school now and in big school we cry quietly," said Daniels.

The stoplight was supposed to be an impartial arbiter of student behavior, but Hatt noticed consequences were not doled out in a completely objective manner. "For instance," she says, "white males from middle-class families repeatedly avoided Mrs. Rayburn's surveillance. African-American students, especially black males, who refused a submissive position in the classroom were repeatedly the first to get in trouble and received the harshest reprimands. Hence, being good became about one's relationship with authority and teacher attitude rather than whether one broke rules more than others."

• *The Shoe Tyer's and Phone Number Club* – The second artifact that caught Hatt's attention was a poster with a picture of a shoe and a telephone and a list of the students who could tie their shoes and recite their telephone numbers. "Students did not learn home phone numbers or how to tie their shoes at school," she says. "Mrs. Rayburn and Mrs. Daniels gave parents responsibility for these tasks, refusing to tie students' shoes. If a student could not tie his or her shoes, he or she either had to find someone in the Shoe Tyer's Club to do it or walk around with shoes untied. Children able to tie their shoes were framed as intelligent.

On the first day of school, Daniels noticed a girl tying her own shoes and said, "You're so smart! Did you tie your shoe by yourself? We have a Shoe Tyer's Club. You're gonna be part of it. Two thumbs up!" Jackson, on the other hand, never joined the Shoe Tyer's Club; his mother, a single parent, worked full time while raising him and two siblings. "Membership in the Shoe Tyer's Club was construed as a 'big deal,'" says Hatt, "yet differences in students' home situations and the unfairness of teachers' expectations were left unrealized, unchallenged, and unapologized for. The concept of 'smartness' makes one's ability to tie shoes seem based on one's innate smartness rather than familial circumstances and teacher implementation."

"Smartness was related to a student's prior knowledge of taught material," continues Hatt. "For example, students already able to count to high numbers or who knew the seasons were often called 'geniuses' or were told they were 'so smart.' In addition, when students demonstrated they knew material before it was taught, they were typically given privileges such as getting nap towels first or being first in line. Through the discourse of smartness students were taught being referred to as 'smart' was a form of praise." They made "good choices," were "responsible," and knew how to "do school," which meant they were smart. Privileges like leading the calendar activity every morning and taking part in show-and-tell didn't go to students whose cars weren't on green or students who weren't in the Shoe Tyer's or Phone Number Club.

One day a student brought in a toy snow leopard for show and tell. A boy correctly named the animal and another boy said, "Aren't you smart! You're a genius!" "His words and intonation directly mimicked Mrs. Daniels's when she would tell students they were smart," says Hatt. "Encouraging students to appropriate authoritative discourse in the classroom overshadowed students' own voices, and students thereby became ventriloquists of teachers' voices of authority. Because students adopted teacher discourse, student agency became limited; Mrs. Rayburn in effect became the author of their words, interpretations, and meanings, and students became stratified along the lines of who could best approximate the teacher's authority."

"What is taught in schools includes who 'is' and 'is not' smart and what smartness means," Hatt concludes. "Determinations are based on teachers' expectations mediated by knowledge of students' socioeconomic backgrounds and racial identities …. If we fail to pay attention to how smartness operates in schools and within larger society, we miss a critical opportunity to reimagine and reinterpret smartness, particularly for low-income students and students of color. We also miss the opportunity to explore how we perpetuate it ourselves. We must see smartness as a tool of control and social positioning. Only then can we begin to disrupt smartness in everyday schooling practices, empowering students to frame and author their lives."

"Smartness as a Cultural Practice in Schools" by Beth Hatt in *American Educational Research Journal*, June 2012 (Vol. 49, #3, pp. 438–460), summarized in Marshall Memo 439.

---

2. The Influence of Mindsets

Beliefs about intelligence have a major impact on teaching and learning, says Carol Dweck (Stanford University) in this *Principal Leadership* article. Teachers, administrators, students, and parents tend to see intelligence in one of two ways:

• *Fixed*—How bright you are is determined at birth. "Some students are smart and some are not, and that's that."

• *Malleable*—Intelligence can grow as a result of effort and instruction. "A growth mindset doesn't imply that everyone is the same or that anyone could be Einstein," says Dweck, "but it does imply that everyone's intellectual ability can grow—and that even Einstein wasn't Einstein before he put in years of passionate, relentless effort."

Having a growth mindset is especially important for students who become aware of negative stereotypes about their abilities—for example, many girls (with respect to science and math) as well as many African Americans and Latinos.

To test this theory, Dweck and two colleagues monitored hundreds of New York City students who entered seventh grade with similar math achievement. Over a two-year period, students with a fixed mindset did less well than those who believed their intelligence could be developed, and the achievement gap between the two groups widened with each passing semester.

Why? "Because they believed that their intellect could be developed, students with the growth mindset focused on learning, believed in effort, and were resilient in the face of setbacks," says Dweck. "Students with the fixed mindset, however, worried more about looking smart and not making mistakes, thought that needing to make an effort to learn meant that their intelligence was deficient, and became discouraged or defensive in the face of setbacks because they believed that setbacks reflected limitations in their intelligence." When they got a bad grade on a test, these students thought about cheating on future tests because they believed they didn't have the ability to do well by legitimate means.

Can the growth mindset be taught? Dweck and her colleagues picked seventh graders whose math scores were steadily declining and divided them into two groups:

• Students in the control group were taught study skills in eight workshop sessions;

• Students in the intervention group learned study skills and were also taught about the malleability of intelligence—that the brain is like a muscle and the more it's used, the stronger it becomes—that when they learn something new, their brains form new connections, making them smarter.

"Students were galvanized by the idea that the growth of their minds was under their control," says Dweck. One boy who had been a troublemaker heard this message and said, "You mean I don't have to be dumb?"

Here's what the study revealed. Despite instruction in study skills, the math achievement of students in the control group continued to get worse. Intervention-group students, on the other hand, showed marked improvement. Teachers (who didn't know which students were in which group) immediately noticed the difference in intervention-group students' attentiveness, study habits, motivation, homework completion, and achievement.

Dweck was so impressed with the results of this study (and others like it) that she and her colleagues developed *Brainology*, a software program designed to teach students the growth mindset, and tested it in twenty New York City schools. Virtually all students reported positive changes in their ideas about learning and study habits. "Most exciting," says Dweck, "many reported using the image of their neurons making new connections to motivate themselves in school, saying that they pictured their neurons forming new connections when they paid attention in class and that when tempted to not study, they rejected that idea on the grounds that new connections would not be formed."

Do teachers' mindsets make a difference? Dweck reports a German study showing that low-achieving students who had teachers with the fixed-ability mindset made no progress, whereas students with teachers with the growth mindset improved to become moderate or high achievers. Dweck has found that adults with the fixed-intelligence mindset tend to make snap judgments, quickly putting people into categories. "This means that once they have decided that someone is or is not capable," she says, "they are not very open to new information to the contrary …. When teachers decide that certain students are not capable (or when principals decide that certain teachers are not capable), they may not take steps to help them develop their potential."

The differences in how students are treated by teachers is stark. For example, when dealing with a student who just failed the first math test of the year, a fixed-mindset teacher typically comforts the student and says that not everyone can be good at math. A growth-mindset teacher tells the student he or she can do better, offers encouragement, and teaches specific learning strategies and study skills. Students are quick to pick up on their teachers' beliefs, says Dweck, as was demonstrated by a study of college athletes. "The more that athletes thought their coaches believed in hard work over natural talent," she says, "the better the athletes did that year. Students know what educators value—they pick up their messages and act on them …. It is essential for educators to communicate that they hold a growth mindset."

The way adults deliver praise is particularly powerful in shaping mindsets. "When adults praise students' intelligence after a student performs well," says Dweck, "they send a fixed-mindset message: you're intelligent and that's what I value in you. When adults praise effort (or strategies), however, they send a growth-mindset message: you can build your abilities through effort." Students who are praised for ability go to pieces when they fail or encounter frustrating tasks. Students who are praised for effort are undaunted by challenges and continue to improve.

Recent studies show that teachers' mindsets are key to closing the achievement gap. Students who believe that ability is fixed are haunted and discouraged if they believe their racial group or gender is less able. But students who see ability as malleable, even if they know their race or gender has underperformed historically, are willing to work on changing history through effective effort and working with their teachers. "When black and Latino students adopt a growth mindset," says Dweck, "their grades and achievement test scores look more similar to those of their nonstereotyped peers. When female students adopt a growth mindset, their grades and achievement test scores in mathematics become similar to those of their male classmates. In these studies, every group seemed to benefit from holding a growth mindset, but the stereotyped groups gained the most."

"Mindsets and Equitable Education" by Carol Dweck in *Principal Leadership*, January 2010 (Vol. 10, #5, pp. 26–29), summarized in Marshall Memo 319.

3. Walking the Talk on Growth Mindset in Mathematics Classes

"We live in a society that perpetuates the myth that math ability is an innate gift," says Kathy Liu Sun (Santa Clara University) in this article in *Teaching Children Mathematics*; "some people have it, and others don't." To counter fixed-mindset thinking, many educators make a point of using growth-mindset language—*You can grow your math brain*—and emphasize the importance of hard work, persistence, and learning from mistakes.

But these exhortations are not enough, says Sun: "Decades of research have shown that people's beliefs are shaped through social interaction; experiences shape beliefs and vice versa. When we tell children what to believe, we are placing the onus of having a growth mindset on them without carefully attending to how our instruction and classroom contexts might shape their beliefs."

For example, Sun has observed teachers who use growth-mindset language but unwittingly send fixed-mindset messages in some of these ways:

- When a student answers a question incorrectly, the teacher quickly moves on to another student (the message—we need to protect students from feeling embarrassed when they make a mistake).
- Some students are not given the opportunity to engage in rigorous math tasks (the message—only certain students can grow their math ability).
- Conceptually difficult tasks are given only to students who finish quickly (the message—speediness is a marker of math prowess).
- Several leading questions funnel students' thinking toward the solution (the message—students can't solve challenging problems independently).

How can this happen when the teacher has good intentions? It's because we all have growth and fixed mindsets in our heads, says Sun, and specific classroom situations can trigger instructional actions that undermine our growth-mindset aspirations. This happens most frequently when we assess student work, see student mistakes and struggles, and compare students to one another. "When these triggers arise," she says, "we should pause to reframe our response to better align with growth-mindset math instruction." Some general suggestions:

• *Put more emphasis on sense-making and less on procedures.* Focusing on procedures and spending a lot of time on drill and practice conveys a narrow definition of success—that it's all about doing the procedure correctly. Procedural accuracy is only a small part of mathematics, and rewarding it distorts the broader curriculum and limits the number of students who can excel, thereby conveying a fixed-mindset message. The alternative is posing questions, making students' thinking visible, unpacking ideas, making sense of problems, emphasizing conceptual understanding, allowing multiple ways to demonstrate mastery, and saying again and again that there is more to math than procedures and speed.

• *Stop using deficit language.* Labeling students "high" or "low," "fast" or "slow," undermines the message that all students can improve at mathematics, says Sun. The key is communicating the expectation "that all students can contribute to mathematics learning, not just those who have traditionally been successful." One strategy is *assigning competence*—making a point of recognizing the contribution a student made to a group that includes students at different achievement levels. "Assigning competence is more than praising behavior," Sun explains, "it clearly acknowledges how a student's contribution extends the mathematical thinking. The more we open our eyes to see what all students are capable of accomplishing mathematically, the more they will continue to impress us."

• *Maintain rigor as students struggle and make mistakes*. "We may talk about the importance of failure in our classes," says Sun, "but we can unconsciously counter this message by superficially dealing with a mathematical error by making the math 'easier' for students who are struggling." These actions are well-intentioned, but they water down the curriculum and don't support growth mindset. "Responding to struggle and failure in ways that genuinely support a growth mindset," she continues, "means that we give challenging work, persist alongside students when they make an error, and maintain the intellectual rigor of the task." When students falter, Sun encourages teachers to ask open-ended questions, press for conceptual understanding, unpack misconceptions, explore students' thinking, talk through errors in a nonjudgmental way, and emphasize the role of struggle in growing our mathematical brains. We should also seek out "low-floor," "high-ceiling" tasks that maintain intellectual rigor while being accessible to all students. The website https://www.youcubed.org offers math problems along these lines.

"Beyond Rhetoric: Authentically Supporting a Growth Mindset" by Kathy Liu Sun in *Teaching Children Mathematics*, March 2018 (Vol. 24, #5, pp. 280–283), summarized in Marshall Memo 727.

How Measures of Intelligence Are Used

④ Five Reasons to Stop Using IQ Tests

In this article in *School Administrator*, Robert Sternberg (then at Cornell University) remembers how intimidated he was by the IQ tests he was given as an elementary school student in the late-1950s and early-1960s—and how badly he did. "Today, no reason exists to subject elementary-school pupils to IQ tests," he says. "All the reasons that once seemed so important have since proved to be invalid…. Education leaders can demonstrate their own intelligence by steering away from IQ tests." Here are the justifications that have been offered for these tests in the past, followed by Sternberg's pushback and suggested alternatives:

• *Old rationale 1—To identify a person's true native ability.* The idea was that IQ tests could find what a child was capable of, irrespective of upbringing and social and cultural opportunities. So far, says Sternberg, all the ways we've tried to measure raw intelligence haven't worked.

- Tests that contain questions on vocabulary, arithmetic, puzzle-solving, and general information inevitably measure a person's past social and cultural opportunities.
- Tests that use abstract geometric symbols produce results that are highly correlated with the amount of Western schooling a child has had.
- Tests that measure reaction-time or brain-functioning turn out to be unreliable.

The bottom line is, says Sternberg, "No existing IQ or other test can separate past opportunities from test performance."

In addition, New Zealand researcher James Flynn has found that, over time, improvements in nutrition, medical care, technology, and schooling have produced a steady increase in IQ around the world—about three points every decade, or thirty points between 1900 and 2000. "The only reason the average IQ remained at one hundred," says Sternberg, "is that test publishers kept renorming the tests, setting new expectations for what constituted a score at a certain level."

The alternative, he suggests, is asking students questions in areas they're interested in and know something about, for example—with Eskimo children, hunting, gathering, and fishing; with Kenyan schoolchildren, herbal medicines against malaria and other diseases. "If you understand the child's knowledge and cognitive skills in a domain that is really meaningful to the child," says

Sternberg, "you will learn what the student is capable of doing in other domains if only motivated to pursue those other domains."

- *Old rationale 2—To predict school achievement.* Since past performance is often a good predictor of future performance and IQ tests contain material that students should have learned in previous grades, it seemed logical that IQ performance would tell us how well a child would perform down the road. But what if a student had mediocre or ineffective teachers in the grades just prior to an IQ test, or had a traumatic experience that affected motivation and performance? For these reasons (and also test anxiety), a one-time IQ assessment can be an inaccurate measure of a student's future potential.

The alternative, says Sternberg, is to look at past achievement—course grades and achievement-test scores—and take into account the context of those data. "This is why college admissions officers increasingly rely on high-school grades to predict college success," he says.

- *Old rationale 3—To identify students with learning disabilities.* The theory was to compare a student's IQ score with his or her achievement in reading, math, or another domain and look for discrepancies. This sounds reasonable, but it hasn't worked well, says Sternberg. "The intelligence test inevitably measures verbal skills, whether in listening, reading, writing, or speaking—so you cannot cleanly separate out measurement of intelligence from measurement of reading (obviously, a verbal skill). The same holds for other content domains." It turns out that students with a disability function about the same in their supposedly disabled domain as students who perform poorly for reasons unrelated to disability; IQ doesn't matter.

The alternative, says Sternberg, is giving diagnostic assessments in specific areas, figuring out what needs to be improved, and working with students in those areas. "You don't need the IQ test and never did," he says. "If you want to know whether the deficit is domain-specific, just compare performance in that domain to performance in other domains. That's all you really need."

- *Old rationale 4—To identify students for gifted programs.* The idea was to select students who are truly smart, not just hard workers and high achievers. "But IQ and achievement tests all measure about the same thing," says Sternberg. For example, results on SAT, ACT, and IQ tests are all highly correlated, even though the first two are supposed to be achievement tests. "You don't need an IQ test to identify students for gifted programming," he says.

The alternative is first to decide what you mean by "gifted." If you say "high IQ," you haven't thought things through, says Sternberg. As Howard Gardner, Joseph Renzulli, David Feldman, and others have found, there's a lot more to giftedness than what IQ tests measure. Performance-based assessments do a much better job—that is, looking at students' actual work in the target area for giftedness—reading, math, science, art, music, and others.

• *Old rationale 5—To draw comparisons of your students to those in other districts.* "However you make comparisons across districts," says Sternberg, "don't use IQ tests. They won't tell you what you want to know." The alternative: use achievement tests.

"Alternative Measures of Intelligence" by Robert Sternberg in *School Administrator*, April 2016 (Vol. 73, #4, pp. 33–35), summarized in Marshall Memo 633.

---

5. Using Tests to Promote Equity

In this article in *The Nation*, Stanford social psychologist Claude Steele argues that tests are often used to triage students: "Based on tests taken early in life," he says, "lower-scoring people and groups get less educational attention, or more of a basic-skills education aimed at bringing them to minimal levels of competence, whereas high-scoring people and groups get a richer education supported by more resources—better-trained teachers, more academically challenging curriculums, better opportunities, etc. The rationale for this … has always been a kind of meritocratic efficiency: maximizing the return on society's investment by investing the most resources in those who, as indicated by test scores, have the ability needed to benefit from those resources."

Steele has seven recommendations to help loosen the grip of this innate ability paradigm on the academic fate of less-advantaged students:

• Stop using the word "ability" in schools and replace it with words like "skill level" or "educational readiness."

• Focus high expectations and demanding and enriched schooling on lower-scoring students, especially in the early grades. "Emphasize getting them to identify with and be excited about their schooling."

• When schools find it necessary to group students by achievement, keep it from being a life sentence. "Provide clear curricular pathways to upward mobility and see to it that some students ascend that pathway as role models."

• Use tests based on specific curriculums to which students have access, and discourage the use of ability and aptitude tests.

• Develop and use multiple, low-stakes, cumulative, curriculum-based assessments.

• Find ways to measure students' motivation and desire, breadth of life experience, work discipline, maturity, and other important attitudes—and use the data to help all students achieve.

• Enlist coalitions of school, church, community, and civil rights organizations to extend out-of-school educational learning opportunities (e.g., tutoring, after-school and weekend programs, test-prep courses, etc.) for minority and low-income children.

Steele concludes: "Major changes in society and in organizations happen when everyone starts working on the same thing. Then things tip. This was true of the *Brown* decision itself. It finally happened when lawyers, social scientists, judges and educators all came together to make it happen. To get rid of test-score gaps, the same coming together is necessary."

"Not Just a Test" by Claude Steele in *The Nation*, May 3, 2004 (Vol. 278, #17, pp. 38–41), summarized in Marshall Memo 40.

6. Ideas and Cautions About Multiple Intelligences

In this *Educational Leadership* article, Seana Moran, Mindy Kornhaber, and Howard Gardner note that Gardner's theory of multiple intelligences has been over-applied in some schools. It's *not* a good idea to group students for instruction based on the eight or nine intelligences, they say, and it's *not* a good use of a teacher's time to prepare eight or nine separate entry points for each lesson.

"Multiple intelligences theory," explain Moran, Kornhaber, and Gardner, "was originally developed as an explanation of how the mind works …. The last thing we wanted to do was to multiply the educators' job nine-fold. Rather, we sought to demonstrate that because students bring to the classroom diverse intellectual profiles, one 'IQ' measure is insufficient to evaluate, label, and plan education programs for all students."

"Adopting a multiple intelligences approach," they continue, "can bring about a quiet revolution in the way students see themselves and others. Instead of defining themselves as either 'smart' or 'dumb,' students can perceive themselves as potentially smart in a number of ways …. The greatest potential of a multiple-intelligences approach to education grows from the concept of a *profile* of intelligences. Each learner's intelligence profile consists of a combination of relative strengths and weaknesses among the different intelligences: linguistic, logical-mathematical, musical, spatial, bodily-kinesthetic, naturalistic, interpersonal, intrapersonal, and [the latest intelligence recently added to the list] existential."

There are two distinct types of intelligence profiles, explain Moran, Kornhaber, and Gardner:

• *A laser profile* – One or two intelligences are very strong and the others relatively weak. The challenge with laser students is if their strong areas are not those assessed by high-stakes tests; teachers have to decide whether to build on the strengths or remediate their weaknesses so they can pass the tests.

• *A searchlight profile* – These students show less pronounced differences in their intelligences. The challenge with them is deciding which area to develop and choosing a career or life path.

The authors liken the interaction of the nine intelligences to a symphony orchestra; as in music, the different "instruments" can interfere with each other, compensate for one another, and enhance each other—adding to or subtracting from overall performance:

• *Interference* – For example, a student may have good social skills (strong interpersonal intelligence) but fail to reach out to others because of weak linguistic intelligence.

• *Compensation* – For example, a student's strong bodily-kinesthetic intelligence may allow him or her to give good oral presentations despite convoluted sentence structure (the authors note that several US presidents fit this profile).

• *Enhancement* – For example, strong spatial intelligence may improve a student's ability to conceptualize a math problem (as was true of Albert Einstein), and strong musical intelligence may help a student write and appreciate poetry.

So a child's overall aptitude is not the sum of the nine intelligences, since interference, compensation, and enhancement may be holding back or augmenting some areas. The teacher's challenge is to look for strengths and weaknesses through the lens of multiple intelligences theory and teach in ways that improve a child's overall performance.

For example, what if three students are having difficulty understanding a story? An unskilled teacher might tackle their problem with a single approach (reading the story over slower and louder). But each student might be having trouble for different reasons: the first may be struggling because of poor reading comprehension skills; the second because of difficulty understanding the dynamics among the story's characters; and the third may have such strong spatial intelligence that he has trouble seeing beyond the physical pattern of the letter symbols (a problem that the young Pablo Picasso experienced). Skilled teachers need to know how to diagnose students' difficulties and orchestrate experiences that help them succeed.

MINDSETS THAT SUPPORT LEARNING

This may include getting students to use their strengths to help classmates with weaknesses—as often happens in the adult workplace. "As the amount of information that students—and adults—must process continues to increase dramatically," conclude Moran, Kornhaber, and Gardner, "collaboration enables students to learn more by tapping into others' strengths as well as into their own. In ideal multiple intelligences instruction, rich experiences and collaboration provide a context for students to become aware of their own intelligence profiles, to develop self-regulation, and to participate more actively in their own learning."

"Orchestrating Multiple Intelligences" by Seana Moran, Mindy Kornhaber, and Howard Gardner in *Educational Leadership*, September 2006 (Vol. 64, #1, pp. 22–27), summarized in Marshall Memo 152.

⑦ Misreading Children's Futures

In this *Kappan* article, Ben Levin (University of Toronto) says it's true that poverty, parental education, family interactions, and ethnicity are strongly correlated with students falling behind in school, dropping out, and not going on to post-secondary education. But all too many educators and parents make the mistake of using these aggregate correlations to predict that a particular eight-year-old will not be successful in life.

This is a serious error, says Levin: "Many studies have found that a large number of students defy negative expectations based on their backgrounds." One Canadian study found that nearly 40 percent of young adolescents with very low reading skills were in post-secondary education six years later, and an American study of failing third graders found that more than 75 percent eventually graduated from high school, including 70 percent from low-SES families. "In every study of this kind," he says, "a significant number of students who seem to have everything against them end up having good results."

It's not that poverty and other factors aren't important, or that we shouldn't be working hard to alleviate social inequalities, or that schools can by themselves overcome entering disadvantages, says Levin: "What is important to keep in mind is that we just don't know how people's lives will turn out …, So, while many people in jail come from high-poverty backgrounds, most people who grow up in poverty … don't end up in jail. For educators, there is a very heartening message in this research. What it says, very clearly, is that our work matters." Small actions by teachers—or just doing their jobs well—can make a tremendous difference to struggling children.

"All this means that schools and educators should be very cautious about thinking we can predict any student's future," Levin concludes, "and even more cautious if that belief leads us, or the student, to lower expectations."

"The One-Legged High Jumper and the Perils of Prediction" by Ben Levin in *Phi Delta Kappan*, October 2012 (Vol. 94, #2, pp. 74–75), summarized in Marshall Memo 458.

Developing Efficacy and Wisdom

8   Helping Students Develop Self-Efficacy

In this article in the *Review of Educational Research*, professors Ellen Usher and Frank Pajares examine the literature on how students develop a sense of efficacy. People's beliefs about their capabilities powerfully affect the way they behave, including:
- The effort they put forth;
- How readily they correct their errors;
- How efficiently they solve problems;
- How willing they are to seek help;
- How well they monitor and assess the quality of their work time;
- The degree of anxiety or serenity they feel as they tackle life's challenges;
- The persistence and perseverance they display in the face of difficulties;
- How they attribute causation;
- Their achievement-goal orientation;
- The choices they make;
- Their level of optimism;
- Their self-concept and sense of worth;
- Their academic achievement across all areas and levels;
- Their college major and career choices.

In short, self-efficacy beliefs are a key factor in students' success. But what is the source of these positive (or on the flip side, negative) beliefs? Usher and Pajares say the research points to four contributing factors:

• *Mastery experiences* – Students' own past successes and failures are important to their sense of competence or incompetence. Mastery experiences are especially powerful when students overcome obstacles or succeed at challenging tasks.

• *Comparing oneself to others* – A second source of self-efficacy comes from stacking their performance up against that of peers. Usher and Pajares say that adolescents are more susceptible to this than elementary-school students.

• *Encouragement from others* – Supportive messages from trusted parents, teachers, and peers boost self-efficacy, particularly when feedback encourages students to measure success in terms of personal growth, not in comparison to others.

• *Emotional and physiological states* – Students can interpret their level of anxiety, stress, and fatigue as a sign of personal competence or incompetence. Previous success or failure can act as a self-fulfilling prophecy.

Which of these is most important to self-efficacy? Usher and Pajares analyzed thirty years of research and found that mastery experiences was by far the most influential. This was true across all studies, all domains, and all types of student (the median correlation was .58). Experiencing mastery was so powerful, say the authors, because "this experience contains the most authentic evidence as to whether students can master subsequent tasks in related domains."

There are links among the four sources, which is not surprising. A student who writes an excellent essay, for example, will probably compare favorably to classmates, receive praise from teachers and parents (and perhaps from peers), and have positive feelings going into the next writing assignment.

Some students can get locked into negative beliefs about their abilities, say Usher and Pajares, thinking they're fixed and unchangeable: "There are few things sadder to a teacher or parent than being faced with capable young people who, as a result of previous demoralizing experiences, self-imposed mindsets, or mindsets imposed before birth, have come to believe that they cannot succeed at a task or activity when all objective indications show that they can." The key is for educators and parents to help young people "become agents of their own psychological health."

"Sources of Self-Efficacy in School: Critical Review of the Literature and Future Directions" by Ellen Usher and Frank Pajares in *Review of Educational Research*, December 2008 (Vol. 78, #4, pp. 751–796), summarized in Marshall Memo 267.

9. Fostering Positive Academic Mindsets

"Four learning mindsets are particularly important in supporting students' academic behaviors, persistence, and performance on academic tasks," say Elaine Allensworth, Camille Farrington, Molly Gordon, David Johnson, Kylie Klein, Bronwyn McDaniel, and Jenny Nagaoka in this report from the UChicago Consortium on School Research:

- I belong in this learning community.

MINDSETS THAT SUPPORT LEARNING

- I can succeed at my schoolwork.
- My ability and competence grow with my own efforts.
- The work has value for me.

When students have these positive mindsets, they apply themselves and are much more likely to be successful in school.

How do students come to embrace these beliefs? Home and community influences are important, but so is the school climate created by administrators and teachers. Conversely, if students believe they don't belong, can't succeed or get smarter, and aren't working on worthwhile endeavors—they are likely to disengage and do less well.

Students' academic mindsets can vary through the course a school day. Moving from one class to another, they may feel more or less confident and accepted, depending on learning conditions and instructional practices used by their teachers. Students at different stages of development enter classrooms with a wide range of psychological "backpacks." In each situation, say the authors, students are asking themselves, "Is school something that 'people like me' care about and are good at?"

What are the PD implications of this complex web of instruction, classroom climate, and student attitudes? "Teachers get better at their craft by reflecting on how their own classrooms might support or interfere with the development of positive student mindsets," say the authors. "Over time, positive mindsets and active engagement in learning not only support deeper understanding and better academic achievement, but they also tend to increase students' enjoyment of learning and development of positive academic identities."

Allensworth and colleagues conclude by suggesting nine teacher actions that develop positive academic mindsets and turn around negative mindsets:

- Setting predictable norms and routines that support respectful interactions among students and teachers;
- Sending clear messages about the nature and purpose of learning and the role of mistakes in the learning process;
- Explicitly connecting new material to students' prior knowledge;
- Helping students "see themselves" in the work by connecting it to their interests, goals, and cultural identities;
- Developing trust by listening to students and responding to their input;
- Creating opportunities for student autonomy and choice as well as for collective learning;

- Showing students models of high-quality work and conveying confidence that they can produce equally good work;
- Providing frequent and specific feedback on students' work and opportunities for students to apply that feedback and progressively improve their performance;
- Using fair grading practices that emphasize growth and improvement.

"Supporting Social, Emotional, and Academic Development: Research Implications for Educators" by Elaine Allensworth, Camille Farrington, Molly Gordon, David Johnson, Kylie Klein, Bronwyn McDaniel, and Jenny Nagaoka, UChicago Consortium on School Research, October 2018, summarized in Marshall Memo 758.

10. Changing Students' Thoughts and Feelings About Achievement

In this article in *Review of Educational Research*, David Yeager and Gregory Walton (Stanford University) look at several successful social-psychological interventions:
- Middle-school students attended eight sessions teaching them that the brain is like a muscle and grows with effort; the students experienced a sharp increase in math achievement for the rest of the school year, compared to no gains for control group students, who were taught study skills.
- A one-hour session designed to buttress the sense of social belonging of African-American college students boosted their GPA over the next three years, cutting the black-white achievement gap in half.
- A fifteen-to-twenty-minute writing exercise in which students were asked to reflect on their core personal values reduced the gap in grades between African-American and white students by nearly 40 percent at the end of the semester, and with booster writing assignments these gains persisted for two years.

How is it possible, ask Yeager and Walton, for brief and low-cost interventions to produce such significant improvements? How can targeting students' thoughts, feelings and beliefs boost academic achievement? Skeptics dismiss the experiments as snake-oil solutions to complicated problems, unworthy of serious consideration.

Yeager and Walton contend that the effects are real and long-lasting "because they target students' subjective experiences in school, because they use persuasive yet stealthy methods for conveying psychological ideas, and because they tap into recursive processes present in educational environments." The authors urge researchers and educators to get a better understanding of why these interventions work and take them to scale.

Yeager and Walton suggest an analogy: A passenger jet weighing many tons is speeding down a runway. We know that it has engines, wings, and a pilot—but how can it possibly get off the ground? The answer is the shape of its wings. They're sculpted (curved on top, flat on the bottom) to create aerodynamic lift. If they were shaped differently, the plane would never fly. Similarly, for struggling students to do well in school, we have to engineer powerful, hidden psychological factors (like the shape of a plane's wings) to provide "lift."

Pursuing this analogy, Yeager and Walton explain how well-planned social-psychological interventions can have such a big impact:

• It's often hard to see the key forces that are at work. "We do not see air flowing over a wing," they say. "Nor do we directly observe how negative intellectual stereotypes or beliefs about the nature of intelligence affect students. We may see the power of these processes only when they are altered."

• People assume that large problems require large solutions. How could small interventions affect problems as daunting as the racial/economic achievement gap? But, say Yeager and Walton, every attitude and behavior exists within a complex field of forces—a "tension system"—in which some forces promote achievement while others restrain it. By increasing a student's motivation to learn or removing a psychological barrier to learning, a small intervention can have an amazing impact—provided that the basic conditions of learning are there.

• It's difficult to see how brief messages can affect students' beliefs and behavior when they receive so many other messages from adults that don't have much effect. The answer is that the messages contained in social-psychological interventions are heat-seeking missiles that go straight to core student beliefs that drive behavior.

• "A key to understanding the long-lasting effects of social-psychological interventions," say Yeager and Walton, "is to understand how they interact with recursive processes already present in schools, such as the quality of students' developing relationships with peers and teachers, their beliefs about their ability, and their acquisition of academic knowledge. It is by affecting self-reinforcing recursive processes that psychological interventions can cause lasting improvements in motivation and achievement even when the original treatment message has faded in salience."

Yeager and Walton go on to give detailed descriptions of four social-psychological interventions that have dramatically improved student achievement. The first two are designed to change students' attributions about academic setbacks, the third and forth to address stereotype threat—students' fear that being a member of a particular gender or racial/ethnic group will lead to low achievement.

• *Intervention 1* – Timothy Wilson and Patricia Linville developed a brief program to teach entering college students that poor academic performance is normal when starting off in a new school, that it doesn't reflect lack of ability, and that grades typically improve as the student adjusts to the new school. One group of students had the intervention, watching videotapes of upperclassmen talking about how their initial jitters and problems wore off as they settled in. The control group saw videotapes of the same upperclassmen talking about their academic and social interests with no mention of first-year grades. A year later, students in the treatment group had higher GPAs than the control group, and this effect gained strength with each passing year; treated students were 80 percent less likely to drop out of college. This intervention has been replicated many times with diverse populations, including adolescents.

• *Intervention 2* – Claudia Mueller and Carol Dweck gave fifth-grade students a moderately difficult set of logic problems. When students were finished, one group (randomly assigned) was praised for intelligence: "That's a really high score. You must be very smart at these problems." The other group was praised for effort: "That's a really high score. You must have worked hard on these problems."—or received neutral praise: "That's a really high score." Next, all students were given a much more difficult set of problems, and all students performed poorly. Then all students were given another set of problems comparable in difficulty to the first set. Here's what happened:

- Students who had been given neutral praise performed at the same level they had on the first set of problems.
- Students who were praised for intelligence solved 30 percent fewer problems and asked to do only easy problems from then on.
- Students who were praised for effort did better than they had the first time around and asked for more challenging problems in the future.

Other studies, including an intervention with middle-school students in New York City who were taught to think of their brains as a muscle that can be developed, have shown similar results.

• *Intervention 3* – At the beginning of a school year, Geoffrey Cohen and colleagues had white and black seventh-graders identify two or three values that were personally important and write about why those values mattered to them. A control group of students was asked to identify values that were not important to them and write about why they might matter to someone else.

Over the next two years, black students in the treatment group earned significantly higher grades than control-group students, reducing the black-white achievement gap by about 40 percent. Improvements in students' GPAs persisted for two years. This intervention has been replicated in numerous studies, including with women in science and Latino adolescents.

• *Intervention 4* – Walton and Cohen gave first-year college students information indicating that students of all ethnicities worried at first about whether they belonged, but that these worries dissipated in time. Students in the treatment group participated in activities designed to drive this message home, including writing essays for the next year's incoming students. Black students in the treatment group improved their grades from sophomore through senior year, cutting the black-white achievement gap by 50 percent. Black students' diaries showed that their sense of belonging improved immediately. Similar interventions have had equally strong effects in studies of female undergraduate engineering students and African-American middle-school students.

Yeager and Walton address two questions on how these interventions bring about significant improvements in student performance:

• *How do the interventions change academic outcomes in the short term?* "They do so," say the authors, "by precisely targeting students' experience in school from the student's perspective and by using impactful delivery mechanisms." To a researcher or a teacher, the interventions may not seem like much. "But to a student sitting at a desk in the third row worrying about whether a poor test score means she is stupid or whether others will reduce her to a negative stereotype, an experience like learning that the brain can grow and form new connections when challenged or being invited to describe personally important values may feel quite 'large'…. These strategies can induce deep processing and prepare students to transfer the content to new settings."

Another factor contributing to the success of these interventions is that they are "stealthy"—that is, they are brief and get at students' belief systems indirectly, not through overt preaching. If students perceive that teachers or other adults think they need help, that perception can undo the impact of an intervention. "In this way," say Yeager and Walton, "the teaching of academic content in school is fundamentally different from the delivery of psychological interventions. Academic content is complex and taught layer on layer. The more math students are taught, in general, the more math they learn. Changing students' psychology, by contrast, sometimes requires a lighter touch."

• *How do social-psychological interventions affect student outcomes over long periods of time?* By setting in motion self-perpetuating social, psychological, and intellectual processes, say Yeager and

Walton. "As students feel more secure in their belonging in school and form better relationships with peers and teachers, these become sources of support that promote feelings of belonging and academic success later. When students achieve success beyond what they thought possible, their beliefs about their potential may change, leading them to invest themselves more in school, further improving performance and reinforcing their belief in their potential for growth." Teachers have higher expectations, students are placed in higher groups, grades improve, and they go from strength to strength.

Yeager and Walton conclude by saying that these interventions can be replicated at scale, but only if they're done right. "There are not quick fixes that can be administered broadly without consideration for local contexts or the meaning students make of them," they say. "When an intervention is taken to scale without the theoretically essential components, it will not have the intended effects." It can't be a worksheet to be handed out or a lesson to "get through." The psychological *experience* needs to be replicated, not the specific activities.

"Social-Psychological Interventions in Education: They're Not Magic" by David Yeager and Gregory Walton in *Review of Educational Research*, June 2011 (Vol. 81, #2, pp. 267–301), summarized in Marshall Memo 389.

Changing Students' Trajectories

11 Useful Applications of Mindset Thinking

In this article in *Education Week*, John Hattie (University of Melbourne) describes what he learned in conversations with Carol Dweck during her recent visit to Australia, for which he prepared by rereading her academic research. Dweck said she was distressed about ways her work on mindsets has been misinterpreted. Her corrections:
- A person is not wholly fixed mindset or growth mindset.
- A growth mindset is not the same as having an open-minded or positive outlook on life.
- It's not all about praising and rewarding effort and believing everyone is smart.
- A fixed mindset is not an adequate explanation for failure; it's not a personality trait.
- Upbeat mission statements and "I can ..." posters won't accomplish very much.

Misinterpretations of the concept may explain why meta-analyses of growth-mindset programs haven't shown major gains, says Hattie: "Too often the interventions are generalized rah-rah attempts to develop a language of growth vs. fixed with little or no attention to the conditions that optimally invoke the strategies of growth; too often the low effects reinforce just how hard it is to change long-developed coping strategies to failure, error, and challenge. The low effects do not mean we should ignore the power of understanding when to be growth and when it is okay to be fixed."

Dweck has never claimed that there is a "growth-mindset" state of mind; it's not an attribute of a person—rather, a way of thinking in a particular circumstance. We're all a mixture of growth and fixed mindsets, says Dweck, and her research has focused on identifying *when* and *where* a growth mindset is most helpful. Some examples:
- When we don't know the answer or feel we don't have the ability to do something;
- When we make an error, reveal deficiencies, or try to hide a mistake;
- When we are criticized, feel threatened, get defensive;
- When we experience failure or do poorly compared to others;
- When we are anxious or in conflict with peers, in "fight or flight" mode;
- When we are overconfident.

In these situations, a fixed mindset can produce suboptimal responses. Activating a growth mindset is a much more effective coping strategy—especially when the challenge is difficult but well-defined and sustained effort and deliberate practice are likely to produce a successful outcome.

The corollary: having a growth mindset is less helpful for easy tasks, or with tasks that are novel and ill-defined and require both creativity and the willingness to abandon unsuccessful strategies. A growth mindset "may not help if it leads to more practice on a task using already failed strategies," says Hattie, "and seeking experts to provide alternative strategies may be more effective than believing that 'I can' and other growth notions." If you encounter a brick wall, a growth mindset may lead to a headache.

"Misinterpreting the Growth Mindset: Why We're Doing Students a Disservice" by John Hattie in *Education Week*, June 28, 2017, summarized in Marshall Memo 693.

---

12. What It Takes to Boost the Performance of Low-Achieving Students

"Americans, like other Westerners, tend to view intelligence as a fixed attribute, like eye color," says Daniel Willingham in this article in *American Educator*. "If you win the genetic lottery, you're smart, but if you lose, you're not." Eastern cultures, including China and Japan, view intelligence as malleable: you can get smarter through effective effort. Which do psychologists believe is the correct view? While it's true that there are differences in children's intelligence, says Willingham, "intelligence can be changed through sustained hard work." Scientists now believe that the genetic role in intelligence is relatively modest.

Here's an example of how we can mistake the role of genes. Identical twin boys are separated at birth and adopted by two different families. By the end of high school, each is an outstanding basketball player. If researchers tracked down the twins, they would notice this striking similarity and might conclude that basketball prowess was genetic. But they would be wrong. The twins did share a genetic characteristic: they were unusually tall. They did well in informal basketball games around their neighborhoods because their parents put up basketball nets at home, and the boys got lots of practice shooting hoops. Each was recruited for his junior-high basketball team and got more playing time. It was practice, not genes, that accounted for their prowess.

"The key idea here is that genetics and the environment interact," says Willingham. "Small differences in genetic inheritance can steer people to seek different experiences in their environments, and it is these environmental differences, especially over the long term, that have large cognitive consequences."

The implications for schools are enormous. Educators need to realize that the genetic intellectual endowment of lower-achieving students often differs very little from that of higher-achieving students. "But they probably differ a good bit from your other students in what they know, their motivation, their persistence in the face of academic setbacks, and in their self-image as students," says Willingham. "I fully believe that these students can catch up, but it must be acknowledged that they are far behind, and that catching up will take enormous effort." Here are his suggestions for closing the gaps:

• *Praise effort, not ability.* Students need to be taught that intelligence is under their control and can be developed through hard work. This message can be sent by praising effective work rather than innate intelligence. It's also important to avoid insincere praise, which devalues the currency.

• *Teach students that hard work pays off.* Willingham shares a conversation he had with one of his students who was on the football team and devoted a lot of time to football practice, neglecting his studies (quoted verbatim):

- Willingham: Is there a player on the team who has a lot of natural ability, but who just doesn't work very hard, goofs off during practices, and that sort of thing?
- Student: Of course. There's a guy like that on every team.
- Willingham: Do the other players respect him?
- Student: Of course not. They think he's an idiot because he's got talent that he's not developing.
- Willingham: But don't they respect him because he's the best player?
- Student: He's not the best. He's good, but lots of other guys are better.

"Academics is just the same," says Willingham. "Most people have to work really hard at it. There are a few who get by without working very hard, but not many. And nobody likes or respects them very much." Most people instinctively understand the relationship between hard work and talent development in other fields but need to have the parallel explicitly drawn in the realm of intellectual development.

• *Treat failure as a natural part of learning.* To develop intellectually, students need to take on tasks that are a little beyond their reach, which means being able to deal with failure and use it as feedback. Michael Jordan once said, "I've missed more than nine thousand shots in my career. I've lost almost three hundred games. Twenty-six times, I've been trusted to take the game-winning shot and missed. I've failed over and over and over again in my life. And that is why I succeed." Teachers need to stress the importance of learning from failure and model this themselves.

• *Don't take study skills for granted.* Willingham suggests that teachers make a list of all the tasks they ask students to do at home and then analyze the skills they need to complete that work successfully. Do they know how to study for a quiz? Do they know how to assess the importance of different things they've read and heard and seen? Do they know how to plan and organize their time?

• *Be realistic about what it will take.* Low-achieving students need to work harder than higher-achieving students to catch up. They need time and support to pull that off.

• *Show students you believe they can improve.* This can be in direct statements of support and caring, and indirectly by not praising second-rate work. The hidden message in phony praise is, "Good job – for someone like you." A better follow-up comment would be, "I appreciate that you finished the project on time, and I thought your opening paragraph was interesting. But I think you could have done a better job organizing it. Let's talk about how."

"Can We Make School More Enjoyable—and Effective—for 'Slow' Students Too?" by Daniel Willingham in *American Educator*, Spring 2009 (Vol. 33, #1, pp. 10–11), summarized in Marshall Memo 280.

---

13. How Geniuses Are Made

In this *New York Times* article, David Brooks contrasts the "romantic" view of genius—a "divine spark" in a few remarkable individuals like Mozart and Einstein—with the modern scientific view, which he says is "more prosaic, democratic, even puritanical" and "pierces the hocus-pocus." According to Brooks, "What Mozart had … was the same thing Tiger Woods had—the ability to focus for long periods of time and a father intent on improving his skills. Mozart played a lot of piano at a very young age, so he got his 10,000 hours of practice in early and then he built from there …. The key factor separating geniuses from the merely accomplished is not a divine spark. It's not IQ, a generally bad predictor of success, even in realms like chess. Instead, it's deliberate practice. Top performers spend more hours (many more hours) rigorously practicing their craft."

Here's how Brooks describes the developmental trajectory of a highly accomplished writer:

• In childhood, verbal ability is slightly above average—just enough to gain some sense of distinction.

MINDSETS THAT SUPPORT LEARNING

• The child happens to meet a writer with whom he or she shares some biographical traits and a sense of affinity—perhaps having the same birthday or coming from the same town or ethnic group. This gives the child "a glimpse of an enchanted circle" he or she might someday join.

• An early loss like the death of a parent can have the effect of infusing "a profound sense of insecurity and fueling a desperate need for success."

• With this ambition, the child reads novels and biographies that provide core knowledge of the field, creating mental groupings such as Victorian novelists, magical realists, Renaissance poets, and so on. "This ability to place information into patterns, or chunks, vastly improves memory skills," says Brooks, allowing the budding adolescent to "see new writing in deeper ways and quickly perceive its inner workings."

• The next stage is focusing intently on technique, in this case on getting better at writing through writing a lot. "By practicing in this way," says Brooks, "performers delay the automatizing process. The mind wants to turn deliberate, newly learned skills into unconscious, automatically performed skills. But the mind is sloppy and will settle for good enough. By practicing slowly, by breaking skills down into tiny parts and repeating, the strenuous student forces the brain to internalize a better pattern of performance."

• At this point it's important for the maturing writer to have a mentor who provides a constant stream of feedback, correcting even the smallest errors and pushing tougher challenges. By now the developing writer is redoing problems dozens of times, ingraining habits of thought that will be crucial to understanding and solving future problems.

This view of how genius develops "takes some of the magic out of great achievement," says Brooks, but he believes we need to be redirected from the old, innate-ability paradigm. "Public discussion is smitten by genetics and what we're 'hard-wired' to do," he says. "And it's true that genes place a leash on our capacities. But the brain is also phenomenally plastic. We construct ourselves through behavior …. It's not who you are, it's what you do."

"Genius: The Modern View" by David Brooks in the *New York Times*, May 1, 2009, summarized in Marshall Memo 285.

Professional Learning Suggestions for Chapter One: Beliefs About Intelligence and Ability

Fostering a Positive Mindset in Your School

When students believe they can't learn, it's likely they won't. Just about everything students say and do comes from their beliefs. To add a second layer, the teacher's own beliefs about intelligence and student ability also deeply influence whether students learn or not. When observing classes, Kim and Jenn frequently see the powerful impact—both positive and negative—of teachers' explicit and implicit beliefs about student abilities. The PD activities below are designed to help teachers better understand what mindset looks like, explore their own mindsets, and plan for ways to foster a growth mindset in students.

I. Understanding Mindset and Its Impact on Students

These first few activities help teachers better understand what mindset is and how it affects students' beliefs.

A. Anchor teachers' ideas about intelligence in their own experiences.
Have teachers think about and discuss the following questions in pairs:
- Think about a time you faced a significant challenge. How did you respond? Think about a failure. How did you react? Think about mastering a skill. What was the experience of mastering a skill like for you?
- Ellen Usher and Frank Pajares (article-summary 8, "Helping Students Develop Self-Efficacy") share a few factors that research shows contribute to one's beliefs about self-efficacy. Think back to your childhood. Were your own beliefs about self-efficacy influenced by: a) *mastery experiences* (your successes or failures), b) *comparing yourself to others* (stacking up your own performance against that of peers), or c) *encouragement by others* (supportive messages from parents, teachers, or peers)? Note that the authors say that mastery experiences *most* influence a student's sense of self efficacy.

- Think about your students. Do you think a certain mindset is particularly affecting certain students and their approach to learning?
- Be honest, where do you fall in your belief about whether intelligence can be attributed to genes or the environment on a scale of one (genes) to ten (environment)?

B. *Further understand mindset and consider how mindset affects students' beliefs and actions.*

1. To help teachers develop the fuller understanding of mindset popularized by Carol Dweck, have them read article-summary 2 ("The Influence of Mindsets") and use the following protocol to discuss it. Make sure they walk away with a clear understanding of "fixed" versus "growth" (called "malleable" in the article-summary) mindset:

Three Levels of Text Protocol
Modified from the School Reform Initiative
http://schoolreforminitiative.org/doc/3_levels_text.pdf

Goal: To help teachers understand *mindset* and the implications for their teaching and their classrooms by reading the article on three levels: literal level, interpretation level, and implication level.

1. Teachers read the summary of the article in the chapter and underline passages that resonate with their ideas about and experiences with mindset.

2. Do one to three rounds (five minutes for each round). Each round consists of—
   - One person shares the following (for up to three minutes total):
     Level 1: Read aloud the underlined passage(s) and what it means. (Read a passage no one has shared yet).
     Level 2: Say what s/he thinks about the passage (interpretation, connections to own experience with *mindset*).
     Level 3: Say what s/he sees as the implications for addressing mindset in the future.
   - The group responds to what has been said (for up to two minutes total).

After reading and discussing the article-summary with the protocol, ensure that teachers have a clear idea of how mindset affects student *beliefs* by having them fill out the following chart alone or in pairs:

PROFESSIONAL LEARNING SUGGESTIONS FOR CHAPTER ONE

How Does Having a Fixed or Growth Mindset Affect Student *Beliefs*?		
How would you view…	…if you had a *fixed* mindset	… if you had a *growth* mindset
Ability/Intelligence		
Success and Failure		
Enjoyment of a challenging activity		
Learning		
Effort		
Other:		

2. With teachers, discuss the fact that your mindset affects more than just your *beliefs*, it also affects your *actions*, as many of the article-summaries suggest. Ask teachers how two students might respond differently to a low grade on a test. What would each *say* and *do*? Note: there's a sample response below.

Students with a Fixed Mindset	*Students with a Growth Mindset*
SAY – "What's the point of taking these tests when I'm just too dumb anyway." DO – The student might not study the next time, or cheat next time, because the student believes s/he is just too dumb.	SAY – "I guess I didn't really know the material." DO – The student might ask for help studying next time, ask the teacher if s/he may retake the test, or put more effort into studying.

Next, ask teachers to discuss how having a *fixed* or *growth* mindset might affect a student's study habits, motivation, homework, and achievement.

C. Discuss ways teachers inadvertently reinforce certain beliefs about intelligence.

1. Have teachers read the Beth Hatt article-summary 1 ("Learning to be 'Smart' in Kindergarten") and the Kathy Liu Sun article-summary 3 ("Walking the Talk on Growth Mindset in Mathematics Classes") and discuss the following:
- In these two article-summaries, what are some ways that teachers inadvertently reinforce certain beliefs about intelligence?
- What other factors have you seen teachers value that suggest to students that they are

"smart" (e.g., arriving on time or writing neatly) or "dumb" (e.g., giving easier assignments to some students)?
- What's the difference between an adult praising a student's *effort* versus praising a student's *ability*?
- If you were a school leader and observed Mrs. Rayburn's class (from Hatt article-summary 1), what feedback would you give her?

2. The Kathy Liu Sun article-summary 3 is a great one for a math team. Before reading it, ask the math teachers to take a stab at filling in the chart that follows—that is, to consider what the underlying *message* might be when math teachers engage in the common behaviors on the left. It's okay if they aren't sure and can't fully fill it out. Next, have the team read the Kathy Liu Sun article-summary 3 and use the Three Levels of Text protocol introduced earlier to discuss it. After this discussion, teachers can go back to the chart if they didn't complete it. Finally, give the math teachers time to come up with ideas for developing a growth mindset in their classes—and here's another resource, from Jo Boaler, that might help: https://www.youcubed.org/.

Teacher Action	Inadvertent Message to Students
When a student answers incorrectly, the teacher quickly moves to another student.	
Some students are not given the opportunity to engage in rigorous math tasks.	
Conceptually difficult math tasks are only given to students who finish quickly.	
The teacher provides leading questions to point the student to the answer.	

II. How Ability Testing Affects Students

For years educators have seen ability testing (like the IQ test) as objective and neutral. We now know that they are neither. Below are two ways for teachers to understand and counter the effects of these types of tests.

PROFESSIONAL LEARNING SUGGESTIONS FOR CHAPTER ONE

A. Understand the detrimental effects of ability testing on students.

Have teachers read Robert Sternberg article-summary 4 ("Five Reasons to Stop Using IQ Tests") and Claude Steele article-summary 5 ("Using Tests to Promote Equity") and discuss:

- What are some of the problems with the age-old IQ tests *and* the ways these tests are used?
- Discuss how tests can have a long-lasting negative impact on students.
- Why is it particularly important to pay attention to the effects of ability testing on girls (in math and science), African-American, and Latino students?

B. Choose three actions to counter the harmful effects of ability testing.

First, have teachers read Claude Steele article-summary 5. Next, in pairs, have teachers discuss and choose the top three suggestions (from the box below) for countering beliefs about innate ability that they believe work best in your school:

Actions to Counter Harmful Effects of Ability Testing

- Stop using the word "ability" and use "skill level" or "educational readiness" instead.
- Hold high expectations and provide challenging curriculum for lower-scoring students, particularly in younger grades.
- If you must group students by achievement, don't group students in those groups forever with no way out.
- Discourage aptitude tests and instead use tests based on specific curriculums to which students have had access.
- Develop and use multiple, low-stakes, curriculum-based assessments.
- Find ways to measure students' motivation, work discipline, maturity, and other attitudes—and use the data to help all succeed.
- Enlist community, church, and civil rights organizations to extend out-of-school learning opportunities (tutoring, afterschool, weekend, test-prep courses, etc.) for minority and low-income students.

III. Implications for Teaching—How to Instill a Growth Mindset in Students

Now teachers should have a clear understanding that "People's beliefs about their capabilities powerfully affect the way they behave" (Usher and Pajares). In this section, teachers will begin to

MINDSETS THAT SUPPORT LEARNING

think about the implications of this for their classrooms. How might they influence students' sense of self-efficacy or students' beliefs about intelligence?

A. Have teachers choose the ways they feel most compelled to influence students' beliefs.

Have teachers read the following list of fourteen ways mindset or sense of self-efficacy affects people outlined in the Ellen Usher and Frank Pajares article-summary 8 ("Helping Students Develop Self-Efficacy").

Then ask them, from these many behaviors (in the chart below) that are affected by a student's sense of self-efficacy, to choose three that they think are the *most* damaging to students. Why? Which three do they feel, as teachers, most compelled to influence? How?

Fourteen Ways Students' Sense of Self-Efficacy Affects:		
1. The effort they put forth;	6. How readily they correct their errors;	11. How efficiently they solve problems;
2. How willing they are to seek help;	7. How well they monitor and assess the quality of their work time;	12. The degree of anxiety or serenity they feel as they tackle life's challenges;
3. The persistence and perseverance they display in the face of difficulties;	8. How they attribute causation;	13. Their achievement-goal orientation;
4. The choices they make;	9. Their level of optimism;	14. Their self-concept and sense of worth.
5. Their academic achievement across all areas and levels;	10. Their college major and career choices;	

B. Have teachers craft language that reinforces a growth mindset.

A number of the article-summaries mention the importance of changing the way we compliment students from praising *ability* to praising *effort*. See: Dweck article-summary 2 ("The Influence of Mindsets"); Yeager and Walton article-summary 10 ("Changing Students' Thoughts and Feelings About Achievement"); and Willingham article-summary 12 ("What It Takes to Boost the Performance of Low-Achieving Students").

PROFESSIONAL LEARNING SUGGESTIONS FOR CHAPTER ONE

Share with teachers the results of the experiment in Yeager and Walton article-summary 10, in which two groups of students were either praised for effort or intelligence on one set of problems. When both groups were given a second set of more challenging problems, the effort group performed *better* the second time and the intelligence group solved 30 percent fewer challenging problems in the second set.

Have teachers fill out the third column in the chart that follows, alone or in pairs, by crafting the language they could use to ensure they praise student *effort* rather than *ability*:

Praise	How Students Internalize This	What We Could Say Instead
"You learned that so quickly! You're so smart!"	*If I don't learn something quickly, I'm not smart.*	
"Look at that drawing. Is he the next Picasso or what?"	*I shouldn't try drawing anything hard or they'll see I'm no Picasso.*	
"You're so brilliant, you got an A without even studying!"	*I'd better quit studying or they won't think I'm brilliant.*	

C. Beyond language, what else can teachers do to foster a positive academic mindset?

The Allensworth et al. article-summary 9 outlines four crucial mindsets that are key to promoting positive academic behaviors in students. Have teachers look at these four mindsets and brainstorm implications for their teaching and classrooms:

Four Key Mindsets Students Should Have	Implications for Teaching and Classrooms
1. I belong in this learning community.	
2. I can succeed at my schoolwork.	
3. My ability and competence grow with my own efforts.	
4. The work has value for me.	

After teachers have brainstormed their own ideas, have them read the nine suggested teacher actions in the Allensworth et al. article-summary 9 (and reprinted below) and choose three to implement. As teachers choose, remind them that Usher and Pajares (article-summary 8) analyzed thirty years of research and found that the factor that is *most important* in helping students develop a positive sense of self-efficacy is experiencing mastery.

Nine Teacher Actions That Develop Positive Academic Mindsets

- Set predictable norms and routines that support respectful interactions among students and teachers.
- Send clear messages about the nature and purpose of learning and the role of mistakes in the learning process.
- Explicitly connect new material to students' prior knowledge.
- Help students "see themselves" in the work by connecting it to their interests, goals, and cultural identities.
- Develop trust by listening to students and responding to their input.
- Create opportunities for student autonomy and choice as well as for collective learning.
- Show students models of high-quality work and convey confidence that they can produce equally good work.
- Provide frequent and specific feedback on students' work and opportunities for students to apply that feedback to improve their performance.
- Use fair grading practices that emphasize growth and improvement.

D. Have teachers develop a lesson plan to introduce the growth mindset to students.

As Dweck (article-summary 2) found in her research, the growth mindset *can* be taught to students. Give teachers a solid block of time as a work period to collaboratively design a lesson to introduce mindset to students. Teachers can work collaboratively across grades or disciplines since this lesson does not need to be specific to a particular content area or grade level. They may wish to choose from the following ideas:

PROFESSIONAL LEARNING SUGGESTIONS FOR CHAPTER ONE

Ideas to Include in a Lesson Plan to Introduce Mindset to Students

- Teach students the science that shows the brain continues to grow and change (neuroplasticity).
- Share picture books that promote the growth mindset. Teachers can search online for "growth mindset picture books."
- Have the teacher and/or the students give real-life examples of times they have learned from failure or have succeeded due to effort. Or share examples about famous people like the one Willingham shares in article-summary 12 about Michael Jordan: "I've missed more than 9,000 shots in my career. I've lost almost 300 games. Twenty-six times, I've been trusted to take the game-winning shot and missed. I've failed over and over and over again in my life. And that is why I succeed." Teachers can search online for "famous failures."
- Have students search online for quotes about the growth mindset and create posters for the class.
- See the mindset-boosting videos on Youcubed.org or other videos like "The Power of Yet."
- Have students create a poster comparing the "growth" versus "fixed" mindset with language *they* can use to reinforce their own growth mindset:

    Fixed-mindset comment: "I'm just bad at math."

    Growth-mindset comment: "I just haven't mastered this math topic *yet*."
- Take a look at this growth-mindset lesson plan available free from Khan Academy, which includes links to videos: https://cdn.kastatic.org/KA-share/Toolkit-photos/FINAL+Growth+Mindset+Lesson+Plan.pdf

IV. The Leader's Role in Creating a Growth-Mindset School

While it's useful to have individual teachers foster a growth mindset within their own classrooms, it is even more powerful when the principal builds a culture that supports a growth mindset across the entire school. Below are four activities you can reflect on alone as the leader or use with a leadership team.

MINDSETS THAT SUPPORT LEARNING

A. Assess your school—do you already have a growth-mindset culture?

Would you describe your school environment as more in line with the growth or fixed mindset? Look at the questions below to help you assess your school environment:

> - Is there room for staff (or students) to make mistakes and learn from them?
> - Do leaders and teachers look honestly at the brutal realities of what's not working at the school? Do they ask tough questions to probe into and reveal these realities?
> - Do teachers and staff receive regular feedback? Is this feedback judgmental or presented in a way that promotes learning?
> - Do the principal and the school leaders receive regular feedback?
> - How does the staff generally respond to this feedback?
> - Is there a big emphasis on staff graduating from a fancy college? Is there an emphasis on talent? Or does the school send the message that learning and perseverance are valued?
> - Have resources (time, money) been put into developing a leadership team? Have mentoring or other programs been put into place to develop staff (suggesting a belief in the potential of people to grow)? Or does the school operate with the belief that there is one great genius at the top and the rest of the staff are there to carry out the leader's vision?
> - Does the leader surround him/herself only with people who support the leader? Or are there any critics in leadership positions at the school?
> - Are the school's leaders presented as resources for learning?

B. Model the growth mindset as the leader.

Modeling is one of the most powerful ways to set the tone for a positive mindset about learning and growth. Together with your leadership team, read this entire chapter and create a list of five things you can all commit to that will model a growth mindset for the school community. These might be anything from sharing a book you are reading to showing that you are continually learning, to ending each meeting by asking for feedback.

PROFESSIONAL LEARNING SUGGESTIONS FOR CHAPTER ONE

Five Growth-Mindset Practices the Leaders Will Model
1.
2.
3.
4.
5.

C. Come to consensus on ten ways to promote a growth mindset throughout the school.

Together with the leadership team, or a special task force to support growth mindset, read this entire chapter and come up with ten ways to promote a growth mindset that all teachers will commit to improving. You may want to first bring a draft of this to the entire staff so they can tweak and fine-tune it so that you have their buy in. Then create a poster for the staff room and consider having "mindset intervisitations" for teachers to give each other feedback on ways they see growth mindset supported in each other's classrooms. Below is an example of what this might look like.

MINDSETS THAT SUPPORT LEARNING

Top Ten Ways Our Staff Promotes a Growth Mindset

1. *Model the growth mindset:* "I put so much effort into this lesson plan so I'm sure it's going to be a good one!" "Let's work on a challenging problem we can really learn from."

2. *Don't label yourself or others:* "Oh, I'm so bad at math," or "She's such a good speller!" Refrain from using labels for ability like "high" and "low."

3. *Praise effort and struggle not intelligence:* "I'm so pleased that you persevered on that challenging problem." "This final paper is excellent. You can see the results of all of those drafts you struggled through."

4. *Emphasize the joy of learning for its own sake:* "I loved learning about a topic last night that was completely new to me."

5. *Point out the effort of famous people:* Ask students why Michael Jordan was such an amazing basketball player. Then point out how many thousands of hours he practiced.

6. *Normalize failure as a necessary part of growth:* When students get a test back, give them time to reflect on what they got wrong, why they got it wrong, and how they can now learn the material. When students make a mistake in front of the class, "Thank you—that mistake gives me an opportunity to teach everyone an important point."

7. *Help students create concrete plans for growth:* If students receive a failing grade with no prospects for improvement, they are more likely to succumb to a fixed mindset. Hand out action plans *before* tests/assignments so students can have a plan of attack—and give out another one *after* the test/assignment to give students concrete steps to learn what they do not know.

8. *Hold high expectations and provide high-rigor tasks for all:* Be aware of your bias—are you sending different messages about capability to girls, black and Latino students, or students from lower socio-economic backgrounds?

9. *Do everything so students succeed academically (provide clear goals, models of high-quality work, regular and honest feedback with time for revision, etc.):* Research shows that mastery experiences are powerful in shaping the student mindset, "I can succeed at my schoolwork."

10. *Take time to build student belonging in the classroom:* Build trust, listen carefully, and create the kind of class culture in which students believe, "I belong in this learning community."

PROFESSIONAL LEARNING SUGGESTIONS FOR CHAPTER ONE

D. Hire for growth mindset.

It's much harder to develop growth mindset in your teachers than it is to hire those who have a growth mindset to begin with. See the chapter in *The Best of the Marshall Memo: Book One* about hiring or read through this chapter on your own and develop three interview questions or tasks you could use to ascertain whether a candidate has a growth or fixed mindset about him/herself or his/her students.

Interview Questions to Detect Growth Mindset in Teacher Candidates
1.
2.
3.

Chapter Two:
Students' Social-Emotional Development

The goal of education is not acquiring knowledge alone, but developing the dispositions to seek and use knowledge in effective and ethical ways.
—David Light Shields

Research has confirmed what parents and educators have always known: academic preparation is not enough to ensure life success. Equally important are the "soft skills"—empathy, tenacity, self-control, optimism, and more. There's quite a lot of research and anecdotal evidence on social-emotional development, but applying it day to day is a challenge many schools are only beginning to address. The Covid-19 crisis and its aftermath have shone a bright light on these issues. We've seen more clearly than ever the inequities and social-emotional challenges that must be addressed.

The articles in this chapter fall into four groups: character and moral education; cautions on social-emotional learning; curriculum content; and programs that make a difference.

Character and Moral Education – David Light Shields says teachers and a school's culture should foster students' intellectual character, moral character, civic character, and performance character. Jay Greene argues that if advocates of social-emotional learning connect it to its roots in character education and religion, there will be more impact on students and more connections with families and local communities. Joel Westheimer says it's not enough for schools to teach students to be personally responsible and participate in civic life; we also need to raise their consciousness on issues of social justice.

Worries About Social-Emotional Learning – Angela Duckworth says that noncognitive skills such as "grit" are important to students' future success and can be taught, but cautions against using measures of social-emotional skills for high-stakes accountability. Grover "Russ" Whitehurst argues that there are three reasons to tap the brakes on implementing "soft" skills in schools: vague definitions, distinguishing innate personality traits from behavior, and the tendency to overdo accountability.

Curriculum Content – Paul Tough says students who have experienced toxic stress can achieve in school if they are led to embrace these beliefs: I belong in this academic community; my ability and competence grow with my effort; I can succeed at this; and the work has value. Daniel Willingham identifies students' ability to self-regulate as a key success factor and describes the ways parents, teachers, and schools can foster this ability. Hunter Gehlbach argues that social perspective-taking—the ability to make sense of other people's thoughts and feelings—is the most important social-emotional skill. Rebecca Bailey and three colleagues advocate specific grade-by-grade content for social-emotional learning programs and say schools need to be more responsive to students' in-the-moment needs and experiences and address SEL issues throughout the school.

Programs That Make a Difference – Jeffrey Benson and Rachel Poliner describe some key factors that make for successful middle- and high-school advisories. Mara Schanfield gives practical advice on implementing an advisory program, including mission, logistics, curriculum, governance, and accountability. Karyn Gorski describes how competitive debating helps students acquire three forms of cultural capital: using critical feedback; analyzing complex ideas; and being resilient in the face of failure. And Jan Hoffman describes a summer camp designed to help adolescent girls deal with the pressures of "Girlworld" and become more assertive, confident, and authentic.

Questions to Consider

- Are social-emotional skills innate, or can they be taught by families and schools?
- How much responsibility do schools have to teach social-emotional skills?
- Can schools repair the damage when students have experienced trauma?

Character and Moral Education

① Four Facets of Character

"We have too often equated excellence of education with the quantity of the content learned, rather than with the quality of the character the person develops," says University of Missouri–Saint Louis professor David Light Shields in this article in *Phi Delta Kappan*. "The goal of education is not acquiring knowledge alone, but developing the dispositions to seek and use knowledge in effective and ethical ways. When we focus on the character of the learner, rather than the content of learning, we address what's likely to be sustained through time and circumstance."

Shields argues that the true purpose of education is to develop intellectual, moral, civic, and performance character in students and the collective character of the school. "Together," he says, "the four forms of personal character define what it means to be a competent, ethical, engaged, and effective adult member of society. Isn't that what we want from our education system?" Here are his comments on each facet:

• *Intellectual character* – A person who is strong in this area is curious, open-minded, reflective, strategic, skeptical, and truth-seeking, says Shields. These are qualities that span different school subjects and extend to all parts of life. When teachers are focused on building intellectual character, they tend to use more inductive, exploratory methods rather than rote learning, making clear *why* students are being asked to learn curriculum content.

• *Moral character* – "At its core, moral character reflects a disposition to seek the good and right," says Shields. "The goal is to develop a disposition to seek goodness, not inculcate a specific list of preferred virtues." He sees the school's role as helping students become sensitive to moral considerations and gain "the cognitive capacity to think deeply and clearly about moral issues and principles."

• *Civic character* – "A thriving nation depends on citizens who participate in governance and civic life," says Shields, noting that developing civic character has always been one of the primary goals of U.S. schooling. This includes knowing how government works, but also developing "a capacity for self-transcendence," he says. "It requires a disposition to consider the common good and to work toward it in collaboration with others." For schools, this means "cultivating respect for freedom, equality, and rationality; an appreciation of diversity and due process; an ethic of participation and service; and the skills to build the social capital of trust and community."

- *Performance character* – The dispositions embedded in this kind of character are perseverance, diligence, courage, resilience, optimism, initiative, attention to detail, and loyalty—all of which help people manage themselves and do their best. These qualities can work for good or ill, says Shields: "A person could be courageous in stealing cars or persistent in hiding the truth. One can be loyal to ignoble people." So performance character—developed through young people's work in school, athletics, music, art, and other domains—needs to be harnessed to moral ends.

To support the development of students' individual character, schools need a *culture of character*, says Shields: "What we seek in terms of individual virtues must be developed simultaneously as group norms."

- To develop intellectual character, a school needs a culture of thinking.
- To develop moral character, it needs a culture of love and justice.
- To develop civic character, it needs a culture of service and engagement.
- To develop performance character, it needs a culture of quality and excellence.

The individual virtues are constantly interacting with the school's culture, he says, each enhancing the other.

"Character as the Aim of Education" by David Light Shields in *Phi Delta Kappan*, May 2011 (Vol. 92, #8, pp. 48–53), summarized in Marshall Memo 386.

2. Rethinking Social and Emotional Learning

In this American Enterprise Institute paper, Jay Greene (University of Arkansas) salutes the goals of social and emotional learning (SEL), but says this new label "represents a set of educational priorities that are as old as education itself." In the past it was often called character education. Greene believes that SEL advocates won't achieve their goals "if they fail to acknowledge the moral and religious roots of SEL, do not consider its history and how past efforts have managed to succeed, and attempt to reinvent those past efforts from scratch on a technocratic foundation that is at odds with what allows SEL to be effective." In fact, he says, embracing previous incarnations may make social-emotional learning more appealing and motivational to many educators and parents.

Greene recalls the cardinal virtues described by Socrates in *The Republic*—prudence, courage, temperance, and justice—which were later incorporated into Christian theology. There is

MINDSETS THAT SUPPORT LEARNING

almost a one-to-one correspondence with the core competencies identified by the Collaborative for Academic, Social, and Emotional Learning (CASEL), but SEL advocates have rebranded the traditional virtues, de-emphasizing teaching character and morality and the religious overtones. Here's how Greene sees the "translation" of the age-old virtues to the modern, secular lingo.
- Prudence: Responsible decision-making, which includes identifying and solving problems, reflecting, and ethical responsibility;
- Courage: Self-awareness, which encompasses self-confidence, growth mindset, and self-efficacy;
- Temperance: Self-management—including impulse control, diligence, grit, and self-discipline;
- Justice: Social awareness and relationship skills—embracing empathy, respect for others, and teamwork.

SEL proponents seem to be attempting a fresh start, says Greene—distancing their precepts from historical thinking. "But a fresh start for SEL stripped of its moral and religious roots is neither possible nor desirable," he argues. "Moral and religious ideas are inherent in SEL, which is why they have always been connected."

In 1940, says Greene, there were well over one hundred thousand school districts in the US, and local school boards had to be responsive to their often-small communities. Although schools were nominally secular, they had plenty of religious overtones: Christian holidays, pledges invoking God, and character education. Today, there are fewer than fourteen thousand school districts in the nation, and school boards work with much larger districts with greater religious and cultural diversity. In addition, state and federal mandates to raise student achievement provide boards with a rationale for focusing on academics, not character education. The result has been less emphasis on the "soft skills" in US public schools.

"Even if people don't understand why character education disappeared over the past few decades," says Greene, "they noticed and were alarmed by its absence. The SEL movement is a reaction to this educational void. But rather than learning from and building on its long history, SEL advocates seem determined to build their effort from scratch on a secular and technocratic basis."

Greene sees four problems with the current implementation of SEL in schools. First, without the moral dimension, there's the possibility that social-emotional learning could be used for amoral purposes. For example, diligence, grit, and self-management (temperance) could be employed to ruthlessly dominate others. Having a value-based and ethical goal is important.

Second, exercising SEL is impossible in certain circumstances. Preaching self-efficacy and grit in a math class is an empty exercise if the curriculum and the teaching are ineffective. "Expecting students to pull themselves up by their bootstraps when they have no boots can be quite damaging," says Greene. "Context matters for SEL."

Third, there's the challenge of motivating students to put SEL ideas into practice. "Why should students be conscientious?" asks Greene. "Why should they believe they can improve outcomes for themselves and others through their own effort? Why should they be honest, punctual, and careful in their work? Simply telling students that these are desirable qualities does not make them believe it. Telling them that their future employers will reward them is clearly insufficient." Historically, religious beliefs have provided the motivational fuel for *why* people should be concerned with others and exert effort, and why they should be honest, punctual, and diligent. That is what's behind the term "Protestant work ethic."

Finally, Greene believes the psychological basis for SEL is not robust. "How is grit really different from conscientiousness or effort?" he asks. "How is growth mindset really different from locus of control or self-confidence? … Because the psychological concepts are fuzzy and the measures are highly sensitive to context, any attempt to centrally command and control progress toward SEL goals is a fool's errand. These SEL measures are also easily gamed and manipulated if used for anything beyond research purposes."

So what is to be done? Greene suggests that educators defer the operational questions of how to teach and measure social-emotional skills, learn from the history, and rethink the broader context of SEL in schools. "The main challenge with SEL," he asserts, "is not how to do it, but what social and political conditions allow any approaches to be effective." His main points:

• *Accept that SEL is all tied up with morality.* While not necessarily teaching religion, we shouldn't shy away from the moral and religious roots. "Doing so," says Greene, "will wipe some of the flaky, New Age feeling away from SEL and allow it to draw support from a broad section of the country that is legitimately concerned with the values that their children are learning."

• *Make SEL real by telling stories.* These might include the Good Samaritan, Hillel, Rosa Parks, and other exemplars of morality in action.

• *Acknowledge that effective SEL requires local control.* "Different communities have legitimate differences over the concrete moral examples of SEL concepts," says Greene. "SEL advocates need to embrace the moral diversity that effective SEL instruction requires." Social-emotional learning in school will get more traction if it aligns with what children are taught at home.

- *Recognize that school choice would help but is not essential.* Greene likes the idea of decentralizing control over schools so people with similar values send their children to like-minded schools.

- *Avoid attempting to centrally measure and incentivize it.* "SEL instruction can only be effective if local communities authentically adopt and pursue it," says Greene, "which requires that they be allowed to put their own moral preferences into SEL abstractions."

"The Moral and Religious Roots of Social and Emotional Learning" by Jay Greene, American Enterprise Institute, June 2019, summarized in Marshall Memo 793.

3. Educating for Full Civic Participation

In this *Kappa Delta Pi Record* article, Joel Westheimer (University of Ottawa) says schools have always tried to instill moral values, good behavior, and character in their students. But what exactly does that mean? For Westheimer, the question is personal: his parents were German Jews who escaped the Nazi Holocaust, but millions of others were not so fortunate. "How could such a highly educated, mature democracy descend into such unimaginable cruelty and darkness?" he asks. What did German schools teach about obedience, civic participation, and dissent? And how can today's schools help kids to "acquire the essential knowledge, dispositions, and skills for effective democratic citizenship to flourish?"

These questions are pertinent: a 2017 Pew poll showed that 22 percent of Americans favor a political system in which a strong leader can make decisions without interference from Congress or the courts. Polls in other western democracies show a similar undercurrent, accompanied by disdain for the free press, civil liberties, and the courts—and open hostility toward foreigners and ethnic "others." Researching schools' efforts to teach civic virtues and individual morality, Westheimer has found mediocre practices and a failure to distinguish among, and effectively prepare young people for, three kinds of citizenship:

- *Personally-responsible citizen* – The key virtues here are honesty, responsibility, integrity, hard work, self-discipline, and compassion. A responsible citizen obeys laws, pays taxes, helps those in need (for example, contributing to a food drive), and lends a hand in times of crisis.

- *Participatory citizen* – Basic knowledge for participation (taught in schools and families) includes how government works at the local, state, national, and global level; the importance of voting; and the role of civic and religious organizations. The difference between this kind of citizenship and the one above is activism: "While the personally responsible citizen would contribute cans of food for the homeless," says Westheimer, "the participatory citizen might organize the food drive." An active citizen is tuned into society-wide issues, economic and environmental concerns, and knows collective strategies for accomplishing things.

• *Social justice-oriented citizen* – The key at this level is critical thinking about fairness, equality, opportunity, and the root causes of injustice. "If participatory citizens are organizing the food drive and personally responsible citizens are donating food," says Westheimer, "social justice-oriented citizens are asking why people are hungry and acting on what they discover to address root causes of hunger (e.g., poverty, inequality, structural impediments to self-sufficiency)."

Westheimer's research over the last two decades has found that the third form of citizenship is least often addressed in schools, which focus mostly on volunteering, charity, obedience, and the three branches of government. That's necessary but not sufficient, he believes: "Education that teaches students to follow the rules, obey authority figures, be honest, help others in need, clean up after themselves, try their best, and be team players is rarely controversial. But without an analysis of power, politics, and one's role in local and global political and economic structures, students are unlikely to become effective citizens who can work with others toward improving the world."

How can schools do a more effective job getting students to think about the origins of major social problems and how they can be solved, Westheimer asks. "We need citizens who can think and act in ethically thoughtful ways. A well-functioning democratic society benefits from classroom practices that teach students to recognize ambiguity and conflict in factual content, to see human conditions and aspirations as complex and contested, and to embrace debate and deliberation as a cornerstone of democratic societies." He suggests the following steps for schools:

• *Teach students to ask questions*. Totalitarian societies have one top-down version of the truth and discourage dissent, even making it illegal. In democratic societies, questioning and constant rethinking of traditions are engines of progress. "Education reformers, school leaders, and parents should do everything possible to ensure that teachers and students have opportunities to ask these kinds of questions," says Westheimer.

• *Expose students to multiple viewpoints*. Students might gather newspaper articles or textbook chapters from different states and countries and ask how they are different, how they are similar, and why. Teachers should get students thinking about how issues that seem trivial to them might be a big deal to others. "Critical empathy" is something teachers should work hard to instill, says

Westheimer. "This is the kind of teaching in a globalized world that encourages future citizens to leverage their civic skills for the greater social good rather than for their own particular interests."

• *Teach controversial issues.* Schools may think they're doing this by covering slavery, Nazism, and laws that denied voting rights to women—but what about the #MeToo movement, women's reproductive rights, misinformation campaigns using social media, and debates about what's included in the school curriculum? "Engagement with contemporary controversies from a range of perspectives and using multiple sources of information is exactly what democratic participation requires," says Westheimer.

• *Focus on the local.* Civic education becomes much more immediate when students study and engage in projects in their immediate surroundings—school, neighborhood, town, state. A recent example of this was how students at Stoneman Douglas High School in Parkland, Florida responded to gun violence at their school. "Their ability to connect a very personal experience with the ways in which government, policy, and social and economic forces shape their lives," says Westheimer, "allowed them to participate on a national scale and, no doubt, prepared them for a life of effective civic engagement."

• *Be political.* Even when teachers are careful not to express their own views, some topics are controversial, with students feeling uncomfortable about the views expressed by classmates. "Democracy can be messy," says Westheimer. "Rather than let fear of sanction and censorship dictate pedagogical choices, however, teachers should be supported and protected, encouraged to use political debates and controversy as teachable moments in civic discourse."

• *Use teachable moments across the school.* Although these issues will be primarily addressed in civics and social studies classes, there are opportunities in other subject areas, assemblies, the cafeteria, and hallways. "How classrooms are set up, who gets to talk when, how adults conduct themselves, how decisions are made, how lessons are enacted—all these inevitably serve as lessons in citizenship, in how we live with one another in complex and diverse local, national, and global communities," concludes Westheimer. "Whether teachers explicitly teach lessons in citizenship or not, students learn about community organizations, the distribution of power and resources, rights, responsibilities, and justice and injustice."

"Can Education Transform the World?" by Joel Westheimer in *Kappa Delta Pi Record*, January–March 2020 (Vol. 56, #1, pp. 6-12), summarized in Marshall Memo 822.

Worries About Social-Emotional Learning

④ Should Schools Assess Students on Social-Emotional Skills?

In this *New York Times* article, "grit" guru Angela Duckworth (University of Pennsylvania) says she's pleased with the growing recognition of noncognitive skills as a key element in students' life success, including these three clusters:
- Tenacity, self-control, and optimism—these help students reach their goals;
- Social intelligence and gratitude—these support acts of relating to and helping others;
- Curiosity, open-mindedness, and zest for learning—these enable independent thinking.

Working with a number of district, charter, and independent schools, Duckworth and her colleagues have found that providing feedback on these attributes increases students' self-awareness and improves their behavior and academic achievement. It's especially helpful to compare students' self-assessment on key traits with assessments done by their teachers.

But Duckworth is alarmed that some educators are incorporating assessments of character into schools' high-stakes accountability systems. "We're nowhere near ready—and perhaps never will be—to use feedback on character as a metric for judging the effectiveness of teachers and schools," she says. "We shouldn't be rewarding or punishing schools for how students perform on these measures."

Duckworth's concern springs from two limitations inherent in students rating themselves on character traits:

• *Reference bias* – Different schools have different standards for what constitutes "coming to class prepared" (one of the self-control attributes). In one school, it might mean that when the bell rings, you're at your desk with your notebook open, last night's completed homework in front of you, and your full attention on the teacher. In another school, the look-fors might be more relaxed. Researchers found that students' self-ratings varied considerably depending on the norms of their schools, and weren't objectively reliable.

• *Incentives for gaming the system and cheating* – Attaching high stakes to character attributes can create extrinsic rewards and punishments that displace the hoped-for intrinsic motivations to behave better. "While carrots and sticks can bring about short-term changes in behavior," says Duckworth, "they often undermine interest in and responsibility for the behavior itself."

Duckworth concludes with these observations on the burgeoning study of noncognitive skills:
- Character matters.
- Character is not just innate—it can be cultivated by specific interventions.
- Getting students to self-assess on character traits can lead to important self-discovery.
- The ways in which we give students feedback on character can be improved.
- Scientists and educators need to collaborate to improve character education.
- Measures of character should not be used as high-stakes accountability metrics.

"Don't Grade Schools on Grit" by Angela Duckworth in the *New York Times*, March 27, 2016, summarized in Marshall Memo 631.

5. Cautionary Notes on Social-Emotional Learning in Schools

In this Brookings *Evidence Speaks* paper, Grover "Russ" Whitehurst takes a critical look at the "soft skills" being embraced by many US schools. The ESSA provision that states must include at least one nonacademic measure in their accountability plans has opened the door to social-emotional learning as a measure of school success. One consortium of California districts has proposed giving 40 percent weight to this domain, including a component with students' self-assessments of growth mindset, self-efficacy, self-management, and social awareness. "Surely soft skills are important and schools have an important role in shaping them," says Whitehurst. "But the reality is that research on soft skills is soft." His three main concerns: vague definitions, distinguishing traits from behaviors, and accountability:

• *Vague definitions* – Social-emotional competencies include character, virtue, personal qualities, emotional intelligence, noncognitive skills, and twenty-first-century skills—everything from completing homework to optimism, social awareness, and a growth mindset. "The complexities and challenges for schools and educators of including such disparate behaviors, thoughts, and dispositions into the overarching grab bag of soft skills are large," says Whitehurst. "Schools that try to do everything are likely to accomplish nothing well. Thus, the first challenge for soft skills education reform is a coherent answer to the question: What are we talking about and trying to influence?"

Whitehurst believes that right now we don't have enough clarity on what exactly it means—for example, for a student to engage in "responsible decision making" and how that's different for a second grader as opposed to a high-school senior. "Without specificity at the level of what students need to learn and examples of how to teach it, there is no clear path to the development of curriculum and instructional practices, teacher training, or meaningful assessment and accountability." Therefore, Whitehurst concludes, it's "premature and unhelpful for educators to define a school's mission, select its curriculum and programs, measure its success, and be held accountable for something as amorphous as the various synonyms for soft skills."

• *Distinguishing traits from behaviors* – For the last one hundred years, psychologists have been trying to understand human personality; their efforts closely parallel the current work on social-emotional skills, including the desire to define broad patterns of human behavior through questionnaire data and the goal of identifying individual differences that predict later outcomes. Nowadays, psychologists pretty much agree on the "Big Five" OCEAN personality traits:

- Openness to experience;
- Conscientiousness;
- Extroversion;
- Agreeableness;
- Neuroticism.

Psychologists also agree that: (a) a person can be high or low or somewhere in between on each one; (b) an individual's placement on one trait doesn't predict placement on any of the others; and (c) each trait doesn't predict specific behaviors in particular situations—rather, a tendency to respond in similar ways in a wide range of circumstances.

The research on soft skills is relatively new, so it's not surprising that there isn't a strong consensus. In fact, says Whitehurst, there's "a Tower of Babel when it comes to constructs and measures." But there are some parallels with the Big Five—for example, in the Chicago Consortium's description of social skills, *cooperation* and *empathy* are similar to agreeableness, *assertion* is similar to extroversion, and *responsibility* is similar to conscientiousness. And some social-emotional learning programs have used the Big Five traits in developing their questionnaires.

The problem, says Whitehurst, is that OCEAN personality traits and most of those being used in current social-emotional learning programs are "highly heritable." Studies of identical twins reared together and apart have shown that between 40 and 50 percent of the variance in OCEAN personality traits is due to genes, whereas only 7 percent is due to environment. Can schools implementing social-emotional learning programs change these deeply embedded personality traits?

That's an empirical question, says Whitehurst, and the results from a rigorous study of the

KIPP charter schools are not encouraging. Along with academic achievement, KIPP is strongly committed to and seriously invested in improving students' character, which the organization sees as crucial in its own right and a pathway to students' future success. The study showed that KIPP schools have been successful at improving students' math and reading achievement, but on twelve social-emotional skills, students did markedly better on only one—collaboration with peers.

The theory of action underpinning social-emotional learning programs in schools goes like this:
- Soft skills are causally linked to students' academic and life success.
- Schools can affect soft skills through curriculum, school climate, and focused training.
- The school's impact on soft skills leads to improved student outcomes in other domains, including academic achievement.

The KIPP study and others like it suggest that almost all the social-emotional skills measured are very resistant to change—or at least that schools haven't yet figured out how to change them.

• *Accountability* – Whitehurst says there are many unanswered questions on the validity of indicators of social-emotional skills; on separating the value-add of schools from factors outside the school; on isolating the impact of individual teachers; on identifying the kind of training needed to improve teachers' skills at strengthening their students' soft skills; on the relationship of proxy measures (like suspensions) and questionnaire items (like a student's response to a question about mindset); and on the way disruptive students with low social-emotional skills affect the students around them.

"We are at the very beginning of understanding what educators should be doing in schools to advance students' soft skills, how the outcomes of those efforts can be measured, and who should be held responsible for what, and how," Whitehurst concludes. Given all that, he has six recommendations:

- Focus on improving student behavior, not personality traits and dispositions. "Encourage and reward students for persistence and hard work rather than trying to increase their grit," he says. "Provide opportunities for students to learn to work productively with others instead of focusing on their development of cooperation and empathy. Instead of trying to increase students' conscientiousness, provide task-relevant instruction on how to manage time and complete assignments—and meaningful consequences for doing so. Arrange classroom instruction and other school-based activities so that all students can experience success and growth based on their work rather than trying to get students to see themselves as self-efficacious or to have a growth mindset."

STUDENTS' SOCIAL-EMOTIONAL DEVELOPMENT

- Develop rules and expectations for respectful social interactions, communicate them clearly, provide opportunities to master them, and implement meaningful consequences for students who don't.
- Use measures of soft skills that are naturally occurring and useful as feedback at the classroom and individual level.
- Focus on students who are significantly off-track in their social-emotional behavior or self-management skills.
- Pay particular attention to teachers, coaches, and other adults in the school who have a track record of problems with interpersonal interactions with students.
- Put in place systematic ways to learn from and improve reform efforts.

"Hard Thinking on Soft Skills" by Grover "Russ" Whitehurst in a Brookings *Evidence Speaks* paper, March 24, 2016, summarized in Marshall Memo 665.

Curriculum Content

6. Successfully Educating Children Who Have Experienced Toxic Stress

In this article in *The Atlantic*, author Paul Tough notes that research on noncognitive skills—resilience, conscientiousness, optimism, self-control—has captured the attention of educators and parents as a key variable in student success. "But here's the problem," he says. "For all our talk about noncognitive skills, nobody has yet found a reliable way to teach kids to be grittier or more resilient. And it has become clear, at the same time, that the educators who are best able to engender noncognitive abilities in their students often do so without really 'teaching' these capacities the way one might teach math or reading—indeed, they often do so without ever saying a word about them in the classroom."

So how are noncognitive skills shaped? For fortunate children, they come from a number of subtle, intricate environmental forces at home and in classrooms. Kids who grow up with calm, consistent, warm, and responsive parenting, and without significant adversity, internalize these messages: *You're safe; life is going to be fine. Let down your guard; the people around you will protect you and provide for you. Be curious about the world; it's full of fascinating surprises.* Almost all of these children will do well when they enter schools.

But toxic stress at home produces physiological and neurological adaptations that have a very negative effect on children's development. There is a strong correlation between adverse experiences—abuse, neglect, and adult dysfunction—and later problems with health and behavior. "When parents behave harshly or unpredictably—especially at moments when their children are upset—the children are less likely over time to develop the ability to manage strong emotions and respond effectively to stressful situations," says Tough. "A highly sensitive stress-response system that's constantly on the lookout for threats can produce patterns of behavior that are self-defeating in school: fighting, talking back, acting up, and more subtly, going through each day perpetually wary of connection with peers or teachers."

When these children reach middle and high school, problems escalate. Teachers and principals tend to assume that when students misbehave, "they're doing so because they have considered the consequences of their actions and calculated that the benefits of misbehavior outweigh the costs," says Tough. "So our natural response is to increase the cost of misbehavior by ratcheting up punishment." Suspension rates for poor and minority youth are orders of magnitude higher than for their more-affluent and white peers. But the forces leading to misbehavior are far from rational, and harsh punishments are ineffective in motivating troubled youth to behave, concentrate, and succeed.

What this suggests, says Tough, is that we need to rethink classroom pedagogy, taking into account the burdens with which many children are entering school. A promising approach is self-determination theory, advocated by Edward Deci and Richard Ryan of the University of Rochester. They believe people are driven by three basic needs—competence, autonomy, and human connection—and that intrinsic motivation kicks in when these needs are being satisfied.

"The problem," says Tough, "is that when disadvantaged children run into trouble in school, either academically or behaviorally, most schools respond by imposing more control on them, not less. This diminishes their fragile sense of autonomy. As these students fall behind their peers academically, they feel less and less competent. And if their relationships with their teachers are wary or even contentious, they are less likely to experience the kind of relatedness that Deci and Ryan describe as being so powerfully motivating for young people in the classroom. Once students reach that point, no collection of material incentives or punishments is going to motivate them, at least not in a deep or sustained way …. If we want students to act in ways that will maximize their future opportunities—to persevere through challenges, to delay gratification, to control their impulses—we need to consider what might motivate them to take those difficult steps."

Deci and Ryan say that if teachers are able to create an environment that fosters competence, autonomy, and connection, students are much more likely to feel motivated to work hard. What can teachers do to create this dynamic in classrooms?

Tough believes the scholar doing the most thoughtful work on this question is Camille Farrington, a former high-school teacher now working at the University of Chicago Consortium on School Research. The 2012 report she wrote with her colleagues, "Teaching Adolescents to Become Learners" (available at http://bit.ly/1pwnNJ3) contains some answers. "There is little evidence that working directly on changing students' grit or perseverance would be an effective lever for improving their academic performance," the report said. "While some students are more likely to persist in tasks or exhibit self-discipline than others, *all* students are more likely to demonstrate perseverance if the school or classroom context helps them develop positive mindsets and effective learning strategies."

Farrington's report drew a distinction between stable character traits like grit, which are difficult to change, and academic perseverance, which is highly dependent on the specific context. A student might demonstrate academic perseverance in math but not in history, in tenth grade and not in eleventh. "In essence," says Tough, "what Farrington found was this: If you are a teacher, you may never be able to get your students to *be* gritty, in the sense of developing some essential character trait called grit. But you can probably make them *act* gritty—to behave in gritty ways in your classroom. And those behaviors will help produce the academic outcomes that you (and our students and society at large) are hoping for."

The key to academic perseverance, says Farrington, is students' academic mindset, and that is directly affected by the messages that teachers communicate minute by minute, day by day. Farrington has distilled the voluminous mindset research to four key beliefs that, if students embrace them, produce academic perseverance:

- *I belong in this academic community.*
- *My ability and competence grow with my effort.*
- *I can succeed at this.*
- *This work has value for me.*

But there are two problems: First, many students who experienced trauma early in their lives are resistant to these beliefs—they're more likely to think, *I don't belong here. This is enemy territory. Everyone in this school is out to get me.* Second, many U.S. schools don't do a very good job nurturing these four beliefs, especially with disadvantaged youth. In fact, "no excuses" discipline policies often create a downward spiral of negative beliefs that are diametrically opposed to the Farrington four.

The good news, Tough says, is that a small number of educators are using the recent insights about the impact of toxic childhood stress to reshape school environments. "These efforts," says Tough, "target students' beliefs in two separate categories, each one echoing items on Farrington's list: first, students' feelings about their place in the school (*I belong in this academic community*), and then their feelings about the work they are doing in class (*my ability and competence grow with my effort; I can succeed at this; the work has value for me*)." Tough cites two examples of promising efforts:

• Turnaround for Children, whose intervention teams of three to four people are working in schools in New York City, Newark, and Washington, DC, that address the psychological needs of potentially disruptive students, help teachers become more strategic and less confrontational with classroom management, and encourage student-centered instructional approaches like cooperative learning.

• EL Education (formerly Expeditionary Learning), which is working in 150 schools nationwide to develop students' academic mindsets using two strategies: belonging and relationships (through Crew, a daily, multiyear discussion and advisory group for students); and highly active, engaging classroom pedagogy—lots of student discussion, group activities, demanding long-term projects conducted by groups of students, and regular student self-assessments, including student-led report card conferences.

"Teachers and administrators at EL schools talk quite a bit about character," says Tough, "their term for noncognitive skills. The central premise of EL schools is that character is built not through lectures or direct instruction from teachers but through the experience of persevering as students confront challenging academic work …. In general, when schools do try to directly address the impact that a stress-filled childhood might have on disadvantaged students, the first—and often the only—approach they employ has to do with their students' emotional health, with relationships and belonging." But belonging isn't enough. To be truly motivated, students also need to believe they are doing work that is challenging, rigorous, and meaningful.

"How Kids Really Succeed" by Paul Tough in *The Atlantic*, June 2016 (Vol. 317, #5, pp. 56–66), summarized in Marshall Memo 638. This article is excerpted from Tough's book, *Helping Children Succeed: What Works and Why* (New York: Houghton Mifflin Harcourt, 2016).

7. What Parents and Teachers Can Do to Teach Self-Regulation

In this article in *American Educator*, University of Virginia psychologist Daniel Willingham reports that in recent years cognitive scientists have increased our understanding of "self-regulation"—people's ability to inhibit impulsive responses, control emotions, pay attention, defer gratification, and plan and control behavior. Three examples:
- A fifth-grader does his schoolwork despite the temptation to look out the window at a construction crew pouring a new cement sidewalk.
- A fourteen-year-old girl practices piano in preparation for a concert even though she'd rather hang out with her friends.
- A preschool boy's carefully-built block structure is knocked over accidentally by another student, but he methodically starts rebuilding it.

Not surprisingly, strong self-regulation is correlated with social competence, empathy, and whether a student is liked by teachers; a lack of self-regulation is associated with disobedience, aggression, and temper tantrums.

"This capacity turns out to have enormous consequences for academic and social success," says Willingham. "And, as teachers observe daily, children differ widely in how much of this capacity they seem to have."

Why are some children so much more proficient at self-regulation than others? Willingham says it's partly an inherited trait, but genetic tendencies can be affected by parenting practices and classroom factors. Here's what recent research has shown:

• *Parenting* – Observational studies have identified warmth, organization, and predictability as important influences on children. When parents give their children meaningful praise and encouragement, show affection, provide structure and routines with some room for autonomy, are sensitive to children's needs, and provide an intellectually stimulating environment (books, questions, complex sentences)—self-regulation flourishes. When parents are critical, cold, indifferent, and physically or verbally controlling, self-regulation withers. There's also a chicken-and-egg interaction between temperament and how parents react; a child with weak self-regulation might elicit more controlling and punitive parenting, which further stunts self-regulation.

• *Classroom factors* – Even children who enter preschool with weak or nonexistent self-regulation skills can learn at school what other children learned at home, and the basics are the same: warmth, organization, and predictability. "Children learn self-regulation through practice," says Willingham. "A well-organized classroom requires that children practice inhibiting their own moment-to-moment desires in favor of acting in accordance with the pace set by the teacher." Warmth is as important as organization and routines, helping students learn empathy and emotional regulation.

Tools of the Mind is an early-childhood program designed to improve self-regulation, working memory, and cognitive flexibility. Its forty activities include dramatic play, collaborative turn-taking, and self-talk around self-regulation. Promoting Alternative Thinking Strategies is another program for preschool and elementary children. Both seem to make a positive difference, but Willingham says more research is needed.

As for the impact of everyday teaching practices, the research is mixed, largely because children who enter school with strong self-regulation aren't changed by what teachers do in this domain. But studies that focus on preschoolers and first-graders who enter with weak self-regulation show that certain instructional behaviors benefit the children most in need:

STUDENTS' SOCIAL-EMOTIONAL DEVELOPMENT

- Teacher sensitivity – Being consistent, positive, warm, and appropriately responsive to children's cues, versus being overcontrolling (imposing a learning agenda on children without heeding their cues) or detached (unaware of what children are doing and not supervising them actively enough).
- Classroom management – This includes planning and organization, consistency, and focusing on developing students' independent and small-group work.
- Understanding the role of negative emotions – When children are frustrated, angry, stressed, or depressed (perhaps because of something at home), they're more likely to act impulsively, in the same way that adults who are upset are more likely to eat too much, overspend, act aggressively, or engage in risky sexual behavior. "Negative emotions seem to make people act in the moment, and to disregard future consequences," says Willingham. "Indulging provides short-term relief from anxiety, and so seems rational in the moment …. When a student does act impulsively, a calm, warm correction and redirection of the student is more likely to prevent further impulsive acts than a rebuke that makes the student feel bad."
- Dealing with lapses – When a dieter eats a brownie, it can lead to giving up on the diet. Successful classrooms try to keep impulsive students from "falling off the wagon," and when they do, provide warm and reassuring support so that they can successfully get back on the wagon.
- Removing cues – Impulsive behavior is enabled by temptations and opportunities, in the same way that a recovering alcoholic's resolve is undermined by being at a party where drinks are being served. This goes back to classroom management—structuring classroom routines to minimize opportunities for poor self-regulation to manifest itself. Willingham describes a first-grade classroom that had just acquired a rabbit as a classroom pet, providing a constant distraction to children sitting nearby. The teacher placed an attractive wall hanging between the rabbit's cage and the area where children were sitting. Problem solved.

"Helping students better self-regulate is a daunting task because it seems such a personal, permanent quality of an individual," concludes Willingham. "But researchers have shown that it is open to change, and they also have shown that good self-regulation is associated with a broad spectrum of positive academic and social outcomes, and that poor self-regulation is associated with greater risk of correspondingly bad outcomes. These facts highlight the urgency for teachers to do all they can to help students grow in this area."

"Can Teachers Increase Students' Self-Control?" by Daniel Willingham in *American Educator*, Summer 2011 (Vol. 35, #2, pp. 22–27), summarized in Marshall Memo 393.

8 Zeroing in on the Key Skill of Perspective Taking

In this *Phi Delta Kappan* article, Hunter Gehlbach (University of California–Santa Barbara, and Panorama Education) says the current attention to social-emotional learning will have a longer shelf life than other trendy topics. But Gehlbach cautions that implementing social-emotional learning in schools raises some important questions:

- Which "soft" skills matter most?
- Which of these proficiencies can teachers actually change? For example, is it realistic that schools can make students more caring?
- Aren't some social-emotional skills really values that should be addressed by families?

The danger with social-emotional learning, says Gehlbach, is that we'll "get excited about it, implement a handful of versions, find ourselves daunted by the vast array of components that need to be taught and assessed, become frustrated, and then move on to the next big thing."

But Gehlbach believes this won't happen if we focus on "a single, teachable capacity that anchors almost all of our social interactions: *social perspective-taking*, or the capacity to make sense of others' thoughts and feelings. The motivation and ability to 'read' other people," he continues, "vividly imagining their unique psychological experience, provides the compass by which we navigate our social world. This capacity allows us to interpret the motivations and behaviors of our friends and neighbors, or to see situations from the point of view of strangers, or to understand and appreciate values and beliefs that diverge from our own. Without it, we cannot empathize, engage in moral reasoning, love, or even hold a normal conversation."

Research suggests that perspective-taking is linked to less stereotyping of others, responding less aggressively to provocation, and developing better relationships with those with different beliefs—in other words, there's a ripple effect to a number of other social-emotional competencies.

Gehlbach believes perspective-taking can be integrated into any class at any grade level, and suggests three precepts for teachers to keep in mind:

• *Make it a classroom expectation for students to talk about others' perspectives.* Instead of asking, "Why did the British appease Hitler?" a teacher might ask, "What are some possible reasons the

British may have wanted to appease Hitler?" Students can also be asked to play devil's advocate or restate a classmate's opinion before responding to it. "When disagreements or interpersonal conflicts arise," says Gehlbach, "it should be considered the norm for students to explain their side of the story and to listen while the other side explains theirs."

• *Encourage students to be social detectives, not judges.* It's easy for students to jump to conclusions about a teacher giving low grades because she's mean, or about a classmate starting a rumor because he's spiteful. But they can be weaned away from shoot-from-the-hip characterizations by asking questions like, *Why might she have done that?* or, *What's his version of what happened?* "The more students get in the habit of investigating others' perspectives rather than rushing to judge them," says Gehlbach, "the more skilled they'll become at looking for clues that might illuminate others' decisions and behaviors."

• *Provide low-stakes opportunities for practice.* Perspective-taking is an unfamiliar process for many students, and it has to be okay to make mistakes as they learn.

"Once in the habit of trying to gauge other people's ways of looking at the world," Gehlbach concludes, "they will inevitably become more empathetic, more understanding, and more caring; they will become more thoughtful about how to navigate relationships; and they will become more likely to reach out across cultural groups rather than withdrawing into their own clique."

"Learning to Walk in Another's Shoes" by Hunter Gehlbach in *Phi Delta Kappan*, March 2017 (Vol. 98, #6, pp. 8–12), summarized in Marshall Memo 678.

9. A More Flexible Approach to Social-Emotional Learning in Schools

In this *Phi Delta Kappan* article, Rebecca Bailey, Laura Stickle, Gretchen Brion-Meisels, and Stephanie Jones (Harvard Graduate School of Education) affirm the importance of social-emotional learning (SEL)—especially for students who enter school with any kind of disadvantage. But in their work with educators implementing SEL programs around the US, the authors have found the following challenges:

- Some SEL curriculums don't reflect students' experiences, and at times oversimplify or ignore students' real-world problems.
- Many SEL programs aren't aligned with children's stages of development, often teaching the same set of skills across the grades.

- Scripted lesson plans don't allow teachers to respond to students' concerns in real time.
- Thirty-minutes-per-week SEL blocks are insufficient and tend to get preempted by academic priorities.
- Educators seldom get enough training and support to implement SEL programs or to engage in their own social-emotional growth.

The authors' takeaway: "There is a pressing need for an approach to SEL that is more flexible and feasible to implement and adaptable to individual and place-based needs while still achieving meaningful outcomes for children." Here are the characteristics they advocate:

• *Teach age-appropriate social-emotional skills at each level.* In the pre-school years, children develop basic emotional skills such as recognizing and communicating feelings and managing anger and sorrow. Executive function skills emerge around age four and develop during the early years of school. Here's a grade-by-grade sequence of appropriate SEL learning in the elementary grades:

- Kindergarten – Stop and think power: Learning to wait, share, take turns, and practice self-management following classroom routines.
- Grade 1 – Focus power: Increasing the amount of time students can pay attention to adults' instructions, listen to peers, and concentrate on tasks and activities.
- Grade 2 – Remember power: Becoming more independent and carrying out multistep tasks, following directions, and making and carrying out detailed plans.

In the next two grades, students use these foundational skills to understand the world through others' eyes and resolve conflicts:

- Grade 3 – Empathy and perspective-taking: Recognizing and responding to others' feelings, needs, wants, ideas, and perspectives—and caring about friendships with peers;
- Grade 4 – Conflict resolution skills: As relationships become more complicated, students need adult guidance on how to deal with disagreements and conflicts when they arise.

In the upper-elementary grades, students must learn to integrate multiple skills, building and maintaining positive, healthy relationships:

- Grade 5 – Relationship skills: At this age, students have a growing desire to connect with others, and relationships with peers and supportive adults, as well as issues in their communities, are often the most important factors in their lives.

An effective social-emotional learning curriculum should address the right skills at each level.

• *Social-emotional learning should occur in classrooms and also in hallways, cafeterias, and playgrounds.* "SEL instruction is most effective when children have frequent opportunities to practice SEL skills in various contexts," say the authors. All staff should be trained in a set of basic, uncomplicated "active ingredients" of social-emotional learning for each grade level. "Focusing on these strategies, rather than comprehensive curricula or scripted lessons, enables teachers and staff to address challenges or opportunities as they arise. This approach can also increase consistency throughout the school community and smooth students' transitions between classrooms and grades."

- *SEL works best when teachers respond to students' specific needs and experiences.* To get students truly engaged, say the authors, teachers need to be trained and empowered to use students' experiences in school, at home, and in their communities. Educators need ideas and resources and a clear sense of what is essential and what is optional (or may be adapted). They should use teachable moments to get their students practicing SEL skills in response to everyday challenges—for example, addressing conflict effectively, managing emotions, and paying attention. Teachers using this approach found they addressed two or three situations a day in the elementary grades, one a day in middle school.

The authors report that a pilot program in a summer school produced significant gains in students' social-emotional skills and was well received by teachers. Educators also liked having detailed strategies at their fingertips, including a pack with detailed descriptions for each strategy and general guidance on how to implement strategies over time—in other words, a mix of autonomy and structure.

"Re-Imagining Social-Emotional Learning" by Rebecca Bailey, Laura Stickle, Gretchen Brion-Meisels, and Stephanie Jones in *Phi Delta Kappan*, February 2019 (Vol. 100, #5, pp. 53–58), summarized in Marshall Memo 773.

Programs That Make a Difference

10. The Secret Sauce of Effective Advisory Programs

In this *Educational Leadership* article, consultants Jeffrey Benson and Rachel Poliner say that many secondary schools have had difficulty implementing advisories. From their work in schools, the authors identify some key elements of advisories that work:

• *The advisor's role* – The purpose of advisories is community building and youth development, which is unfamiliar territory for many teachers. Some feel awkward with sitting in a circle and holding open discussions and default to keeping students in straight rows and giving writing assignments, rather than having them talk to each other. "These teachers may feel more comfortable in the short term," say Benson and Poliner, "but they aren't taking the risk of learning to be an advisor."

Principals and the advisory team can take some specific steps to help: clearly describing the advisor's role vis-à-vis the advisory curriculum, discipline issues, and parent contact; articulating the specific short- and long-term goals of advisories; and being careful to refer to *advisor, advisee,* and *advisory meeting* rather than *teacher, student,* and *class period.*

• *Professional development* – The most effective PD is run like an advisory group—small, extending through at least one school year, and using rituals to establish a sense of community. It's helpful to have a text (one Massachusetts high school read Carol Dweck's *Mindset*) and think about schoolwide norms and practices (such as finding a replacement for wishing students "Good luck" before important athletic or academic events).

• *Content, format, rituals, and materials* – Advisory group leaders should have training, materials, and structures to develop four key areas: students' self-assessment and goal-setting; social competence, assertiveness, and sense of autonomy; communication, negotiation, and problem-solving skills; and sense of purpose for the future. "Advisors can help the group craft norms for good discussions, use varied discussion formats and techniques, and coach advisees when needed," say Benson and Poliner. Advisories can discuss students' time-management struggles, high and low points of the past week, service projects, hobbies and passions, and career goals. Advisories can also be the forum in which a major event in the news is discussed—for example, when students in one Boston school returned from their spring 2013 vacation marked by the Boston Marathon bombing, the principal blocked out a longer advisory period first thing in the morning, gave teachers discussion prompts and information on counseling resources, and held a staff discussion after school.

• *Structures* – Benson and Poliner describe two different approaches to scheduling: one high school has thirty-minute advisories twice a week; another has a ten-minute check-in midmorning every day and a forty-minute advisory once a month.

• *Groupings* – Small is better, say the authors. One school found that with groups of twenty, even with two advisors in the room, students acted the way they did in regular classes. The school split the groups in two and found alternative spaces to meet. Groupings can be by grade or mixed-grade, and it's best to keep groups and their advisors together for several years.

• *Aligning with school mission and context* – "The values promoted in advisory should be expressed throughout the school," say Benson and Poliner. This means connecting advisory to counseling, schoolwide student leadership programs, induction of new students and staff, school spirit activities, and discipline policies.

• *Assessment and feedback* – Each school's advisory coordinating team needs to use surveys, focus groups, and classroom visits to continuously assess what's working and what's not with scheduling, grouping, curriculum, and materials.

• *Stamina* – Schools need to make necessary adjustments and stick with advisories over time, conclude Benson and Poliner. Done right, they can make a major difference to school climate, staff efficacy, and students' lives.

"Designing Advisories for Resilience" by Jeffrey Benson and Rachel Poliner in *Educational Leadership*, September 2013 (Vol. 71, #1, pp. 50–55), summarized in Marshall Memo 502.

---

11. Additional Suggestions for Advisories

"Implementing a successful advisory program is a complex endeavor," says Boston consultant Mara Schanfield in this article in *ASCA School Counselor*. "The chances of success dramatically increase if it is implemented with patience, collaboration, and a school counselor's leadership." Here are her suggestions:

• *Purpose* – Advisories, which meet on a regular basis within the school day, make it possible for a cadre of staff members to get to know a small group of students well, putting them in a position to solve problems that might not be detected in a large school—for example, students who are consistently missing breakfast, being bullied, showing signs of depression, or might need special-education services. Advisors serve as the primary contact point with parents, providing one person in the school who knows each child well and can make more frequent and well-informed calls to a manageable number of parents. Advisors can also be trained to write seniors' college recommendation letters, greatly reducing the load on core-subject teachers. At their best, advisories personalize a large school and develop trust and strong relationships that can fundamentally shift the school's culture, engage students, connect families, and improve student outcomes—including achievement, graduation rates, and post-secondary success.

- *Basics* – The first priority is purpose. "An effective advisory program has a clear mission that is closely aligned with the school's goals for student achievement," says Schanfield. For example, a school trying to meet accountability benchmarks in English language arts should focus its advisories on literacy. Second is a champion—the principal or another leader who keeps the flame alive through difficult times. Third is administrative support: training for advisors, curriculum materials (a frequent problem in failed advisory programs), the absolute minimum of interruptions during advisory time, advance notice of changes in the advisory schedule, pulling students out of advisory only for emergencies, time for advisors to make family phone calls, and fostering patience for the long-term benefits that a successful advisory program should produce for students and teachers. Finally, operational support, usually provided by counselors: fitting advisories into the schedule and school calendar; assigning students to groups; getting students to the right places at the right time; adding new students to advisory groups; and dealing with students who need to change their group.

- *Curriculum* – Advisory programs need a curriculum, and Schanfield mentions three that she thinks are solid: *The Advisory Guide* by Rachel Poliner; *Top 20 Teens* by Paul Bernabei; and a curriculum developed by the Chicago Public Schools. But she believes there should always be flexibility to adapt or depart from the curriculum. "An effective advisory program places emphasis on interactions," says Schanfield. "Essentially, advisory curriculum isn't 'delivered' but rather facilitated." This is new territory for many results-oriented teachers, and they need lots of support to be successful.

School counselors play a key role, providing training and support (for example, running "Advisory for Advisors," where teachers can share ideas and support one another); working one-on-one and in small groups with teachers; and finding other supportive roles for teachers who are not cut out to be successful advisory leaders. On the curriculum, counselors can suggest themes (bullying prevention, for example), suggest topics for a grade level (post-secondary planning for seniors), and empower advisors to take advantage of teachable moments (something that comes up in the news). "Advisors who share power and allow students to drive activities are often impressed by the results," says Schanfield, citing a high school where students took the initiative to suggest a rewriting of the school's discipline policy after what they considered an unfair expulsion.

• *Governance and accountability* – Schanfield recommends an advisory board with counselors, administrators, teachers, students, family, and community representatives as members. This board should meet regularly and ensure that ideas are thought through and good policy decisions are made. The board should also track a number of measurable items:
- Student attendance in advisories;
- School attendance on advisory days;
- Requests to transfer in and out of advisory groups (tracked by advisor);
- Student mobility to other schools;
- Attrition;
- Teacher retention;
- Discipline referrals;
- Suspensions.

Schanfield also recommends surveying advisors and students at least twice a year, including interviews and informal conversations, to get a sense of buy-in and effectiveness.

"Advisory Advice" by Mara Schanfield in *ASCA School Counselor*, May/June 2010 (Vol. 47, #5, pp. 18–22), summarized in Marshall Memo 346.

---

12. High-School Debate and "Cultural Capital"

In this *American Journal of Education* article, Karlyn Gorski (University of Chicago) reports on her six-month study of two urban high-school teams taking part in the interscholastic Chicago Debate League. Observing their practice sessions and competitions and interviewing students and their coaches, Gorski concluded that debate allowed students to acquire three forms of cultural capital: being confident asking for and using critical feedback; deconstructing and analyzing complex ideas; and building on their already existing ability to face failure with resilience and persevere. These attributes equipped debaters to compete more successfully on what Gorski describes as the profoundly uneven playing field of US secondary schools.

Gorski says that students from all backgrounds enter classrooms with cultural capital, but certain kinds are more valued than others by dominant institutions like schools—which gives an advantage to more-privileged students. For example, sociologists have found that most middle-class children feel empowered to demand customized interactions with authorities like teachers and doctors; poor and working-class children, on the other hand, learn to display a "sense of constraint" marked by compliance with rules and practices. Similarly, middle-class kids learn to navigate problems at school using "strategies of influence," while working-class students are taught to use "strategies of deference." In college, more-entitled students are comfortable interacting with instructors, while students from high-poverty schools often exhibit discomfort, which doubly disadvantages them.

Gorski provides further commentary on the three forms of cultural capital she observed students developing on the debate teams:

- *Using feedback* – "Debaters learned, through repeated interactions with peers and authorities in the debate space, to request high-quality feedback that they could use to their own advantage," says Gorski. "Feedback was seen as crucially important to improving one's debate skills, and strategies for responding to it were seen as valuable beyond the debate setting …. When feedback was given, it was rarely accepted as adequate. 'Anything else?' was a constant refrain from debaters after receiving criticism…. Comfort placing demands on figures of authority, such as requests for assistance, accommodations, and attention, is a form of dominant cultural capital that is highly valued in educational settings."

- *Evaluating complex ideas* – Debate preparation constantly exposed students to challenging arguments and ideas. Competing, along with being asked to take both sides of an argument, sharpened students' analytic skills. In the process, says Gorski, debaters acquired "habits of mind" and "sophisticated skills of interpretation and analysis" that they had not learned at home or in classrooms. "Familiarity with complex literatures, as well as the strategies debaters use to understand them, set these students up for success in challenging courses throughout high school and college."

- *Resilience* – Being able to bounce back from a specific failure is especially important for disadvantaged youth, says Gorski; she calls this "adaptive cultural capital" and adds that it's especially important for disadvantaged students. Debate is uniquely suited to fostering this ability since debaters are constantly told that losing is a valuable experience. Gorski quotes one student: "You're not always gonna win in life, you're not always gonna be number one, you're not always gonna be the top, the best, and get everything. So, when you lose, you got to learn how to take that losing and know what to do with it." Many debaters regarded learning, rather than winning, as the goal, and developed specific strategies for dealing with—and learning from—defeats.

Is it possible, asks Gorski, that students who go out for debate already have these three cultural attributes? It's true that competitive debaters enter high school with higher eighth-grade test scores than non-debaters, and there is some self-selection with students who choose an academically challenging extracurricular. "However," says Gorski, "it is important to note that even if all of the debaters are driven, motivated, prosocial, and academically excellent students, the key finding presented here still holds: it is possible for certain doubly disadvantaged students to gain dominant and adaptive cultural capital within their underresourced neighborhood schools …. They built these skills over time and spoke often of the differences between their confidence and capabilities before and after joining the debate team. In their own perspectives, debate was a crucial factor in their ongoing development." One girl spoke of her "debate brain … that's where my whole mind turns on; it like, sucks everything up." This student said her "debate brain" turned on only in tournaments, not at school, where regular classes didn't provide enough intellectual stimulation and actionable feedback.

"'My Voice Matters': High-School Debaters' Acquisition of Dominant Adaptive Cultural Capital" by Karlyn Gorski in *American Journal of Education*, February 2020 (Vol. 126, #2, pp. 293–321), summarized in Marshall Memo 821.

---

13. Helping Teen Girls Deal with the Hidden Culture of Female Aggression

In this *New York Times* article, Jan Hoffman reports on the Girls Leadership Institute, a two-week summer camp that helps young adolescent girls deal more effectively with the unspoken rules of "Girlworld" and learn to do things as simple as making direct eye contact when they're asking for what they want. "By the time a girl turns 14," writes Hoffman, "she knows the rules of Girlworld by heart. If you can't do the pose—hand on hip, eye roll, hair toss—have enough self-respect to go hide in a corner. Let your hair fall over your face, cover your mouth when you speak, and always end declarative sentences like this?"

The girls who come to the camp are a mixed bunch—loners and alpha girls, chameleons and bullies, easterners and westerners, black and white, rich and poor. "Here is where they just get to breathe," says Hoffman. "They hug with abandon, often in five-girl pile-ons, their braces glinting in the sunlight … they relearn how to have fun, to remember the creative giddiness they enjoyed only a few years earlier." In one activity, they all act deliberately, unashamedly dorky, led by the camp's founder, former Rhodes Scholar Rachel Simmons (in whose office is a framed note from an eighth grader: "Dear Rachel: You are the most immature adult I've ever met and I love you!").

Among the workshop topics: Reputations, Ending Blame, and Self-Defeating Habits. In the latter, when a girl uses phrases like "I kind of …" or "I don't know if this is right but …," the other girls blow kiddie siren whistles. "The effect is playful, not humiliating," says Hoffman, "enduring but not punitive." There is a No Fat Talk Day and a daily shout-out to appetite: "Food, good! Food, good," chant the girls as they begin breakfast.

The genesis of the camp was when eight-year-old Rachel Simmons was tormented by a popular girl named Abby, who proceeded to poison her friends' minds against her. "Every time Rachel rounded a corner, she imagined she heard snickering," writes Hoffman. As an adult, Simmons carried this hurt inside as she went from one high-profile job to another. "I had been living for these accomplishments, not for who I was," she said. "And that's when I began thinking about why it still bothered me so much that Abby made my friends run away from me before Israeli dance class in third grade."

Simmons dropped out of the Rhodes Scholar program, flew home from England, interviewed hundreds of girls, and ultimately published two best-selling books, *Odd Girl Out* (2002) about what she calls "the hidden culture of female aggression," and *The Curse of the Good Girl* (2009), about "the pleasers"—girls who run from conflict and subjugate their pizzazz to being seen as humble, well-mannered, and liked by everyone. Some of Simmons's observations about the psychology of Girlworld:

- Girls fear rocking the boat in their all-consuming relationships, so they're not good at addressing everyday conflicts.
- Many girls are terrified to face a dispute head on. "In Girlworld, 'Can we talk for a sec?' means 'OMG the end is near!'" says Simmons.
- Aggressive girls fight dirty and mean, taking command of the cafeteria table and spreading rumors about their victims.
- Bullied girls, seething with anger, feel emotionally paralyzed.
- Much of this is unnoticed by adults.

There is a middle ground between being a "mean girl" and a "nice girl," says Simmons. One step is using more precise emotional language—not *annoyed, angry, whatever*, for example—but *excited,*

STUDENTS' SOCIAL-EMOTIONAL DEVELOPMENT

nervous, tense, and *hurt*. Another is being direct about what you are feeling and helping friends get in touch with how their behavior is (often unintentionally) affecting you. Simmons urges girls to think of a conflict with a friend "as an opportunity to negotiate for what you want." Rather than using phony Girlworld apologies like "So-ree!' and 'Just kidding!', Simmons has girls be more authentic and specific: "I'm am sorry I checked my phone when you were talking."

If girls learn to resolve tensions with their friends, she believes, they will be better able to ask for promotions and raises as adults and to be treated respectfully by those they love.

Can self-confidence and assertiveness be taught in a two-week camp? For many girls, it's just a break from the action and the nastiness starts all over again in the fall. But for some, the Girls Leadership Institute is transformational. One girl said, "I was in the middle. Not a loser, but not popular. I used to walk around with my head down, not wanting to call attention to myself. People treated me carefully because I was shy." She says that now people are happy to be around her. "I think that's because when you seem more confident, you make others feel more confident."

"Girls Interrupted" by Jan Hoffman in the *New York Times*, Aug. 15, 2010 (pp. ST1, 9), summarized in Marshall Memo 347.

Professional Learning Suggestions for Chapter Two: Students' Social-Emotional Development

Developing Nonacademic Skills in Students

The activities in this section will help leaders and/or teachers consider the role of schools in building "soft skills" in their students. It begins with developing a better understanding of what these skills are and then considering how these skills might be developed at school.

I. Understanding "Soft Skills"

Before faculty and leaders think about *which* social-emotional skills they might want to teach students and *how* they want to do it, they will benefit from exploring some foundational issues concerning social-emotional learning. The exercises below have staff think through the rationale for social-emotional learning, the ideal nonacademic skills they would like to see in their graduates, the difference between skills they teach and traits that might be inherited, and potential obstacles that might get in their way.

A. Consider the rationale for teaching "soft skills" in school.
Give staff the two questions below. Tell them to be prepared to discuss their thoughts on these two questions after they read two of the following three article-summaries (their choice): "Four Facets of Character" (David Light Shields article-summary 1), "Rethinking Social and Emotional Learning" (Jay Greene article-summary 2), and "Educating for Full Civic Participation" (Joel Westheimer article-summary 3).

> *Should "soft skills" be taught in school?*
> *Can "soft skills" be successfully taught in school?*

Conduct a large-group discussion for people to share their opinions based on what they've read in these article-summaries and *in their own experience.* Have them share any examples of students successfully acquiring nonacademic skills in school or not acquiring them!

PROFESSIONAL LEARNING SUGGESTIONS FOR CHAPTER TWO

B. Outline the characteristics of your ideal graduate.

Some schools conduct an activity in which faculty sketch the academic skills they would like to see in their ideal graduate (critical thinking, problem solving, etc.). In this exercise, have teachers outline the *noncognitive* skills they would want in their graduates.

First have everyone read "Four Facets of Character" (David Light Shields article-summary 1), and use his categories of four different types of character skills they would want to see in their students by the time they graduate (from elementary, middle, or high school, depending on the grades at your school). Divide staff into small groups to fill out a chart on large paper like the one below:

C. Explore the differences between "traits" and "behaviors" and consider which skills are teachable.

Several of the article-summaries discuss the differences between traits that are more inherited versus skills that can be more influenced or even taught. Have staff read two of the article-summaries that explore this issue: "Cautionary Notes on Social-Emotional Learning in Schools" (Grover Whitehurst article-summary 5) and "Successfully Educating Children Who Have Experienced Toxic Stress" (Paul Tough article-summary 6).

Next, have staff consider *their own* personality traits using the "Big Five" OCEAN personality traits in the Whitehurst article-summary. Focus on the first three traits and ask teachers to do a forced choice—stand next to one wall if you are on one end of the continuum below or next to the opposite wall for the opposite end of the continuum:

    O = Openness to experience (inventive/curious versus consistent/cautious);

    C = Conscientiousness (efficient/organized versus easy-going/careless);

E = Extroversion (outgoing/energetic versus solitary/reserved).

Once staff have chosen a wall, ask them to discuss with those on the same side: *Why do you think you have this personality type? Do you think it was inherited or influenced by your environment/context/people?*

After you've done this for the three personality types above, bring everyone together for a large-group discussion:

What is the difference between a "behavior" and a "trait"?
Which skills can we influence in schools and which are harder to teach?

D. Explore concerns about teaching social-emotional skills.

Before staff teach anything, ask them to discuss concerns they have with teaching social-emotional skills. Next, have them read two article-summaries that focus on some concerns with teaching these types of skills, "Should Schools Assess Students on Social-Emotional Skills?" (Angela Duckworth article-summary 4) and "Cautionary Notes on Social-Emotional Learning in Schools" (Grover Whitehurst article-summary 5). After they've read these article-summaries, have them add to their earlier discussion and consider ways to surmount obstacles. You might use a table like the one below to organize your brainstorm:

Concerns about Teaching Social-Emotional Skills	Suggestions to Surmount These Obstacles

II. How to Foster Social-Emotional Learning in Students

If your school would like to discuss how to foster social-emotional learning skills in students, below are some activities to generate ideas for how to do this. First have the group focus on the WHAT (what skills do we want to develop?) and then the HOW (how do we want to do this?).

A. Come to consensus on which social-emotional skills your school values most.
Go back to the brainstormed lists of intellectual, moral, civic, and performance skills that the

PROFESSIONAL LEARNING SUGGESTIONS FOR CHAPTER TWO

small groups created (with the stick-figure image of a graduate). Have each group hang their large paper on a wall (or post it virtually). Next, let groups add *additional skills* that they've learned from reading other articles. If they haven't yet read other article-summaries, divide up the following article-summaries and have each small group read one or two:

> "Rethinking Social and Emotional Learning" (Jay Greene article-summary 2)
> "Educating for Full Civic Participation" (Joel Westheimer article-summary 3)
> "What Parents and Teachers Can Do to Teach Self-Regulation" (Daniel Willingham article-summary 7)
> "Zeroing in on the Key Skill of Perspective Taking" (Hunter Gehlbach article-summary 8)
> "A More Flexible Approach to Social-Emotional Learning in Schools" (Rebecca Bailey et al. article-summary 9)

Once groups have added skills they'd like to see in their graduates, give each staff member five Post-it notes to vote for the top five character skills they would want your school to teach (or do this virtually and have staff "like" or vote for their top five character skills).

Have someone compile the five most popular character skills and conduct a discussion about what these mean. Use some type of consensus decision-making approach to come to agreement about these five skills. You don't need 100 percent agreement, but you may want to send this task to a smaller group (like the leadership team) to decide. Or you can use the following definition of consensus:

The group has arrived at consensus when:
→ *All points of view have been heard.*
→ *The will of the group is evident even to those who most oppose it.*

B. Consider implications for implementing social-emotional learning at your school.
Now that your school has outlined WHAT social-emotional skills to emphasize, it is time to think about HOW. Have staff go back to the articles to think about what they have learned from each article-summary that might have an implication for the classroom or the school. Particular article-summaries to focus on include the following: Greene article-summary 2, Westheimer

article-summary 3, Whitehurst article-summary 5, Tough article-summary 6, and Bailey et al. article-summary 9.

Ask them to apply what they've read to the implementation of social-emotional skills in the classroom and the school using a chart like the one that follows:

Article-Summary	*Implications for the Classroom*	*Implications for the School*
Greene (2)		
Westheimer (3)		
Whitehurst (5)		
Tough (6)		
Bailey et al. (9)		
Other article-summaries		

C. Discuss possible structures to deliver social-emotional learning.

Some schools have advisories—others have homerooms, town meetings, or other structures in place that would give teachers time to introduce nonacademic skills. In some schools, teachers have their students all day (such as elementary schools) and can use some of that time for nonacademic skill development. Still other schools that have none of this time set aside, yet have school-wide character skills they expect teachers to weave into their academic instruction.

Discuss which of the above structures or programs would fit best for your school. Then, regardless of whether that structure is an advisory program or not, look at the recommendations in the two article-summaries on advisory programs (10 and 11) and discuss the elements that need to go into a successful program:

- A clear purpose
- Professional learning
- Small groupings
- A coordinator/champion
- Assessment of the program and feedback
- Planned content/program/curriculum
- Materials
- Alignment with school mission
- Operational support
- Rituals for the class
- Time
- Flexibility

Which do you have in place now? Which structures would need to be developed to improve your school's chance of successfully teaching these five "soft skills"?

D. Conduct research to find a program.

If you feel that you need more resources before having your school dive into social-emotional learning, you may want to have a small group do some additional research. To begin, have them read this short article about choosing the right social-emotional learning program: https://www.gse.harvard.edu/news/uk/17/06/selecting-right-sel-program and look at the accompanying report which highlights twenty-five programs. Next, have them take a look at a few of the programs mentioned in this chapter. For example, review Tough article-summary 6, which mentions Turnaround for Children and EL Education, and/or Willingham article-summary 7, which mentions Tools of the Mind and Alternative Thinking Strategies. Have this small group report back with information about any promising programs that might work for your school.

III. Engage Parents in Thinking About and Fostering Social-Emotional Learning

Parents clearly have a role to play in the development of their children's social-emotional skills. Parents may not even realize that they are their children's first and most important teachers! Choose one of the article-summaries, such as "What Parents and Teachers Can Do to Teach Self-Regulation" (Willingham article-summary 7), and invite parents for a morning coffee (in person or virtually) to read and discuss the article-summary and its implications for what they might do *at home* to reinforce the social-emotional skill development you hope to do at school!

Chapter Three:
Race and the Education of American Students

Cultural competence is having an awareness of one's own cultural identity and views about difference, and the ability to learn and build on the varying cultural and community norms of students and their families. It is the ability to understand the within-group differences that make each student unique, while celebrating the between-group variations that make our country a tapestry.
—National Education Association

Now more than ever, the issue of race is a front and center in US schools and communities; each of us is responsible for thinking and acting in a moral and responsible way. There are schoolwide and districtwide obligations as well; we don't expect one teacher to bring every student in a classroom to proficiency in reading. Similarly, addressing racial issues is a collaborative endeavor; we need the understanding and support of our colleagues.

The articles in this chapter address five dimensions that are top-of-mind in schools today: implicit bias and microaggressions; discussing the undiscussable; challenges for students of color; stereotype threat; and cultural proficiency.

Implicit Bias and Microaggressions – Sarah Fiarman remembers how, as a white teacher, she absorbed unconscious bias like breathing in smog—involuntarily, without awareness—and suggests ways to anticipate and name bias, be accountable, and create systems to reduce it. Michael Shepherd reports on his study of teachers unconsciously judging students' verbal responses less favorably based on race and voice intonation. Robin Ely, Debra Meyerson, and Martin Davidson suggest ways to think through and deal with "identity abrasions"—insensitive comments, microaggressions, defensiveness—that occur when people of different cultures interact.

Barry Gilmore describes how middle-school girls spotted biases in the books they were reading (for example, passive female characters) and recognized unconscious biases they themselves brought to their reading.

Discussing the Undiscussable – Peggy McIntosh describes the contents of the "invisible knapsack" of privilege that white Americans carry around, making their lives quite different from that of people of color. Gislaine Ngounou and Nancy Gutierrez say it's essential that schools have ongoing discussions of racial issues with a systems perspective, a willingness to experience discomfort, sharing of personal stories, and no expectation of closure. Jacqueline Darvin proposes that vignettes can be an effective way to process and respond to culturally fraught situations. Hahna Yoon describes some techniques she's learned to deal with insensitive comments, including asking for clarification, separating intent from impact, and sharing what she herself used to say and what she says now.

Challenges for Children of Color – Kevin Mahnken reports two studies in which teachers gave harsher discipline consequences to students with African-American names than they did to students they believed were white. Orlando Patterson says the "cool pose culture" has captured the bottom fifth of young black males, keeping them from performing up to their potential, and points to some possible solutions. Christopher Emdin says many black male students have internalized an anti-school ethos from the culture around them and suggests how schools can help them be their true selves. Pedro Noguera casts doubt on all-male classrooms as a solution to the achievement issues of black and Latino boys and describes schools that have impressive high-school graduation rates for all students.

Stereotype Threat – Joshua Aronson describes how negative societal expectations can debilitate the performance of certain groups and suggests classroom strategies to counteract this dynamic. Claude Steele says that a pervasive societal stigma holds African-American students back from committing full effort in school and describes how "wise schooling" can elicit the full potential of all students.

Cultural Proficiency – Andy Molinsky says that when interacting with people from other cultures, we need to be sensitive to six ways they're different: directness, enthusiasm, formality, assertiveness, self-promotion, and self-disclosure. Jennifer Gonzalez and Zaretta Hammond argue that cultural competence is not the same as multicultural and social-justice education and goes beyond strategies to improve relationships and self-esteem—so the bottom line is closing achievement gaps. Derek Mitchell, Jesse Hinueber, and Brian Edwards say it's impossible for schools to be colorblind. Rather, they should focus explicitly on the achievement of African-American students; foster adult learning about race, culture, class, and power; build strong relationships with students; and foster noncognitive skills and student agency. Hilary Dack and Carol Ann Tomlinson urge educators to recognize and appreciate cultural variance, tune in to culturally influenced learning patterns, look beyond cultural patterns to see individuals, and plan inviting learning experiences. Justin Minkel suggests five ways that white teachers can use literature, guest speakers, and upstanding and culturally sensitive actions to boost the achievement of children of color.

Questions to Consider

- Why does academic achievement differ across racial and economic groups?
- Which classroom practices widen achievement gaps, and which narrow them?
- Can white teachers be effective with black and brown students?

Implicit Bias and Microaggressions

① Coming to Grips with Implicit Bias

In this article in *Educational Leadership*, former principal Sarah Fiarman remembers an epiphany she had as a teacher. Between classes, she expressed annoyance that a few students were frequently having side conversations while she was teaching. A colleague said she might be noticing this behavior among black students but not among whites. "Sure enough," says Fiarman, "when I observed more carefully in my next class, white students were doing the same thing. Without realizing it, I had selectively noticed the misbehavior of just one subset of students." As a white teacher who prided herself on racial sensitivity, she was chagrinned that she, like so many others, had absorbed an unconscious bias "in the same way we breathe in smog—involuntarily and usually without any awareness of it."

Implicit biases are present in people of all backgrounds—unconscious preferences based on gender, race, sexual orientation, and other aspects of identity, usually favoring one's own group—but sometimes, among stigmatized populations, favoring the dominant group. Researchers have found that black students are often punished more harshly than white students for the same infractions, and there are differences in who gets called on in class, the level of questions, praise and correction, how educators communicate with families, and whether a parent's assertive advocacy is seen as pushy or appropriate. Fiarman's suggestions:

• *Increase awareness.* "School leaders need to help their staffs understand that unconscious bias is not deliberate," she says, "it doesn't reflect our goals or intentions. Normalizing talking about it allows educators to examine and discuss their biases more freely and productively." Leaders can also suggest online tools, articles, and books—giving colleagues time to read, reflect, and discuss. This can lead to the kind of realization Fiarman had about her chatty students.

• *Name it.* The teacher who helped Fiarman see her blind spot wasn't trying to make her feel bad; she was being helpful, and her words were received in that spirit. How does a school facilitate such interactions? Singleton and Linton (2006) suggest four agreements for courageous conversations about specific incidents:

  - Speak your truth.
  - Expect to experience discomfort.

- Stay engaged.
- Expect and accept a lack of closure.

Colleagues can work on being nondefensive and deal with questions like: *What leads you to that conclusion? Would this decision be different if the family or child were of a different race or background? How would you make this decision if this were your own child?*

Fiarman describes a tense meeting with an African-American family. As the principal, she took a risk and said, "If I were in your shoes, I might worry that the school was treating my son differently because he's black. I want you to know that we're thinking about that too. We don't want to be the school that disproportionately disciplines black boys." This helped create a climate that produced a positive plan.

• *Anticipate bias and create systems to reduce it.* Forty years ago, symphony orchestras began auditioning musicians behind a screen, and the percent of female players increased from 6 percent in 1970 to 21 percent in 1993. In classrooms, calling on students using popsicle sticks eliminates the possibility of bias. It's also helpful for leaders to make decisions collaboratively, not in isolation or in anger, so there's time to slow down and hear from others.

• *Build empathy.* One study showed that when teachers administer a simple questionnaire to students and learn about common interests and experiences, grades and behavior among minority students improve and gaps close. Another study found that intentionally building positive relationships with students can cut the suspension rate in half. "When teachers simply had opportunities to relate to or consider the perspectives of their students—and to be reminded of the value of this perspective-taking–they were more likely to change their behavior," says Fiarman.

• *Hold ourselves accountable.* "Numbers keep us honest," she says. Tracking discipline referrals, the rigor of classroom questions, the quality of student work, and other data by race, gender, and other variables is a useful check on what's really happening.

"Deconstructing our unconscious bias takes consistent work," Fiarman concludes. "We can't address it once and be done. We need to recognize these unwanted, deep-rooted beliefs and limit their influence on us. Then our actions will match our intentions."

"Unconscious Bias" by Sarah Fiarman in *Educational Leadership*, November 2016 (Vol. 74, #3, pp. 10–15), summarized in Marshall Memo 659.

---

2 Unconscious Bias in Secondary-School Science Classrooms

In this article in *Urban Education*, Michael Shepherd (California State University–Fresno) reports on his study of 128 California teachers evaluating the verbal responses of ninth graders to open-ended science questions. The teachers (a racially and gender-diverse sample from private, charter, and traditional public schools) listened to a randomized mix of recordings of identically worded student responses to these questions (three examples of the stock responses are included after each question):

What is the goal of a scientific method?

> *To get the best data you can get.*
>
> *To test and prove hypotheses.*
>
> *To set a standard way for checking information.*

Why are scientific models useful?

> *Because they give you a physical example of something.*
>
> *Because they give us new ways of looking at things.*
>
> *Because they provide a visual element.*

Why is it important that scientific investigations be repeated?

> *Because there might not be enough data.*
>
> *In case something was left out the first time.*
>
> *So that they are guaranteed to be right.*

After hearing each recorded response, teachers rated how well they believed students answered the question on an eight-point Likert scale—from *not-so-well* to *very well*. Teachers heard ten randomized student responses to each question, and the rating sessions lasted ten to fifteen minutes.

Unbeknownst to the teachers, students had been recorded repeating stock answers spoken by Shepherd. (Students didn't *read* the answers because Shepherd found that when they read, they sounded like they were reading, and he wanted students to sound somewhat spontaneous.) Students made two recordings of each response with identical wording, but with a telling difference: first they spoke with rising intonation at the end ("upspeak"), then with falling intonation (which comes across as more confident and authoritative). The scripts were in standard English, but it was possible for teachers to tell students' race and ethnicity via subtle linguistic cues—and teachers could tell almost all students' gender.

Here's what Shepherd concluded after a careful analysis of all the teachers' ratings of students' responses:
- There was very little difference in teachers' evaluations of male versus female students.
- Responses spoken with rising intonation (by male and female students) were rated significantly lower than identical responses spoken with falling intonation. Shepherd notes that in classrooms (and life), rising intonation is much more common among females.
- Responses spoken by African-American and Latino students were rated significantly lower than identically worded responses spoken by white students.
- There was no significant correlation between teachers' gender, race, ethnicity, and social class and their ratings, nor with the type of schools in which teachers worked.

Shepherd believes his study shows that unconscious biases are at work in many classrooms, with significant impact. Students' self-efficacy, motivation, and achievement suffer when they notice (perhaps unconsciously) that their verbal responses, seemingly just as good as those of their classmates, are evaluated less favorably. These subtle signals interact with the stereotype threat experienced by students of color, and by female students in STEM classes, resulting in a cumulative impact on school performance—and whether students end up pursuing careers in science, technology, engineering, and mathematics.

"Effects of Race/Ethnicity, Gender, and Intonation on Secondary Science Teachers' Evaluation of Spoken Responses" by Michael Shepherd in *Urban Education*, June 2020 (Vol. 55, #5, pp. 730–752), summarized in Marshall Memo 837.

3. Getting Past "Walking on Eggshells" with Race and Gender

In this article in *Harvard Business Review*, Robin Ely, Debra Meyerson, and Martin Davidson say that, despite the reduction of overt prejudice and discrimination, "identity abrasions" occur every day—for example:
- *A white person confuses the names of two Asian-American co-workers.*
- *An African-American leader is addressed less formally than her white male counterparts.*
- *A woman's idea is misattributed to a male colleague.*

Identity abrasions can also occur on the other side—when majority-group members are fearful of being accused of being prejudiced or treating others unfairly and tiptoe around the issue of race and gender—for example, a white manager fears she will be perceived as racist if she gives critical feedback to a Latino subordinate.

For those who believe they are targets of insensitive behavior and those who are accused of being insensitive, Ely, Meyerson, and Davidson offer these suggestions:

• *Pause and reflect.* Anger is a common reaction to a threat to our identity. "We react by casting blame and judgment, which most often incites defensiveness in others," they say. "Taking time—even a few moments—to identify our feelings and consider our responses will help us to respond more effectively."

• *Connect with others.* "When we experience an identity abrasion," say the authors, "our impulse is to focus inward—to justify, explain, and defend ourselves." Instead, we should focus outward, "on goals that are larger than we are, such as advancing broad social ideals, contributing to a task, or striving to achieve an organization's mission. Goals such as these connect us with others by infusing our lives with meaning. Meaningful goals remind us of what is at stake in a given situation, giving us a reason to engage with others even if we feel threatened."

• *Question yourself.* This is the most difficult step, especially for women and people of color whose concerns have so often been dismissed or trivialized. But it's still important to ask, "What am I missing in the way I'm seeing this situation? How might my desire to be proven right or innocent be distorting my view of reality or of the other person?"

• *Get genuine support.* "Unfortunately," say the authors, "most of us seek help from the wrong people, seeing those who challenge our point of view as threats and those who reinforce it as allies. Receiving reinforcement may be comforting, but it often doesn't confer much learning …. What we need is the counsel of trusted colleagues who can help us identify choices we make about how to behave or what to believe, as well as what alternatives are available."

• *Shift your mindset.* "We have found that people who are able to turn identity abrasions into opportunities have the capacity to radically shift their way of thinking—about themselves, their situations, and other people," say Ely, Meyerson, and Davidson. "The fundamental shift is away from a mindset that says, 'You need to change,' to one that asks, 'What can I change?'"

What can leaders do to support these five actions? They need to create a safe environment; assiduously model self-questioning; build close relationships with diverse populations within the organization; and make clear that a learning orientation is key to organizational success. The authors conclude: "When people treat their cultural differences—and the conflicts and tensions that arise from them—as opportunities to seek a more accurate view of themselves, each other, and the situation, trust builds and relationships become stronger."

"Rethinking Political Correctness" by Robin Ely, Debra Meyerson, and Martin Davidson in *Harvard Business Review*, September 2006 (Vol. 84, #9, pp. 78–87), summarized in Marshall Memo 151.

4. Examining Our Own Biases Reading Young Adult Literature

In this article in *English Journal*, Barry Gilmore (a principal, author, and former English teacher) describes what happened when he recommended Nicola Yoon's *Everything, Everything* to a student; she wanted to know whether it passed the Bechdel test. "I can't stand to read things that are totally boy-centered," said the girl. "I mean, it can be a lot about boys, but that can't, like, totally be what it's about." Of course, she had to explain the Bechdel test to Gilmore, who'd never heard of it: *Does a work of fiction contain at least one scene in which two or more women (preferably named characters) discuss something other than a male?* Thinking about the book he'd recommended, Gilmore was relieved that, in addition to the main narrative about a girl falling in love with a boy, it did include scenes in which the girl speaks to her mother and a female nurse about other subjects.

What interested Gilmore in the girl's question "was that she had keyed in to an area of bias I, with nearly 25 years of experience in schools, had missed entirely. Her response drew out an implicit bias in my thinking and reading. What else, I wondered, had I missed?" To find out, he convened a group of seventh- and eighth-grade girls and asked them about other trends they'd noticed in the young adult fiction they were reading. Some responses:

- In many works of fiction, especially fantasy, strong girls are presented as being strong because they have older brothers (who usually bully them); girls rarely gain strength from growing up with sisters.
- The skin color or race of white characters is almost never discussed in an initial description, while it is with members of minority groups, often comparing their color to food: almonds, coffee, caramel, cappuccino, chocolate, mocha.
- Minority characters are often "white people wearing costumes," that is, a token character who brings no authentic experience to the story.

Clearly these girls were perceptive about the message literature sends that many people don't notice. "If our goal is to encourage critical reading and textual analysis," Gilmore wonders, "what activities or assignments might encourage and reward the sort of critical observation achieved by the girls with whom I spoke? And, importantly, what role can young adult literature play in broadening the exposure of students to a variety of voices and perspectives?"

Gilmore saw clearly the importance of students reading literature with characters different from themselves; research shows that this is crucial to developing empathy for people of different races, nationalities, religions, and sexual orientation. But broadening the scope of what's read in school poses difficult choices for English teachers who might not have enough time to have students read both *Animal Farm* and *The Absolutely True Diary of a Part-Time Indian*.

Gilmore pursued the subject of implicit bias in subsequent meetings with his group of middle-school girls. They claimed they were all for leadership by girls and women, and were surprised when he showed them the results of a study by Richard Weissbourd saying that many boys and girls harbored biases against female leadership. Gilmore had the girls look at a number of young adult novels and they recognized assumptions they made about characters whose gender or race was ambiguous. He asked them to identify an implicit bias they might bring to their reading and write it on an anonymous sticky note and post it on the wall. These were some of the biases revealed:

- *I think I assume that characters are white until I know they aren't.*
- *I always think of characters as skinny.*
- *I think the names of characters tell me how they look.*
- *I don't know if I have implicit bias but I probably do and don't know it.*
- *I guess I assume that certain characters are poor (skin color).*
- *I read this book called* Grasshopper Jungle *about a boy who was maybe gay and I couldn't finish it because I didn't like reading about it.*

"These were the same girls who had adeptly pointed out examples of implicit bias from their own reading," says Gilmore. "In our discussion, the girls themselves recognized this fact: they were annoyed by the implicit biases of authors, but they also brought their own biases to reading."

These realizations are helpful to students—and their teachers. Gilmore suggests three classroom practices that support a fuller understanding of texts and readers' biases:

• *Identity charts* – In the middle of a page at the front of their reader's and writer's notebooks, students write their name in a circle and draw lines out to jottings of various aspects of their personality—interests, hobbies, place names, gender, race, and other characteristics. One girl's chart included: *brown hair, brown eyes; stage crew; terrible at sports/clumsy; "How I Met Your Mother";*

Jewish; student, 8th grade, middle school; daughter, Mom, Dad, Spike (dog); "Terrible Three" (friends); books/reader; Kiera Cass; Rick Riordan; John Green!

The point of this exercise is to bring to the fore and recognize what we bring to texts as readers. Discussing identity charts, one class noticed: (a) Some students listed race and others didn't. (The teacher's question—How does our awareness of race as a piece of our identity change the way we read?) (b) Most of the white and Hispanic students listed a specific country of origin, while most black students identified themselves by race. (The teacher's question— How do our understandings of place of origin and race combine to affect our reading point of view?) (c) Some students used adjectives on their charts and others used only visible activities or characteristics. (The teacher's question—How do authors decide how to describe and introduce characters to us?)

• *Fishbowl discussions* – Three to five students sit in a small circle in the middle of the classroom and conduct a discussion of a text while the rest of the class sits in an outer circle taking notes and not speaking. When a student in the center finishes speaking, someone in the outer circle (which includes the teacher) may tap him or her on the shoulder and take that place in the discussion circle. Ideally, almost everyone gets to participate in the discussion by the end of the class. Gilmore has found it helpful to have several statements in his back pocket to introduce at an opportune moment, including:

- There are aspects of this character's background important to a full understanding of the character that a casual reader might easily miss.
- This character (or story), as good as it is, plays into some common stereotypes and misunderstandings.
- This character (or author) brings both explicit and implicit bias to the story.

After a recent fishbowl discussion of Katheryn Erskine's *Mockingbird*, a twelve-year-old boy wrote the following reflection: "I always thought of people with Asperger's as weird. I guess I've had a few kids in my school with this or something like it. I know it changes how I read this book, but I got really into Caitlin's story and the way she told it, so I think that can help me look at things in a different way instead of just the way I always saw it."

• *Graphic organizers* – Gilmore suggests having students draw a Venn diagram of their own characteristics compared with those of a character in a novel. This is helpful, he says, "Because the goal of incorporating bias into our thinking is to produce richer bridges between ourselves and others (whether they are characters, groups, or real people) …." Making Venn diagrams with *To Kill a Mockingbird*, one girl listed Scout's characteristics: *smart, strong, takes risks, brother, strong father.* She listed her own: *sisters, black, shy, don't speak up, love to dance, strong mother.* In the overlap space, she wrote: *courage, adventurous, tomboy, Christian, South.* After reading several other books involving African-American characters, this girl wrote a culminating poem:

> White and black,
>
> Age nine and age thirteen,
>
> From the country and from the city,
>
> Both Southern,
>
> Both tomboys,
>
> Both girls,
>
> Both more than people see.
>
> I can't know you, but I can understand you …

"Literature is important in part because it opens for us areas of human experience we might not access otherwise," Gilmore concludes. "We shouldn't make the mistake of believing that all aspects of that experience lie close to the surface or that we can capture them with a simple list of themes on a whiteboard; each student brings unique biases to the act of reading—and so do authors, and so do we. 'In order for students to examine their own beliefs,' notes Melissa B. Schieble, 'teachers must make their assumptions and ideals transparent.'

"Yet it's important to note," Gilmore continues, "that lessons in implicit bias should not be framed or received as instructions to feel guilty or condemnations of entire groups as racist, sexist, or otherwise prejudiced." *Implicit bias can be overcome with rational deliberation.* "It does not necessarily lie within a teacher's power to expose each individual's implicit biases, nor would we want that power, but it is within our power and responsibility to offer every student an opportunity to recognize implicit bias, both in his or her own reading life and in the literature we bring to school, and thus to make the implicit explicit. It's not a crime to communicate what we don't mean. It is, however, a shame not to take the time to examine our communication and to try to say what we do mean, which includes the message that the reading life of every adolescent is important and valued."

"Saying What We Don't Mean" by Barry Gilmore in *English Journal,* September 2017 (Vol. 107, #1, pp. 19–25), summarized in Marshall Memo 705.

Discussing the Undiscussable

⑤ The Daily Effects of "White Privilege"

"I was taught to see racism only in individual acts of meanness, not in invisible systems conferring dominance on my group," says Peggy McIntosh (Wellesley College) in this widely discussed 1989 article in *Peace and Freedom Magazine*. "As a white person, I realized I had been taught about racism as something that puts others at a disadvantage, but had been taught not to see one of its corollary aspects, white privilege, which puts me at an advantage."

McIntosh began to look at her unspoken advantages as "an invisible weightless knapsack," and compiled a list of what it confers. "As far as I can tell," she says, "my African-American coworkers, friends, and acquaintances with whom I come into daily or frequent contact in this particular time, place and time of work cannot count on most of these conditions." Here is a selection from McIntosh's list of fifty items, quoted directly:

- If I should need to move, I can be pretty sure of renting or purchasing housing in an area which I can afford and in which I would want to live.
- I can be pretty sure that my neighbors in such a location will be neutral or pleasant to me.
- I can arrange to protect my children most of the time from people who might not like them.
- I can be pretty sure that my children's teachers and employers will tolerate them if they fit school and workplace norms; my chief worries about them do not concern others' attitudes toward their race.
- I do not have to educate my children to be aware of systemic racism for their own daily physical protection.
- I can go shopping alone most of the time, pretty well assured that I will not be followed or harassed.
- I can be sure that my children will be given curricular materials that testify to the existence of their race.
- Whether I use checks, credit cards, or cash, I can count on my skin color not to work against the appearance of financial reliability.
- I can talk with my mouth full and not have people put this down to my color.

- I can swear, or dress in second-hand clothes, or not answer letters, without having people attribute these choices to the bad morals, the poverty, or the illiteracy of my race.
- I can speak in public to a powerful male group without putting my race on trial.
- I can do well in a challenging situation without being called a credit to my race.
- I am never asked to speak for all the people of my racial group.
- If a traffic cop pulls me over or if the IRS audits my tax return, I can be sure I haven't been singled out because of my race.
- I can take a job … without having my co-workers on the job suspect that I got it because of my race.
- I can be pretty sure of finding people who are willing to talk with me and advise me about my next steps, professionally.
- I can be late for a meeting without having the lateness reflect on my race.

"Many, perhaps most, of our white students in the United States think that racism doesn't affect them because they are not people of color," says McIntosh, "they do not see 'whiteness' as a racial identity. In addition, since race and sex are not the only advantaging systems at work, we need similarly to examine the daily experience of having age advantage, or ethnic advantage, or physical ability, or advantage related to nationality, religion, or sexual orientation."

"Describing white privilege makes one newly accountable," McIntosh concludes. Having described it, one must ask, "what will I do to lessen or end it?"

"White Privilege: Unpacking the Invisible Knapsack" by Peggy McIntosh in *Peace and Freedom Magazine*, 1989, summarized in Marshall Memo 793.

---

6. Orchestrating Productive Discussions About Race

In this article in *Phi Delta Kappan*, Gislaine Ngounou (Phi Delta Kappa International) and Nancy Gutierrez (New York City Leadership Academy) say that to undo racial inequities in schools, educators need to have difficult conversations on a number of sensitive topics, including: how race affects discipline practices; which students are placed in basic and advanced classes; which teachers are assigned to which students; which parents are seen as "engaged." One-shot PD experiences won't work, nor will lectures on racial bias, PowerPoint presentations of data and research, or making social justice one more initiative. "Rather," say Ngounou and Gutierrez, "conversations about these issues have to be frequent, ongoing, and handled with great care and skill."

It's easy for school leaders to overestimate their own skill at leading such discussions, to underestimate the amount of time it will take to dig into issues of racial inequity, and to naively assume that everyone is equally ready to engage. "Not that school and district leaders can afford to wait for just the right moment to dive into a discussion about race and equity," say the authors; "if that were the case, the discussion might never begin." But timing and preparation are important, and so is sensitivity to the emotions, beliefs, and experiences of their colleagues. They suggest four guiding principles:

• *There needs to be a systems-thinking approach.* These issues aren't an add-on, a box to be checked off. Inequity affects every part of the organization and people's work, and discussions need to involve teachers, administrators, nonteaching staff, parents, students, community leaders, and others.

• *There has to be a willingness to experience discomfort.* "It's important to create and maintain a supportive learning environment," say Ngounou and Gutierrez, "while at the same time pushing people to confront truths and realities that may make them feel uncomfortable." People need skilled facilitators to help them "find their entry points into the conversation, to examine their own actions and reactions, to acknowledge that they have been shaped by their own experiences, and to look for concrete ways in which they can have positive influences on their students and colleagues."

• *Personal stories are important.* Leaders and their colleagues need to explore how race (and awareness of race) has shaped their lives, including their experiences in schools. It also helps to discuss books, articles, and films that relate to the challenges educators and students face in school.

• *Don't expect closure.* An initial discussion will do little more than pry open the "worry box"—a mix of feelings, fears, and goals behind current practices. Much more time is required to make significant progress. "Questions about race, equity, and schooling reach people at a level that is deeply personal, emotional, and moral," conclude Ngounou and Gutierrez, "and they need to be able to work through what they have uncovered." There may never be a tidy resolution, but having these conversations is "nonnegotiable."

"Learning to Lead for Racial Equity" by Gislaine Ngounou and Nancy Gutierrez in *Phi Delta Kappan*, November 2017 (Vol. 99, #3, pp. 37–41), summarized in Marshall Memo 713.

---

7 Using Vignettes to Address Hidden Professional Issues

In this article in *Principal*, Queens College–City University of New York professor Jacqueline Darvin suggests using "cultural and political vignettes" to get teachers (especially new teachers) thinking about the unspoken challenges of the profession. Here's an example (from Sonia Nieto's book, *The Light in Their Eyes: Creating Multicultural Learning Communities*):

> *A new student from India comes to your school and on her first day in the cafeteria, she begins eating rice with her hands. Several children make fun of her. You are her teacher and happen to be in the lunchroom when this happens. What do you do?*

Asked to react to this scenario, educators divide sharply on whether the teacher should intervene immediately, later, or not at all. The facilitator's goal is to get teachers to explore multiple perspectives and avoid responding in ways that are biased, stereotyped, or narrow. Points like these often come up:

- Intervening might make the girl feel worse by calling attention to her eating habits.
- Intervening might give the girl the message that her cultural values and customs are "wrong"—that she needs to be "more American."
- Failing to intervene might lead to a serious incident.
- Talking privately to the girl about "the American way of eating rice" and letting her decide what to do.
- Sitting beside her and eating French fries "the American way," thus demonstrating to the girl and those teasing her that eating with one's hands is acceptable in certain situations.

There isn't a single right response to this situation, and facilitators should help teachers expand their perspective by asking questions such as whether all Indian people eat rice with their hands and whether there are other variables in why people eat in a particular way.

Role-playing is another way to handle vignettes—assigning roles to teachers, giving them a moment to think through what they will do, and having the audience support them as they work through the situation and then discuss how it went, including the importance of nonverbal communication—gestures, posture, and intonation.

Darvin suggests several more cultural and political vignettes for professional development discussions:

- You are upset with a student who does not make eye contact when he talks to you, even after you have asked him several times to do so. Why might this student be behaving in this way? How might this type of misunderstanding be avoided or reconciled?

• The father of one of your students comes to see you during a parent-teacher conference night. His son is doing poorly in your class and blames you and the school for his son's problems. What can you say and do to improve this situation? What pitfalls should you avoid?

• You notice that students tend to self-segregate along racial lines in your class discussion groups. Do you address this situation or simply let students continue working this way all year? If you decide to intervene, what would you do and why?

• Some of your sixth-grade students have same-sex parents. You have heard students making homophobic comments and have even witnessed teasing of male students who display typically feminine characteristics and female students who display typically masculine traits. Should you address this situation in your class? If so, how?

"Novice Teachers Need Real Professional Development" by Jacqueline Darvin in *Principal*, March/April 2012 (Vol. 91, #4, pp. 28–31), summarized in Marshall Memo 428.

8. Strategies for Addressing Insensitive Comments

"For many of us, microaggressions are so commonplace that it seems impossible to tackle them one at a time," says Hahna Yoon in this *New York Times* article. *Should I respond? Is it worth it? Am I over-reacting? Do I just need to grow a thicker skin?* Yet each incident bothers her, whether it was her fourth-grade teacher assigning her the part of a "slant-eyed child" in a school play or a stranger in the online dating world saying he "loves Asian women." The constant drip-drip of these everyday slights affects people's mental and physical health, says Yoon, making them feel like outsiders in their own land and even, in combination with other issues, leading to suicidal thoughts.

What are microaggressions? Yoon did some research and learned that the term was coined in the 1970s by Harvard psychiatrist Chester Pierce, and more recently updated in several books by Derald Wing Sue, a professor of counseling psychology at Columbia. His definition: everyday slights, indignities, put-downs, and insults that members of marginalized groups experience in their day-to-day interactions with individuals who are often unaware that they have engaged in an offensive or demeaning way. The first step, says Yoon, "is to recognize that one has occurred and dissect what message it may be sending." If the person is in your everyday life, it's probably a good idea to address it. But it's important to think it through.

For starters, says Kevin Nadal, a psychology professor at John Jay College, there are five questions to ask oneself (quoted directly):
- If I respond, could my physical safety be in danger?
- If I respond, will the person become defensive, and will this lead to an argument?
- If I respond, how will this affect my relationship with this person (e.g., co-worker, family member, etc.)?
- If I don't respond, will I regret not saying something?
- If I don't respond, does that convey that I accept the behavior or statement?

Having considered these questions and decided to go ahead and speak up, it's important to think about goals. "Do you simply want to be heard?" asks Yoon. "Or are you more interested in educating the other person and letting them know they did something wrong?"

Microaggressions can happen so quickly that there isn't time to formulate the ideal response. Diane Goodman, a social justice and diversity consultant, recommends committing to memory three alternative approaches so they're readily available:
- Asking for clarification— for example, "Could you say more about what you mean by that?" or "How have you come to think that?"
- Separating intent from impact—for example, "I know you didn't realize this, but when you [comment/behavior], it was hurtful/offensive because [consequence of comment/behavior]. Instead, you could [different language/behavior]."
- Sharing your own process—for example, "I noticed that you [comment/behavior]. I used to say/do that too, but then I learned [different language/behavior]."

Underlying these approaches is the idea of helping microaggressors see that they're not being attacked. "If we want people to hear what we're saying and potentially change their behavior," says Goodman, "we have to think about things that will not immediately make them defensive."

How about microaggressions in the digital space? On Facebook, Twitter, and other platforms, the damage can spread more widely, but there are also more opportunities for people to push back from the safe distance of cyberspace. One approach is pasting in a link that speaks to a particular kind of insensitive comment or image. However, if it's an impersonal message or meme from a stranger, the best thing is probably to ignore it and move on.

Yoon concludes by emphasizing the importance of drawing boundaries and finding support

MINDSETS THAT SUPPORT LEARNING

among allies. Discussing common experiences with a few friends can facilitate the coping process, as well as "developing pride in your community, sharing stories with people from it and taking action to make changes on a local and political level, reflecting on the challenges of your ancestors and practicing self-care and staying healthy—physically and spiritually."

"How to Respond to Microaggressions" by Hahna Yoon in *The New York Times*, March 3, 2020, summarized in Marshall Memo 828.

Challenges for Children of Color

9 Unconscious Racial Bias in School Discipline

"Classroom discipline is, let's face facts, a fraught subject," says Kevin Mahnken in this *Education Gadfly* article. "Few areas of education discourse are more in need of illuminating research." Mahnken reports on two experiments by Stanford University researchers Jason Okonofua and Jennifer Eberhardt on implicit psychological bias. In the first, teachers were shown the disciplinary records of students with stereotypically Caucasian and African-American names, each describing two incidents of petty insubordination. After reading each report, teachers were asked to say how irritated they felt, how seriously they took the infraction, and how great a hindrance they believed it would be to their teaching. The results were striking: when teachers read about the second incident involving students with "black" names, they felt significantly more troubled, more likely to recommend harsher punishment, and more likely to see the student as a "troublemaker." This did not happen with students with "white" names.

In a second experiment, teachers were shown descriptions of the same disciplinary incidents and asked whether they could imagine suspending the hypothetical students at some point in the future. Teachers were far more likely to say the behavior of students with names like Darnell or Deshawn was indicative of a pattern that would lead to suspension. The more likely teachers were to think the student was black, the more likely they were to perceive the misbehavior as part of a troubling pattern.

"The results of this report hold weighty implications for education reformers," concludes Mahnken. "The effects of suspension on a child's academic career—indeed, his life as a whole—could potentially be cataclysmic; it disrupts learning in the event and correlates with delayed academic advancement down the line. Clearly, there is room for right-thinking people to disagree on competing approaches to discipline and how to safeguard the interests of kids who step into the classroom ready and eager to learn. But if the facts behind this debate are suffused with indisputable evidence of racial bias, reformers need to find a way of addressing it."

"Two Strikes: Race and the Disciplining of Young Students" by Kevin Mahnken in *The Education Gadfly*, June 3, 2015 (Vol. 15, #21), summarized in Marshall Memo 590. The full study was published in *Psychological Science* (May 2015, Vol. 26, #5, pp. 617–624).

10 Working with the "Cool Pose Culture"

In this *New York Times* article, Harvard sociology professor Orlando Patterson examines the anti-achievement culture embraced by the bottom fifth of African-American male students. It's not peer pressure against "acting white" that's causing them to do so poorly in school, says Patterson; that theory has been shown to be largely false except for students attending a small number of mixed-race schools. So, what is the explanation? One of Patterson's students returned to her high school and interviewed her black male former classmates to find out why so few of them graduated and went to college. It turned out they were perfectly aware of the consequences of their actions. "We're not stupid!" they said indignantly.

The reason for their low achievement, she found, was that the "cool pose culture" was simply too gratifying to give up. "For these young men," says Patterson, "it was almost like a drug, hanging out on the street after school, shopping and dressing sharply, sexual conquests, party drugs, hip-hop music and culture, and the fact that almost all the superstar athletes and a great many of the nation's best entertainers were black." Living in this subculture is immensely fulfilling and garners respect from white peers—which explains why most young black men and women have higher self-esteem than other ethnic groups, regardless of how badly they are doing in school.

Patterson calls this the "Dionysian trap" for young black men—one that is all the more seductive because it is accepted and encouraged by mainstream American culture and corporations. "Hip-hop, professional basketball, and homeboy fashions are as American as cherry pie," he writes. "Young white Americans are very much into these things, but selectively; they know when it is time to turn off Fifty Cent and get out the SAT prep book. For young black men, however, that culture is all there is—or so they think. Sadly, their complete engagement in this part of the American cultural mainstream, which they created and which feeds their pride and self-respect, is a major factor in their disconnection from the socioeconomic mainstream."

Can we change this culture—or should we try? Patterson believes that three "gross misconceptions" prevent many academics and educators from making the effort:

• *Misconception 1: Cultural explanations blame the victim.* This argument is "utterly bogus," says Patterson. "To hold someone responsible for his behavior is not to exclude any recognition of the environmental factors that may have induced the problematic behavior in the first place. Many victims of child abuse end up behaving in self-destructive ways; to point out the link between their behavior and the destructive acts is in no way to deny the causal role of their early victimization and the need to address it."

• *Misconception 2: Cultural explanations are deterministic, leaving no room for human agency.* Nonsense, says Patterson. "The same cultural patterns can frame different kinds of behavior, and by failing to explore culture at any depth, analysts miss a great opportunity to reframe attitudes in a way that encourages desirable behavior and outcomes."

• *Misconception 3: Cultural patterns cannot change.* Not true, says Patterson, pointing to the way Jim Crow, "that deeply entrenched set of cultural and institutional practices built up over four centuries of racist domination and exclusion of blacks by whites in the South," was dismantled within a single generation.

"The tragedy unfolding in our inner cities is a time-slice of a deep historical process that runs far back through the cataracts and deluge of our racist past," concludes Patterson. "Most black Americans have by now, miraculously, escaped its consequences. The disconnected fifth languishing in the ghettos is the remains. Too much is at stake for us to fail to understand the plight of these young men. For them, and for the rest of us."

"A Poverty of the Mind" by Orlando Patterson in the *New York Times*, March 26, 2006, summarized in Marshall Memo 132.

11. "Reality Pedagogy" to Engage Black Male Students

"To address the low achievement of black males," says Teachers College–Columbia professor Christopher Emdin in this article in *Phi Delta Kappan*, "schools must be willing to accept that there are ways of looking at the world, modes of communication, and approaches to teaching and learning that are unique to black males. At the same time, educators must also acknowledge that these unique ways of being are just as complex as those of other students. The tie that binds all students is the desire to be academically successful."

It's not racist to point out differences in black males, says Emdin. These differences aren't genetic or developmental, but are "social and psychological baggage" that these young people bring to the classroom. "A wide variety of black male images in media—music, movies, and television programs—take characteristics of black culture, tie them to anti-school identities, violence, and misogyny, and use them as forms of entertainment. This means the world is inundated with scenarios that leave a false perception of black males that these youths must deal with when they enter classrooms…. Black males are being socially typecast and face a constant internal dilemma of fitting into expectations embodying these false characteristics or finding spaces where they can engage in practices that are counter to the perceptions."

The struggle to figure out who they should be in the classroom prevents many black male students from engaging in learning and often manifests itself in rudeness and disruption—this from boys who, says Emdin, are quiet and attentive in church or at community events "where their true selves are welcome." The "cool pose" of disinterest in academics may be at war with their true selves, but many students are trapped by perceptions, especially if they have played a certain classroom role for years.

Emdin has developed the "five Cs of reality pedagogy," tools for teaching black males that he says have produced positive results:

- *Cogenerative dialogues* – Voluntary, academically mixed groups of four to six black male students talk with their teacher (before or after school or during lunch) about how the teacher can better meet their specific academic needs—in a climate that allows them to "present their true selves to the teacher." Ground rules ensure that all participants have an equal chance to speak, that all discourse is respectful of other participants, and that an action plan is generated.
- *Coteaching* – The teacher preps a black male student to teach a class, observes him teaching it, asks questions as a "student" during instruction, debriefs afterward, and uses techniques from the student's lesson in his or her own classes.
- *Cosmopolitanism* – By this, Emdin means getting all students to take on roles that make them responsible for each other and help the class run smoothly. Making black male students part of this process and shifting roles periodically during the year helps them become an integral part of the classroom culture.
- *Context* – Teachers integrate artifacts from black male culture into their lessons—for example, creating rap songs about academic content, using pictures from local parks to explain science concepts, and using pop culture magazines to enhance English lessons. "There must be a willingness to visit their neighborhoods, watch the television programs that they watch, and listen to the music that they like," says Emdin.
- *Content* – This involves teachers encouraging black male students to pose questions about academic content and being willing to say, "I don't know" and "That's a good question." "Acknowledging that education isn't about a completed body of knowledge and that the teacher does not have

all the answers expands student perceptions about the nature of learning," says Emdin. "When black males understand that they aren't merely being expected to memorize material from an accepted body of information, they become more willing to behave differently in this new classroom environment."

"Yes, Black Males Are Different, but Different Is Not Deficient" by Christopher Emdin in *Phi Delta Kappan*, February 2012 (Vol. 93, #5, pp. 13–16), summarized in Marshall Memo 425.

---

12 What Works and What Doesn't Educating Male Students of Color

In this article in *Phi Delta Kappan*, NYU professor Pedro Noguera reviews the discouraging statistics on African-American and Latino male students: they are less likely to be placed in programs for high achievers, more likely to be classified as learning disabled and placed in special education; they have the highest suspension and expulsion rates, well over half drop out; and they are the least likely to enroll in or graduate from college.

Even students of color who grow up in middle- and upper-income families lag significantly behind. Nationwide, there is a 31-point gap between the high-school graduation rate of white and black males (78 percent versus 47 percent). The states with the highest black-white male graduation gaps are Nebraska, New York, Wisconsin, Ohio, and Illinois. On the flip side, four states graduate a higher percentage of black than white male students: Maine, North Dakota, New Hampshire, and Vermont.

Are single-gender classrooms and schools the answer, as some believe? "The need to act on the problems confronting black and Latino males is apparent," says Noguera, "but no research supports the notion that separating young men is the best way to meet their academic and social needs…. Clearly, there is no magic to be found in merely separating boys of color from their peers." The all-male classroom idea is based on what he calls "highly questionable research" that boys learn differently than girls; in fact, neurologists have not found this to be true. Isolated success stories notwithstanding, researchers in the US and abroad haven't found positive benefits from all-boy classrooms.

"Most of these initiatives," says Noguera, "are being carried out by individuals who are sincere and well-meaning about their desire to 'save' young men of color, but in many cases, they lack a clear sense of how to approach their work…. Many single-sex schools have been created without a clear sense of instructional supports that the students they serve will need. They also haven't created a learning climate conducive to academic success and positive youth development. Not surprisingly, these schools are foundering, and the students they serve are not thriving."

Noguera then reports on his research in New York City, where he and his colleagues have found more than twenty high schools that consistently graduate over 80 percent of their black and Latino males—schools like Frederick Douglass Academy and Thurgood Marshall Academy in Harlem and Eagle Academy in the South Bronx. Some of these successful schools are all-male, but others aren't, which suggests that sex segregation is not the key variable. In fact, at Thurgood Marshall, ninth-grade boys are paired with high-achieving twelfth-grade girls for mentoring.

What is driving these schools' impressive results? Strong, positive relationships between teachers and students, personalized learning with mentors, counseling, other supports that intervene early and effectively when problems arise—and strong, effective, nonauthoritarian principals who are regarded as big brothers and father figures. "These are safe schools where students feel as though they can be themselves," says Noguera, "where the peer culture reinforces the value of learning, and where character, ethics, and moral development are far more important than rigid discipline policies."

"Saving Black and Latino Boys: What Schools Can Do to Make a Difference" by Pedro Noguera in *Phi Delta Kappan*, February 2012 (Vol. 93, #5, pp. 8–12), summarized in Marshall Memo 425.

Stereotype Threat

13 Addressing Stereotype Threat

In this article in *Educational Leadership*, Joshua Aronson describes research showing that even among college students with identical SAT scores and economic backgrounds, there were significant achievement gaps. Aronson and his colleague Claude Steele suspected that another factor was suppressing the achievement of students of color—something not related to their intelligence and skills. They conducted a series of experiments and identified "stereotype threat," the way in which cultural stereotypes of intellectual inferiority impaired the performance of stigmatized groups. Aronson and Steele believe that if educators understand how stereotype threat works, they can successfully close the persistent achievement gaps in American schools.

Large numbers of Americans have negative stereotypes about different groups (for example, half of white Americans believe that blacks are less intelligent), and most children become aware of these beliefs by first grade. Students who are on the receiving end of negative stereotypes are acutely aware of how others see them, and in evaluative situations (e.g., being called on in class or taking a test) they experience what Aronson describes as "an additional degree of risk not experienced by nonstereotyped students. The very real possibility looms that they will confirm the stereotype's unflattering allegations of inferiority, in the eyes of others and perhaps in their own eyes as well …. Such feelings can make black students more apprehensive than white students about being evaluated and about the prospect of failure. They will often begin to question whether they truly belong in an arena that prizes academic talent."

Having identified stereotype threat, Aronson and Steele tried to find ways of reducing its anxiety-producing effects in the classroom. In one experiment, they sat two groups of college students down to take a challenging standardized test: one group was told that the test was intended to measure their intellectual ability; the second was told that it was not a test of ability—just a measure of the psychology of verbal problem-solving. The performance of black students in the first group was far lower than that of black students in the second group, who solved twice as many problems. (The performance of white students was the same in the two groups.) In another study, Aronson and Steele found that when students were asked to identify their race before they took a test, black students performed much worse than whites; when they were not asked their race, performance was comparable.

These studies suggest that human intellectual performance is quite fragile; it can be affected by anything that threatens a person's sense of competence, feeling of belonging, and trust in other people. Stereotype threat activates these feelings in stigmatized students, causing a marked deterioration in their performance.

Stereotype threat doesn't cause stigmatized students to give up or try less hard. Instead, it gives them an "I'll show you" attitude—and they try *too hard*. Applying extra effort is effective with easy or well-learned tasks and in situations where all that's needed is just trying harder. But with challenging tests, *relaxed concentration* leads to optimal performance. Anxious students striving to redeem themselves and their group do less well in such situations—and the negative effects of stress seem to be most pronounced for students who care the most about their performance.

African-American students are not the only ones affected by stereotype threat. It has been shown to affect any group where there is a commonly-held stereotype about lower ability: female students on math tests; Latino students on verbal tests; elderly people on tests of short-term memory; high-scoring white male engineering students when told that their performance would help understand the mathematical superiority of Asians.

Research has shown that stereotype threat kicks in as early as sixth grade; by this age, children are concerned with what others think of them, see that society has negative expectations of certain groups, and have absorbed the American belief about innate intellectual ability. By middle and high school, stereotype threat has a marked impact on students' performance and the kinds of classes they take. It leads minority students and girls to avoid challenge when they feel they are being evaluated: "When given a choice of problems ranging in difficulty, they generally select easy, success-ensuring tasks. One of the most pernicious effects of stereotype threat is that it creates an atmosphere in which *looking* smart is more important than *getting* smart."

Aronson believes several strategies effectively counteract the effects of stereotype threat. He says that implementing these in schools will cause stigmatized students' test scores, motivation, and enjoyment of school to "soar."

• *Using cooperative classroom structures* in which students work interdependently; such classrooms reduce competition, distrust, and stereotyping.

• *Teaching students that intelligence is expandable rather than fixed*. "When we teach students to reconsider the nature of intelligence," says Aronson, "to think of their minds as muscles that get strengthened and expanded—*smarter*—with hard work, we find that their negative responses to stereotype threat diminish."

• *Teaching students about stereotype threat.* "Learning that their test anxiety results from a common response to stereotyping," he says, "helps students interpret their struggles in a less pejorative and anxiety-producing way and results in higher test scores."

• *Exposing minority students to role models* who have triumphed over similar academic struggles with hard work and persistence.

Aronson concludes by cautioning against believing that one single factor will close the achievement gap. It's not just stereotyping. It's not just the family. It's not just the schools. It's all of the above, and we need "to think complexly about the problem … to find a way for all children to thrive in school."

"The Threat of Stereotype" by Joshua Aronson in *Educational Leadership*, November 2004 (Vol. 62, #3, pp. 14–19), summarized in Marshall Memo 62.

---

14. "Wise Schooling" of African-American Students

What causes the widening racial achievement gap? asks Claude Steele (Stanford University) in this article in *Atlantic Monthly*. The conventional wisdom says it's the legacy of slavery, continuing segregation, job discrimination, dysfunctional schools, broken families, drugs, violent neighborhoods, the "acting white" pressures from peers, and the social isolation of black students.

But Steele says these factors don't fully explain the persistent gap because: (a) achievement still lags among middle-class blacks who have the same advantages as their white peers; (b) the gap exists even among black students with strong academic preparation; (c) surveys show that the poorest black parents value education at least as highly as white parents; and (d) some schools have improved black achievement even though the external problems remained.

Steele believes the most important cause of the chronic underachievement of African-American students is *stigma*, "the endemic devaluation many blacks face in our society and schools," which leads them to hold back from identifying with education. The good news is that some educators have overcome the power of racial stigma with "wise schooling," unleashing the full potential of all their students. There's considerable evidence, says Steele, that "wiseness" is "the missing key to the schoolhouse door," allowing students to overcome even significant obstacles. He describes four programs that have found the key:

• James Comer transformed two low-achieving New Haven elementary schools by establishing a valuing and optimistic atmosphere in which a child can identify with learning. "After all," says Comer, "what is the difference between scribble and a letter of the alphabet to a child? The only reason the letter is meaningful, and worth learning and remembering, is because a *meaningful* other wants him or her to learn and remember it." Comer's program has many components—teacher training, parent workshops, coordination of information about students—but Steele is convinced that the most important ingredient is ensuring that "the students—vulnerable on so many counts—get treated essentially like middle-class students, with conviction about their value and promise. As this happens, their vulnerability diminishes, and with it the companion defense of disidentification and misconduct …. Comer's genius … is to have recognized the importance of these vulnerabilities as barriers to *intellectual* development, and the corollary that schools hoping to educate such students must learn first how to make them feel valued."

• In the 1970s, Berkeley mathematics professor Uri Treisman dramatically boosted the calculus performance of his black freshmen, allowing them to outperform white and Asian peers and graduate from college at similar rates. The central technique was group study of calculus concepts, but the underlying driver of success was "wiseness," systematically allaying black students' racial vulnerabilities. The program stressed their potential to learn, enlisting them in a challenging honors workshop with difficult work beyond course requirements. "Working together," explains Steele, "students soon understand that everyone knows something and nobody knows everything, and learning is speeded through shared understanding. The wisdom of these tactics is their subtext message: 'You are valued in this program because of your academic potential—regardless of your current skill level. You have no more to fear than the next person, and since the work is difficult, success is a credit to your ability and a setback is a reflection only of the challenge.' The black students' double vulnerability around failure—the fear that they lack ability, and the dread that they will be devalued—is thus reduced. They can relax and achieve."

• Jaime Escalante used the same approach—assurance combined with challenge—to get extraordinary achievement in AP calculus from Chicano high-school students in East Los Angeles.

• Xavier University has had great success producing African-American medical students not by providing remediation but by saying, "You may be somewhat behind at this time but you're a talented person. We're going to help you advance at an accelerated rate."

RACE AND THE EDUCATION OF AMERICAN STUDENTS

Steele closes with a list of five school factors that reduce black students' vulnerabilities and help them develop a strong identification with schooling:

- *Teachers who truly value their students.* "If what is meaningful and important to a teacher is to become meaningful and important to a student," he writes, "the student must feel valued by the teacher for his or her potential and as a person."
- *Remediation defeats; challenge strengthens.* "The challenge and the promise of personal fulfillment, not remediation (under whatever guise), should guide the education of these students," says Steele. "Their present skills should be taken into account, and they should be moved along at a pace that is demanding but doesn't defeat them. Their ambitions should never be scaled down but should instead be guided to inspiring goals even when extraordinary dedication is called for. Frustration will be less crippling than alienation."
- *The first condition won't work without the second, and vice-versa.* "A valuing teacher-student relationship goes nowhere without challenge," writes Steele, "and challenge will always be resisted outside a valuing relationship."
- *Racial integration helps – but is not essential.* "Segregation, whatever its purpose, draws out group differences and makes people feel more vulnerable when they inevitably cross group lines to compete in the larger society," argues Steele. The only exception is segregated schools that beat the odds and produce especially robust academic achievement and confidence, but those are few and far between.
- *A truly inclusive curriculum.* "The particulars of black life and culture—art, literature, political and social perspectives, music—must be presented in the mainstream curriculum of American schooling, not consigned to special days, weeks, or even months of the year, or to special-topic courses and programs aimed essentially at blacks," says Steele. "Such channeling carries the disturbing message that the material is not of general value. And this does two terrible things: it wastes the power of this material to alter our images of the American mainstream—continuing to frustrate black identification with it—and it excuses in whites and others a huge ignorance of their own society. The true test of democracy, Ralph Ellison has said, "is … the inclusion—not assimilation—of the black man."

"Race and the Schooling of Black Americans" by Claude Steele in the *Atlantic Monthly* (currently *The Atlantic*), April 1992, pp. 68–78), summarized in Marshall Memo 145.

Cultural Proficiency

15. Cultural Competence 101

In this *Harvard Business Review* article, Sarah Cliffe interviews Brandeis University professor Andy Molinsky about his research on dealing with cultural differences without violating one's sense of self. When people interact across cultural boundaries, says Molinsky, they first have to figure out what the cultural norms are and how they differ from their "home" culture along six dimensions:

- Directness
- Enthusiasm
- Formality
- Assertiveness
- Self-promotion
- Self-disclosure

Then people need to figure out the "zone of appropriateness" as they deal with people from different cultural backgrounds. Finally, they have to figure out what adaptations are needed (and that they're willing to make) and practice until they are comfortable.

"We tend to exaggerate what's required," says Molinsky. The key is being sensitive while figuring out your comfort zone. "Does giving criticism more directly (for example) make you feel sick to your stomach or just strange and uncomfortable? People's answers vary greatly. The gap is about who you are as much as it is about your culture. If there's a big gap between what's considered appropriate and what you're comfortable with, that's the place to start."

Here's another example. A manager asks his employees for their ideas, but the norm in this organization is that managers make top-down decisions. People interpret his reaching out as a sign that he doesn't have any ideas of his own and isn't a competent leader. The manager figures this out and ends up using a hybrid approach: he continues to ask people to contribute ideas because he believes it will help them grow professionally, but then makes top-down decisions on his own.

When leaders are trying to adapt to a new culture, says Molinsky, they sometimes feel inauthentic ("This is just not me."), less than competent, and resentful. "We know in theory that we need to adapt to different cultural norms," he says, "but it's really hard, stressful work. And when you're stressed, you're generally at your least creative and productive. So you resent the whole situation." But he's found that if leaders hang in there, they get over the hump and may even learn interesting things about themselves—perhaps aspects of the culture that are a better fit with their personality.

Building relationships across cultural barriers is "huge," says Molinsky. "Once someone has gotten to know you pretty well, they're going to cut you some slack when you screw up, which you will. You'll cut yourself some slack too if you feel that you're known and trusted and that people wish you well." Self-conscious commentary on culture can be a helpful part of building relationships and trust. A Dutch manager giving a presentation in Chicago knew that back home, he would never include a joke in a business presentation. But in this American setting, he said, "I'm about to do something very un-Dutch" and put up a relevant Dilbert cartoon.

Bicultural people have a big advantage in multicultural situations, says Molinsky. "They've already learned how to code-switch—how to make an almost unconscious calculation about which set of behaviors to use depending on where they are. They don't have the deep, magnetic default that most people do."

"'Companies Don't Go Global, People Do,'" an Interview with Andy Molinsky by Sarah Cliffe in *Harvard Business Review*, October 2015 (Vol. 93, #10, pp. 82–85), summarized in Marshall Memo 603.

---

16 What's Really Involved with Culturally Responsive Teaching?

In this *Cult of Pedagogy* article, Jennifer Gonzalez says that "culturally responsive teaching" has been getting a lot of attention recently, which is a good thing given the increasing diversity of US classrooms. "The not-so-good news," says Gonzalez, "is that in some cases, teachers *think* they're practicing culturally responsive teaching when, in fact, they're kind of not. Or at least they're not quite there. And that means students who might really thrive under different conditions are surviving at best."

Gonzalez asked Zaretta Hammond, an author and consultant specializing in this area, to share some common misconceptions and set them straight:

• *Misconception 1: Culturally responsive teaching is the same as multicultural or social justice education.* In fact, each of these address diversity from a different angle. Multicultural education is "the celebration of diversity, what we usually see in schools," says Hammond. "While those are really noble things and critical to a high-functioning classroom and school climate, it doesn't have anything to do with learning capacity." It's great for students to see their cultures reflected in school, but it won't affect their cognitive abilities. Better than focusing on "surface culture," she says, is learning about collectivism, an ideology common in many of the cultures from which students come. Understanding collectivism helps teachers reach diverse students.

Social justice education "is about building a lens for the student, really being able to look at the world and seeing where things aren't fair or where injustice exists," says Hammond. Again, this is important, but it doesn't address students' learning capacity. For example, learning about social justice doesn't address the issue of a student who is three grades behind in reading.

Culturally responsive teaching, by comparison, "is about building the learning capacity of the individual student," says Hammond. "There is a focus on leveraging the affective and the cognitive scaffolding that students bring with them." The test of culturally responsive teaching, then, is whether students of color, English language learners, immigrant students, or any with disadvantages are learning. If they're not succeeding, a teacher's approach might need to be more culturally responsive.

• *Misconception 2: Culturally responsive teaching must start with addressing implicit bias.* "You need to get to implicit bias at some point," says Hammond. "It's just not the starting point. If you start there, you can't pivot to instruction. Whereas when you understand inequity by design, you can actually talk about instruction but also come back to talk about micro-aggressions. The sequencing of that is really important."

• *Misconception 3: Culturally responsive teaching is all about building relationships and self-esteem.* "There's a big effort afoot in terms of social-emotional learning programs," says Hammond, "trying to help students gain self-regulation, and build positive relationships with students. Here's what the schools are finding that do surveys: After a few years of this kind of work, their positive climate has gone up, satisfaction surveys among adults as well as kids are really high, but the achievement doesn't move." It's certainly true that building trusting relationships is important as an "on-ramp" to higher-level cognitive work by students, but it's a means to that end, not an end in itself.

• *Misconception 4: Culturally responsive teaching is about implementing certain strategies in the classroom.* For example, some teachers add call-and-response to their classroom routines and think that will reach diverse students. But while this is a good first step, the real question is whether call-and-response is being used to deepen student thinking. "Teachers need to interrogate their practice a little more robustly," says Hammond, "because it's not an off-the-shelf program, it's not two or three strategies. It's not plug and play."

Hammond advocates three broader approaches to making instruction more culturally responsive: First, gamify it—that is, make routine curriculum work (like memorizing science vocabulary) into a game that involves repetition, solving a puzzle, or making connections between things that don't seem related. Second, make it social—that is, organize learning so that students rely on each other, building on their communal orientation. Third, storify it—that is, create a coherent story or narrative about the subject matter.

Perhaps the most counterintuitive thing about culturally responsive teaching is that it's not just for certain groups of students. "This kind of teaching is good for all brains," says Hammond. "So what you're doing to actually reach your lowest-performing students is going to be good for your highest-performing students." In short, Gonzalez adds, "the instructional shifts that will make the biggest differences don't always look 'cultural' at all, because they aren't the kind of things that work only for diverse students."

"Culturally Responsive Teaching: 4 Misconceptions" by Jennifer Gonzalez and Zaretta Hammond in *Cult of Pedagogy*, September 10, 2017, summarized in Marshall Memo 703.

---

17. Strategies for Boosting the Achievement of African-American Students

In this *Phi Delta Kappan* article, Derek Mitchell, Jesse Hinueber, and Brian Edwards (Partners in School Innovation) say it's unwise for schools to try to be colorblind. "Although the impulse is understandable and the sentiment is admirable," they say, "… we cannot avoid being affected by racial currents in society, whether we acknowledge them or not …. Schools that do achieve strong results for black students address racial dynamics carefully yet directly, empower students to bring their whole selves to school, and teach in ways that leverage students' experience and cultures." Here are the details of what these schools do:

• *Direct attention, strategies, and resources to black student achievement.* This includes looking at multiple indicators (grades, discipline data, graduation rates) while treating students' race and culture as central to their identity—as assets to build on. For example, the Oakland, California schools have seen positive results from the Manhood Development Program, which focuses on the contributions of Africans and African Americans from ancient times to the present, emphasizes careers and civic engagement, brings in peer mentors, and features role models in school assemblies.

• *Foster adult learning about race, culture, class, and power.* "Teachers of all races can successfully serve black students," say Mitchell, Hinueber, and Edwards, "and professional development can accelerate the process. School leaders play an important part by providing time and support for professional learning, modeling an assets-based approach toward students and staff, and demonstrating profound respect for students and families." Ongoing PD topics should include historical school experiences of black students, implicit bias, teacher expectations, courageous conversations, discussion protocols, and key aspects of culturally responsive instruction. One particularly important point: teachers need to give honest and helpful feedback to students, not fall into the common trap of overpraising black students in an effort to boost their self-esteem. The most successful teachers are "warm-demanders."

• *Build strong relationships between educators and black students.* Effective schools "don't search for a silver-bullet instructional strategy," say the authors, "but, instead, understand that trusting relationships are essential to creating a thriving academic community." This means building rapport with students and their families (home visits are very helpful), allowing more student and family voice in parent conferences, and building a firm alliance with students focused on achievement. Teachers might think of the curriculum as mirroring students' backgrounds, providing windows to expose students to other cultures, and building bridges that connect the two. This kind of curriculum goes beyond superficial items like food, dress, and music—focusing on "deep culture," how kinship and fairness are defined.

• *Foster noncognitive skills and student agency.* This includes giving students a sense of belonging (*I am part of this academic community.*), value (*This work is important to me.*), growth mindset (*With effort, my skills will keep on improving.*), and self-efficacy (*I can do this.*). One particularly effective gap-closing strategy is having students reflect on and write about the principles that guide their lives.

"Looking Race in the Face" by Derek Mitchell, Jesse Hinueber, and Brian Edwards in *Phi Delta Kappan*, February 2017 (Vol. 98, #5, pp. 24–29), summarized in Marshal Memo 673.

18. Four Steps to Cultural Competence

"All people are shaped by the culture in which they live," say Hilary Dack and Carol Ann Tomlinson (University of Virginia) in this *Educational Leadership* article. "The shaping process is both subtle and pervasive, and it can be difficult for all of us to grasp that people shaped by other cultures will see and respond to the world differently than we do." As a result, it's easy for educators to interpret unfamiliar student behaviors as expressions of disinterest, deficiency, disrespect, or defiance. Dack and Tomlinson suggest four ways to become better attuned to differences so all students flourish:

• *Recognize and appreciate cultural variance.* Good teachers have always been "students of their students," say the authors; now it's important to be students of their cultures, "attuned to their languages, appreciating their experiences and histories, and valuing their lenses on the world." This might include joining students at concerts, plays, movies, and other events reflecting a diverse array of cultures.

• *Tune in to culturally influenced learning patterns.* Some students' backgrounds are collectivist while others are more individualistic, say Dack and Tomlinson. "Some will have learned to revere their teachers from a distance, others to negotiate with their teachers as they would with a peer, and still others—that they owe their teachers no respect until it's earned …. Each new layer of understanding provides a platform for creating a classroom in which all comers can feel at home." Here are a few other cultural continuums on which individual students are arrayed:

- Needs to observe <---> Needs to test ideas
- Needs external structures <---> Creates own structures
- Competitive <---> Collaborative
- Conforming <---> Creative
- Reserved <---> Expressive
- Fixed sense of time <---> Flexible sense of time
- Information-driven <---> Feeling-driven

A teacher noticed that several students were uncomfortable responding to quick-response questions and on-the-spot writing prompts. Advised by a colleague that these students had been taught to value reflection over speed, and to listen and reflect before speaking, the teacher made two adjustments: first, she gave advance warning of an upcoming question by saying, "I want to hear from a couple of additional students on this topic. Then I'm going to ask for your thinking." Second, early in a lesson she said, "As we conclude our lesson today, I'm going to ask you to summarize your understandings in writing." These minor tweaks made a noticeable difference to the comfort and performance of formerly reticent students—and not just those the teacher originally had in mind.

• *Look beyond cultural patterns to see individuals.* Although there are learning-style patterns within cultures, there are plenty of individual differences. Students who appear to be part of a homogenous group can vary tremendously because of differences in gender, school experience, parental support, time in the US, and personal temperament. "True cultural sensitivity requires person sensitivity as well," say Dack and Tomlinson.

• *Plan inviting curriculum and instruction.* This means teaching history, literature, music, language, and contemporary issues in ways that make as many connections as possible to students' varied cultures and experiences. "In other words, the curriculum leads students to explore content through universal lenses rather than only parochial ones," say the authors. "A teacher who looks at students as individuals – no matter what their cultural experiences are—will attend to their varied points of readiness, their interests, their exceptionalities, their status among peers, and so on when planning curriculum and instruction." And from a pedagogical perspective, it's wise to try to hit as many points on the continuums listed above as possible, either in unit and lesson plans or the choices students are able to make.

For example, in preparing students for a challenging assessment, a teacher might give two options: a quiz bowl in which students compete in teams to answer sets of questions, or a tag team in which students collaborate in groups to propose answers to the same questions, explain their thinking, and ask one another for elaborations to clarify their thinking.

Dack and Tomlinson close by quoting John Hattie on the characteristics of classrooms that invite students to learn:

- Respect – Every student is valuable, able, and responsible.
- Trust – Each student contributes to the learning process.
- Optimism – Each student has the potential to be successful.
- Intentionality – Every step of a lesson invites each student to learn.

"Inviting All Students to Learn" by Hilary Dack and Carol Ann Tomlinson in *Educational Leadership*, March 2015 (Vol. 72, #6, pp. 10–15), summarized in Marshall Memo 576.

---

19. A White Teacher's Suggestions for Doing Right by Students of Color

In this article in *Education Week Teacher*, Arkansas teacher Justin Minkel notes an important "disconnect" in US schools: 80 percent of K–12 teachers are white, while 51 percent of students are children of color. "White teachers like me have to love our students of color enough to learn how to teach them well," says Minkel. His suggestions:

- *Small daily actions* – "Our students of color are often starved for anything and anyone relevant to their identities and experiences," he says. His first graders were enraptured when he showed a YouTube clip of the *Hamilton* cast performing at the White House.
- *Literature* – "Children of color need books to be mirrors as well as windows," says Minkel. There's no shortage of material, starting with Scholastic's "We Need Diverse Books" catalog https://bit.ly/2MEaiX3. High-quality books and magazines need to be prominent in guided reading groups, readalouds, and classroom libraries for independent reading. Texts about people of color shouldn't shy away from issues of oppression, but there should be a balance. One mother reported that her children had this to say about the books they were reading in school: "It's always about slavery and racism. Once in a while, can't we read about black kids just chillin'?"
- *Guest speakers* – There are all too many negative images of African Americans and Latinos in the media, says Minkel: "We have to provide our students a constant stream of writers, artists, mathematicians, scientists, engineers, and other competent and caring men and women of color to counter that poisonous programming."
- *Upstanding* – "When you hear other white people—including fellow teachers—make racist comments, speak up," says Minkel. "It's OK if your face turns red, you blurt out something that doesn't quite line up as a sentence, or it takes you 12 hours to come up with the line you wish you had said. The important thing is to make a little gash in that conversation so the comment does not go unnoticed or unchallenged. Part of white privilege is the ability to speak against racism without being quickly discounted by white people in power as people of color often are."
- *Listening* – "I continue to marvel at the patience, kindness, and generosity of spirit shown to me by African-American and Latino friends and colleagues," says Minkel. "To learn from them, I have to remind myself to stop talking and instead listen deeply to their experiences, perspectives, and advice …. We can't be afraid to ask a question of a colleague of color for fear we'll look foolish or clueless."

"How Can White Teachers Do Right by Students of Color?" by Justin Minkel in *Education Week Teacher*, August 15, 2018, summarized in Marshall Memo 749.

Professional Learning Suggestions for Chapter Three: Students' Social-Emotional Development

Educating Educators About Racism

This chapter takes on the critical topic of racism and the downward force it exerts on students of color. As educators, failure on our part to confront and disrupt racism makes us complicit in the academic, psychological, and socio-emotional suffering that students of color endure. American schools have a responsibility and opportunity to model antiracism policies and practices for their local communities, country, and the global community. It is a responsibility we have not taken seriously enough.

Below are fourteen professional learning suggestions that attempt to answer the question: *What can we do about this?* We can engage in professional learning activities that help us come into consciousness and see racism in and around us. Given that we are in education, we can commit to being diligent students of antiracism so that, knowing better, we can do better to weaken its impact. And finally, we can support and empower our students of color.

I. Come into Consciousness

The adults in your school will be at varying levels of knowledge, readiness, self-awareness, and experience when it comes to the topics of racism, white privilege, and unconscious bias. The following activities are intended to help people "come awake" to the reality, pervasiveness, and destructive impact of racism by educating, heightening self-awareness, and introducing a foundation of common language that staff can use to talk about these difficult issues.

A. Uncover implicit bias.
We can't fight an enemy when we are unconvinced or unaware of its presence. Thus, a necessary step in combating racism is to see it plainly in ourselves. Taking an implicit bias test is a common and effective way to "show rather than tell people" that they have implicit bias, even though they don't act in consciously racist ways. Some prefer to introduce an implicit bias test *after* engaging in a provocative book study or a dynamic speaker with expertise in this area. This way, staff are

PROFESSIONAL LEARNING SUGGESTIONS FOR CHAPTER THREE

enlisted emotionally and nondefensively with the issue and have a more intense desire to learn and grow when this tool is introduced.

1. As a springboard for a faculty meeting, have faculty take any or all of the tests below, especially if you sense that there are some who need help moving from—*I don't see color, and talking about racism brings unnecessary contention and division*; *I'm not racist*; and/or *I don't act in consciously racist ways*—to a place of understanding/belief about their own unconscious bias.

   a. The Implicit Association Test (IAT) https://implicit.harvard.edu/implicit/takeatest.html

   b. Antiracist Educator Questionnaire and Rubric https://bit.ly/30yFprN

   c. Diversity and Inclusion Self-Assessment https://bit.ly/2Bkxw0L

2. Once people have taken one or more of these tests, have small group discussions and a large-group debrief where you discuss: where these biases come from, what they mean, what we can do about them. Remind people not to expect closure.

B. Understand white privilege.

Have staff read article-summary 5, summarizing Peggy McIntosh's renowned essay "White Privilege: Unpacking the White Knapsack." Written in 1989, it was considered a groundbreaking article and is still considered by many the authoritative text on the subject of white privilege. In the essay, McIntosh "unpacks" and makes visible an invisible knapsack of fifty unearned benefits of being white. After reading the article, divide staff into small groups and have them discuss the following:

- What were your initial reactions to this list of unearned privileges?
- Did any particular privileges on this list stand out to you? Why?
- Which if any of these privileges affected your experiences as a K–12 student? How?
- Which of these privileges affect your experience as a K–12 teacher? How?
- Which privileges on this list make you most uncomfortable? Why?
- Which privileges on this list have you had the fewest opportunities to think about?

MINDSETS THAT SUPPORT LEARNING

> *Facilitator Tips:*
> - Explain the word "systemic" and think about why US people, especially white people, have trouble seeing systemically. Explain the myth of meritocracy that argues that the unit of society is the individual and that whatever one suffers or ends up with must be whatever that individual either wanted, worked for, earned, or deserved. When this myth survives successfully, it suppresses knowledge of systemic oppression and its "upside," systemic privilege.
> - Help adults in your school (and encourage them to help students) see racism systemically and structurally rather than see "racism" as the actions of uneducated/racist/hateful individuals making individual choices.
> - McIntosh has advised that this work goes best when participants draw on their own personal experiences, not their opinions. Opinions invite argumentation, whereas when someone shares an experience it elicits curiosity and empathy. As facilitator, if you find discussion veering towards opinions, request that people share their lived experiences and stories instead.

C. Use white privilege to undo systems of unearned privilege.

In large- and small-group discussions, have staff brainstorm ways to use their white privilege to undo systems of privilege.

　1. Facilitate a large-group discussion of the following questions:
- Why is it important to be aware of our white privilege? What happens when we are not?
- In what ways can we use unearned privilege to weaken *systems* that are biased in our school? Why would we want to?
- How could we use our white privilege to do the following seven things:

Pay attention and be alert	Speak up/assert/ take initiative	Be an ally/do advocacy work
Make associations	Defer (allow others to decide/ lead)	Lobby/campaign
Recognize and act against both external and internalized forms of oppression and privilege		

PROFESSIONAL LEARNING SUGGESTIONS FOR CHAPTER THREE

2. Divide staff into small groups. For each group, create a chart with the above on the horizontal axis and the following different roles on the vertical axis:

- As an individual teacher
- As a group of teachers (department, grade)
- As an entire school faculty
- As a district or region

Ask each group to appoint a "table recorder" who can capture what people brainstorm in the table. When small groups have had sufficient time to brainstorm, go around and have each reporter share an idea for each cell of the chart. Share these in a large version of the chart in the front of the room or use a Google form so everyone can share and see all ideas.

D. Anticipate and manage white fragility.

As a brief introduction to white fragility, show the following nine-minute video and discuss its implications:

"White Fragility," by Robin DiAngelo: *https://www.youtube.com/watch?v=6O27_yBQ8Qc*

II. Commit to Being Diligent Students of Antiracism

After initially coming into consciousness as was suggested in Part I, educators need to dive more deeply into becoming students of antiracism. This section provides suggestions for a range of resources and media to help educators "come awake" and see and fully understand the systemic nature of racism.

A. Establish common language.

Make no assumptions that students, teachers, administrators, or parents have heard of or understand the terminology related to antiracist or antibias education. Failing to communicate these terms opens the door to misperceptions and even false accusations about both why and what you are trying to do. Post these definitions on your school/classroom websites as well as on walls in the school so that they serve as continual reminders. In addition to avoiding misunderstanding, we should learn antiracist terminology because it has been said that we cannot think about, much less discuss, things that we have no vocabulary for. The more vocabulary we have for a topic like racism, the more precise and effective our conversations can be. As a means of equipping staff to engage in those conversations, make establishing a common language a professional learning objective. Racialequity.org has an excellent lexicon of terms that you can select from: https://www.racialequitytools.org/glossary#anti-racism.

1. Decide on a manageable number of initial terms that you think are most important for the group to have common language and understanding around.

2. Share and type them up on a handout with a box beneath each one.

3. In small groups, going clockwise, have the first person read the definition, have the group members write a sentence in the box that uses the term. It can be about an experience they had; it can be a paraphrase of the definition; or it can be a question.

4. After one minute, go around the circle and have each person read what they wrote. There need not be discussion about each term until the very end. Then, move onto the next definition and have the next person in the circle read that definition; repeat the process. This is an activity you can return to for introducing new terminology or refreshing old terminology as often as needed.

B. Learn from the nineteen article-summaries in this chapter.

The sections that follow provide a wide range of resources your staff can use to better understand racism and antiracism. In addition, the nineteen article-summaries in this chapter can add to this effort. Have staff jigsaw the readings so everyone can benefit from all of them:

1. Let staff choose which of the five sections of article-summaries they prefer to read (it's helpful to include choice when you can in a PD activity):
   - Implicit Bias and Microaggressions
   - Discussing the Undiscussable
   - Challenges for Children of Color
   - Stereotype Threat
   - Cultural Proficiency

2. Ask staff to read all of the articles in the section they choose before a staff meeting, or carve out time during a staff meeting.

3. At the staff meeting, put staff into groups with one representative from each of the five groups and have them each share:
   - *In a nutshell, what is the main idea of each article-summary you read?*
   - *What most resonated with you about the article-summaries you read and why?*

PROFESSIONAL LEARNING SUGGESTIONS FOR CHAPTER THREE

- *What implications or next steps did you take from the article-summaries you read?*

4. Come back together as a large group. Have one large piece of newsprint for each of the nineteen article-summaries on the walls (or do this online) and let everyone walk around and write their takeaways on each paper.

5. Discuss the strongest takeaways staff had from the article-summaries in this chapter.

C. Set up faculty book studies.

Another powerful way to help people "come awake" and see the systemic nature of racism is to engage in faculty-wide book studies.

1. Create a document that links each of the book titles that follow to a brief synopsis of the book (e.g., on Amazon, Good Reads or BuzzFeed) and share the long list with your leadership team. Ask them to read synopses of the books and authors and decide on one for the entire faculty to read over the summer, or offer a choice of a couple which faculty can read a few chapters at a time and meet in "book-clubs" to discuss over the course of one school term. Note that this is by no means an exhaustive list, and a group should be assigned to update this list regularly.

- *Waking Up White* by Debby Irving
- *Tell Me Who You Are: Sharing Our Stories of Race, Culture & Identity* by Winona Guo and Priya Vulchi
- *How to Be an Antiracist* by Ibram X. Kendi
- *So You Want to Talk About Race* by Ijeoma Oluo
- *Citizen: An American Lyric* by Claudia Rankine
- *The Fire Next Time* by James Baldwin
- *The Fire This Time: A New Generation Speaks About Race*, edited by Jesmyn Ward
- *Why Are All the Black Kids Sitting Together in the Cafeteria?* Beverly Daniel Tatum
- *I'm Still Here: Black Dignity in a World Made for Whiteness* by Austin Channing Brown
- *Me and White Supremacy: Combat Racism, Change the World, and Become a Good Ancestor* by Layla F. Saad

2. Work with your leadership team curriculum coordinator to come up with specific outcomes for each book club that will help the school take action/move forward in its antiracist agenda. Appoint a "reporter" for each small group who can record in a common document for the members of the group: key concepts from the book, enduring understandings, essential questions, and recommendations for how the school can apply what the book teaches.

MINDSETS THAT SUPPORT LEARNING

D. Use film, documentaries, and short videos to teach and learn.

A picture is worth a thousand words. Use documentary, film, short video or a *TED Talk* as an engaging springboard for antiracist professional learning.

   1. Choose a documentary, film or *TED Talk* from the list that follows for faculty to view all together, individually, or asynchronously in assigned small groups.

   - A Curated List of *TED Talks* to Help You Understand Racism in America: www.ted.com/playlists/250/talks_to_help_you_understand_r
   - Films and TV series to watch:

13th (Ava DuVernay) documentary — Netflix	*If Beale Street Could Talk* (Barry Jenkins) — Hulu
American Son (Kenny Leon) — Netflix	*Just Mercy* (Destin Daniel Cretton)
Black Power Mixtape: 1967–1975 — Available to rent	*King in The Wilderness* — HBO
Blindspotting (Carlos López Estrada) — Hulu	*See You Yesterday* (Stefon Bristol) — Netflix
Clemency (Chinonye Chukwu) — For rent	*Selma* (Ava DuVernay) — Available to rent
Dear White People (Justin Simien) — Netflix	*The Black Panthers: Vanguard of the Revolution* — For rent
Fruitvale Station (Ryan Coogler) — Available to rent	*The Hate U Give* (George Tillman Jr.) — Hulu with Cinemax
I Am Not Your Negro (James Baldwin doc) — For rent	*When They See Us* (Ava DuVernay) — Netflix

   2. Follow the viewing with a whole group discussion to share key learning. Assign break-out groups to make concrete recommendations for action inspired by the documentary, film, or *TED Talk*.

E. Enlist experts.

Be prepared for the fact that conversations about racism and unconscious bias can be met with a range of emotions from participants, such as: guilt, shame, anger, denial, sadness, dissonance, and discomfort. This is because the real work of antiracism is very personal; it challenges people's sense of self. Robin DiAngelo terms this internal discomfort and difficulty in confronting racism in oneself and one's own community "white fragility." Given this, there might be value in bringing in skilled facilitators with experience helping adults find entry points into the conversation, nondefensively examine their own actions and reactions, engage in activities that show them how they have been shaped by their own experiences, and look for concrete ways in which they can have positive influences on their students and colleagues. The following organizations and individuals have expertise in training on antiracism and cultural competence.

   - Diversity Equity and Inclusion Extension: deiextension.org

PROFESSIONAL LEARNING SUGGESTIONS FOR CHAPTER THREE

- Race Forward: https://www.raceforward.org/trainings
- Robin DiAngelo, Keynotes on White Fragility: https://robindiangelo.com/services/
- Latasha Morrison (bethebridge): Anti-Racism Coaching and Training https://latashamorrison.com/consultant-speaker/
- Teaching Tolerance: www.tolerance.org
- Center for Racial Justice Education: https://centerracialjustice.org/
- Research for Better Teaching: http://www.rbteach.com

Facilitator Tips:
Using an expert antiracist organization or facilitator does not relieve you of the responsibility or initiative to learn. As diligent students of this issue, you must do the ongoing work individually and institutionally to deepen your understanding of this issue. Before bringing in experts, do prework as a faculty (articles, book study, establishing common language) and communicate with the expert specific areas of learning and growth that you would like their help to go deeper into.

III. Support and Empower Students

This section includes several activities that directly support and empower students.

A. Hold ourselves accountable; disaggregate the data.
Often students of color are blamed for not putting in the necessary effort required to achieve high levels of academic success when, in reality, racial inequity and institutional racism are at play.

1. Ask teachers to bring data disaggregated by race to a professional development session, or gather and disaggregate the data by race for teachers prior to a PD session. This can be data related to students underperforming in classes, students who have been disciplined/suspended, students who are being "counseled out" of a school because the school doesn't seem able to meet their needs, students who have been referred for IEPs or labeled with a learning need, or students who have been recommended to higher level courses (e.g., AP).

2. Display the definitions of *racial equity* and *institutional racism* (one source: *Flipping the Script: White Privilege and Community Building* by Maggie Potapchuk, Sally Leiderman, Donna Bivens, and Barbara Major, 2005) and discuss them.

3. Following a data analysis protocol, ask hard questions about where and why students of color are over or underrepresented. Invite discussion about whether data showing a disproportionate number of students of color could be evidence of institutional racism and/or racial inequity—and if we were to assume these two things are at play, what we could do in response.

4. Plan action steps aimed at countering racial inequity and institutional racism and agree to test these actions over an appropriate enough period of time to gather data about their impact on the data.

B. Equip students to respond to microaggressions.

Have staff do a "live read" of article-summary 8, "Strategies for Addressing Insensitive Comments," about how to respond to microaggressions. This means you carve out time during a staff meeting for reading the article on the spot. Next, have them read "21 Racial Microaggressions You Hear on a Daily Basis," which can be found at: https://www.buzzfeed.com/hnigatu/racial-microagressions-you-hear-on-a-daily-basis.

1. Display the term "microaggression" and its definition for staff to read. Have a large-group discussion of this definition.

2. Have staff watch this video all together: *#HatchKids: Students Give Examples of Microaggressions* https://www.youtube.com/watch?v=8RfwnibEd3A

3. After everyone has read the two articles and seen the video, have a large-group discussion: *Does anyone want to share an example of microaggressions you have experienced personally or witnessed? What are some ways we, as staff, might respond when we hear microaggressions? What do you think of the effectiveness of the three suggestions Hahna Yoon shares in article-summary 8 in the chapter:*

- Asking for clarification, for example, *"Could you say more about what you mean by that?"*
- Separating intent from impact**,** for example, *"I know you didn't realize this, but when you … (comment/behavior), it was hurtful/offensive because …."*
- Share your own process, for example, *"I noticed that you … (comment/behavior). I used to do/say that too, but then I learned …."*

4. Divide staff into trios. First ask them to choose a microaggression from the articles, video, or the examples that came from the group. Next, have them role-play being in a situation

PROFESSIONAL LEARNING SUGGESTIONS FOR CHAPTER THREE

where they are on the receiving end of one of those microaggressions and where they choose to respond with one of the options discussed.

5. Give staff time (individually or in grade-level/subject-alike groups) to come up with a plan for:
- When and how they can teach their students what "microaggressions" are. (Some might opt to use the very same video and article, others might go about it differently—in a way that is better matched to their students.)
- How they will equip students to respond to microaggressions (e.g., role play, create a regular space for students to share/advise one another about the intent and impact of their words).

C. Empower students to surmount stereotype threat.

Have the entire staff do a live read of article-summary 13, "Addressing Stereotype Threat," and pay close attention to the suggestions at the end of the piece to combat stereotype threat.

1. Divide staff into small groups to come up with strategies for Aronson's suggestion: *Teaching students that intelligence is expandable rather than fixed.* There are countless examples of visuals, videos and mini lessons that teachers around the world are using to teach students that their intelligence is expandable. Give the small groups time to explore these resources online and then come together to share ideas from their online searches *and* from their own classrooms for ways to teach students that their intelligence is expandable. Then have everyone commit to trying one to two strategies before the next PD session, and be sure to check in on the implementation of these strategies and how students responded.

2. Share this definition of stereotype threat with the large group and discuss it:

> *Stereotype threat* refers to the risk of confirming negative stereotypes about an individual's racial, ethnic, gender, or cultural group. The term was coined by the researchers Claude Steele and Joshua Aronson, who performed experiments that showed that black college students performed worse on standardized tests than their white peers when they were reminded, before taking the tests, that their racial group tends to do poorly on such exams. When their race was not emphasized, however, black students performed similarly to their white peers.

3. Show this brief video: https://www.youtube.com/watch?v=failylROnrY of Claude Steele talking about his book *Whistling Vivaldi*. Before beginning the video ask each person to

capture one thing from the video that they would like to share back with the group that helps clarify either:
- What is stereotype threat?
- Why it is important to understand its impact?
- What can teachers do to help students feel "identity safe" enough to flourish?

4. Have faculty form small groups and create a poster in which they:
- Provide a definition of *stereotype threat* (in their own words);
- Accompany it with a visual of some sort (symbol, cartoon);
- Include one reason why educators need to be aware of this;
- Brainstorm two to three tips for teachers about how to mitigate the impact of stereotype threat;
- Come up with one idea for what teachers could say to students or do with students to mitigate stereotype threat.

D. Integrate antiracism into the curriculum.
Integrating antiracist teaching and learning into our curriculum is critical if we are to take a stance against racism in a systemic and sustained way.

1. Share/reshare the definition of antiracism with teachers. Ask them the question:
   - In what ways is the course/curriculum that you teach antiracist?
   - What evidence would you offer for or against that claim?

2. In subject-alike and grade-level teams, give teachers time to examine examples and resources that they could integrate in their curriculum. At the end of the time, have each group share something they reviewed, what they liked about it, and how/where/when they could integrate it into their curriculum.

3. To ensure action and accountability, prepare a form where each grade level or department makes a commitment to how they will integrate antiracist topics/ lessons/units/resources into their curriculum. Set a period of experimentation with this (start and end date) and set a date when people will reconvene as a whole group to present what they have experimented with, what they have learned, and what they plan to keep doing and/or experiment with next.

E. Let students be our teachers about how to do this work better.
In article-summary 11, "'Reality Pedagogy' to Engage Black Male Students," Christopher Emdin

PROFESSIONAL LEARNING SUGGESTIONS FOR CHAPTER THREE

offers some concrete suggestions about how to let students be our teachers in this antiracism work. For many teachers who are accustomed to leading learning and always being the one to offer expertise and guidance about "how" to do things, this will have to be a conscious effort and mindset shift.

1. As a large group, discuss the following:
   - Invite staff to share experiences about times students have been *their* teachers about how to do some aspect of teaching/learning more effectively. Explain that in antiracist work, staying in "learner mode" (regardless of how much experience with antiracism we believe we have) and letting students and parents of color be our teachers is critically important.
   - Next, ask teachers if they have ever been accused by a student of being racist.

2. Break staff into groups of three and have them read Christopher Emdin article-summary 11. Ask them to select one of his "five Cs of reality pedagogy" to discuss with their colleagues.

3. Have a chart with the explanation of each of the five Cs taped on a different wall or section of the room. Ask faculty to go to the chart with the reality pedagogy they would like to explore. Once faculty are in these five groups, give them time to reread the strategy and then discuss and record the following:
   - What gets in the way of this happening?
   - What would help us do what this article suggests?
   - What do we predict the impact of doing these things would be?

4. Take time in the PD session to make some commitments about what you will try, how long you will give yourselves to experiment with this, and a date (future PD session) when you will share what you did and how it went. Using a form is not a bad idea.

Chapter Four: Partnering with Families

Teachers are the experts in pedagogy, but families are one hundred percent the experts on their children. We need one another.
—Kristin Ehrgood

Families are central to children's success, but which forms of home involvement have the greatest impact? The articles in this chapter explore four dimensions of this question: parenting for school success; home-school communication; parent-teacher conferences; and the value of homework and at-home activities.

Parenting for School Success – Ron Ferguson, Jeff Howard, and Martin Walsh say that five high-leverage parenting practices make all the difference for children from birth to age three. Margaret Talbot describes a Providence, Rhode Island, program that monitors parents' verbal interactions with their young children and coaches parents to increase the amount of conversation. Angel Harris and Keith Robinson say that parents can "set the stage" for their children's school success by providing specific conditions at home, and argue that this stage-setting is more important than traditional school-involvement activities. Eva Pomerantz, Elizabeth Moorman, and Scott Litwack show how teachers' actions can bring out the best in parents' interactions with their children—or reinforce the negative.

Home-School Communication – June Kronholz describes a program that trains and pays teachers to make visits to their students' homes and the difference those visits have made. Sarah Sparks reports on a study of how parents prefer to be notified of school and classroom events. Robert Evans and Michael Thompson suggest ways educators can deal successfully with antagonistic parents.

Parent-Teacher Conferences – Sarah McKibben suggests eight ways schools can improve the quality of parent-teacher conferences. Jun-ah Choi describes a conference with her son's kindergarten teacher that didn't go well and suggests how teachers can avoid the mistakes this teacher made. Amy Goodman reports on the successful implementation of student-led report card conferences in an Alaska middle school.

Homework and At-Home Activities – Alexandria Neason questions the value of homework, especially at the elementary level, and suggests how to improve the way homework is assigned and assessed. Bruce Jackson theorizes that the "good homework habits" encouraged in elementary schools backfire when students reach the secondary grades. Bill Henderson details his Boston elementary school's tenacious and successful efforts to increase the amount of reading struggling students did at home.

Questions to Consider

- What can families do at home to maximize their children's school success?
- What are the best ways for schools and families to communicate?
- Why is homework so often seen as a waste of time?

Parenting for School Success

1. Early-Childhood Practices That Prepare Children to Thrive in School

In this article in the *Bay State Banner*, Ron Ferguson (Harvard Achievement Gap Initiative), Jeff Howard (The Efficacy Institute and the Black Philanthropy Fund), and Martin Walsh (Mayor of Boston) describe the Boston Basics Campaign and their effort to get its message to day-care centers, hospitals, community agencies, and schools. "Our goal," say Ferguson, Howard, and Walsh, "is to help parents and caregivers adopt five easy practices that research has proven are essential to brain development from birth to age three."

- *Maximize love and manage stress.* "Showing affection and patience at every opportunity helps children build confidence to explore the world on their own," they say.

- *Talk, sing, and point.* "Talking and singing to infants and toddlers stimulates their brains and develops their skills," they say. "Pointing helps them connect words to the associated objects."

- *Teach counting, grouping, and comparing with everyday objects.* "Having fun with numbers, names, shapes, and patterns is how children learn to understand their world," they say. "And it prepares them to learn and love math."

- *Let children explore through free movement and play.* "Curiosity is a child's built-in engine for learning," say Ferguson, Howard, and Walsh. "It's our job to encourage it and provide safe outlets. At home or in the playground, help kids dive into their environment and develop their 'mind's eye.'"

- *Read and discuss stories.* "Whether made-up or factual, the people, places and events of stories are the building blocks for our children's imagination and much of their learning later in life," they say.

"We know that raising kids is hard," conclude the authors, "and it's only made harder by the stresses of work, money, illness, violence, and more. So we want to make our entire city a relentlessly supportive place for all those who care for young children." Introductory videos can be viewed at https://boston.thebasics.org.

"Five Simple Habits to Help Our Children Thrive" by Ron Ferguson, Jeff Howard, and Martin Walsh in the *Bay State Banner*, March 17, 2016, summarized in Marshall Memo 629.

2. Changing the Way Parents Talk to Their Children

There are many similarities among families, says Margaret Talbot in this article in the *New Yorker*: all parents show affection, discipline their children, and try to teach them good manners. But there are big social-class differences in the number of words children hear in their homes: an average of 2,150 an hour in professional families, 1,250 in middle-class families, and 620 in poor families.

The city of Providence, Rhode Island, is trying to do something about the vocabulary gap with a program called Providence Talks. "Head Start is awesome," says former mayor Angel Taveras, who launched the project. "But we've gotta do something even *before* Head Start." The city's caseworkers are making frequent visits to young mothers of limited means and coaching them on the power of simply talking more with their children.

"Changing how low-income parents interact with their children is a delicate matter, and not especially easy," says Talbot. "The way you converse with your child is one of the most intimate aspects of parenting, shaped both by your personality and by cultural habits so deep that they can feel automatic." Talbot observed one caseworker on a home visit, noticing how she sat cross-legged on the floor with the mother and her two-year-old daughter, praised the mom's efforts, and interacted warmly with the child. "Whenever she's saying a few new words, it's important to tell her yes, and add to it," said the caseworker. "So if she sees a car you can say, 'Yes, that's a car. It's a big car. It's a blue car.'" The child said, "Boo ca!" and the caseworker said, "Right! Blue car! Good job!" The mother said her daughter was stuck on the word "guppy" from a TV show ("everything's 'guppy, guppy, guppy'") and she's been correcting her ("No, that's not a guppy. That's a doll.") The caseworker gently redirected Mom: "Well, I think now the important thing won't be so much telling her no but just adding words and repeating them, so she'll start repeating them on her own."

As part of the Providence Talks program, toddlers wear a small iPod-size device one day a month and it records and analyzes verbal interactions: the words spoken by adults in the child's vicinity, all the child's vocalizations, a TV in the background, and all the exchanges in which the child says something and an adult replies, or vice versa. Caseworkers are able to show parents a graph of how many words the child is hearing and speaking, the up and down trends during the day, and details like more words being spoken when the TV is off. "The fact that we have this report in a graph form makes it nonjudgmental," says Andrea Riquetti, the director of Providence Talks. "We can say, look, here's the data. Look how much you were talking at eleven o'clock! How can we do this for another half hour? As opposed to a home visitor telling a parent, 'You're not talking to your child enough.'"

Some commentators note that the quality of spoken words is as important as quantity. It's important that parent and child are both paying attention to and talking about the same thing—a cement mixer on the street, a picture in a book—and the ensuing conversation and gestures are fluid and continue over time. "It's not just serve and return," says Kathy Hirsh-Pasek of Temple University. "It's serve and return—and return and return."

"Though cultural factors may well explain why some low-income parents talk relatively little with their toddlers, the most obvious explanation is poverty itself," says Talbot. "When daily life is stressful and uncertain and dispiriting, it can be difficult to summon up the patience and the playfulness for an open-ended conversation with a small, persistent, possibly whiny child."

In addition, poorer families may be unconsciously preparing their children for jobs and lives in which they won't have much power and autonomy—hence the high value on discipline and respect for parental authority. *Unequal Childhoods*, a classic 2003 study by sociologist Annette Lareau, found that middle-class families mostly practiced what she called "concerted cultivation": adults engaged children in lots of back-and-forth conversation, with the verbal jousting giving kids intellectual confidence. Working-class and poor families, on the other hand, tended to take an "accomplishment of natural growth" approach: children's lives were less customized, discipline consisted of directives and sometimes threats of physical punishment, and there was less talk and less drawing out of children's opinions.

Lareau doesn't think one approach is better than the other. The middle-class approach takes a lot of parents' time. She found that poor and working-class children were more polite to adults, less whiny, more competent, and more independent. Still, middle-class families' approach prepared their children better for success in school and professional careers. "It taught children to debate, extemporize, and advocate for themselves," says Talbot, "and it helped them develop the vocabulary that tends to reap academic rewards."

"The biggest question was whether Providence Talks could really change something as personal, casual, and fundamental as how people talk to their babies," says Talbot. She believes the program's potential is as the first of a series of sustained interventions. Some of the children will likely attend preschool programs that will help them build on any language gains. Providence Talks will also help identify kids who could benefit from speech therapy and other support.

"The word 'empowering' is overused," Talbot concludes, "but a clear strength of Providence Talks is that it seemed to instill confidence in parents. Those rising graphs promised that parents could make a demonstrable difference in their children's lives. The parents I met did not seem to feel chided by the data, and they liked the idea of competing with their partners or themselves to log higher word counts." Caseworker Riquetti has the last word: "It's a chance to talk with parents about how they can positively interact with their kids. Sometimes in their busy lives, their stressful lives, they miss out on that."

"The Talking Cure" by Margaret Talbot in the *New Yorker*, January 12, 2015, summarized in Marshall Memo 569.

3. Rethinking Traditional Ideas About Parent Involvement

In this article in the *Russell Sage Foundation Journal of the Social Sciences*, Angel Harris (Duke University) and Keith Robinson (formerly at University of Texas) say that the at-home activities that really make a difference are what they call *stage-setting*. In the same way that a theater's behind-the-scenes workers support actors' on-stage success, parents can support children's school achievement by the *life space* and *messages* they orchestrate:

- Providing a secure home and neighborhood environment so children don't have to worry about food and shelter and getting to and from school safely;
- Taking steps to get their children attending good schools;
- Supporting academics and non-school activities like ballet and piano lessons;
- Caring about children's overall success, but not pressuring and overcontrolling;
- Putting a desk rather than a TV in a child's bedroom;
- Having lots of books and magazines in the home;
- Conveying the critical importance of academic achievement to life options;
- Showing confidence in the child's intelligence and ability to do well in school;
- Fostering a positive academic identity and a sense of responsibility to not let the family down.

"A busy parent with a demanding career can be a successful stage-setter with minimal direct involvement in his or her child's schooling," say Harris and Robinson. "This hypothetical parent's influence is at work under the surface, subtly shaping the children's self-concept, aspirations, and future possibilities. By not micromanaging students' homework and school activities, parents may produce more-autonomous children who are better equipped to make their own way through the challenges of middle and high school."

Harris and Robinson note that in poorer communities it's more challenging for parents to set the stage for children's success; there may be weaker neighborhood institutions and public services, fewer college-educated adults in the home and neighborhood, and less access to museums and other enriching experiences. In addition, say the authors, "over the course of a year a majority of the poorest families experience at least one of the following deprivations: eviction, crowded housing, disconnection of utilities, no stove, no refrigerator, or housing with upkeep problems …. These conditions inhibit the development of educational skills, depress school achievement, and discourage teachers."

Studies show that parents of all income levels want their children to be successful in school. What matters is how those hopes play out day to day. The winning combination, say Harris and Robinson, is parents conveying the importance of education *and* creating an educationally supportive home environment. This broadens children's horizons, enriches their psyches, and sets them up for success.

Harris and Robinson go on to say that "stage-setting explains a greater share of the link between social class and achievement than traditional forms of parental involvement." It's only because stage-setting is so closely correlated with social class that it appears that SES is determining student achievement. "To be clear," they say, "we acknowledge that affluent parents are more involved than their less-advantaged counterparts. It is also true, however, that many educators find the anecdotally observed relationship between parent involvement and high achievement too appealing to ignore and thus promote parental involvement as the answer to most of the problems within K–12. We propose instead that affluent parents have created a space that sets their children up for success largely independent from their involvement."

This means that schools need to rethink the idea of parental involvement, conclude Harris and Robinson. "Rather than pushing parents to be more involved in traditional school-based activities, educators should help parents understand and shape the factors that truly make a difference in their children's academic success—messages about academics and certain home conditions."

"A New Framework for Understanding Parental Involvement: Setting the Stage for Academic Success" by Angel Harris and Keith Robinson, the *Russell Sage Foundation Journal of the Social Sciences*, September 2016 (Volume 2, #5), summarized in Marshall Memo 710.

4 Unpacking the Research on Parental Involvement

In this article in *Review of Educational Research*, Eva Pomerantz, Elizabeth Moorman, and Scott Litwack (University of Illinois/Urbana-Champaign) say that parenting styles vary along four continua:
- controlling <-> autonomy-supporting,
- ability-focused <-> effort-focused,
- negative-affect <-> positive affect,
- negative beliefs about children's potential <-> positive beliefs about potential.

Research has shown that on each continuum, the right-hand side is more conducive to children's school and life success.

Teachers can't dictate parenting style, but the way they interact with families can influence at-home interactions one way or the other. When teachers encourage children's autonomy, focus on effort, have positive affect, and convey positive beliefs about children's ability—parents may pick up on those themes. When the classroom culture is controlling, focuses on innate ability, and conveys negative beliefs about children's ability—parents may shift in those directions. This will be especially true of parents who already believe that children need to be controlled, that ability is fixed, and have doubts about their children's potential.

These insights have direct implications for how schools interact with parents. First, teachers should give parents information on the malleability of children's ability and help parents develop the skills they need to help their children with their schoolwork. This should contribute to effective help at home—with upbeat affect.

Second, schools should reduce the pressure on parents. Studies have shown that parents who feel driven to improve their children's school performance tend to adopt controlling and negative-affect styles, which can bring out the worst in terms of beliefs about ability and potential. Expectations should be high, but educators should focus parents on the process of learning rather than students' performance.

Third, educators should emphasize the importance of parents' positive affect and positive beliefs about their children's potential. For example, teachers should assign homework that is interactive, allowing children to share what they are learning in school. Parent workshops should be upbeat and positive, because that affect may carry over to parents' interactions with their children. And, schools should constantly highlight children's improvement with respect to standards rather than comparing them to other children.

"The How, Whom, and Why of Parents' Involvement in Children's Academic Lives: More Is Not Always Better" by Eva Pomerantz, Elizabeth Moorman, and Scott Litwack in *Review of Educational Research*, September 2007 (Vol. 77, #3, pp. 373–410), summarized in Marshall Memo 199.

Home-School Communication

5 Teachers Making Home Visits

Research says that engaging parents in their children's education is key, says former *Wall Street Journal* reporter June Kronholz in this article in *Education Next*, but traditional strategies—back-to-school nights, parent-teacher conferences, potlucks, helping with homework—are not reaching parents who are alienated from their children's schools. In addition, there are many barriers: schools that are miles from students' homes, transportation difficulties, and security precautions—locked doors, sign-ins, ID badges.

Kronholz describes a different approach: teachers making home visits. She accompanied a team of Washington, DC, educators on a visit to the home of a particularly troubled and unsuccessful second grader. Sitting at the dining room table with the boy's mother, who was deeply worried about him, they learned how he idolized his older brother, that he loved helping with classroom chores, that he was keenly aware that he was older than his classmates, that he felt good at math, and that he loved when his teachers texted pictures of him to his mother. Asked about her aspirations for her child, the mother said, "I want so much for my son. Him trying to succeed. Maybe not succeeding, but just trying." She agreed to visit the school to see a class project, and also consented to have her son tested for learning disabilities.

Debriefing after the visit, the teachers said the most important thing was establishing a relationship with the mother. "A lot of our families have lost trust in our system," said one teacher, "but being in her house, that was her zone." Perhaps it would turn the tide with this troubled student. Discussing another home visit, a teacher said, "The kids see the parents and the teacher interacting. They see our relationship. They see we're working together."

The Flamboyan Foundation has followed the lead of Montessori schools, KIPP, and other educators in training and paying teachers to visit students' homes. Kristin Ehrgood, who launched Flamboyan in 2008, says, "Teachers are the experts in pedagogy, but families are one hundred percent the experts on their children. We need one another." Flamboyan is the DC partner of the Parent/Teacher Home Visit Project, a Sacramento-based nonprofit established in 2002 that now has 432 participating schools in seventeen states and the District of Columbia. The organization's protocol goes like this:

- Each school applying must have at least half its teachers willing to make home visits and a supportive administration (visits are voluntary for teachers).
- Teachers visit homes in pairs—for safety and so they can share impressions.
- Teachers don't take notes or even carry a notebook so they don't look like social workers or truancy officers.
- Teachers are paid at the district's hourly rate, often using Title I funds.
- Home visits are get-to-know-you style, positive, and not academically focused, except in high schools where time is spent on the mechanics of college admission.
- Teachers have a script of questions to ask families:

  Tell me about your child's experiences in school. Tell me about yours.
  Tell me your hopes and dreams for your child's future.
  What do you want your child to be someday?
  What do I need to do to help your child learn more effectively?
- Parents are invited to a specific school function.
- Parents are asked to share one (only one) expectation they have for their child.

"It's a very different dynamic than the parent-teacher conferences," says Karen Mapp, a parent expert at the Harvard Graduate School of Education. "We can get teachers the information they need to reach students individually." Knowing that a child is crazy about soccer can help a teacher choose the right books or incorporate a related math activity.

Kronholz reports that home-visiting teachers around the US have similar worries: "The call is hardest," says Jessica Ghalambor, a seventh-grade teacher in Sacramento. "You're inviting yourself over." In addition, "There's an immigration fear, a CPS [Child Protection Services] fear." Teachers get specific guidance from trainers on how to address their jitters:

- What's the best way to approach parents for a visit? A helpful starting point is saying, "This really will help me to be a better teacher for your child."
- What if the parent refuses to have a visit? Call back, but don't press; other parents will persuade them to come around.
- What if there is evidence of abuse or neglect? Work through your principal to report it to protective services—but also, "Check your assumptions," said one trainer; "homes don't look like the home you grew up in."
- What if the parents don't speak English? Arrange to bring a translator.

- What if the child lives in a homeless shelter? Meet in a neutral location like a park or coffee shop.
- What if the family wants to feed you? It's your choice whether to enjoy the meal or politely pass.

The research on home visits is scanty and hardly conclusive, Kronholz reports. But when she asked Steven Sheldon of John Hopkins University whether funding for home visits might be better spent on an additional reading teacher, he said, "What goes on at home, all of that is part of the problem and all of it is part of the solution."

Washington, DC teacher Ghalambor, after making a successful visit to the home of a super-shy eighth grader who was way behind in reading, said, "I know there's no scientific basis, but the very next day you could see the change. I could tell she knew I cared." On their own turf, parents are willing to share traumas that are haunting their children, and students are more willing to open up to a teacher who has seen their bedroom and patted their dog. Later, when it's time for a difficult conversation about a child's discipline problems or special-education testing, things go more smoothly. But the main purpose is building relationships and nurturing trust so students learn better.

"Teacher Home Visits" by June Kronholz in *Education Next*, Summer 2016 (Vol. 16, #3, pp. 16–21), summarized in Marshall Memo 640.

6. Getting a Foot in the Door with Text Messages to Parents

In this article in *Education Week*, Sarah Sparks reports on a study of a school program that sent parents text alerts when a child was in danger of failing, or was frequently absent. A study found that how parents were recruited into the program made a big difference. Here's what researchers from Columbia and Harvard discovered in a study in a dozen middle and high schools in Washington, DC:

- When schools asked parents to go to a website and sign up for alerts, fewer than half of one percent did so.
- When parents were sent a text with a link to the signup, 11 percent signed up.
- When parents were asked if they wanted *not* to get the information, 95 percent stayed in.

Lisa Gennetian of New York University comments that opting parents into a program by default may seem contrary to the spirit of parent agency and empowerment. "We are a country that embraces choice," she says, "and I think things like opt-out fly a little in the face of this idea of choice."

But even though parents enrolled in the program only passively, the text alerts benefited their children: overall course failure rates fell by 25 percent and grade-point averages improved by a third of a letter grade. What's more, at the end of the school year, these parents were more likely to want more information about their children's schooling in the future. "Parents don't know what they don't know," said study co-author Todd Rogers; "if you give them actionable information, they act on it." What's more, he added, "Parents don't get the choice to receive report cards."

"Make One Change to Parent Outreach, and Study Finds Fewer Students Fail Classes" by Sarah Sparks in *Education Week*, November 12, 2018, summarized in Marshall Memo 764.

7. Dealing with Very Difficult Parents

In this article in *Independent School*, psychologist/consultants Robert Evans and Michael Thompson say that school leaders they're working with report an increase in problem parents, including a small minority who engage in what can only be described as adult-to-adult bullying. "These parents are habitually rude or demanding or disrespectful," say Evans and Thompson, "engaging in personal attacks on teachers and administrators, demeaning and threatening them. They repeatedly violate the school's policies, values, and norms of conduct." The authors have identified three types:

- *Righteous crusaders* who berate the school for not dealing with a problem that no one else sees—for example, "My daughter says you don't like her."
- *Entitled intimidators* who want special treatment for their child. "They demand that rules be waived, exceptions made, policies upended," say Evans and Thompson—for example, firing a teacher they dislike or having their child placed in a particular class.
- *Vicious gossips* who continually find fault with the school or certain teachers and broadcast their complaints, often to a group of "vigilantes" recruited by the lead parent. There may be

an element of truth in their complaint, but it's pursued in a relentless, destructive way that defames and victimizes people in the school.

What explains the increase in adult bullying that Evans and Thompson describe? They believe it springs from three sources:

• *A rising tide of anxiety* – Parental nerves get frayed when there are a lot of changes and a lot of choices. In recent years, that's exactly what's been happening in the US socially, economically, and technologically. No wonder parents worry about how their children will fare as adults and are more inclined to advocate aggressively for the best possible school experiences.

• *A culture of loneliness* – Some parents may be isolated from other families and their children may not take part in the kind of regular free-play experiences with other children that were common in previous generations. This may result in a lack of parental perspective on how children navigate normal aspects of growing up, which may prevent some parents from keeping in perspective the common ups and downs of the school day.

• *Educator denial of parent mental health issues* – A few parents have genuine personality disorders that lead them to twist the facts and see things that others don't. "Although all of us who are parents can lack perspective when it comes to our own offspring," say Evans and Thompson, "a few have a profoundly distorted view of their children or a deeply rooted mistrust of institutions, notably the school."

For conscientious educators, encounters with bullying parents can be profoundly distressing. Thrown off balance by intense criticism and unreasonable demands, teachers and administrators may try to placate, persuade, convince, and accommodate a righteous crusader, entitled intimidator, or vicious gossip. But these tactics are unlikely to be successful. Evans and Thompson offer these suggestions:

- Have administrators, not teachers, deal with very challenging parents. "Managing bullying parents is a job for those who can speak for the school," they say.
- If a teacher has had a bad encounter with such a parent, he or she should never again meet alone with the parent.
- Realize that bullying parents are externalizers, which means self-observation is not their strong suit. They're unlikely to ask, "Am I doing something to upset people or that keeps them from seeing things my way?"
- Rational discussion is not going to work. "No matter how intelligent they may be, bullies demonstrate arrested social/emotional development," say Evans and Thompson. "Educators

will rarely go wrong by treating a bully parent exactly the way they would an outrageous and aggressive high-school student."
- "The ideal approach can be summarized in three words:" they continue, "'limits, limits, limits.' Bullies deserve thoughtful attention and an invitation to be reflective, but when these don't suffice, they need to know—unequivocally—the minimum nonnegotiable conditions of belonging in the school community."
- Some possible lines: "You have every right to your opinion, but you cannot swear at us." "We hear clearly that you want us to change your son's grade, but we will not do so."

What's most difficult for educators is not becoming defensive in the face of an onslaught of criticism and invective. Evans and Thompson suggest keeping this idea in the forefront of one's mind: "Whatever we did, we did nothing to make this person as crazy as he or she sounds at this moment." Avoiding defensiveness and being persistently curious about how the parent sees the situation can lower the temperature. "At the heart of any inquiry should be a desire to learn what the parent is hoping for and what his or her biggest fear is," say the authors. "Often, the biggest bullies are, underneath, deeply frightened. Once you set boundaries on their behavior, it may be possible to get to the heart of the matter. But not always."

"Parents Who Bully the School" by Robert Evans and Michael Thompson in *Independent School*, Spring 2016 (Vol. 75, #3, pp. 92–98), summarized in Marshall Memo 626.

Parent-Teacher Conferences

8 Improving the Quality of Parent-Teacher Conferences

"For some parents, teacher conferences are more like speed dating than substance," says Sarah McKibben in *Education Update*. Many parents don't believe meetings with teachers are worth the trip, and attendance declines steadily as students move through the grades, from 89 percent in primary grades to 57 percent in high school according to one study. McKibben reports on some ideas for improving this dynamic:

• *Rebrand.* A more inviting name for these perennial meetings is "progress conferences." This is more positive and doesn't seem to exclude foster parents and guardians.

• *Build relationships and trust up front.* Home visits, frequent e-mailing or texting, and partnering around academic issues build the groundwork for face-to-face conferences.

• *Finesse the childcare issue.* Ohio high-school teacher Allison Ricket invites parents to bring along other children and provides crayons and paper in an area at the back of her classroom where they can entertain themselves during conferences.

• *Accommodate.* Some parents need an interpreter (children shouldn't be asked to translate) or perhaps support with disabilities.

• *Change the dynamic.* It makes a difference if a teacher sits side by side with family members and doesn't hold a clipboard or pad of paper. Open hands suggest an open mind.

• *Clarify learning outcomes.* Surprisingly, only 7 percent of parents in a National Parent Teacher Association survey in K–8 schools said they were informed of grade-level curriculum expectations in conferences. One idea from the Flamboyan Foundation (dubbed Academic Parent-Teacher Teams) is convening parents three times a year to talk as a group about curriculum expectations and teaching ideas, with parents following along in their children's individual progress folders. Parents then have a single one-on-one parent conference once a year.

• *Involve students.* Progress conferences are much more helpful when students are at the table reporting on their progress, challenges, and goals. Advisory group meetings focus on preparing students to lead parent conferences and lobby their parents to attend.

• *Listen.* "Parents usually come in having an idea of what they want to talk about, so I like to be open and ready for whatever they need," says Ricket. Although she has students' grades and portfolios on hand, she lets parents go first and is careful to empathize with any concerns they have.

"Parent-Teacher Conferences: Outdated or Underutilized?" by Sarah McKibben in *Education Update*, September 2016 (Vol. 58, #9, pp. 1, 4–5), summarized in Marshall Memo 653.

---

9. A Conference That Didn't Go So Well

In this article in *Phi Delta Kappan*, Jun-ah Choi (St. Peter's University, New Jersey) describes the first parent conference she had with her son Michael's kindergarten teacher. In her volunteering visits to the school up to that point in November, Choi had been greeted warmly and told how much her son loved school. She was expecting a good two-way conversation with the teacher about the questions she as a parent had, the boy's family life, and how she and her husband were raising him—culminating in a teacher-parent partnership to further his education. Instead, the teacher showed Michael's work, explained the progress he'd made in math and reading, and said he was a good kid but that he sometimes was silly and misbehaved. Exactly how? He had a hard time following the "do-not-pop-the-bubble" rule, meaning he got into other children's space, touching and hitting others in a playful way.

"I left the conference feeling disappointed, humiliated, and dumbfounded," says Choi. "According to this teacher's mental framework, children are either respectful or disruptive, and she had already put Michael in the second category. I didn't want to be on the defensive, I didn't want to apologize for my son's behavior, and I didn't want to try to educate the teacher. How could I carry out a conversation with someone who does not know me and does not try to know me, who offers no analysis and insights but only judgment? So I bowed out. I politely said thank you, and I left."

"I had expected something fundamentally different," Choi continues. Instead, that year and the next, all she heard was her son's status "on the spectrum from struggling to smart and where he stood on the obedience spectrum (from disruptive to respectful)." Teachers seemed oriented around how parents could help *them* by getting children to obey school rules, helping out in the cafeteria, and raising money—all to make teachers' challenging jobs easier. "But do they care who I am," asks Choi, "how I raise my son, what my struggles are as a parent? ... For immigrant and nonwhite families like mine, the absence of genuine, two-way communication tends to be especially hurtful."

Choi's South Korean upbringing, and the way she and her husband were raising Michael, involved a lot of touching and cuddling to show love and no clear boundary between "your" space and "my" space. What's more, Choi was used to living in a cramped apartment where all spaces are shared and children don't have their own bedrooms. Choi expects that as her son gets older, he'll learn to "code-switch" and use different behaviors in school, but in kindergarten he felt negatively labeled. "Mommy," he said, "I am in the bad behavior group at school." Choi worries that he's internalizing the belief that his home culture is inferior.

"I wish that my son's teachers would meet me at the very beginning of the year and engage me in a conversation that continues all year long," Choi concludes. "I wish that they would invite me to look at the curriculum and share my perspective. I wish that I had chances to offer my insights about the rules and values that are practiced at my child's school …. Had the school invited me to do so, I would have gladly discussed the issue of cultural mismatch and helped Michael's teacher put his 'misbehavior' in context. Had there been any real effort to build trust between me and the teacher, I would have been more than willing to lend a hand and become more involved."

"Why I'm Not Involved: Parental Involvement from a Parent's Perspective" by Jun-ah Choi in *Phi Delta Kappan*, November 2017 (Vol. 99, #3, pp. 46–49), summarized in Marshall Memo 713.

10 Student-Led Parent Conferences

In this *Middle School Journal* article, literacy support teacher Amy Goodman describes how Anchorage, Alaska, schools implemented student-led parent conferences, spanning two days. District leaders took a number of steps to support the initiative: they increased the amount of early-release time available for conferences from six and one-half hours to thirteen hours, trained teachers in half-day workshops, and systematically prepared students for their new role. Each school set up blocks of time for the conferences, during which core-subject teachers circulated and elective and physical-education teachers provided information on students' performance in their subjects.

MINDSETS THAT SUPPORT LEARNING

From the beginning, the conferences were billed as *student-led* and *teacher-supported*. Here were the responsibilities communicated to teachers, students and parents:

- Teachers:
  - Help students compile a final portfolio with three to four work samples from each core subject.
  - Show students how to use sticky notes to write insightful "talking points" for each work sample.
  - Have students write goals in each subject area (and revisit these later in the year to measure progress).
  - Have students complete behavior and/or work-habits checklists.
  - Provide an agenda for students to follow during the actual conferences to help with time management.
  - Provide class time for students to rehearse for their conference.
  - Make sure all teachers discuss student progress with each family during the actual conferences.
  - Offer parents the opportunity to sign up for an additional conference if they prefer meeting with teachers by themselves.
- Students:
  - Choose work samples that reflect your progress in each core subject area as well as some weak areas.
  - Use sticky notes to append "talking points" for each sample that help explain your learning; avoid "show and tell."
  - Set serious goals for improvement in each subject area.
  - Be honest about your behavior and work habits in each core subject.
  - Use your agenda to help pace yourself during the actual conference.
  - Practice for the conference with a partner, making sure your portfolio is organized.
  - When teachers drop in during the conference, pause politely and let them speak.
  - Encourage your parents to sign up for an additional conference if they want more information.
- Parents:
  - Request a conference time that fits your work schedule; if a conflict arises, reschedule with the team.

- Bring your child with you; the student leads this type of conference with support from teachers.
- Listen carefully to what your child has to say about his/her work samples; ask clarifying questions.
- Expect your child to synthesize his/her learning; this is not "show and tell."
- Review your child's goals carefully; offer specific support your family can provide.
- Behavior and work habits are critical to success; analyze these carefully.
- When teachers drop in, ask them questions to better understand your child's progress in each subject area.
- Schedule another conference if you need to meet privately with the teachers.

Goodman concludes with data on the first year of implementation, including parent attendance rates ranging from 65 to 91 percent (with increases between 7 and 21 percent from the previous year) and very positive reactions from parents, who said the conferences were valuable and informative, said their children were well-prepared, felt they had a much better understanding of what was being studied in each subject area, and knew more about how their children learned, their child's effort, study skills, and classroom behavior. In addition, parents complimented the school on the way all teachers circulated during the conference time and the way elective and physical education teachers provided information on their subjects.

"Student-Led, Teacher-Supported Conferences: Improving Communication Across an Urban District" by Amy Goodman in *Middle School Journal*, January 2008 (Vol. 39, #3, pp. 48–54), summarized in Marshall Memo 218.

Homework and At-Home Activities

11 Rethinking Homework

In this *Education Update* article, Alexandria Neason reviews the research on the impact of homework, which is decidedly mixed. One study showed a correlation between completing homework and better scores on unit tests, but the link was weaker in elementary schools. Other studies found no strong evidence of homework leading to higher grades. "We still can't prove it's effective," said education professor Cathy Vatterott, author of a 2009 book on homework. "The research is flawed and idiosyncratic."

What's indisputable is that lower-income students find homework more challenging, and not completing homework has a disproportionate impact on their grades. Myron Dueck, a Canadian school leader and author, says one of the most serious effects of homework is "the exacerbation of social and economic inequities that already exist." Students who are struggling with food insecurity, unstable housing, noisy and distracting home environments, inadequate computer access, after-school jobs or child care, and the normal challenges of adolescence often find homework too much to handle. And indeed, studies of high-school dropouts cite homework as one of the top reasons for throwing in the towel.

Given this gap-widening effect ("We are basically punishing them for their poverty," says Vatterott) what should schools do? Neason summarizes some possible policy tweaks:

• Beef up the rigor and engagement of in-school lessons so that missing homework takes less of a toll on achievement. One district made a point of including music and sensory objects in heavily scaffolded classroom lessons.

• Give students opportunities to complete homework in school, providing a conducive study environment and good computer access.

• Use homework to reinforce already-mastered skills or to complete assignments that were launched in class, versus introducing new material. "Homework should reinforce students' confidence in their abilities, not shatter it," says Neason.

• Don't assign busywork. Each homework assignment should have a clear rationale and add value.

• Don't assign homework that requires students to buy special materials like poster board.

• Don't portray homework as a test of responsibility. Students may be ashamed to tell teachers about out-of-school struggles that make homework difficult for them to complete.

• Rethink the weight of homework on grades. Students might be graded on what they learn rather than on process pieces such as homework assignments. One approach is to make homework optional and check for understanding with a quick quiz the next day.

• Rethink 0–100 grading scales, which have a devastating effect when a student gets a zero for missed homework. A 6-5-4-3-2-1 scale mitigates this effect.

• A variation on this is limiting homework to 10 percent of students' grades or giving a grade of incomplete with time to complete it, perhaps during lunch or recess.

• At the elementary level, eliminate homework entirely. Some elementary schools have stopped assigning homework and encourage students to play and read after school.

"Does Homework Help?" by Alexandria Neason in *Education Update*, January 2017 (Vol. 59, #1, pp. 1, 4–5), summarized in Marshall Memo 670.

12. A Theory About Homework

In this *Kappan* article, recently retired California teacher Bruce Jackson puts forward an intriguing hypothesis on why the "good homework habits" that we strive to give students in elementary school fall apart when they get to high school.

As an urban high-school teacher, Jackson noticed a stubborn resistance among a number of promising students to doing his geometry homework. Students who started the year with significant gaps in their math education really needed to study and do problem sets every night. If they did that, it was entirely possible for them to overcome their math deficits and pass. But very few did their homework, and as a direct result, most of them failed, even though they said they wanted to go to college. "Why would so many students willingly waste a year sitting through geometry class and earn zero credits toward graduation?" Jackson wondered. All they had to do was spend forty to fifty minutes a day at home—and there was free tutoring available at lunch and after school. *What were they thinking?*

When asked directly, Jackson says, these students "offer a charming variety of excuses, evasions, defensive maneuvers, *mea culpas*, and doleful expressions, many well-practiced from prior confrontations with parents or counselors. Almost all say that to succeed they would need to start doing all their homework. They further insist that they want to be successful." But then they didn't follow through. Jackson began to believe that this behavior pattern originated in elementary schools and operated in ways that students and adults didn't fully grasp. Here's his theory:

- In elementary school, homework is usually assigned without a strong belief that it improves achievement (research confirms that K–5 homework has little impact), but with the goal of instilling "good work habits" and responsibility. School boards, superintendents, and principals insist on homework and many parents expect it, so elementary schools are firmly in this pattern. The problem, says Jackson, is that doing homework becomes a sign of childhood dependency and submission to adult authority. "Good boys and girls obediently do their homework; rebellious boys and girls do not. Parents and schools with the necessary will power and resources can ensure that their third-graders *will* do their homework. Most 8- and 9-year-olds, after all, will submit to sufficiently adamant adults, at least for a while. But homework isn't intrinsically pleasurable, and the seeds of future rebellion are sown. Along with the other indignities of childhood, homework has become something to be outgrown. Like broccoli or lima beans, it can be endured until one gains enough size, strength, and mental agility to create persuasive cover stories for what happened to it."

- In middle school, the rebellion against homework picks up steam, especially among boys getting homework assignments from female teachers. "Young males in American society are under intense social pressure to show rebellious, risk-taking behavior," writes Jackson, "and for boys with few positive male role models, the need to establish masculine credentials by rejecting 'feminizing' submission to authority is particularly strong." The peer group begins to see doing homework as a liability: "only nerds, grinds, and other social 'losers' maintain such 'goody-goody' habits," says Jackson. "Even moderate zeal around homework risks affecting contact with friends and limiting access to the currency of social interchange: 'what's hot' on the Web and in film, TV, video games, music, gossip, and consumer goods." When homework compliance starts to fall off, teachers are often so overwhelmed with the number of students that they don't follow up. Teachers may keep students who don't do homework after school, but this punishes teachers as much as it does students, and many lose the will to continue. "Over time," says Jackson, "students determined to avoid homework discover that they can outlast most teachers in a battle of wills."

- As fewer and fewer students do homework, teachers are caught in a self-reinforcing cycle. If lessons depend on students doing homework, and few students are doing it, the lessons will flop. So teachers tend to assign nonessential homework—busywork or "skills review." Here's the cycle:
    - Fewer students doing homework
    - Less classwork based on homework

- Less homework that matters
- Even less reason for students to do homework.

"Once this powerful feedback loop is in place," says Jackson, "individual efforts to counter it are often self-defeating. Students still completing homework become more isolated and less able to justify their actions to their friends or themselves. Teachers trying to emphasize homework face a double load: one lesson plan for those who have done the assignment plus a separate one to keep the rest occupied and out of trouble. How much easier to give up and go with lesson plans that minimize the importance of homework."

• In high school, except for a small number of seriously college-oriented students, the culture has internalized the very opposite of what we thought we were teaching. "'Good homework habits' are now an unhappy memory from early childhood dependency," writes Jackson. "Obedience to parents and teachers is problematic and rarely practiced outside their immediate presence. Students have furthermore learned that homework is not really important to passing courses, that it's mostly make-work to keep them busy, that nothing serious happens if they don't do it. Finally, except for those in the 'brains' crowd, taking homework seriously has become incompatible with their hoped-for social identity. For most students, the prevailing norm is to 'get by without showing off,' and far too many figure they can get by without doing much homework."

• The real tragedy of this, says Jackson, is that in high school, homework really *is* important! And it's a social leveler too, allowing students with weaker academic backgrounds to compete with better-prepared peers and make it to college. But the students who need it the most are the least likely to do it.

So what is to be done? Alfie Kohn and others decry "excessive" homework and advocate abolishing it in the elementary grades or cutting way back. Jackson concedes that children from well-to-do families might do fine without homework, given their ready access to books, the Internet, recreational programs, the arts, and college expectations. "But for families without these class-based resources," he says, "how else but through homework can students catch up academically with their more advantaged peers? Alfie Kohn worries about over-homeworked children 'missing out on their childhood.' Yet students in the low-income areas where I've worked spend long hours in homes where television, video games, or older siblings are the only babysitters, and outside, the streets are unsafe. If this childhood is to be 'protected' from the intrusion of homework, what chance do these students have of matching their middle-class peers in academic proficiency?"

Jackson thinks he has the solution: making elementary homework meaningful and enjoyable. Here are some components:

- A well-designed home reading program that gets students hooked on independent reading, builds a self-sustaining reading habit that doesn't depend on obedience, tokens, or rewards, and cuts down on TV viewing and video game use.
- Giving homework assignments that provide recognition and an academic payoff in school and help internalize the idea that individual effort outside school pays off. "No one seriously contends that virtuoso performances in music or sports are achieved without extensive practice," says Jackson. "Why should academic performances be different?"
- Assigning projects that don't "feel" like homework and motivate students to produce high-quality products. Such long-term work, says Jackson, "may do far more for building an academic identity than any number of stars, happy faces, or letter grades."

"Despite the ambiguities of research," he writes, "carefully planned homework can be a great equalizer at the elementary level" and can serve as the foundation for a different and far more productive homework dynamic in middle and high schools.

Jackson concludes with a call for better research—and says the best insights for improving homework may come from action research by middle- and high-school teachers. He urges them to get to know their students and parents, loop with their students for as many years as possible, seek to understand the conditions under which homework gets done, and strive to make the homework they assign "truly doable, worth doing, and in some way rewarding to the students themselves."

"Homework Inoculation and the Limits of Research" by Bruce Jackson in *Phi Delta Kappan*, September 2007 (Vol. 89, #1, pp. 55–59), summarized in Marshall Memo 200.

13. A Boston School Boosts Home Reading

In this article in *Principal*, former Boston principal Bill Henderson describes the steps he and his colleagues took after abysmal standardized-test scores placed their students' achievement near the bottom of the city's elementary schools. The school's leadership team agreed on some basic goals: more instructional time on reading; improving the quality of classroom instruction; getting more books into students' hands; and providing more help to kids who were reading below grade level. But there was strong sentiment that these strategies wouldn't result in higher achievement unless students spent a lot more time reading at home. Here is the ten-year story of how Henderson and his colleagues worked on that challenge:

- *A contest* – The first step was offering prizes to students who read the most books. Some students read a lot, but as the year progressed, it became evident that less-proficient readers were giving up because they thought they had no chance of winning. Other students tried to game the system by reading lots of short, easy-to-read books. The school distributed prizes to the winners at the end of the year, but teachers had no illusions that they had changed many students' reading habits. If anything, they had reinforced existing inequalities.

- *More reading material* – The following year, the school used every possible approach to get more books into students' hands:
    - Expanding the school library's collection;
    - Stocking classroom libraries;
    - Taking students to neighborhood libraries and getting them library cards;
    - Giving students free books through Reading Is Fundamental;
    - Giving students a book on their birthday;
    - Setting up a swap cart where students could exchange used books and magazines;
    - Bringing in vendors to sell books to families at rock-bottom prices;
    - Requesting book donations from the community.

All these measures exposed children to a lot more reading material, and that was good. But many students still weren't reading regularly at home.

- *Reading contracts* – The following year, the school developed a contract that required students to read or be read to at least four days a week at home. The goal for kindergarten through second grade was at least fifteen minutes a day, grade three-to-five students at least twenty minutes. Families could skip days when they were busy or had a crisis, and children could read independently or be read to by any relative or family friend. The school pushed the reading contracts at parent meetings, teacher conferences, and in school bulletins and newsletters. However, the results were disappointing. Fifty percent of students participated at least 75 percent of the time, and those students showed steady growth in reading proficiency. But the other 50 percent were not reading regularly at home. Most disturbing was the fact that the students who were not reading at home were generally the least-proficient readers, students whose families qualified for free or reduced-price meals, and students with special needs.

• *Parent workshops* – At the beginning of the following school year, a committee of parent leaders asked Henderson to send a strong letter to all parents emphasizing the benefits of reading at home. They also held a series of parent workshops on the importance of home reading. But those who showed up for the workshops were parents whose children were already honoring the reading contract. It was obvious that a more aggressive approach was needed.

• *A literacy show* – At the beginning of the next year, the school council decided to hold a literacy show in which students dressed up as children's book characters and performed skits. Parents packed the auditorium and loved watching their children on the stage, and Henderson took advantage of the turnout to deliver a strong message about how children's future academic progress depended largely on how much they read at home. But there were still a good number of homes in which very little reading was taking place.

• *Home visits and calls* – The following year, some parents decided to address this issue by visiting the homes of all newly-enrolled students. Twelve parents received training and technical assistance from the Boston-based Institute for Responsive Education and proceeded to visit homes, giving a book to each family, talking up the importance of home reading, and discussing ways that each family could fulfill the reading contract. The visiting parents also called and/or visited the homes of parents who were not participating regularly in home-reading; as fellow parents, they were usually well received. The school council upped the ante, making performance on the reading contract part of each student's report card. Teachers checked off each student's level of participation and sent warning notices to nonparticipating students midway through each marking period. This initiative, combined with the others, brought participation in the home reading program to 84 percent—a significant accomplishment, but the school was not satisfied.

• *Reaching the hard core* –An analysis of the 16 percent of nonparticipating students revealed the same pattern as before: almost all of these students came from low-income homes, had special needs or reading problems, and were reading below grade level. In other words, they were the students who needed the program the most. "The hard reality," says Henderson, "was that unless we could change the reading patterns of these children, their chances of academic success were limited." And as students got older, it would be increasingly difficult to change their habits.

The next fall, parent and staff leaders held a pizza party, inviting only the families of the students who were not participating in the home reading program. Invitations were sent, follow-up phone calls made, transportation arranged, and parents were encouraged to bring along younger siblings so child care would not be an issue.

PARTNERING WITH FAMILIES

Two-thirds of the targeted families showed up—real progress—and after a pizza feast parents went to the auditorium while children stayed in the cafeteria with adult volunteers to do arts and crafts projects and watch a movie. Parents were frank about why it was so difficult to honor the reading contracts. Some parents vented about the stress of being single parents trying to find time after work to make dinner, clean up, and get their children ready for bed. Others said that they had to work in the evening and leave their children with an older sibling or relative. Many said their children were hooked on television and video games.   Parent leaders listened sympathetically to these concerns, acknowledging their own parenting difficulties. Then they led the group in brainstorming strategies for getting children reading *despite* the barriers: setting a specific time and/or place for reading; restricting TV time; reading to all children in the household together; asking a relative or family friend to read with children; contacting teachers for suggestions on the best reading materials; and calling each other for ideas and support. Coming from fellow parents in much the same circumstances, the suggestions hit home.

After this meeting, the school paired a number of students who were not reading at home with parent and community volunteers, who read with them at the neighborhood library. The school also began to check on some students whose participation in the reading contracts seemed dubious, quizzing them on their books to make sure they were really fulfilling their contracts. And the school reached out to its expanding population of Vietnamese-American families, telling them through translators about the importance of home reading, giving them easy-to-read English books, and assuring them that home reading in Vietnamese was perfectly acceptable.

By the middle of the next school year, all these efforts had 95 percent of students participating regularly in the home reading program, and reading at home was firmly established as part of the school's culture. As participation increased, the school's standardized-test scores also rose, reaching the national average and putting the school near the top of Boston's elementary schools. Of course, other factors contributed to this dramatic improvement: more instructional time; extensive staff development; adopting best teaching practices; and tutoring for high-need students. But Henderson believes that regular reading practice is critically important to reading proficiency—and that the home reading program has been the most effective venue for extensive practice. "Hopefully," he concludes, "we have implanted a reading habit that will stay with them throughout their lives."

"Home Reading: The Key to Proficiency" by Bill Henderson in *Principal*, September 2000 (Vol. 80, #1, pp. 46–48), summarized in Marshall Memo 147.

Professional Learning Suggestions for Chapter Four: Partnering with Families

Improving Your School's Partnership with Families

Families are our students' fiercest allies. Yet schools don't always maximize their relationships with families. In some of the schools Kim and Jenn have visited, family involvement looks no different than when we were in school! It's time to broaden our ideas of parent involvement to more than attending parent-teacher conferences and baking cookies for school fundraisers. The PD activities below will help leadership teams and teachers reconceptualize their relationships with families so they can breathe new life into traditional parent involvement, parent-teacher conferences, home-school communication, and efforts to support reading at home.

I. Rethinking Parent Involvement

These first few activities will help teachers rethink traditional ideas of parent involvement, and the third will have your leadership team compile at-home suggestions for supporting school success.

A. Have early childhood and elementary teachers build on effective home practices.
Both the Ferguson, Howard, and Walsh article-summary 1 ("Early-Childhood Practices That Prepare Children to Thrive in School") and the Talbot article-summary 2 ("Changing the Way Parents Talk to Their Children") include implications for at-home practices families can adopt to better prepare their children for school success. Have your early childhood or early elementary teachers read these two article-summaries and discuss:

- What are some implications of these article-summaries for our work with students?
- What should we be sure to do in our classrooms if students come to school *without* having had families who engaged in the five practices in the first article-summary: 1) maximize love, manage stress; 2) talk, sing, point; 3) teach counting, grouping, and comparing; 4) let the child explore through free movement and play; and 5) read and discuss stories. What should we be sure to do for students who have been exposed to fewer words (as described in the second article-summary)?

PROFESSIONAL LEARNING SUGGESTIONS FOR CHAPTER FOUR

B. Encourage teachers to rethink traditional ideas about parent involvement.

1. First, ask teachers to brainstorm everything they think of when they think of "parent involvement."

2. Next, have teachers read the Harris and Robinson article-summary 3 ("Rethinking Traditional Ideas About Parent Involvement") to expand their ideas about what parent involvement might include.

3. Have the whole group discuss: Now that you've read this article-summary, what ideas do you have about what parent involvement could be?

4. Have teachers brainstorm ways they can reinforce the at-home suggestions in the article-summary in their classroom. They can use the chart that follows to compile ideas from the article-summary and to add more of their own:

Ways to Create an Educationally Supportive Environment at Home	Ways to Convey the Importance of School and Communicate Beliefs in the Students

C. Have your leadership team compile a list of suggestions to share with families for ways to support school success at home.

1. Have your leadership team read the first four article-summaries in this chapter about "Parenting for School Success."

2. As a group, compile a list of implications from these article-summaries for ways families might support their children at home.

3. Turn these implications into a list: "Top Ten Ways for Families to Support their Children's Academics at Home" (using something like the format that follows). Next, either share this list with families in some type of newsletter or electronic communication, or consider creating a workshop for parents to discuss these ideas.

> "Top Ten Ways for Families to Support their Children's Academics at Home"
>
> 1.
> *Example or sentence starter:*
> 2.
> *Example or sentence starter:*
> 3.
> etc.

II. Building Better Home-School Communication

Home-school communication is all about building trust. The first two activities help a leadership team assess the effectiveness of home-school communication efforts and brainstorm ways to improve it. The third activity helps teachers develop the much-needed skill of handling upset parents.

A. Self-assess the effectiveness of your school's current home-school communication efforts.
Create a self-assessment form (like the one that follows) that a leadership team can fill out to begin to determine how the school can better communicate with families.

PROFESSIONAL LEARNING SUGGESTIONS FOR CHAPTER FOUR

> **Sample Self-Assessment of Your School's Current Home-School Communication Efforts**
> Rate each item from 1 (not at all/very poorly) to 5 (always/extremely well).
>
> ___ We provide opportunities for *two-way* communication so parents can share concerns, questions, and thoughts.
>
> ___ We provide a variety of *different* types of communications to meet parents' varying schedules and preferences for communication type (newsletters, e-mails, blogs, phone calls, home visits, etc.).
>
> ___ We are particularly aware of the technology that younger parents (like millennials) prefer to use for communication and we reach out in a variety of those ways (Twitter, Instagram, Facebook, etc.).
>
> ___ We expect that teachers communicate with families about positive news in addition to problems.
>
> ___ School leaders proactively share positive news about the school via a variety of media (school website, Twitter, YouTube, etc.).
>
> ___ We clearly communicate who at the school parents should contact for which types of concerns.
>
> ___ We offer communications in the languages that our families feel most comfortable with.
>
> ___ We train our staff in effective communication skills to help with interacting with families.
>
> ___ We provide opportunities for parents to learn what is happening in their children's classes (through a curriculum night, the school website, ongoing updates throughout the year, classroom visits, etc.).
>
> ___ We ensure that parents understand their child's progress (through regular progress reports, by explaining assessment results and by alerting them early on when their child is struggling).

B. Be proactive about building communication with families.
The Kronholz article-summary 5 ("Teachers Making Home Visits") and the Sparks article-summary 6 ("Getting a Foot in the Door with Text Messages to Parents") are about building relationships with families through communication.

1. Have the school leadership team read these two article-summaries and review the results from the self-assessment.

2. Discuss the readings and self-assessment results along with the following quotation from the Kronholz article-summary, "Teachers are the experts in pedagogy, but families are one hundred percent the experts on their children. We need one another."

3. Based on the discussion, brainstorm all of the ways the school might enhance home-school communication. Although your school might not be able to create an opt-out approach to text messages or conduct home visits, consider the *goals* of these programs as you brainstorm—that is, to build trust, relationships, and communication.

C. Prepare teachers to deal with upset parents.

The Evans and Thompson article-summary 7 ("Dealing with Very Difficult Parents") deals with particularly problematic parents. The leadership team may want to read this article-summary to get ideas for putting into place a policy or guidelines for what teachers should do when encountering these more extreme parental behaviors. However, most of the "difficult" interactions with parents will not be so challenging. To help prepare teachers for these situations, do the following:

1. In pairs, have teachers think about and then share the last time they had a difficult interaction with a parent. They should not use any family member's name—keep this anonymous. (This is not a gripe session!)

2. Next, have them discuss why they think this particular situation became "difficult."

3. As a large group, have teachers skim the Evans and Thompson article-summary 7 to get some ideas of the *sources* of parent frustration. Then have the teachers brainstorm *other* reasons parents may get upset. (If teachers don't come up with it, share that parents may get upset when they feel a lack of one or more of these three key elements: safety, respect, or justice.)

4. Brainstorm tips for the best ways to respond in heated situations: take a breath, keep eye contact, focus on a mutual goal (what's best for the student), listen, validate the parent's point of view even if you don't share it, etc.

5. Role-play or discuss how teachers would use the suggestions from above to better handle a sticky situation with a parent. Pass out slips of paper and have each teacher write down one or more scenarios of heated situations they've previously experienced with parents (again, without names!). Put all of these papers into a bag or bowl. Have pairs of teachers choose one

PROFESSIONAL LEARNING SUGGESTIONS FOR CHAPTER FOUR

scenario and then either discuss what they would do, or role-play (if your school has a culture of using role-plays) the parent and the teacher.

III. Improving Your School's Parent-Teacher Conferences

The following activities will engage a leadership team in planning improvements to the structure of your parent-teacher conferences and will prepare teachers to proactively plan for parent-teacher conferences so they don't make common mistakes.

A. Have your leadership team create a plan to improve parent-teacher conferences.

If schools hold parent-teacher conferences (and Kim and Jenn have never seen a school that doesn't), they want attendance to be as high as possible. Unfortunately, this isn't always the case, and in fact, attendance declines as students move from primary school (89 percent) to high school (57 percent). Have your leadership team consider changing the structure of parent-teacher conferences at your school to increase attendance and effectiveness:

1. Have the leadership team discuss what is and isn't working about the current parent-teacher conference structure.

2. Have the team read the McKibben article-summary 8 ("Improving the Quality of Parent-Teacher Conferences") and the Goodman article-summary 10 ("Student-Led Parent Conferences") and consider the idea of adopting student-led conferences.

3. After reading these two articles, discuss:
   - What might be some of the reasons for the decline in attendance at parent-teacher conferences from elementary school to middle, and then high school?
   - What might be some of the benefits of student-led conferences? Drawbacks?
   - What kind of preparation was necessary for the Alaska schools to successfully implement student-led conferences?
   - What do you think are some of the biggest obstacles our school might have in putting student-led conferences in place?
   - What are some implications from these two articles for how we might improve our own parent-teacher conferences?

B. Prepare teachers for upcoming parent-teacher conferences.

1. In preparation for upcoming parent-teacher conferences at your school, have teachers read the Choi article-summary 9 ("A Conference That Didn't Go So Well").

2. Next, have teachers discuss the following questions to avoid making the same mistakes as those in the article-summary *and* to make their own parent-teacher conferences as beneficial as possible:
   - What went wrong from Jun-ah Choi's perspective?
   - How might we avoid this at our own parent-teacher conferences?
   - What other ideas do we have to maximize the benefits of parent-teacher conferences (build relationships, support student learning at home, address concerns either party has about the student, etc.)?

IV. Supporting Students' Continued Learning at Home

Imagine the benefits if homework were used for real learning and if families supported student reading at home. The following two activities help teachers and leaders find ways to better support student learning at home.

A. Help teachers understand and overcome the problems with assigning homework.

1. Have teachers brainstorm a list of what they believe works and what doesn't work with homework, using a chart like the one that follows. Make sure they discuss and consider:
   - How much is homework contributing to student learning?
   - How do actual homework practices in your class compare to your ideal view of how homework should function?

What Works with Our Current Homework Practices?	What's Problematic About Our Current Homework Practices?

PROFESSIONAL LEARNING SUGGESTIONS FOR CHAPTER FOUR

2. Ask teachers to read the Neason article-summary 11 ("Rethinking Homework") and then discuss:
- What problematic issues with homework does the article-summary introduce?
- What implications does this have for how we should handle homework?

3. Have teachers return to the lists they brainstormed in the previous chart and add more ideas after reading the article-summary.

4. As a school, or by departments or grade teams, commit to three changes to improve homework practices that address what is problematic about current homework practices.

B. *Consider ways to boost student reading at home.*

1. Have teachers and/or school leaders read the Henderson article-summary 13 ("A Boston School Boosts Home Reading") and do the "Three Levels of Text Protocol" to discuss it. See p. 34 in Chapter One for this protocol.

2. Consider which practices from the article-summary your school might adapt or adopt to increase student reading at home. While Henderson's school did not find complete success with any *one* of the innovations mentioned in the article-summary, when implemented together they did lead to improvements in at-home reading. Discuss the questions below and use the chart on the following page to organize your ideas:
- Which of the article-summary's practices to boost reading at home would work best at our school?
- Which practices would simply not be a fit for our context?
- Which of the practices would be the easiest and which would be the most difficult to implement at our school?
- Which practices would require the most investment (of time, money, resources) and which would involve the least?
- Given everything discussed above, choose a few of the practices to implement and create a timeline to do so.

MINDSETS THAT SUPPORT LEARNING

Practices to Boost at-Home Reading	Resources Needed to Implement This	Timeline for Implementation (Who, What, When, Where, How)

B. EFFECTIVE PEDAGOGY

Chapter Five: **The Key Elements of Good Pedagogy**
Words of Wisdom for Teachers   175
Keys to Engaging Students   181
Effective Feedback   190
Professional Learning Suggestions   197

Chapter Six: **What Makes Learning Stick**
Brain Science and Memory   205
The Retrieval Effect   211
Study Skills   217
What Should Students Memorize?   223
Professional Learning Suggestions   228

Chapter Seven: **Proficiency in Reading, Writing, and Oral Language**
Implementing Effective Literacy Instruction   235
Maximizing Reading Success   240
Teaching and Assessing Writing   248
Building Strong Vocabularies   258
Professional Learning Suggestions   265

Chapter Eight: **Differentiation and Personalization**
Why Differentiate and Personalize?   275
Differentiation by Pushing for Mastery   284
Low-Tech Differentiation   292
High-Tech Differentiation   296
Professional Learning Suggestions   303

Chapter Five:
The Key Elements of Good Pedagogy

We do not create understanding directly. We create it indirectly.
Understanding is a byproduct of experience. Our job as teachers is to create that experience.
—Fred Jones

Some teachers make teaching look easy, which can be disconcerting for those of us who had a tough first year in the classroom and needed lots of mentoring and hard work to get up to speed. Researchers have burned the midnight oil trying to extract the secret sauce of good teaching, and professors and professional developers strive to pass along what's been learned to front-line educators.

The growing knowledge base on effective teaching is addressed in a series of chapters in the two *Best of Marshall Memo* books. In Book One, positive classroom discipline, planning units and lessons, assessment for learning, and grading practices are covered in chapters eight, nine, ten, and eleven, respectively. In Book Two, student beliefs, race, families, memory, literacy, and differentiation are addressed in chapters one, three, four, six, seven, and eight.

The chapter you're reading now has a narrow focus: the art and science of successfully teaching a lesson. The articles fall into three buckets: words of wisdom for teachers; keys to engaging students; and effective feedback.

Words of Wisdom for Teachers – Robert Marzano says teaching is an art and a science and asks teachers to reflect on ten key questions as they work with students every day. William Powell and

EFFECTIVE PEDAGOGY

Ochan Kusuma-Powell analyze the unconscious tendencies that can undermine teachers' aspirational goals as they work with students. Christopher Reddy describes the "curse of knowledge," the difficulty many teachers have empathizing with students who don't understand, and how to overcome it. Mark Wise and Beth Pandolpho urge teachers to focus on what's important, strategically use different classroom formats, circulate purposefully, check the whole class for understanding, get students doing the real work, and allow time for reflection.

Keys to Engaging Students – Paul Bambrick-Santoyo and Stephen Chiger suggest that teachers pose thought-provoking questions and then have all students write before an all-class discussion. Cathy Seeley describes You/We/I teaching: students tackle a problem; the teacher circulates; the class discusses solutions; and the teacher connects with the objective. Fred Jones describes how to get students working harder than their teacher with Say/See/Do teaching: students immediately put what's been taught to work. Bradley Ermeling and Genevieve Graff-Ermeling describe a Japanese approach to observing and helping students during the heart of each lesson.

Effective Feedback – John Hattie says that giving and getting feedback is the only way teachers know their impact—and have an impact—on learning. Grant Wiggins says that effective feedback is goal-referenced, tangible and transparent, actionable, user-friendly, timely, ongoing, and consistent. Dylan Wiliam argues that feedback is helpful only if learning tasks are designed to make students' thinking visible, students do some mental heavy lifting, and the process develops their capacity for self-assessment. Matthew Maurer, Edward Bell, Eric Woods, and Roland Allen describe the highly constructivist approach used by cane instructors who teach blind people how to independently navigate busy city streets.

Questions to Consider

- Is teaching an art or a science?
- Are the skills of good teaching teachable?
- How can lessons be structured so students are doing more of the work?

Words of Wisdom for Teachers

1) The Art and Science of Good Teaching

In this interview in *Principal Leadership*, researcher/author Robert Marzano talks about the balance between art and science in classroom teaching. Marzano says he used to believe that teaching could be reduced to a science: "if you do X, Y, and Z, then D is going to happen." But over the years, he's changed his mind. "Research in education can only get us to a certain point with regard to teaching," he says, "and that is to identify the broad areas of effective instruction, where you say that in general, good teachers set goals, and in general, good teachers give feedback, and so on. But that's as far as it can go. The art part of effective teaching is where individual teachers figure out the best ways to use specific strategies in the context of their content area, their students, and their personalities. That's art, in the sense that people have to adapt the research to their specific situations. There's no cookie-cutter approach to teaching, but good teaching does include certain things in general."

There isn't one right way to teach. The bottom line, says Marzano, is whether students are learning. He suggests that teachers reflect on their classroom effectiveness by asking themselves these ten questions:

- What will I do today to establish and communicate learning goals, regularly check for understanding, track progress, give students feedback, get them involved in looking at progress, and celebrate success?
- What will I do today to help students effectively interact with new knowledge—including breaking it down into understandable chunks using a variety of media, anecdotes, and narratives; putting students in groups; getting them making predictions, elaborating and reflecting on the material, and responding in writing?
- What will I do today to help students practice and deepen their understanding of new knowledge?
- What will I do today to help students generate and test hypotheses about new knowledge?
- What will I do today to engage students—including the use of games and simulations, low-stakes competition, physical movement, friendly controversy, unusual information, and opportunities for them to relate new content to their own lives?

- What will I do today to establish or maintain classroom rules and procedures?
- What will I do today to recognize and acknowledge adherence and lack of adherence to classroom rules and procedures?
- What will I do today to establish and maintain effective relationships with students—including a balance between guidance and control and cooperation and concern?
- What will I do today to communicate high expectations to all students—including sensitively eliciting class-wide participation and finding the appropriate affective tone for students who are used to low expectations from adults?
- What will I do to develop effective lessons organized into a cohesive unit, making it clear to students where each lesson fits into the big picture?

These attributes of excellent teaching have emerged from decades of research, and Marzano says that effective teachers use many of them in their classrooms—although hardly anyone uses all ten.

In the past, Marzano has written about the importance of teaching being visual and dramatic, but he's worried that some teachers are spending too much time struggling to add these dimensions to their classrooms. "All *visual* means is that instead of telling students about something, show them," he says. "Use slides, use the Internet, show it with pictures. *Dramatic* does not necessarily mean it is acted out, although you could do that—it really just means a story." Using stories greatly increases students' retention of information, he says.

Asked about teacher expectations, Marzano says flatly, "the jury is in;" research clearly shows that high expectations are crucial to student success. But he says we need to go beyond believing that all children can learn. He suggests the following steps:

- Identify which students you have higher and lower expectations for (be honest!).
- Identify differences in the way these two categories of students are treated in the classroom (e.g., being asked more questions, being asked easier questions, being given more wait-time when they don't answer correctly).
- Identify specific strategies that can be used for "low-expectation" students.

"One of the most profound things I've seen teachers do is try this out in their classroom," says Marzano. He's found that it produces concrete strategies for making sure that all students are treated the same: "Ask a lot of questions of all students and make sure that you ask all students the same number of questions," he says. "Ask difficult questions of all students. Stay with them. When students don't answer correctly, draw out what they do know and clarify what they don't know. Over time, this creates a culture where kids get the message, Hey, my teacher is serious here. Students' expectations become, I give my best thinking and it's OK for me to be wrong."

"Producing Learning: A Conversation with Robert Marzano" by Jan Umphrey in *Principal Leadership*, January 2008 (Vol. 8, #5, pp. 16–20), no free e-link available, summarized in Marshall Memo 217.

② Hidden Assumptions That Undermine Teaching

"When we articulate our assumptions, we can examine and evaluate their implications and decide if they're aligned with our deeply-held beliefs about teaching and learning," say veteran international educators William Powell and Ochan Kusuma-Powell in this *Phi Delta Kappan* article. Drawing on the work of Robert Kegan and Lisa Laskow Lahey, they list some goals embraced by many teachers:

- I would like to see all my students achieve success.
- I want to better meet the needs of diverse learners in my class.
- I want to be more student-centered.
- I want to personalize learning so every student can feel included and invited to learn.

But here are some unconscious tendencies that pull teachers in another direction:

- I like to feel in control of the classroom.
- I need to be needed.
- I want students to feel I am indispensable to their learning.
- I don't want to try something new, fail, and look like a fool.
- I tend to think that the way I learn is the best way for my students to learn.

And here are some of the ways these tendencies manifest themselves in the classroom:

- I have a tendency to jump in to "save the day." I like to be helpful.
- I look for (or manufacture) situations in which students depend on me for their learning.
- Sometimes I don't listen well.
- I have difficulty appreciating that other people may learn differently.
- I've taught this way for many years, and it works for most kids.

And here are the underlying assumptions that need to be confronted for transformational change to occur:

- I assume I won't feel professional satisfaction unless all learning in the class comes from me.

- I assume that success (mine and students') is monolithic and defined by outside forces over which I have no control.
- I assume that failure (mine and students') is something to be avoided, rather than something to be learned from.
- I assume that to engage in public learning may be a sign of weakness (that I don't know everything I'm supposed to know) and may make me look like a fool.

"Overcoming Resistance to New Ideas" by William Powell and Ochan Kusuma-Powell in *Phi Delta Kappan*, May 2015 (Vol. 96, #8, pp. 66–69), summarized in Marshall Memo 587. These thoughts are adapted from *Immunity to Change: How to Overcome It and Unlock the Potential in Yourself and Your Organization* by Robert Kegan and Lisa Laskow Lahey (Boston: Harvard Business Press, 2009).

3. The Curse of Knowledge

In this *Edutopia* article, Christopher Reddy explores the problem of a teacher knowing content really well and forgetting how difficult it was to learn it in the first place, creating an empathy gap with students who are having difficulty learning. The teacher can't get into the students' state of mind, making it much more difficult to teach effectively. A teacher suffering from the curse of knowledge may assume that the lesson's content is "easy, clear, and straightforward," says Reddy. "We assume that connections are apparent and will be made effortlessly. Assumptions are the root cause of poor instruction. And acknowledgement is the first step to recovery." Reddy suggests these steps to counteract this all-too-common classroom dynamic:

• *Fill in background knowledge.* It's very difficult for students to understand new content without a foundation of facts and concepts, says Reddy: "Conceptual knowledge in the form of facts is the scaffolding for the synthesis of new ideas." Teachers should not assume that students have all the prerequisite puzzle pieces to understand what's being taught.

• *Tell stories.* Vivid narratives are one of the most powerful ways for students to make a personal connection to curriculum content, says Reddy: "Everyone loves a great story because our ancestral past was full of them. Stories were the dominant medium to transmit information. They rely on our innate narcissistic self to be effective learning tools—we enjoy stories because we immediately inject ourselves into the story, considering our own actions and behavior when placed in the situation being described."

- *Inject emotion.* Psychologist Barbara Fredrickson has found that playing a short, humorous film clip or making a quick joke can change the emotional valence of a classroom, creating emotional links between teacher and students.
- *Use more than one learning modality.* Students are attuned by a variety of learning styles and intelligences, and presenting visually, kinesthetically, orally, and musically connects with more students.
- *Use analogies and examples.* An effective analogy highlights a connection, and getting students to form connections is at the core of learning. Similarly, giving lots of examples helps students scan their knowledge inventory for possible connections.
- *Use novelty.* "New challenges ignite the risk-reward dopamine system in our brains," says Reddy. "Something that is novel is interesting, and something interesting is learned more easily because it is attended to." Teachers should look for ways of presenting content with a different spin.
- *Have students retrieve what's been learned.* Effective teachers check for understanding at regular intervals, strategically spacing the mini-tests to maximize long-term retention and provide feedback to teacher and students on what's being learned and what continues to be a struggle.

"The Teacher Curse No One Wants to Talk About" by Christopher Reddy in *Edutopia*, December 18, 2015, summarized in Marshall Memo 621.

4. Six Pointers for Rookie Teachers

"Teaching is one of the only professions in which new hires bear the full responsibilities of the profession beginning on their first day on the job," say New Jersey educators Mark Wise and Beth Pandolpho in this *ASCD Inservice* article. Here are their suggestions on how new teachers can avoid "siren calls" that might lure them to ineffective practices:

- *First things first*—avoiding the compulsion to "cover" everything in the curriculum. Like movie directors, teachers must make choices on which elements will move the story (learning) forward and which need to be cut. When planning lessons, teachers need to put in the essential elements (the "big rocks") first, making it easier to make on-the-fly decisions about what to abandon or shorten.
- *Choose the right format or strategy*—avoiding faddish practices that don't fit the situation.

EFFECTIVE PEDAGOGY

Teachers can have students sit in rows, groups, a circle, or a fishbowl. They can lecture, stage a debate, have students think/pair/share, or rotate through stations. And they have many options with technology. The question is not what's coolest, but what is best for the learning objective.

• *Circulate with a purpose*—avoiding the tendency to walk around monitoring compliance. The right questions in the teacher's mind: *What am I looking for? What am I listening for? What is the evidence? What will I do if I don't see it? Is this a time for an all-class mini-discussion?* All those questions lead back to the planning objective: how can I make students' thinking visible quickly and efficiently so I know if they are "getting it"?

• *Check the understanding of the whole class*—not calling on only the students who raise their hands. Teachers should use systems that accurately assess all students' learning in real time so as to reveal misconceptions and errors and make good decisions on immediate next steps.

• *Produce mental sweat*—not doing the heavy lifting for students. "We want our students to succeed," say Wise and Pandolpho, "but when we over-scaffold, even with the best intentions, we are not doing our students any favors." It's not enough to teach students how to "do school." To be prepared for college and life, students need to work hard, make mistakes, get feedback, fix problems, and become autonomous learners.

• *Allow time for reflection*—avoiding the pressure to "move on." Especially in middle and high schools, students traipse from class to class with little time to consolidate what they're taking in. They need time and space to jot answers to big-picture learning questions, followed by small-group discussions: *What new information did I learn? How does this connect to what I already know? What questions do I still have?*

"Tips for New Teachers: Avoiding the Siren Calls" by Mark Wise and Beth Pandolpho in *ASCD Inservice*, August 16, 2018, summarized in Marshall Memo 753.

Keys to Engaging Students

5. Getting Every Student Thinking and Working

In this *Educational Leadership* article, Paul Bambrick-Santoyo and Stephen Chiger (Uncommon Schools) describe the following classroom interaction: students read a highly engaging text (the lyrics of "Birmingham Sunday," a Richard Fariña song about the 1963 church bombing), then the teacher asks a well-framed question about the phrase "falcon of death" and calls on three eager students who share thoughtful insights. Other students chime in, and the teacher has the class spend the remaining ten minutes of the class writing independently about the song's use of figurative language.

"By its design," say Bambrick-Santoyo and Chiger, "this lesson placed the greatest amount of cognitive work not on the students as a whole, but on two or three students who happen to be both excellent readers and bold speakers. The other students didn't have to articulate their own interpretations of the text until they'd already heard someone else do so. In effect, the three students who dominated the conversation put the jigsaw puzzle together. The others got to admire the big picture once it was complete, but they didn't actually place a single piece."

Because discussion preceded writing, most of the class was able to avoid doing the intellectual heavy lifting, and when students did write, most were recording others' insights, not their own. In addition, the teacher's feedback wouldn't come until hours or days later. In scenarios like this, say Bambrick-Santoyo and Chiger, "Writing becomes a tool for evaluation, not instruction. The reality is that people's understanding isn't complete until they can piece their own thoughts together and write them down."

A better approach is for the teacher to have students read the text, pose a good question, and then ask all students to respond in writing *before* an all-class discussion. "This changes the whole experience," say the authors. "Now every student has a crack at the puzzle, even the ones who wouldn't normally raise their hands." And while students are writing, the teacher can:

- Circulate strategically. It's smart to start with students who get their thoughts on paper the most quickly, giving others time to get into the task.
- Give immediate feedback. Zoom in on a particular facet of the assignment rather than trying to read through everything students are writing.

- Plan feedback. Anticipate the kinds of thinking students might use and how to respond.
- Keep the feedback short. Whispering a comment or jotting a note can take as little as fifteen seconds, making it possible to see more students.

While circulating, the teacher can also gather insights on particularly good thinking and what's causing confusion. During the all-class discussion that follows, the teacher can focus on those, perhaps having the class compare two students' responses and debate which was strongest.

Many accomplished writers discover what they know and feel *as they write*, say Bambrick-Santoyo and Chiger. "Our students are no different. Until we see what students can articulate in writing, we don't know what they comprehend—and on some level, neither do they. To strengthen our students as readers, the place to start is with their writing …. Give your students time to write during class, and give them feedback that responds to their craft and their comprehension. Great writing is a communication of great thinking, so strengthen reading and writing in tandem, not in isolation."

"Until I Write It Down" by Paul Bambrick-Santoyo and Stephen Chiger in *Educational Leadership*, February 2017 (Vol. 74, #5, pp. 46–50), summarized in Marshall Memo 672.

6 You/We/I Teaching

In this *Educational Leadership* article, math educator and writer Cathy Seeley recalls the logical, straightforward way she learned how to teach math: explain the concept, guide students as they work with examples, and then have them apply what they've learned as they work independently. The problem with this pedagogy, she says, is that it "may set students up for frustration and failure, especially when they're faced with challenging problems they haven't been taught how to solve."

The alternative is what Seeley calls *upside-down teaching*—teacher-structured but with students doing most of the work. Here's how it works. The teacher presents a problem that students don't know how to solve, provides support as they wrestle with it, then joins with them to connect their solutions to the mathematical goal. As students work, the teacher circulates, asks questions to clarify students' thinking, and thinks strategically about which students to call on to share

their work—and in what sequence. The upside-down lesson reverses the conventional I/We/You sequence. Now it's:
- *You* tackle a problem.
- *We* talk together about your thinking and your work.
- *I* help connect the discussion to the lesson goal.

"The focus is on students coming up with ideas, solutions, approaches, and models," says Seeley, "even as the teacher facilitates the discussion …." It's important to create a climate where it's okay to make mistakes, students listen to each other's contributions, and the ultimate solution is a group endeavor.

Why is this approach effective? Because, says Seeley, "constructively struggling with mathematical ideas can engage students' thinking and help them learn to persevere in problem solving." Upside-down teaching also helps students develop a growth mindset—the belief that they can get smarter through effort, strategy, and persistence.

The key to launching such lessons is a "low-floor, high-ceiling task," one that has multiple entry points so all students can access the task at some level—and there's also plenty of depth. As students work, the teacher looks over students' shoulders and might say:
- *How did you decide to divide by seven?*
- *Can you draw a picture of what you just said?*
- *Let me know when you've decided between your three different models.*

When the class comes back together, students present their findings and the teacher asks clarifying questions, facilitates the discussion, makes good use of errors and misconceptions, and closes by making explicit the connections between students' work and the mathematical goal of the lesson. Seeley describes four examples of upside-down lessons, with a video of each:

• Second graders watch a video of the Cookie Monster grabbing an unopened package of cookies, eating several, and putting the package back on a kitchen counter. "What did you notice about the video?" asks the teacher. "What did you wonder?" The question: how many cookies were eaten? Students work in pairs, the class reconvenes, and the teacher highlights different approaches and summarizes with a subtraction equation. http://bit.ly/22dMIic.

• A sixth-grade teacher shows students she can achieve the perfect shade of purple paint by mixing two cups of blue paint with three cups of red paint. Students are challenged to figure out, and model with colored cubes and drawings, how many cups of red and blue paint would be needed to make twenty cups of perfect purple paint. http://bit.ly/1Od4lbH.

- A twelfth-grade teacher has students examine a tire from her car, noting its dimensions and characteristics, and then asks what would happen if someone replaced her tires with bigger ones: how would the car's speed, gas mileage, odometer accuracy, and space the car would take up on the road or in a parking space be affected? http://bit.ly/2yuzCY3.
- A precalculus teacher draws a graph on the board with coordinates labeled in two different colors and tells students there might be an error in the coordinates shown in red. http://bit.ly/2hK2tgR.

"Turning Teaching Upside Down" by Cathy Seeley in *Educational Leadership*, October 2017 (Vol. 75, #2, pp. 32–36), summarized in Marshall Memo 707.

7. Say/See/Do Teaching

In this article, author/consultant Fred Jones presents several insights from his books and workshops:

- *Who's doing the work here?* – A perennial issue in classrooms, says Jones, is that too much instruction consists of teacher talk—extended lectures in high school and even in elementary school: "Too much sitting. Not enough doing." This is a problem because the human brain has very poor long-term memory for information that comes in through our ears. Too much teacher-talk results in cognitive overload, student anxiety, and valuable information going in one ear and out the other. It also results in discipline problems when: the teacher assigns independent work; lots of students need help (*What part don't you understand? All of it!*); and frustration, disengagement, and acting-out behavior increase. Jones is skeptical of cooperative learning as a solution; too often student groups talk about other stuff or one student does all the work while the others coast.

"What if, after we give our students a 'chunk' of input, we had them do something with it *immediately*?" asks Jones. This suggests a two-step model: reduce the amount of "stuff" we give kids in one segment and then have them immediately do something with the information before they have time to forget.

The ineffective model: input, input, input, input, *output*.

A better model: input, *output*, input, *output*, input, *output*.

"Learning by doing focuses on *performance*," says Jones. "The teaching of performance is usually referred to as *coaching* …. Assessment is continuous, not something that is separated from performance and delayed until its relevance is lost …. You explain what to do next. You model what to do next. Then you have the student(s) do that step while you watch like a hawk. If there is an error, you fix it immediately before it becomes a bad habit. You may repeat that step a few times to iron out the kinks. Then, when you are satisfied with performance, you proceed to the next step …. Typically, therefore, three-quarters of the teacher's time is spent in work-check and feedback while three-quarters of the students' time is spent in *doing*." This process is even more streamlined when there is a visual instructional plan or exemplar posted at the front of the room that students can refer to at any point.

• *Say/see/do teaching* – The key to corrective feedback is giving it during initial acquisition and having high standards, says Jones. To use an athletic analogy, a basketball coach explains to his players how to bend their knees to play defense, models it, and then asks them to do it. If one player has his knees only slightly bent, the coach immediately corrects him: "I'm going to put my hand on your shoulder. Keep bending your knees as long as I'm pushing down …. There, that's it. That's how defense feels."

"Good coaches know that you walk a razor's edge when you teach someone to perform a skill," says Jones. "There is no neutral ground upon which to land. If your trainee does not learn to do 'it' right, he or she learns to do it wrong. The only alternative to a good habit is a bad habit. Bad habits are very hard to break. Coaches, therefore, are perfectionists. In the words of Vince Lombardi, legendary coach of the Green Bay Packers, *Practice does not make perfect. Only perfect practice makes perfect.*"

Next comes structured practice—walking students through performance with continual assessment and immediate feedback, having students repeat the performance, slowly at first, with the teacher watching closely to spot and correct errors. This works with skills as different as playing the guitar, using a tool in a wood shop, learning effective public speaking, or blocking a scene for a play. "With additional practice, speed and fluidity gradually develop," says Jones. "But a good coach makes sure that correct performance is *never* sacrificed for speed …. Students, of course, always want to go for speed too soon. They want to 'run and gun' in basketball or play 'hot licks' with the guitar like their heroes. The eternal struggle of the teacher in building perfect practice is to slow students down until they can increase speed *without* increasing error …. *Teaching* something means teaching your students to do it *right*. To Coach Lombardi's dictum you can add the words of UCLA basketball coach John Wooden: *You haven't taught until they have learned.*"

- *Teaching concepts versus skills* – Jones disagrees with the common notion that social studies is more conceptual than mathematics or playing a musical instrument. "All skills are simply conceptual operations that are expressed through performance, perfected through feedback, and made permanent through practice," he says. "Social studies teachers can be seduced into thinking that their subject is uniquely 'conceptual' if they rely heavily on lecturing. When input is divorced from output, teachers tend to drift into a 'mentalistic' model of learning—the notion that understanding occurs as a direct result of input …We do not create understanding directly. We create it *indirectly*. Understanding is a byproduct of experience. Our job as teachers is to create that experience. Without doing something with conceptual input *quickly*, it will simply dissipate—another example of 'in one ear and out the other.'"

In the humanities, the challenge is how to get students to *do* a concept. Jones describes three ways to accomplish this:
  - Talking—for example, brainstorming as a class, turning and talking with a partner, partner teaching (pairs of students taking turns reteaching the skill to each other), or a formal debate. "Most students graduate from high school without any significant experience in public speaking," says Jones. "Organizing thoughts for an oral presentation, learning to 'sell' those ideas while on your feet, and conquering the anxiety of public speaking are key life skills."
  - Writing—for example, a brief in-class essay can work wonders, with students then sharing their writing in groups of four, choosing the best one, and marking the strongest passages in the margin. "Writing and rewriting are the crucibles in which the fragments of ideas that pass for understanding in our consciousness are forged into clarity," says Jones. "Only through writing do we produce rigorous thought."
  - Performing—for example, working out problems at the board, role-playing in class, or acting out a scene.

"Teachers who focus on performance," says Jones, "repeatedly ask themselves, 'What will the students be able to do when they leave my class that they could not do when they entered?'"

- *Teaching so it sticks* – "The twin goals of instruction are *comprehension* and *retention*," says Jones. "We want the students to *get* it and to *keep* it." The secret is using the three learning modalities effectively: verbal (say), visual (see), and physical (do). "Each modality has unique strengths and weaknesses when it comes to comprehension and long-term memory. If you teach to the strengths and avoid the weaknesses, your job can be a lot easier."

THE KEY ELEMENTS OF GOOD PEDAGOGY

- Verbal – Its strength is comprehension—being able to convey complex meaning. The weakness is long-term memory—*in one ear and out the other*. "When we teach by talking," says Jones, "we rapidly load information into the verbal modality—the one in which there is almost no storage. This is a prescription for teacher exasperation and student failure …. Even if students were to do something with the material before the end of the period, memory loss between input and output would be great."
- Visual – This can produce instant comprehension—*a picture is worth a thousand words*—and it's terrific for embedding information in long-term memory. But not everything can be a picture.
- Physical – This can produce deep understanding—*we learn by doing*—but it's somewhere between verbal and visual in terms of memory; continuous practice is needed to maintain skills, and at some point we have learned how to ride the bicycle and never forget.

The strengths and weaknesses of these three have been understood since ancient times—the oft-quoted Chinese proverb: *I hear, and I forget. I see, and I remember. I do, and I understand.*

The three modalities can be welded together in the classroom in the simple three-part model: *Say, see, do.* Let me explain what to do next. Watch as I show you, Now you do it. This pattern is repeated as teachers move through the content, constantly checking for understanding and coaching students through practice. "When we accept that learning takes place *one step at a time*," says Jones, "and that we learn by doing, the nature of teaching snaps into focus. We teach *performance*. Even with conceptual material, if the student cannot 'do' the concept accurately, usually by talking or writing, we cannot say that learning has taken place.

"Focusing on performance immediately faces us with the issue of *excellence*," he concludes. "We must build *correct* performance. The only alternative is *incorrect* performance …. As the saying goes, 'It is always cheaper to build it right the first time.'"

A final "Fredism": "If you find yourself working harder than the students, it is definitely time to rethink your approach to teaching. It is time to return to fundamentals—learning by doing one step at a time …. *It is not your job to work yourself to death while the students watch.*"

"Fred Jones Tools for Teaching" broadsheet, April 2010, summarized in Marshall Memo 331.

EFFECTIVE PEDAGOGY

8 A Japanese Method of "Teaching While Walking Around"

In this *Educational Leadership* article, Bradley Ermeling and Genevieve Graff-Ermeling reflect on the inefficiency of the time they as teachers spent circulating during lessons: "We saw that the unplanned, cursory exchanges we had with students when they were working on an assignment in class mostly reiterated previous instruction and seldom advanced student learning. We came to understand that the teacher's role during student work time in class—what we chose to focus on, how long we spent with each team or individual, what we chose to say or not say—had crucial instructional value."

It turns out that Japanese teachers have fine-tuned "between-desks instruction." Here's what it sounds like after an eighth-grade math teacher in Japan gives his students a problem and circulates for fifteen minutes:

- "Yes, write your explanation on the paper next to the problem."
- "This $180 - 10x$ you wrote – whose money is this?"
- "So you counted all the way? Is there an easier method to find the answer?"
- "If you try combining this and that, you can make a mathematical expression."
- "So you wrote a simultaneous equation – OK!"

This process of observing and helping students as they wrestle with a problem is called *kikan-shido*. The teacher's goal is to spend relatively short amounts of time with each student—not getting bogged down with students who are having major difficulty—so it's possible to see every student and notice patterns that need to be addressed with the whole class.

Kikan-shido is more organized and purposeful than it appears. Teachers construct a clear mental image of what will be happening and think through a series of questions:

- What materials will I need to distribute?
- What are my goals as I circulate?
- How will I distribute my time with various groups?
- What key understandings or misconceptions will I be looking for?
- What probing questions will I use to check for understanding or advance thinking?
- What will I be careful not to say or do that might decrease the rigor of the task?
- When should I engage in chit-chat to provide encouragement and build rapport?

"Carrying a copy of the lesson plan on a tablet or mobile device during *kikan-shido* is also useful," say Ermeling and Graff-Ermeling; "teachers can review the plan on the spot and take notes as they observe."

They acknowledge it takes a while to perfect teaching between the desks—several months of practice, trial-and-error, and refinement—"persevering long enough to understand the nuances of effective implementation." But when *kikan-shido* is working well, there will be big improvements in student achievement. One teacher, upon receiving her students' scores—far better than they'd ever done before in her twenty-eight years of teaching—closed the door "and cried and cried and gave thanks. I have to believe I changed the way I taught, that making them struggle really bridged the gap."

"Teaching Between Desks" by Bradley Ermeling and Genevieve Graff-Ermeling in *Educational Leadership*, October 2014 (Vol. 72, #2, pp. 55–60), summarized in Marshall Memo 556.

Effective Feedback

9 Making Feedback to Students Effective

"Gathering and assessing feedback are really the only ways teachers can know the impact of their teaching," says Australian educator John Hattie in this *Educational Leadership* article. The problem is that not all feedback is effective. Hattie offers these suggestions for making feedback work:

- *Clarify the goal.* "The aim of feedback is to reduce the gap between where students are and where they should be," says Hattie. "With a clear goal in mind, students are more likely to actively seek and listen to feedback." The teacher might provide scoring rubrics, a completed example, the steps toward a successful product, or progress charts.

- *Make sure students understand the feedback.* "When we monitor how much academic feedback students actually receive in a typical class, it's a small amount indeed," says Hattie. Teachers need to check with students to see if they're getting it. This may involve asking them to interpret written comments and articulate next steps.

- *Seek feedback from students.* Do they need help? Different strategies? Another explanation? Teachers who listen to students can adapt lessons, clarify work demands, and provide missing information—all of which helps students do better.

- *Tailor feedback to students.*   Novice students benefit most from task feedback, somewhat more proficient students benefit from process feedback, and highly competent students thrive on feedback aimed at self-regulation or conceptual understanding.
    - Task feedback – How well the student is doing on a particular task and how to improve.
    - Process feedback – This might be suggested strategies to learn from errors, cues to seek information, or ways to relate different ideas.
    - Self-regulation feedback – This helps students monitor, direct, and regulate their own actions as they work toward the learning goal—and helps build a belief that effort, more than raw ability, is what produces successful learning.

To move students from mastery of content to mastery of strategies, to mastery of conceptual understanding, teachers need to give feedback that is *at* or *just above* their current level.

- *Use effective strategies.* One tip is to scope out entering misconceptions and have students think them through. Another is providing students with formative assessment information, giving them specific information on strengths and weaknesses. A third is to start with effective instruction and learning experiences. "Teachers need to listen to the hum of students learning, welcoming quality student talk, structuring classroom discussions, inviting student questions, and openly discussing errors," says Hattie. "If these reveal that student have misunderstood an important concept or failed to grasp the point of the lesson, sometimes the best approach is simply to reteach the material."

• *Avoid ineffective feedback.* Researchers have found that praise and peer feedback are problematic. "Students welcome praise," says Hattie. "Indeed, we all do. The problem is that when a teacher combines praise with other feedback information, the student typically only hears the praise …. The bottom line seems to be this: Give much praise, but do not mix it with other feedback because praise dilutes the power of that information." As for peer feedback, Graham Nuthall monitored students' peer interactions through the school day (using microphones) and found that most of the feedback students receive during the day is from other students—and much of it is incorrect. Peer feedback needs clear structure, such as a rubric and a set of guiding questions.

• *Create a climate of trust.* Students must understand that errors and misunderstandings are part of learning and not be afraid of negative reactions from peers—or the teacher—if they make mistakes.

"Know Thy Impact" by John Hattie in *Educational Leadership*, September 2012 (Vol. 70, #1, pp. 18–23), summarized in Marshall Memo 451.

10. The Elements of Effective Feedback

"Decades of education research support the idea that by teaching less and providing more feedback, we can produce greater learning," says author/consultant Grant Wiggins in this *Educational Leadership* article. But feedback is a fuzzy term: "Basically," says Wiggins, "feedback is information about how we are doing in our efforts to reach a goal."

In some situations, we get feedback that is immediately informative: hitting a tennis ball, telling a joke, seeing if students are attentive. But when people give us feedback, it often takes the form of value judgments or advice. Aren't judgments and advice helpful? Not if you want to cause learning, says Wiggins. Telling a student, *Good work!* or *This is a weak paper,* provides no actionable information. Telling a student, *you need more examples in your report,* or telling a baseball player, *You might want to use a lighter bat*, is in most cases, annoying. "Unless it is preceded by descriptive feedback, the natural response of the performer is to wonder, 'Why are you suggesting this?'"

Here are examples of effective feedback. For good work, *Your use of words was more precise in this paper than in the last one, and I saw the scenes clearly in my mind's eye.* Or, *Each time you swung and missed, you raised your head as you swung so you didn't really have your eye on the ball. On the one you hit hard, you kept your head down and saw the ball.* To be effective, says Wiggins, feedback needs to be:

• *Goal-referenced* – "Information becomes feedback if, and only if, I am trying to cause something and the information tells me whether I am on track or need to change course," he says. A teacher might say, *The point of this writing task is to make readers laugh.* So, when rereading your draft or getting feedback from peers, ask, *How funny is this? Where might it be funnier?*

• *Tangible and transparent* – "Alas, far too much instructional feedback is opaque," says Wiggins. He tells about a student who was confused by his teacher's frequent jotted comment on his English papers—*vag-oo*. (What the teacher meant was *vague*!)

• *Actionable* – Students need to know specifically what to do. The following pieces of feedback are not concrete, specific, or useful: *Good job! B+. You did it wrong.*

• *User-friendly* – Feedback should not be overly technical or more than the recipient can handle. "Expert coaches uniformly avoid overloading performers with too much or too technical information," says Wiggins. "They tell the performers one important thing they noticed that, if changed, will likely yield immediate and noticeable improvement."

• *Timely* – Too often, students have to wait days, weeks, or even months (in the case of standardized tests) for important feedback on their work. Feedback can arrive more quickly if teachers use technology or peer reviewers.

• *Ongoing* – "What makes any assessment in education formative is not merely that it precedes summative assessments, but that the performer has opportunities, if results are less than optimal, to reshape the performance to better achieve the goal," says Wiggins. "This is how all highly successful computer games work."

• *Consistent* – "Teachers need to look at student work together," he says, "becoming more consistent over time and formalizing their judgments in highly descriptive rubrics supported by anchor products and performances."

Wiggins closes with a sports analogy. His daughter aspired to run a 5:00 mile. As she ran a practice race, her coach yelled out split times, gave feedback ("You're not swinging your arms!"), told her where she stood ("You're on pace for 5:15"), and gave advice ("Pick it up—you need to take two seconds off this next lap to get in under 5:10!"). Wiggins contrasts this to many schools' pacing guides and use of interim assessments. "They yield a grade against recent objectives taught, not useful feedback against the *final* performance standards," he says. All this does is give the teacher a schedule for rolling out the curriculum. "It's as if at the end of the first lap of the mile race," says Wiggins, "my daughter's coach simply yelled out, "B+ on that lap!" To make school feedback more like highly effective sports feedback, he advises gearing interim assessments toward biannual goals and using item analysis to give students (and teachers) real *feedback* on what needs work.

"7 Keys to Effective Feedback" by Grant Wiggins in *Educational Leadership*, September 2012 (Vol. 70, #1, pp. 11–16), summarized in Marshall Memo 450.

11. Getting Students to Do the Heavy Lifting

In this article in *Educational Leadership*, assessment expert Dylan Wiliam reports the startling research finding that students often learn nothing from the comments and grades their teachers write on their papers—in fact, many students learn less when teachers provide feedback than when they write nothing at all. "The apparently simple process of looking at student work and then giving useful feedback turns out to be much more difficult than most people imagine," says Wiliam. "The only important thing about feedback is what students do with it …. If our feedback doesn't change the student in some way, it has probably been a waste of time."

Two examples: An English teacher tells a student that her composition will be better if she reverses the sequence of the third and fourth paragraphs. The composition will improve, but the teacher did the intellectual heavy lifting and the student probably learned very little. Similarly, if a teacher corrects arithmetic errors, there's nothing left for the student to do except calculate the score. "The real issue is purpose," says Wiliam. "We need to use the information we obtain from looking at the student's work—even though that information may be less than perfect—and give feedback that will move the student's learning forward." Here are his suggestions for teachers:

• *Design tasks and ask questions that make students' thinking visible.* This means more prep work for the teacher, especially in math classes, but frontloading well-framed tasks makes it much more likely that students will be engaged and the feedback will be useful. We won't always get it right, says Wiliam, but he reminds us that batting .300 in the major league baseball is considered very good.

• *Make feedback into detective work.* A math teacher might return a twenty-question test to a student with the comment, "Five of these are incorrect. Find them and fix them." This approach ensures that students receiving feedback do as much work as the teacher. It also makes students look at their work with a more analytical eye.

• *Build students' capacity for self-assessment.* The ultimate goal of feedback should be to get students to the point where they can self-correct without the teacher looking over their shoulders. Instrumental music teachers understand this intuitively, and focus the thirty to forty minutes they spend with their students each week on developing the skill of being able to notice mistakes and improve technique in the hours of solo practice between lessons. "Contrast this approach with most content-area teaching in schools," says Wiliam, "where teachers seem to believe that students make most of their progress when the teacher is present, with homework as a kind of optional add-on."

Human nature being what it is, many students find it emotionally challenging to be critical of their own work. A good scaffolding strategy is having a class look at an anonymous piece of work and describe the feedback this person should receive, then have students critique the work of a classmate, and finally self-correct. After a task like this, it's helpful to ask students what they found easy, what they found difficult, and what was interesting. Alternatively, students might be asked what they would do differently if they did the task again. Once students can do this, feedback from others becomes less and less necessary.

"In the end," says Wiliam, "it all comes down to the relationship between the teacher and the student. To give effective feedback, the teacher needs to know the student—to understand what feedback the student needs right now. And to receive feedback in a meaningful way, the student needs to trust the teacher—to believe that the teacher knows what he or she is talking about and has the student's best interests at heart. Without this trust, the student is unlikely to invest the time and effort needed to absorb and use the feedback."

"The Secret of Effective Feedback" by Dylan Wiliam in *Educational Leadership*, April 2016 (Vol. 73, #7, pp. 10–15), summarized in Marshall Memo 631.

---

12 Teaching Blind People to Use Canes and What It Can Teach Others

In this article in *Phi Delta Kappan*, Matthew Maurer (Butler University), Edward Bell (Louisiana Tech University), Eric Woods (Colorado Center for the Blind), and Roland Allen (Louisiana Center for the Blind) note that many educators claim to be constructivists, but when confronted with high-stakes tests, they lose their nerve and resort to traditional rote learning. Educators who train blind people to use canes have figured out a way to avoid this trap. Their students learn to navigate city streets, buses, stores, and office buildings. "The stakes involved are certainly high," say the authors, "but teachers of cane travel maintain a steadfast dedication to constructivism."

Imagine two blind people, they continue. The first is a man in his midtwenties who lost his sight due to diabetes; the second is a girl who was born blind. Neither has the skills and tools with which to navigate in the outside world, and there is a strong tendency for their loved ones and teachers to overprotect them—to do too much for them.

But learning how to get out and travel safely is hugely important to the young man and the girl—and the role of educators can be transformational. "If a blind person can learn to travel independently," say the authors, "the freedom gained is enormous. That person can experience the world firsthand and can decide when and how to do so. The development of solid cane travel skills can deliver that freedom and independence."

Over the last few decades, the National Federation of the Blind has developed a highly effective method of teaching blind people to navigate with canes, and it can best be described as "structured discovery." Cane instructors are usually blind themselves, and if they are not, they wear sleeping shades during lessons so they cannot see. ("As any good teacher knows," say the authors, "what we say has a small impact on learning, while what we do has a much stronger effect.") Cane teachers accompany their students on city streets, guiding them to develop their own understanding and style of getting around a city safely. "The cornerstone of the method is the philosophy that undergirds it," write the authors, "an understanding that students must construct travel strategies for themselves making use of the guidance of experts."

The authors provide a transcript of a dialogue between a cane teacher and a blind teenage girl in the middle of a guided lesson on a busy street. The student hesitates because she thinks she has arrived at an intersection, and the teacher asks her nineteen questions that probe and push her understanding of what is around her, what the texture of the sidewalk is like, what sounds she can hear in each direction, what she can deduce about whether there are buildings around her, and what kinds of tricky circumstances might throw her off (e.g., a parking lot that allows street noises from a block away to travel to her more quickly). The girl, who was faltering and about to give up, regains her confidence, solidifies her skills, and moves on.

"As all educators continue to teach in a climate of high accountability," conclude the authors, "it is important to make use of the most effective techniques at our disposal and to resist the temptation to simply teach students to perform well on written tests. The structured discovery method can serve as a model for us to follow. We must begin by choosing powerful settings for learning. Then we need to take the time and effort to ask questions that lead students, and we must patiently guide their thinking until they construct the knowledge and skills they need."

It's also important to lead by example, they say. "If, as teachers, we can metaphorically don sleep shades, our students may make dramatic emotional shifts in their learning. If we, ourselves, are the active, inquiring learners we wish our students to be, it is likely that they will follow our example."

"Structured Discovery in Cane Travel: Constructivism in Action" by Matthew Maurer, Edward Bell, Eric Woods, and Roland Allen in *Phi Delta Kappan*, December 2006 (Vol. 88, #4, pp. 304–307), summarized in Marshall Memo 164.

Professional Learning Suggestions for Chapter Five: The Key Elements of Good Pedagogy

Improving Pedagogy, Improving Learning

As an instructional leader, one of the principal's main goals is to help teachers understand what good teaching is and to use pedagogical strategies that will improve learning. Below are some activities to help teachers better understand a few key elements of good teaching and plan more effective teaching practices as well.

I. What Is "Good Teaching"?

This introductory section helps teachers think about the assumptions that underlie their teaching, explore what "good teaching" means, and then compare their ideas to what one researcher has discovered about what constitutes effective instruction based on his research.

A. Have teachers explore some of their hidden assumptions about teaching.
Put a large piece of tape on the floor equidistant from two walls of a room and clear furniture out of the way. Tell teachers that our *beliefs* lie at the root of many of our teaching practices as is described in "Hidden Assumptions That Undermine Teaching" (article-summary 2).

>1. Ask teachers to stand on the tape in the middle of the room. Read aloud the following unconscious tendencies and ask teachers to stand along a continuum from one wall (completely agree) to the opposite wall (completely disagree), based on what they believe:
>
>>"I like to feel in control of the classroom."
>>"I don't want to try something new, fail, and look like a fool."
>>"I need to be needed."
>
>2. After reading each statement and having teachers move to the appropriate spot in the room, ask the teachers to discuss with one or two people standing nearby how they think this belief impacts their instruction.

3. As a large group, have teachers discuss or debate whether they think *belief* or *skill* has a greater impact on how successful a teacher's instruction is.

B. Have teachers discuss what they think "good teaching" means before they read anything.
Give teachers five to ten minutes to individually write down how they would describe "good teaching." Have them think about all of the "broad areas of effective instruction." Next, have a large-group discussion about what they believe goes into "good teaching" and capture ideas in some visual way (from newsprint to Padlet).

C. Have teachers read the Marzano article-summary 1, "The Art and Science of Good Teaching."
Now that teachers have discussed their beliefs about good teaching, have them read the article-summary looking for similarities and differences with their own ideas.

1. While they read, have teachers *circle* ideas that they missed in their own descriptions of good teaching and *underline* ideas that they already have included in their own definitions. With a partner, have them discuss what new thoughts they have about effective instruction after reading the article-summary.

2. Next, have teachers look at the ten questions in the Marzano article-summary. Ask them to think about the most recent lesson they taught and self-assess how well they believe they did on each of these ten areas. They can just write a rating (from 1–4) in the margins.

3. Now have teachers take out their plans for the next lesson they plan to teach and adapt them to take into consideration *some* of the ten items in Marzano's list. Keep in mind that they are not expected to incorporate all ten!

II. Increasing Student Engagement

If teachers can increase engagement, they will increase learning. Below are ideas to help teachers consider and begin to plan for new ways to engage students.

A. Conduct a gallery walk to examine quotations about engagement.
Post a few of the following quotations related to engagement (some from the "Say/See/Do Teaching" Jones article-summary 7) around the room or digitally with a program that allows participants to comment. Have teachers walk around the room (or explore the quotations digitally) and post comments with their reactions to them:

PROFESSIONAL LEARNING SUGGESTIONS OF CHAPTER FIVE

"Too much sitting. Not enough doing."

"Learning by doing focuses on *performance*."

"When we teach by talking, we rapidly load information into the verbal modality—the one in which there is almost no storage."

"I hear and I forget. I see and I remember. I do, and I understand."

"If you find yourself working harder than the students, it is definitely time to rethink your approach to teaching."

"The best classroom management tool is an engaging lesson" (Sean Junkins).

"Tell me and I forget, teach me and I remember, involve me and I learn" (Benjamin Franklin).

"Engagement isn't a thing, it's the only thing" (literacy leader Christopher Lehman).

"One of the most powerful ways to engage students is to let them take charge of their own learning."

B. Brainstorm strategies teachers already use to get more than one student to respond or work at a time. While some teachers still call on one student at a time, most have strategies to get more students working, thinking, discussing, and responding simultaneously. Have teachers do a large-group brainstorm to share what they are already doing before reading about some strategies in a few article-summaries in the chapter. As a bonus, have teachers think of ways they could use *technology* to augment the power of any of these engagement strategies.

C. Have teachers read "Getting Every Student Thinking and Working" (Bambrick-Santoyo and Chiger article-summary 5); "You/We/I Teaching" (Seeley article-summary 6); and "Say/See/Do Teaching" (Jones article-summary 7).

    1. Have teachers first discuss how the engagement strategies in the three article-summaries compare to each other. Next, have them compare these three structures to the brainstormed list of ideas the teachers came up with in *Part B* above.

    2. Give teachers a choice (choice increases engagement!) to either choose one of the models in the three article-summaries and create a lesson plan based on that model *or* choose a few engagement strategies that have been discussed and find digital tools to enhance these ideas; for example, what tool might help all students write in response to a prompt *and* be able to comment on each other's writing *before* the class has a discussion?

    3. Each of the three ideas in the article-summaries places more of a focus on what the *student*

EFFECTIVE PEDAGOGY

is doing as compared to what the *teacher* is doing. Discuss this change as a large group and brainstorm ways that teachers might construct lessons differently to focus more on what the *student is doing*. Use the chart below for the brainstorm and note what the teacher and student would be doing for each idea.

Lesson Element (e.g., hook, assessment, exploration, etc.)	What the Teacher Does	What Students Do

D. Have teachers reread the three article-summaries in Part C (5, 6, and 7) looking for and underlining any other elements they will need to consider in order to maximize student engagement (for example, classroom culture, expectations, feedback, perseverance, etc.).

1. In pairs, have teachers share what they underlined and discuss the implications of these elements on their teaching.

2. Have each pair choose one or two elements and brainstorm ways they could address this element in their classrooms. (For example, "In order to build perseverance—which will help with student engagement—when I give a student-centered task I will ask students to work for increasingly more minutes on their own or in pairs each day *before* asking for help from me.")

3. Have each teacher commit to trying one of these suggestions and checking in with their partner after two weeks to discuss successes and challenges.

E. Have math and science teachers watch one of the videos in "You/We/I Teaching" (Seeley article-summary 6).

These videos show how math and science teachers might structure their classes to improve engagement.

1. Divide teachers up by grade level and have them watch the corresponding video. (One is an elementary math class, one is a middle school class, and two are high school classes.)

2. Next, have teachers who watched the same video discuss the structure the teacher used in the video, what worked about it, and how they might tweak or improve it for their own classes.

PROFESSIONAL LEARNING SUGGESTIONS OF CHAPTER FIVE

Then give everyone some time to write down how they would adapt the lesson structure for an upcoming lesson they plan to teach.

3. Finally, have teachers take turns sharing the ideas they came up with to adapt an upcoming lesson, one at a time. After each teacher shares, the group gives feedback and the presenting teacher takes notes. Ask the teachers to either plan to observe another teacher using the new structure over the next few weeks or to check back in to share results after they have taught the lesson.

III. Effective versus Ineffective Student Feedback

According to research, giving students feedback effectively can just about double their learning. However, the key is that it must be done *effectively*. Some incorrect feedback has the power to *detract* from learning. Below are some activities to help teachers understand what makes feedback successful.

A. Do a full-faculty live read and discussion of one of the article-summaries about feedback.
Since all teachers give feedback whether they teach AP Economics or PE, these article-summaries are pertinent to your entire faculty.

1. Choose either John Hattie article-summary 9 ("Making Feedback to Students Effective"), Grant Wiggins article-summary 10 ("The Elements of Effective Feedback"), or Dylan Wiliam article-summary 11 ("Getting Students to Do the Heavy Lifting")—and have the entire faculty read it during a meeting.

2. In small groups, have teachers discuss the chosen article-summary by going around in a circle and having each person share: one thing that resonated with them, one implication for their own feedback, and one commitment they will make to improve their feedback.

B. Compile all of the suggestions for improving feedback from the three article-summaries above (9, 10, and 11).
Some of the article-summaries suggest ways to improve the wording or the content of feedback while others address the conditions that need to be in place to improve feedback. It is helpful to have all suggestions in one place.

1. Have teachers read article-summaries 9, 10, and 11.

2. Alone or in pairs, ask teachers to mine the article-summaries for suggestions and compile them using an organizer like the one below:

Compiled Suggestions to Improve Feedback		
"Making Feedback to Students Effective" (summary 9)	"The Elements of Effective Feedback" (summary 10)	"Getting Students to Do the Heavy Lifting" (summary 11)

C. Have the teachers improve the crafting of feedback to students.
Ask teachers to bring in examples of written feedback they have given to students. (If they don't have any, then this might suggest you need to clarify expectations for teachers giving written feedback.) Or you can use a few of the examples of poor feedback below so they can work to improve them.

1. Ask teachers to read "The Elements of Effective Feedback" (Wiggins article-summary 10) to get ideas for ways to improve the content of their feedback.

2. Next, have them use the seven criteria in the article-summary to improve the examples of written feedback they have brought to this meeting—or to improve the following:

Good work on your math test!
This paper lacks logical organization.
You're running too slowly.

D. Have teachers try using two effective techniques to improve feedback.
Ultimately, we want students to be able to assess the quality of their own work without a teacher's assistance.

1. Have teachers read "Getting Students to Do the Heavy Lifting" (Wiliam article-summary 11).

2. In pairs have teachers discuss the two techniques in the article-summary: *make feedback into detective work* (find the five errors in this piece) and *build students' capacity for self-assessment* (examine an anonymous piece of student work and describe the feedback that should be given).

3. Have each teacher choose one of these two techniques and commit to trying it within the next two weeks and then check in with their partners to compare notes.

Chapter Six:
What Makes Learning Stick

Teachers can tell and talk, but only learners can learn .... It isn't that Sally won't listen or isn't intelligent or won't try harder to memorize what she has been told; it's that she hasn't engaged in the hard work of constructing and reconstructing neural pathways to understanding.
—ALDEN BLODGET

Most of the information that enters our brains every day is lost within a few hours. This is a source of endless frustration for teachers ("I just taught that yesterday!"), but it's a necessary adaptation that prevents cognitive overload for students and adults. The articles in this chapter fall into four buckets: brain science and working memory; the retrieval effect; study skills; and the question of what we need to memorize in the age of Google.

Brain Science and Memory – Alden Blodget describes the hard cognitive work students must do to build and maintain the neural networks that hold important information in their brains. Andrew Watson, Michael Wirtz, and Lynette Sumpter explain the limits of working memory and suggest how teachers can apply this understanding to improve students' retention and reduce classroom stress. Clare Sealy says that embedding important knowledge and skills in students' long-term memory requires skillful (not necessarily jazzy) teaching and hard work by students.

The Retrieval Effect – Pooja Agarwal, Henry Roediger, Mark McDaniel, and Kathleen McDermott describe the power of frequent, low-stakes tests to greatly improve retention. Benedict Carey explains why taking a final exam before instruction improves understanding and memory.

Kathy Ganske remembers how she got her second graders to remember what they've learned each day and week and share it with their families.

Study Skills – Susan Dynarski says research has shown that college students taking notes by hand have significantly better retention and grades than those typing notes on laptops. Benedict Carey reports that studying is most effective when students work with challenging material, study mixed content, use more than one location, space studying over time, and test themselves frequently. Daniel Willingham shares research on how students can commit facts and skills to memory, how they can avoid forgetting, and how they can avoid the trap of overconfidence.

What Should Students Memorize? – Daniel Willingham lists the four ways our brains outperform Google, and suggests the kinds of information that's best committed to memory. Amber Northern shares the Common Core's recommendations on memorizing and becoming fluent with math facts. Molly Worthen argues that having students memorize and recite poetry, which was a staple in US schools until the 1920s, has real value in today's classrooms.

Questions to Consider

- Why do students have trouble remembering our lessons?
- What makes learning stick?
- With Google in their pockets, should students memorize state capitals? Times tables? Anything?

Brain Science and Memory

① The Neuroscience of Learning

In this *Education Week* article, Alden Blodget says that learning something new (how to solve quadratic equations, the history of the Vietnam War) involves building new "wiring," neural networks or circuits, in the brain. Unfortunately, new neural networks aren't permanent—they constantly degrade. Students seem to understand one day, and then the next day they don't. "It's as though they had never seen this stuff before," is a common complaint in faculty lounges. What seemed clear in a quiet classroom with a supportive teacher falls apart when students struggle with the homework in a noisy house with nobody around who can answer their questions.

The process of building and rebuilding neural networks "requires considerable effort from the learner," says Blodget. "The essence of learning isn't memory and recitation; meaningful learning (the sort of learning educators hope to foster) results from an active effort to understand, an effort that promotes the growth of increasingly efficient webs of neural connections among different regions of the brain …. Teachers can tell and talk, but only learners can learn …. It isn't that Sally won't listen or isn't intelligent or won't try harder to memorize what she has been told; it's that she hasn't engaged in the hard work of constructing and reconstructing neural pathways to understanding."

Every time students rebuild neural networks, skills and concepts become more stable and automatic. "The highest level of skill or understanding," says Blodget, "results from repeatedly experiencing this building-rebuilding cycle over time (years), moving through a sequence of increasingly complex levels. That movement is not linear and steady; it is dynamic and messy."

One reason many students don't make the effort to build better circuits is that they're not motivated—what they're learning doesn't matter deeply to them. Neuroscientists have found that attitudes and emotions play a major part in learning, says Blodget: "Just as you cannot separate hydrogen and oxygen and still have water, you cannot separate emotion from cognitive function and still have thinking—or learning." Emotion acts as a rudder for thought.

"Brains and Schools: A Mismatch" by Alden Blodget in *Education Week*, Sept. 11, 2013 (Vol. 33, #3, pp. 30–31), summarized in Marshall Memo 502.

② Not Overloading Working Memory

A little-recognized classroom skill, say Andrew Watson (Translate the Brain) and Michael Wirtz and Lynette Sumpter (St. Mark's School) in this article in *Independent School*, is managing students' working memory. This facet of our brains is distinct from declarative memory (factual information) and procedural memory (how to ride a bike). Working memory is what allows us to hold onto a few pieces of information for several seconds and reorganize them into a new system or structure. "Schools are, in effect, shrines built to honor successful working memory functioning," say Watson, Wirtz, and Sumpter. "Students simply can't think and learn without using working memory all the time."

The problem is that working memory has a surprisingly small capacity; most people can keep only five to seven items in mind at the same time. If we ask students to remember verbal instructions, that information takes up working memory capacity and reduces students' ability to think and learn. The authors confess that, as classroom teachers, "we paid little attention to a cognitive capacity that is essential for our students' learning. For this reason, we probably overwhelmed our students' working memory without ever realizing we had done so."

It's essential, they say, that educators "develop our own expertise in the field of working memory—understand what it is, how it differs from, and contributes to, long-term memory … [and] explicitly discuss and develop teaching techniques to support our students' cognition within their limited working memory capacity."

Here are some classroom and homework activities that run the risk of swamping students' working memory capacity:
- Too much new information at once;
- Verbal instructions, especially if they're long or complex;
- Too many new combinations of information at once;
- Work that combines cognitive and creative effort;
- Work early in the morning or late at night.

Here's how students often react when their working memory is overloaded:
- Difficulty remembering some information while processing other information—for example, long multiplication;
- Atypical difficulties with attention;
- "Catastrophic failure," difficulty adding just one simple step to several previous steps.

Watson, Wirtz, and Sumpter offer the following suggestions for addressing working memory overload:

- Make information visual. "Humans have much more brain real estate devoted to visual processing than to all our other senses combined," say the authors. "Visual depiction reduces working memory demands." This suggests maximizing the use of photos and videos, flowcharts and diagrams, or simply writing down complicated instructions.
- Manage note-taking. "If students are trying to understand an idea while at the same time writing notes, those two processes compete with each other in working memory," they say. "As a result, they're likely not to do either very well." One strategy is to ask students to put their pencils or pens down (or stop typing) when you're explaining new, complex, or important ideas, then have students write notes in silence with the teacher circulating to monitor what's being written.
- Redistribute working memory demands across longer periods of time. "Chunk" material—organize it into an already-familiar pattern.
- Promote attention by reinforcing conceptual frameworks. Explicitly teach strategies—for example, Treviso multiplication.
- Reduce stress, perhaps using mindfulness. Less pressure from time, grades, and peers is helpful, along with cutting down distractions in the classroom.
- Regularly emphasize that struggle is normal.

A teacher at St. Mark's School wrote the following after being exposed to the research on working memory: "I used to think that pushing the bounds of memory was helpful, much like how lifting weights makes you stronger in the long run. I learned it is quite the opposite with working memory, and that overtaxing it can cause our students to shut down. As a result, I have tried to provide more visual cues, word banks, fewer choices, etc., so that students focus on the most important task at hand, instead of trying to juggle too many pieces of information in their working memories."

Another teacher wrote, "I've learned how small and essential working memory is. When planning my lessons, I'm much more intentional about looking for areas where I risk overwhelming working memory. I know what to look for during a lesson to see if students are reaching the point of overload and how to change things up to get them back on track."

"Putting Memory to Work" by Andrew Watson, Michael Wirtz, and Lynette Sumpter in *Independent School*, Fall 2015 (Vol. 75, #1, pp. 56–60), summarized in Marshall Memo 606.

EFFECTIVE PEDAGOGY

3 Understanding Two Very Different Kinds of Memory

In this *Education Next* article, British educator Clare Sealy says it's commonly believed that to make a lesson stick in students' memories, teachers need to make it spectacular, exciting, and unusual. "Memorable events, in this view, should form the template for creating memorable lessons," says Sealy. But she believes that's a myth stemming from conflating two ways in which we remember things:

• *Episodic memory* – These are memories of events each day, and they are formed automatically, with no special effort on our part: what we had for lunch, a joke someone told this afternoon. The downside of episodic memories is that they fade quickly; we won't remember what we had for lunch a month ago unless something very unusual happened at the meal, and *that joke*—what *was* the punch line?

This means that if we as teachers put our faith in episodic memory, we'll be constantly disappointed when we ask our students what they learned the day before. They'll remember all kinds of things, says Sealy: "that you used Post-it Notes, that Mollie was late, that you spilt your coffee, that Liam made a hilarious joke." In other words, students remember the "contextual tags but not the actual learning. Episodic memory is so tied up with context it is no good for remembering things once that context is no longer present." This is especially true when students move to a different classroom, grade, or school. It's not that last year's teachers are lying when they say their students mastered fractions; it's that students' memories were largely episodic, and now the context is different.

• *Semantic memory* – This kind involves much more work—taking notes, studying, and encoding information—but the advantage is that such memories last longer. "Semantic memories have been liberated from the emotional and spatial/temporal context in which they were first acquired," says Sealy. "Once a concept has been stored in semantic memory, it is more flexible and transferable between different contexts. Semantic memory is central, therefore, to long-term learning, learning that can be put to use in novel contexts to solve unexpected problems. Semantic memory is what we use when we are problem-solving or being creative."

Episodic memories are the stuff of life in schools, especially the way students are treated and how adults treat each other. And broadening experiences outside of school (field trips to museums, theaters, historic sites, forests, mountains) are especially important for children whose families are not able to provide them. But the hum-drum semantic memories are the most important takeaways from schooling.

Cognitive psychologist Daniel Willingham says that "memory is the residue of thought." This means, says Sealy, that "teachers have to make sure that lessons give students the opportunity to think about the things we actually want them to remember, rather than some extraneous other thing. We need them to think about the message of the lesson, rather than the medium we use to teach it." And this is why "fun" lessons may be getting in the way of long-term learning; the medium may become more prominent than the message. "When teachers plan lessons," she continues, "we need to be mindful of what children will be thinking about during each part of the lesson, rather than what they will be feeling or doing. Have we planned activities that will ensure children think hard about the right things?"

British school inspectors noticed this phenomenon as they watched elementary students doing science experiments. Checking in with students, observers found that kids could explain what they were doing but not the underlying scientific concepts; there wasn't enough cognitive bandwidth for that. The logical conclusion is that students should be taught the concepts before diving into hands-on experiments. "Once the scientific concepts are secure," says Sealy, "children are much more able to really 'think like scientists,' with the added benefit that the practical activity then consolidates understanding of the previous learning."

The same is true of having students research information on their own; the cognitive work of looking for information and making judgments about its relevance prevents them from grasping and remembering content.

And this insight also applies to classroom mathematical discovery and creative problem-solving. Sealy believes these activities "are completely inappropriate for the initial stage of learning, when children are encountering a concept for the first time. If we want children to become independent problem-solvers, we need to teach them carefully and explicitly so that semantic memory can begin to form. Counterintuitive as it may seem, children do not become independent problem solvers by independently solving problems. This is because when children are trying to solve problems before they know the necessary math to do so, they will be expending considerable mental energy tracking what they are meant to be solving against what they have found out so far, so much so that even when they are successful, they will have forgotten what they actually did en route to finally finding the answer! ... Frustratingly, current *performance* is a terrible guide to knowing whether or not *learning* has actually happened or not."

EFFECTIVE PEDAGOGY

Explicit, step-by-step instruction is essential, she says, followed by retrieval and application at intervals after the initial lesson, with fewer cues and prompts. Only then will students begin to cement knowledge and skills in long-term memory.

It's common for people to say they don't remember anything they learned in school, but this simply means they don't have an episodic memory of specific lessons. That's not a bad thing, says Sealy, because if we remembered everything, our brains would explode. But if we were taught well, we know lots of deeper stuff, says Sealy: "triangles and oxygen, Anne Boleyn and paragraphs, square numbers and ox bow lakes, color-mixing and Lady Macbeth …. That's the beauty of semantic memory. It isn't, and doesn't need to be, tied up with episodic clutter." Those deeper memories, formed by good teaching, serve as a foundation for further learning and all sorts of creative endeavors—even if we don't remember learning them.

Well-schooled people are "knowledge-privileged," says Sealy: "You have been given opportunities to think hard about stuff you didn't know and therefore have a vast repository of semantic memory on hand, readily available whenever you want it. Yet it is all too easy to overlook this privilege and vastly underestimate how much we do in fact know and how much our schooling benefited us. Because we don't remember learning what we know, we don't remember the effort that went into teaching it."

Sealy's concern is that schools that focus on immersing students in "fun" and "involving" lessons may be short-changing this vital area, leaving kids "with an impoverished ability to think or be truly creative …. Before we decide to impose our own agendas onto children's education," she concludes, "we need to check our knowledge privilege before making decisions that will deprive children of their fair share of the rich cultural inheritance our world affords and to which they are entitled."

"The Best Way to Help Children Remember Things? Not 'Memorable Experiences'" by Clare Sealy in *Education Next*, September 26, 2019, summarized in Marshall Memo 812.

The Retrieval Effect

4   How Remembering Improves Remembering

"When we think about learning, we typically focus on getting information *into* students' heads," say Pooja Agarwal, Henry Roediger, Mark McDaniel, and Kathleen McDermott (Washington University–Saint Louis) in this Institute of Education Sciences paper. "What if, instead, we focus on getting information *out of* students' heads?" More than one hundred years of research has shown that "retrieval," calling information to mind, has the effect of strengthening retention, thus enhancing and boosting learning. "Deliberately recalling information forces us to pull our knowledge 'out' and examine what we know," say Agarwal, Roediger, McDaniel, and McDermott. "Often, we think we've learned some piece of information, but we come to realize we struggle when we try to recall the answer. It's precisely this 'struggle' or challenge that improves our memory and learning—by trying to recall information, we exercise or strengthen our memory, and we can also identify gaps in our learning …. Retrieval practice is a powerful strategy for improving academic performance, without more technology, money, or class time."

Research has shown that retrieval is much better for cementing understanding in long-term memory than commonly used strategies like rereading, highlighting, underlining, note-taking, reading review sheets, watching a video, and listening to a lecture. These strategies may produce short-term gains when cramming for a test, but memory researchers have found that they don't produce long-term retention. Counterintuitively, information that feels easy to recall is least likely to stick in our minds.

"Retrieval practice," say the authors, "makes learning effortful and challenging. Because retrieving information requires mental effort, we often think we are doing poorly if we can't remember something. We may feel like progress is slow, but that's when our best learning takes place. The more difficult the retrieval practice, the better it is for long-term learning …. Slower, effortful retrieval leads to long-term learning. In contrast, easy strategies only lead to short-term learning."

What's more, retrieval increases understanding and higher-order functions. It improves students': complex thinking and application skills, organization of knowledge, and transfer of knowledge to new concepts. The process of retrieval also clarifies for students what they *don't* know. Their improved metacognitive sense of what they've mastered and what they haven't gives students a more realistic sense of their academic status and leads to better decisions on how to spend study time.

Agarwal, Roediger, McDaniel, and McDermott pose and answer several questions about retrieval practice:

• *For which grade levels, subject areas, and students is it appropriate?* Researchers have found that it's helpful for all grades, for students at all achievement levels, and for all subject areas. Studies have been done in science, math, social studies, history, vocabulary learning, and foreign language vocabulary.

• *What are the most effective classroom strategies?* It's best to use retrieval with the whole class (using an all-class response system like clickers, Plickers, dry-erase boards, or exit tickets); to use retrieval as a learning strategy rather than a quiz or test; and to always provide feedback to students on their responses.

• *Do teachers need to stop using textbooks and traditional classroom strategies?* There's no need to change textbooks, since retrieval practice works perfectly with review or chapter questions. Nor is there a need to change one's teaching style—questions are still asked of students, but the response is more universal. And retrieval doesn't take more time—it just uses time more effectively, getting more bang for the instructional minute.

• *How is classroom retrieval practice different from "cold calling"?* Retrieval involves calling on *all* students and getting an immediate sense of how well the entire class is understanding what's being taught. "By engaging every student in retrieval practice," say the authors, "every student reaps the benefits for long-term learning."

• *How much retrieval practice is necessary?* The more the better, but spacing it out makes retrieval more challenging and effective. In terms of timing, retrieval is best a short time after a learning experience—but not too short; the more the spacing stretch, the more powerful the benefit.

• *Should retrieval questions be graded?* No, say the authors. Keeping the questions low-stakes helps students feel less pressured and more comfortable making mistakes, which students need to see as beneficial to the learning process. Rather than grades, teachers should provide immediate feedback to correct errors, misunderstandings, and misconceptions.

• *Doesn't retrieval practice increase test anxiety?* Quite the contrary, say Agarwal, Roediger, McDaniel, and McDermott; it decreases worries about high-stakes assessments by improving mastery and confidence and embedding information more deeply in students' memories.

• *What types of questions are best?* Retrieval works equally well for facts, concepts, and higher-order, complex material—ideally mixed together. And it's a good idea to shift between multiple-choice and open-response questions.

"How to Use Retrieval Practice to Improve Learning" by Pooja Agarwal, Henry Roediger, Mark McDaniel, and Kathleen McDermott in an Institute of Education Sciences paper, 2013, summarized in Marshall Memo 610.

5. Using Pretests to Improve Achievement

In this *New York Times Magazine* article, Benedict Carey asks us to imagine that on the first day of a difficult college course, before we had studied anything, we were able to see the final exam. "Would that help you study more effectively?" he asks. "Of course, it would. You would read the questions carefully. You would know exactly what to focus on in your notes. Your ears would perk up anytime the teacher mentioned something relevant to a specific question. You would search the textbook for its discussion of each question." But many people would consider that cheating.

What if you actually *took* the final exam at the beginning of the course? You would do terribly, of course, but the experience would have many of the same positive effects as the "cheating" scenario, sharply improving your overall performance.

How can doing badly on a test produce positive results? It's because of what psychologists call the pretest effect: "the attempts themselves change how we think about and store the information contained in the question," says Carey. Answering incorrectly primes our brain for what's coming later. Failing the pretest provides more learning benefits than conventional studying. In other words, "Testing might be the key to studying, rather than the other way around," he says. "As it turns out, a test is not only a measurement tool. It's a way of enriching and altering memory .... The test, that is, becomes an introduction to what students should learn, rather than a final judgment on what they did not."

It's now clear that conventional studying—reading, rereading, highlighting—is not very effective. Psychologists say that when we study in these ways, we tend to misjudge and overestimate our knowledge and skills. "We are duped by a misperception of 'fluency,'" says Carey, "believing that because facts or formulas or arguments are easy to remember *right now*, they will remain that way tomorrow or the next day. This fluency illusion is so strong that, once we feel we have some topic or assignment down, we assume that further study won't strengthen our memory of the material. We move on, forgetting that we forget." Fluency creates overconfidence and plays tricks on our judgment.

This insight about learning goes back to 1620, when Francis Bacon wrote, "If you read a piece of text through twenty times, you will not learn it by heart so easily as if you read it ten times while attempting to recite it from time to time and consulting the text when your memory fails." In 1916, Columbia University psychologist Arthur Gates conducted experiments and found that the best way to memorize a Shakespeare sonnet was to spend a third of the time trying to memorize it and two-thirds of the time trying to recite it from memory. In effect, testing was a form of studying and constant improvement.

In the 1930s, Herman Spitzer, a doctoral student at the University of Iowa, wondered: if testing is so helpful, when is the best time to do it? He had thirty-five hundred sixth-graders read an age-appropriate article and then divided them into groups, giving them quizzes at different time intervals and then measuring long-term retention. The students who were quizzed earliest had by far the best recall of the material they'd studied, even though all the students had studied for the same amount of time.

Elizabeth Ligon Bjork and Nicholas Soderstrom at UCLA explored this idea, giving some students pretests at the beginning of lectures and comparing long-term retention with students who didn't take pretests. Pretested students did poorly on the tests, but as long as they were given the right answers and explanations soon afterward, the long-term result was significantly higher retention than the control group. Bjork and others have pondered why this happens. Here are some possible explanations:

• First, students get a glimpse of what the teacher intends to teach, which helps them see where instruction is headed and how the information fits into the course narrative. Students who get the pretest preview are more confident in judging what's important and what isn't. Teachers always try to signal this as they teach, but pretested students are more attentive and hear what they're saying better. "Taking a practice test and getting wrong answers seems to improve subsequent study," says Bjork, "because the test adjusts our thinking in some way to the kind of material we need to know."

• Second, wrong guesses puncture students' overconfidence about what they know. A student might be sure he knows that Canberra is the capital of Australia, but when confronted by a multiple-choice item with Sydney, Melbourne, and Adelaide as alternative answers, he's suddenly not so sure. "If you're studying just the correct answer, you don't appreciate all the other possible answers that could come to mind or appear on the test," says Robert Bjork. Pretesting is a kind of "fluency vaccine."

• Third, retrieving is a different mental process than straight studying. The brain is digging out information, along with a network of associations, and that alters and enriches how the network is restored. Guessing operates in similar fashion. "Even if the question is not entirely clear and its solution unknown," says Carey, "a guess will in itself begin to link the question to possible answers. And those networks light up like Christmas lights when we hear the concepts again."

This suggests a limit on the usefulness of pretesting: quizzing students in an unfamiliar language like Arabic or Chinese, in which they have no prior knowledge or associations, won't be helpful. "The research thus far," says Carey, "suggests that prefinals will be much more useful in humanities courses and social-science disciplines in which unfamiliar concepts are at least embedded in language we can parse."

"Exams Measure What We Know, But They're Also One of the Best Ways to Learn" by Benedict Carey in the *New York Times Magazine*, September 7, 2014, summarized in Marshall Memo 553. Carey's book with these and other findings is *How We Learn: The Surprising Truth About When, Where, and Why It Happens* (New York: Random House, 2014).

---

6 What Did You Learn in School Today?

In this article in *The Reading Teacher*, Kathy Ganske (Vanderbilt University) recalls that when she was in elementary school, her father would ask almost every evening what she'd learned in school that day. Knowing the question was coming, she recalls, "I kept my eyes and ears open throughout the day for potential candidates for demonstrating understanding …."

When she became a teacher, Ganske began to ask her students as they waited for their afternoon buses what new ideas, concepts, facts, or processes they would share with someone at home. "At first, students were slow to generate responses," she says, "but that gradually changed. In anticipation of the talk, they sifted through our day's journey, as evidenced by the occasional announcement of 'I'm going to hang on to that one!' that punctuated our classroom learning. The end-of-day wrap-up provided a satisfying sense of closure, and the recap of learning made students aware of what they'd accomplished."

A few years later, Ganske took this a step further: her second graders began to publish a Friday parent newsletter of the week's learning dubbed *The Koko Report* (in honor of the class's bake sale support of Koko the gorilla and the Gorilla Foundation). The newsletter emerged from a meeting on the carpet in which Ganske jotted key content areas on chart paper, had students suggest other events—field trips, visitors, special projects, birthdays—and together they constructed a web of the week's learning. Initially, students had difficulty remembering what had happened during the week, but the routine improved their ability to retrieve information from several days ago. "Unless we make a conscious effort to help them solidify their learning," says Ganske, "they may lose a great deal of it."

Next, students signed up as "reporters" to write brief articles, working in groups of two or three, or occasionally solo. "The talk and recording of information jump-started and deepened students' recollections of our week," says Ganske, "and the web provided support for their beginning writing skills, as did the discussion and feedback that took place in the small groups." Students brought their reports to Ganske, who typed them on a blank newsletter template. After a group edit and the addition of a few teacher comments for parents and guardians, the Koko Report was photocopied and sent home. The whole workshop took forty-five to sixty minutes.

Convinced of the value of daily or weekly closure/remembering/consolidating, Ganske researched the topic and was surprised to find that very few studies had been done to document its impact. "We need to be sure we plan time to cycle back to the what, why, and how of students' learning to help them actively synthesize the parts into a whole," she concludes. "Lesson closure provides space for students to digest and assimilate their learning and to realize why it all matters."

"Lesson Closure: An Important Piece of the Student Learning Puzzle" by Kathy Ganske in *The Reading Teacher*, July/August 2017 (Vol. 71, #1, pp. 95–100), summarized in Marshall Memo 694.

Study Skills

⑦ The Difference Between Taking Notes by Hand and on a Laptop

In this Brookings article, Susan Dynarski explores research from Princeton and UCLA on note-taking in college lectures, and comes down squarely on the side of hand-written notes. "When college students use computers or tablets during lectures," she says, "they learn less and earn worse grades …. Understanding the lectures, measured by a standardized test, was substantially worse for those who used laptops."

Dynarski elaborates: "Learning researchers hypothesize that because students can type faster than they can write, a lecturer's words flow straight from the student's ears through their typing fingers, without stopping in the brain for substantive processing." It's more like a transcript than a summary. "Students writing by hand, by contrast, have to process and condense the material if their pens are to keep up with the lecture."

Taking notes serves two purposes: (a) storing the lecture's ideas for later review, which laptops do better; and (b) cognitive encoding of the information, which handwriting does better. On balance, mental processing and coding are more important, which is why handwritten notes produce superior long-term learning.

But couldn't we train students to be more thoughtful with laptop notetaking, getting them to slow down and summarize? Researchers tried this, and laptop-using students' retention and understanding didn't improve.

There's another reason for not using laptops for note-taking: the powerful temptation for students to engage in social media and online shopping during a lecture. Researchers found this kind of multitasking degraded the learning of those who engaged in it, and also lowered the performance of students sitting nearby, who could see their classmates goofing off. In fact, students looking over the shoulders of multitasking students did *worse* on post-tests (17 percent lower) than the multitaskers themselves (who scored 11 percent lower).

The experiments reported above were conducted in somewhat artificial settings, with students paid to listen to lectures that weren't part of real coursework for grades. Would the findings hold up in a real-world situation? Researchers conducted a study at the US Military Academy at West Point that met this standard. All USMA students take a semester-long introductory economics class with common multiple-choice/short-answer tests graded automatically. Researchers randomly assigned sections to one of three conditions: electronics allowed; electronics banned; and tablet computers allowed (if they were laid flat on desks where professors could observe how they were being used). Instructors teaching multiple sections were assigned more than one treatment condition.

At the end of the semester, students who used electronics in class (the first and third conditions) scored significantly worse than students who were not allowed to use computers or laptops—0.2 standard deviations lower (there was no discernible difference between the laptop and tablet sections).

Would the West Point findings hold up in a community college or four-year college? The researchers argue that disparity would be even more pronounced, since USMA classes are small, professors can more easily monitor inappropriate use of electronics, and West Point students are motivated by the high stakes attached to achievement in every course.

"There may well be particular classroom settings in which laptops improve learning," concludes Dynarski. "Perhaps a coding class, in which students collaborate on solving a programming problem. But for the typical lecture setting, the best evidence suggests students should lay down their laptops and pick up a pen."

"For Better Learning in College Lectures, Lay Down the Laptop and Pick Up a Pen" by Susan Dynarski, Brookings Institution, August 10, 2017, summarized in Marshall Memo 698.

---

8. Research-Based Approaches to Studying

In this *New York Times* article, Benedict Carey reports the latest findings from cognitive science about the kinds of studying that work best for students of all ages. Interestingly, these findings are at variance with the conventional wisdom among parents and educators. For example, Carey says that all the talk about visual, auditory, left-brain/right-brain learners, etc. is unproven. A recent article in *Psychological Science in the Public Interest* found no empirical support for these theories. "The contrast between the enormous popularity of the learning-styles approach within education and the lack of credible evidence for its utility is, in our opinion, striking and disturbing," write the authors. Here's what the research says *does* work:

- *Varying study location* – Alternating between two rooms while studying significantly improves retention. A classic 1978 study found that college students who studied forty vocabulary words first in one room and then in another did far better on a post-test than students who studied the words two times in a single location. Subsequent studies have replicated this finding for a variety of subjects. "The brain makes subtle associations between what it is studying and the background sensations it has at the time," says Carey. "It colors the terms of the Versailles Treaty with the wasted fluorescent glow of the dorm study room, say; or the elements of the Marshall Plan with the jade-curtain shade of the willow tree in the back yard. Forcing the brain to make multiple associations with the same material may, in effect, give the information more neural scaffolding."

- *Mixed content* – Studying distinct but related skills or concepts in one sitting improves retention. "Musicians have known this for years," says Carey, "and their practice sessions often include a mix of scales, musical pieces and rhythmic work. Many athletes, too, routinely mix their workouts with strength, speed and skill drills." In a recent study in *Applied Cognitive Psychology*, University of South Florida researchers Doug Rohrer and Kelli Taylor reported on a study of fourth graders' retention of geometry concepts. Those who studied a mixture of problems scored 77 percent on a follow-up test, compared to 38 percent for students who focused on one kind of problem. "When students see a list of problems, all of the same kind, they know the strategy to use before they even read the problem," says Rohrer. "That's like riding a bike with training wheels." Mixed practice is far more productive. The finding has been replicated in other fields, including an experiment asking college students and older adults to distinguish the painting styles of twelve unfamiliar artists. "What seems to be happening in this case is that the brain is picking up deeper patterns when seeing assortments of paintings," says Williams College psychologist Nate Kornell, one of the authors. "It's picking up what's similar and what's different about them."

- *Spaced studying* – "An hour of study tonight, an hour on the weekend, another session a week from now," says Carey, is a highly effective study strategy. Dozens of studies have shown that spacing improves later recall for the same amount of time. One theory is that when the brain comes back to material after some time has passed, it has to relearn some that's been forgotten before adding new material. "The idea is that forgetting is the friend of learning," says Nate Kornell. "When you forget something, it allows you to relearn, and do so effectively, the next time you see it." Last-minute cramming, on the other hand, may help a student pass a test the next day but is ineffective for long-term memory. "Hurriedly jam-packing a brain is akin to speed-packing a cheap suitcase," says Carey, "… it holds its new load for a while, then most everything falls out. When a neural suitcase is packed carefully and gradually, it holds its contents far, far longer."

• *Frequent assessment with feedback* – "The process of retrieving an idea is not like pulling a book from a shelf," says Carey. "It seems to fundamentally alter the way the information is subsequently stored, making it far more accessible in the future." Washington University–Saint Louis psychologist Henry Roediger has confirmed this in his research (see Article 4 summary): "Testing not only measures knowledge but changes it," he says. "Testing has such a bad connotation. People think of standardized testing or teaching to the test. Maybe we need to call it something else, but this is one of the most powerful learning tools we have."

• *Challenge* – It turns out that a difficult test is better for long-term memory than an easy one. "The harder it is to remember something, the harder it is to later forget," says Carey. "The more mental sweat it takes to dig it out, the more securely it will be subsequently anchored." Researchers call this "desirable difficulty."

"We have known these principles for some time," says UCLA psychologist Robert Bjork, "and it's intriguing that schools don't pick them up, or that people don't learn them by trial and error. Instead, we walk around with all sorts of unexamined beliefs about what works that are mistaken."

"Forget What You Know About Good Study Habits" by Benedict Carey in the *New York Times*, Sept. 7, 2010 (pp. D1, D6), summarized in Marshall Memo 351.

---

9. How Can We Help Students Remember More?

In this article in *American Educator*, University of Virginia cognitive scientist Daniel Willingham sets us straight on four common misconceptions about memory: (a) subliminal learning and memorizing while asleep are ineffective; (b) hypnosis doesn't make memory any more accurate; (c) herbal supplements or pharmaceuticals, despite tantalizing claims and a small number of suggestive findings, don't improve memory; and (d) memory doesn't depend solely on the modality in which we learn new material.

Willingham then shares research on how K–12 students—and adults—really do commit information and skills to memory, how they can avoid forgetting, and how they can tell when they've studied enough.

- *Committing facts and skills to memory* – The key to remembering is *thinking about* what you want to remember, he says. Memory is the "residue of thought, meaning that the more you think about something, the more likely it is that you'll remember it." This has immediate implications for the best way for students to study. It's not enough to tell students to think about what they're studying, and just rereading notes and highlighting them isn't that effective. It can even be detrimental if it creates the illusion that you know the material because you've "studied" it.

What's helpful is giving students a specific task that will force them to think about meaning as they study, for example, asking *Why*, after every sentence or paragraph or segment they read. One study showed that students who did this remembered significantly more than students who read the same material without asking *Why*. Another strategy is for students to write down the main ideas of a chapter and identify how the author elaborates on these points, drawing a diagram of the main and subordinate ideas. A third approach is for students to write an outline for a chapter and then see if they can write a *different* outline, organizing the same material another way.

Willingham notes that SQ3R, a widely touted study method, seems to embody the think-about-it strategy: Survey what you will read, generate Questions as you survey, Read to answer your questions, Recite the important information as you read, and Review when you've finished. Unfortunately, SQ3R doesn't work that well; the reason, he says, is that it's difficult to do well (framing good questions is the hardest part). Mnemonics, on the other hand, can be quite effective because they give us something to think about—cues to our memories. These are especially helpful when memorizing material that doesn't have much intrinsic meaning.

- *Not forgetting what's been committed to memory* – The key to accessing memories is cues or hooks that help retrieve what we've stored in our brains. Without cues, memories are inaccessible, seemingly lost. With the right cues, even distant memories can be retrieved intact. So to minimize forgetting, students need to create distinctive and memorable hooks as they store material. One strategy is distinctive mnemonics to "tag" memories. Here are some examples:
  - Music or rhymes – Setting the material to be remembered to a familiar tune, for example, the alphabet song, or "Thirty days has September …"
  - Acrostic – Creating an easy-to-remember sentence in which the first letter of each word provides a cue to the item to be remembered—for example, "Every Good Boy Does Fine" to remember the order of notes on the treble clef.
  - Mnemonic associations – For example, remembering that the word *principal* ends in *pal*

because she is your *pal*, or remembering that *grammar* ends in *ar* by remembering not to *mar* your work with bad grammar.
- Pegwords – These are useful for memorizing lists of unrelated items. For example, remembering that the number one item on the list will be associated with "bun," the number two item with "shoe," the number three item with "tree," etc., and then creating a visual image of each item with its position word.
- Method of loci – Also useful for memorizing unrelated items, you take a mental walk down a familiar route and associate each item to be remembered with a location on the route.
- Acronym – Creating an acronym using the first letter of each item to be remembered, for example, HOMES for remembering the Great Lakes: Huron, Ontario, Michigan, Erie, and Superior.
- Keyword – Useful for memorizing foreign vocabulary: finding an English word that is close in sound to the foreign vocabulary word and creating a visual image that connects the two, for example, remembering *championes*, the Spanish word for mushrooms, by creating a visual image of a boxing champion in the ring, arms aloft, wearing large mushrooms instead of boxing gloves.

Another memory-retention strategy is distributed studying—not cramming in one session, but studying at several different, spread-out times. A third strategy is over-learning; since we tend to overestimate how much we'll remember and underestimate how much we'll forget, it makes sense to study about 20 percent longer than seems necessary. Another strategy is to test yourself as you go along, replicating the conditions under which you'll actually be tested. Finally, an excellent way to remember is to explain the material to another person—ideally someone who can ask thoughtful follow-up questions.

• *Being certain one has actually committed something to memory* – Most people, children and adults, think they remember more than they actually do. This means that students don't study as much as they need to. One experiment showed that students allocated only 68 percent of the time they needed to master material. Thus, for students to study more effectively, says Willingham, they need to find ways to assess what they know more realistically, and the best way to do that is to regularly retrieve important information and practice useful skills—to make sure they're still in there.

"Ask the Cognitive Scientist: What Will Improve a Student's Memory?" by Daniel Willingham in *American Educator*, Winter 2008–09 (Vol. 32, #4, pp. 17–25, 44), summarized in Marshall Memo 268

What Should Students Memorize?

10 Why Not Just Google It?

In this *New York Times* article, Daniel Willingham (University of Virginia) pushes back on the notion that because students can find pretty much any piece of information online (the capital of Ohio; the quadratic equation), there's no point in having them memorize stuff. Google is certainly good at finding information, says Willingham, but there are four ways that the human brain is superior to the Internet's information.

First, it can quickly determine context and decide if a particular word is the right one for the situation at hand. For example, a student might Google *meticulous*, find that it means "very careful," and write, *I was meticulous about not falling off the cliff*. Context and background knowledge supply what an online search cannot.

Second, in many situations our brains are faster than Google. Retrieving a memorized piece of information—for example, four times nine—is much quicker than opening a browser and accessing the times table. In addition, when students go to the Internet for information, they can lose the thread of solving a problem. That's why the National Mathematics Advisory Panel advocates "quick and effortless recall of facts" as essential to math proficiency. Speedy recall is also vital to reading comprehension. We read best when we know at least 95 percent of the words in a text. "Pausing to find a word definition is disruptive," says Willingham. "Online, the mere presence of hyperlinks compromises reading comprehension because the decision of whether or not to click disrupts the flow of understanding."

Third, our brains are adept at functioning with partial information—for example, we have the idea of *someone who owes money* but not the word (*debtor*). We store the meaning, spelling, and sound or words in separate areas, which is why it's possible to recall one without the others. "Good readers have reliable, speedy connections among the brain representations of spelling, sound, and meaning," says Willingham. "Speed matters because it allows other important work—for example, puzzling out the meaning of phrases—to proceed."

Finally, the brain has a built-in self-improvement function. Every time we retrieve something from memory or use a skill, the connection becomes more robust and the information or skill is easier to access next time. That's why using GPS will not help you remember your way around an unfamiliar city if at a later date you have to navigate without it.

For these reasons, says Willingham, "It's a grave mistake to think Google can replace your memory. It can, however, complement it, if we keep in mind what each does best." The Internet is clearly superior when we need to quickly find arcane or not-worth-remembering information. A rule of thumb: we should commit to memory the facts that we will often need to access quickly—the sounds of letters; core vocabulary; important science, health, and history facts; times tables; the quadratic equation—while taking advantage of the Internet to find random stuff, widen our knowledge and skills, and continuously broaden our memory bank.

"You Still Need Your Brain" by Daniel Willingham in the *New York Times*, May 21, 2017, summarized in Marshall Memo 687.

11. Should Students Memorize Times Tables?

In this Thomas B. Fordham Institute article, Amber Northern remembers her father drilling her on multiplication facts at the kitchen table—*Six times six? Twelve times eleven? Eight times nine?* Although the sessions were arduous, she took "great pride at (eventually) memorizing the entire lot, and I relished the ritual that Dad and I shared as Mom finished the dishes and my near-teen sister chatted forever on the phone."

Not everyone is a fan of memorizing times tables, and some argue that this exercise frustrates and stresses out elementary-school children and is the very opposite of developing a genuine understanding of math concepts. What do the Common Core standards have to say? Interestingly, says Northern, the standards don't ever use the word *memorize*. Instead, they say, "By the end of Grade 2, know from memory all sums of two one-digit numbers," and "By the end of Grade 3, know from memory all products of two one-digit numbers."

What is the distinction between *memorizing* and *knowing from memory*? To find the answer, Northern spoke to one of the principal authors of the Common Core math standards, Jason Zimba, and here's what he said: "Memorizing most naturally refers to a process (such as the one you and your dad engaged in), whereas knowing more clearly refers to an end—and ends, not processes, are the appropriate subjects for a standards statement." Zimba doesn't think there is any ambiguity about what the Common Core requires about multiplication facts. "I do know there are people who wish that the sentence had not been included," he says. "Perhaps their discomfort interferes with their reading comprehension."

What about *fluency* with math facts? asks Northern. Is that the same as knowing the facts? Zimba says Common Core standards separate the two, specifying that students "Fluently multiply and divide within 100, using strategies such as the relationship between multiplication and division (e.g., knowing that 8 x 5 = 40, one knows 40 ÷ 5 = 8) or properties of operations." *Knowing* multiplication facts is different. Fluency "pertains to an act of calculation," he says. "In particular, to be fluent with these calculations is to be accurate and reasonably fast. However, memory is also fast, so the difference between fluency and memory isn't a matter of speed. The difference, rather, has to do with the different nature of calculating versus remembering. In an act of calculation, there is some logical sequence of steps. Retrieving a fact from memory, on the other hand, doesn't involve logic *or* steps. It's just remembering; it's just knowing …. The standards expect students to remember basic facts *and* to be fluent in calculation. Neither is a substitute for the other."

Here's an example with addition facts. Before memorizing them, a second grader might tackle the problem 8 + 7 = ? by thinking, "One more than 7 + 7, which I remember is 14, so 15." Once students have committed the facts to memory, they won't need to go through that extra step. They *just know*, which is synonymous with *knowing from memory*.

Finally, Northern asks Zimba if the Common Core authors are critical of memorization. "Not unless you think that memorizing demands that we work in inefficient ways," he says. There are one hundred different single-digit products to learn; the first nine are 1 x 1, 1 x 2, 1 x 3, 1 x 4, 1 x 5, 1 x 6, 1 x 7, 1 x 8, and 1 x 9. It's highly inefficient to teach those as separate facts, separate from their meanings. "Memorizing single-digit sums and products isn't like memorizing the alphabet," says Zimba. "The alphabet is an irrational sequence with no structure or internal logic. It can't be optimal to memorize the addition and multiplication tables, with all their patterns, the same way we memorize the alphabet sequence. By pointing that out, I'm not critiquing memorization—I'm prompting us to think about the most effective way to reach the endpoint: knowing the single-digit sums and products from memory."

"Does Common Core Math Expect Memorization? A Candid Conversation with Jason Zimba" by Amber Northern, Thomas B. Fordham Institute, July 13, 2016, summarized in Marshall Memo 648.

---

12. Should Students Memorize Poetry?

In this *New York Times* article, Molly Worthen (University of North Carolina–Chapel Hill) says, that before the invention of writing, "the only way to possess a poem was to memorize it." Then, as scrolls and folios provided a way to externally encode some of the content of humans' brains, "court poets, priests, and wandering bards recited poetry in order to entertain and connect with the divine." In early US schools, poetry recitation was "an inexpensive exercise that helped even inexperienced teachers at underfunded schools impart rhetorical skills and nurture moral character."

After the Civil War, as public schools proliferated, textbooks contained anthologies of verse, and memorizing poetry became a fixture at the elementary and secondary level. A 1902 handbook for teachers said that reciting poetry stocked children's minds "with the priceless treasure of the noblest thoughts and feelings that have been uttered by the race." Poems were chosen to model Victorian virtues—piety, noble sacrifice, and valiant acceptance of mortality—as in poems like Thomas Gray's "Elegy Written in a Country Churchyard."

But in the 1920s, educators began to question the relevance of memorizing poetry to students' lives. It was gradually replaced by activities involving self-expression, and by the 1960s had almost disappeared from schools (except in some world language classes). Now, says Worthen, memorizing poetry "has become deeply unfashionable, an outmoded practice that many teachers and parents—not to mention students—consider too boring, mindless, and just plain difficult for the modern classroom. Besides, who needs to memorize when our smartphones can instantly call up nearly any published poem in the universe?"

Worthen is not persuaded. "The truth is that memorizing and reciting poetry can be a highly expressive act," she says, and it's more important than ever: "All of us struggle with shrinking attention spans and a public sphere that is becoming a literary wasteland, bereft of sophisticated language or expressions of empathy beyond one's own Facebook bubble. For students who seem to have less and less patience for long reading assignments, perhaps now is the time to bring back poetry memorization. Let's capitalize on their ear for the phony free verse of Twitter and texting and give them better words to make sense of themselves and their world."

Worthen admits that she is impatient with poetry: "I prefer straightforward prose that tells me what it means." But she's started spending ten minutes a day memorizing carefully chosen poems—a Shakespeare sonnet, some Longfellow, some Gerard Manley Hopkins. She's finding that the close reading and hard work involved in learning a poem by heart gets her in touch with the meaning and the artistry of each poem. "Every time I bumbled through a stanza, I ruminated on each word a little more," she says. "I played with tone and emphasis …. It's time for us to show we care about words again, to rebuild our connection to a human civilization so much broader than our Twitter feeds."

"Memorize That Poem!" by Molly Worthen in the *New York Times*, August 27, 2017, summarized in Marshall Memo 704.

Professional Learning Suggestions for Chapter Six: What Makes Learning Stick

Maximizing Learning

The articles in this section show how findings in cognitive science, neuroscience, and related fields can help teachers maximize learning in their classrooms. The activities below are meant to be conducted for teachers: to help them *learn* about these new findings, *experience* the benefits of these learning techniques firsthand, and *plan* lessons for students based on these ideas.

I. Understand the Science:
What Can Science Teach Us About Maximizing Learning?

The activities below are for teachers to learn about the science of learning from reading several article-summaries, and apply what they've learned to their teaching.

A. Discuss the problem of students forgetting what we teach.
Before teachers read anything, project the following quotation from "How Remembering Improves Remembering" (article-summary 4) and have teachers, in pairs, discuss what they believe it means and what implications it has for teaching and learning:

> "When we think about learning, we typically focus on getting information *into* students' heads."

In a large group, ask teachers, "By a show of hands, how many of you have had the experience of teaching something or assigning a reading, and the students have no idea what they learned after days, weeks, or months have passed?" Discuss this problem along with the quotation as a large group focusing on what teachers think might lie at the root of this problem.

B. Model the power of brain science to boost learning and remembering.
Tell teachers that you are going to give them a pretest with terms you will be discussing today as a way to model the power of the pretest to boost learning. Be sure to let them know that *no one* will see how they did on this test and that, in fact, you assume most educators don't know these terms.

PROFESSIONAL LEARNING SUGGESTIONS FOR CHAPTER SIX

Tell them they will have this very same test at the end of today's session. Now have them take out paper or use their computers to define then following terms:

> *episodic memory, semantic memory, retrieval, fluency illusion, working memory, building and rebuilding neural networks,* and *pretest effect.*

C. Jigsaw readings on brain science and brainstorm implications for teaching.

Have teachers explore some of what science says about memory and learning and think about implications for their teaching.

1. Have teachers choose to read any two of the first five articles-summaries:

    "The Neuroscience of Learning" (article-summary 1)

    "Not Overloading Working Memory" (article-summary 2)

    "Understanding Two Very Different Kinds of Memory" (article-summary 3)

    "How Remembering Improves Remembering" (article-summary 4)

    "Using Pretests to Improvement Achievement" (article-summary 5)

2. In pairs, ask teachers to jot down some insights about learning from cognitive science, neuroscience, and related fields that they've gleaned from the two article-summaries they read using the chart that follows. Tell them to be sure to define any of the terms from the pretest that they came across in the chart as well.

Term	What Does This Term Mean and What Does the *Science* Say?	Any *Implications* for Teaching and Learning?
Building and rebuilding neural networks		
Working memory		
Episodic memory		
Semantic memory		
Retrieval		
Fluency of Illusion		
Pretest effect		

3. Now bring everyone back together and have a large-group discussion. Have teachers share what they learned about the science of learning and what implications this learning might have for teaching and learning. Everyone should have their own copy of the chart above so they can take notes on all of the terms.

EFFECTIVE PEDAGOGY

C. Now that teachers have thought about the science of learning, ask them to discuss the role students must play in their own learning.

As a final activity in this section, ask teachers to discuss the following quotation from "The Neuroscience of Learning" (Alden Blodget article-summary 1), and think about the implications for teaching.

> "Teachers can talk and talk, but only learners can learn …. It isn't that Sally won't listen or isn't intelligent or won't try harder to memorize what she has been told; it's that she hasn't engaged in the hard work of constructing and reconstructing neural pathways to understanding."
> —Alden Blodget

II. Experience Science of Learning Techniques Firsthand

One of the best ways to understand the power of these newer findings is for teachers to experience them firsthand. Below are suggestions for how teachers can experience the power of retrieval and self-testing.

A. Have teachers engage in the second half of the pretesting exercise from earlier.

Exactly as you did before, ask teachers to take out paper or use their computers to define the following terms:

> *episodic memory, semantic memory, retrieval, fluency illusion, working memory, building and rebuilding neural networks,* and *pretest effect.*

Now have a large-group discussion: *How did you do on the second test? Do you think you did as well as you would have if you* hadn't *had the pretest? How did the pretest affect the way you read the articles and listened to the discussion, knowing that you were going to have the exact same test later? How might you use pretests in your own classroom?*

B. Have teachers engage in a self-testing exercise.

Do a little experiment with your teachers. Have teachers experience self-testing firsthand by trying the following technique with a reading.

1. Distribute the following article about puffins from the *New York Times* to the teachers:

    https://www.nytimes.com/interactive/2018/08/29/climate/puffins-dwindling-iceland.html

PROFESSIONAL LEARNING SUGGESTIONS FOR CHAPTER SIX

However, give them only the first half (thirteen paragraphs). Have them read it through once and put it away. Now, on their own, have them write down everything they remember from the article.

2. Next, give teachers the second half of the article (the following thirteen paragraphs), but tell them to stop every two paragraphs to self-test. ("What did I just learn in these two paragraphs?") At the end, have them put away the article and write down everything they learned from the second half of the article.

3. As a large group, discuss how their learning differed when reading the first and the second parts of the article.

Note that you can certainly do this exercise with a more relevant article about teaching and learning, but people might have more prior knowledge about the topic.

III. Study Skills and Memorization

The activities in this section help teachers learn more effective study skills for students, consider their own role in teaching study skills, and finally debate the importance of memorization for student learning.

A. Have teachers consider the importance of teaching study skills to their students.
Teachers have varying opinions about whether it is their job to teach study skills—and if it *is* their job, which skills to teach. Exposing them to the article-summaries that follow will introduce them to more effective study skill methods.

1. To learn more about the types of study skills that help students learn, ask teachers to read two of the following five article-summaries:

"How Remembering Improves Remembering" (article-summary 4)

"Using Pretests to Improve Achievement" (article-summary 5)

"The Difference Between Taking Notes by Hand and on a Laptop" (article-summary 7)

"Research-Based Approaches to Studying" (article-summary 8)

"How Can We Help Students Remember More?" (article-summary 9)

2. Next, ask them to discuss the following in pairs: *Do you believe it is the role of the teacher to actively teach study skills? Which, if any, study skills do you already teach students? From the articles*

you've read, do any new study skills now seem important to teach, and how might you integrate them into your instruction?

B. Have teachers debate the question: Should we teach students to memorize?

There are also conflicting ideas about the role of memorization in students' lives given that they are growing up in a time when they can Google anything. Start by asking if the teachers have any idea of the answer to this question—Do the Common Core State Standards ever mention the word "memorize"? After taking some answers, let them know that one of the articles says that the word "memorize" never actually appears in the Standards.

1. First have teachers read the three article-summaries about memorization: "Why Not Just Google It?" (article-summary 10), "Should Students Memorize Times Tables?" (article-summary 11), and "Should Students Memorize Poetry?" (article-summary 12).

2. Next, ask teachers to literally take a stand to share their beliefs about requiring students to memorize. Have one wall represent, "I completely disagree with having students memorize anything," and the other wall, "I absolutely believe students should be asked to memorize some material." Now have teachers stand anywhere along the continuum. Once everyone is standing, ask a few people to share their opinions.

C. Engage in an exercise to consolidate and solidify learning.

Just like Kathy Ganske did in "What Did You Learn in School Today?" (article-summary 6), have the teachers experience what it is like to solidify their learning from today's session with a closing activity. Distribute index cards to everyone and have them write down what they believe are the most important takeaways from today's discussions and activities about making learning stick. The size of the index cards limits how much they write and keeps this activity brief.

Let teachers know that this type of brief closure activity is useful in the classroom to solidify learning (and they can use it in other professional learning sessions as well).

Chapter Seven:
Proficiency in Reading, Writing, and Oral Language

Too often, when children struggle to read, educators assume the problem lies within the children themselves. But in fact, decades of research have shown that whatever children's innate skills, strengths, and abilities may be, what really matters are the beliefs, attitudes, and actions of the teachers and other adults in their lives.
—Deborah Wolter

Teachers' and school leaders' biggest concern in literacy instruction is the widening achievement gap between children who enter schools with basic reading skills, robust vocabularies, and general knowledge—and those who don't have these advantages. The articles in this chapter address this challenge on four fronts: the best ways to organize literacy programs; maximizing students' reading success; teaching and assessing writing; and helping all students build strong vocabularies.

Implementing Effective Literary Instruction – Irene Fountas and Gay Su Pinnell say four keys to effective literacy programs are: shared vision and values, collective responsibility, teacher expertise, and a culture of continuous professional learning. Richard Allington and Rachael Gabriel say literacy classrooms should have student choice, lots of "just right" reading, students reading for understanding and connecting with personal meaning, talking to peers about reading, and hearing adults reading fluently. Mike Schmoker urges school leaders to conduct a careful audit of their reading programs to make sure students are getting systematic phonics, extensive reading, lots of discussion and writing, and text level acceleration.

Maximizing Reading Success – Maryanne Wolf describes what we have learned about the "reading brain" that allows for early diagnosis of reading problems. Kayla Lewis tells what she learned from Reading Recovery training: observe well, focus on students' strengths, work in the zone of proximal development, talk less, don't "rescue" students, take responsibility, recognize each student's unique profile, work with colleagues, and keep learning. Jan Burkins and Kim Yaris say good literacy programs expose students to a range of reading levels through read-alouds, shared reading, guided reading, and independent reading. Deborah Wolter says struggling readers improve if they have choice among plenty of texts, time to read in comfortable spaces, lots of adult support, and instruction on strategies for dealing with difficulties and reading critically and analytically.

Teaching and Assessing Writing – William Zinsser suggests these principles for effective writing in English: be clear, be simple, be brief, be human, and be logical. Robert Slavin and five colleagues share research on effective writing instruction. Lucy Calkins and Mary Ehrenworth say students will learn to write well if there's a well-articulated grade-to-grade curriculum, exemplars of good writing, teacher collaboration, structured lessons, frequent practice, choice, and prompt feedback. Ruth Culham believes the six-trait writing rubric is a valuable tool for assessing and improving different facets of students' writing during writers' workshop. Vicki Spandel says students should: be familiar with the six-trait rubric, see exemplars of proficient writing, learn how to use the rubric to assess their own writing, and get rich feedback on the rubric traits and also on how their writing touches us.

Building Strong Vocabularies – Robert Pondiscio argues that developing a rich and varied vocabulary is essential to less-fortunate students closing the achievement gap, and that vocabulary is tightly linked to knowledge in literature, history, science, and the arts. Susan Neuman and Tanya Wright believe the vocabulary gap can be closed if less-advantaged students get consistent, explicit, high-quality vocabulary instruction starting in preschool; exposure to a rich knowledge base; and lots of reading. Isabel Beck and Margaret McKeown say the vocabulary gap will close with systematic, skillful, primary-grade teaching of high-value "second tier" words as classes read well-chosen stories.

Questions to Consider

- What do proficient readers and writers do that struggling students haven't mastered?
- What should we see and hear in an effective literacy class?
- What will it take to close the literacy achievement gap?

Implementing Effective Literacy Instruction

① Four Key Elements in Effective Literacy Instruction

"Many good ideas flounder and fail because of haphazard implementation, conflicts, unintended consequences, an inability to sustain effort, and a simple lack of communication," say Irene Fountas (Lesley University) and Gay Su Pinnell (The Ohio State University) in this article in *The Reading Teacher*. "It can be easy to get discouraged." The key to an effective literacy program for all students, they say, is four key elements:

• *Element 1: Shared vision and values* – To stay focused through changes in literacy mandates, leaders, and programs, here's what research and common sense tell us has worked—and will work going forward:

- High expectations for all students, valuing linguistic, ethnic, and cultural diversity;
- Teacher teams taking collective responsibility for the success of each student;
- Using evidence gained from systematic observation and ongoing assessment;
- Effective practices appropriate to whole-class, small-group, and individual contexts;
- Students engaged in authentic inquiry about topics that fuel their intellectual curiosity;
- Students as powerful agents in their own learning, frequently making choices;
- Students thinking, talking, reading, and writing about their world;
- Lots of texts providing rich, diverse examples of genre, theme, topic, setting, and other literary qualities;
- Students reading and processing more than two thousand texts by middle school;
- Students gaining an understanding of their physical, social, and emotional world and their roles as informed global citizens.

These values should guide every literacy decision the school makes and translate to a clear consensus on what a visitor should see and hear in every literacy classroom.

"Educators need to grapple with beliefs, values and a forward-thinking vision," say Fountas and Pinnell, "until they fully understand and believe in them and agree that they can commit to act in unison when they walk out of the meeting room and into their classrooms." The vision and values should be written up and revisited regularly, ensuring that everyone is on the same page, "moving beyond an approach where each teacher applies his or her own methods or philosophy."

This is not about cookie-cutter teachers and classrooms but a deep consensus about what good teaching looks like. "The critical value of an articulated vision for literacy," they say, "is that students are guaranteed access to a coherent educational experience regardless of the teacher, the grade level, or the latest educational mandate."

- *Element 2: Common goals and language and collective responsibility* – Once a shared vision is in place, say Fountas and Pinnell, "the language naturally shifts from *my* students and *my* classroom to *our* students, *our* classrooms, *our* curriculum, *our* school, *our* data, *our* goals, *our* professional learning opportunities, and *our* expectations for students and one another." The school becomes more coherent for students: "they get the same messages about the role of literacy in their lives year after year from all members of the school community." There's also a collective effort to understand the increasingly diverse students in our classrooms and build cultural proficiency in all staff. For educators, common aims and collective work reduce stress. "You have a shared pool of expertise and support upon which you can draw and to which you contribute," say Fountas and Pinnell. "The burden is lighter, the anxiety lower, and your own ability to improve student outcomes is enhanced."
- *Element 3: A high level of teacher expertise* – To prepare students for the literacy demands of the twenty-first century, teachers need to bring their *A game* and help each other develop in four critical areas:
    - A repertoire of techniques for observation and assessments – "The most effective teaching is scientific," say Fountas and Pinnell: "You analyze and respond minute by minute to the precise reading or writing behaviors you observe."
    - A clear vision of proficiency in reading, writing, and talking – For reading, this includes thinking *within* the text (searching for and using information, monitoring and self-correcting, solving words, maintaining fluency, adjusting, and summarizing); thinking *beyond* the text (predicting, making connections, synthesizing, and inferring); and thinking *about* the text (analyzing and critiquing).
    - A deep knowledge of texts, their characteristics, and their demands – Fountas and Pinnell recommend a using a wide variety of texts (not one core text), implemented in interactive read-alouds, shared reading, guided reading, book clubs, and independent reading. Leveled texts are used only in guided reading.
    - Expertise in implementing a range of research-based instructional practices – "The result," say Fountas and Pinnell, "is a coordinated series of instructional contexts that take into

account a student's current abilities but are designed to stretch the student in new ways every day."

This level of teacher expertise and teamwork should produce "thoughtful, literate, and socially responsible young people moving into our society."

• *Element 4: A culture of continuous professional learning* – "Effective teaching is complex and demanding," say Fountas and Pinnell. "It requires far more expertise, information, resources, and problem solving than any one of us could have alone." That's why reflection, collaboration, conversation, communication, open classroom doors, regular team meetings, and mutual support are so essential—fueling energy, teacher agency, and individual acts of leadership. Support and communication are especially important for new teachers.

"It is not as hard as it sounds," conclude Fountas and Pinnell. "Your school may already be engaging in many of these practices, so much is already in place …. The key is implementation of good ideas—trying them on with care, studying them over time, and getting better and better."

"Every Child, Every Classroom, Every Day: From Vision to Action in Literacy Learning" by Irene Fountas and Gay Su Pinnell in *The Reading Teacher*, July/August 2018 (Vol. 72, #1, pp. 7–19), summarized in Marshall Memo 744.

2. The Literacy Experiences Children Should Have Every Day

In this *Educational Leadership* article, Richard Allington (University of Tennessee–Knoxville) and Rachael Gabriel (University of Connecticut–Storrs) present six high-quality experiences they believe all children should have every day if they are to become successful, engaged readers. These experiences are especially important for struggling readers—but tragically, those are the children who are least likely to have them.

• *Every child reads something he or she chooses*. "The research base on student-selected reading is robust and conclusive," say Allington and Gabriel. "Students read more, understand more, and are more likely to continue reading when they have the opportunity to choose what they read."

• *Every child reads accurately*. This means reading material at the "just right" level of difficulty. Spending more time reading doesn't help unless students are reading at 98 percent or higher accuracy. "When students read accurately, they solidify their word-recognition, decoding, and word-analysis skills," say Allington and Gabriel. "Perhaps more important, they are likely to understand what they read—and, as a result, to enjoy reading."

• *Every child reads something he or she understands.* Comprehension is the goal of reading instruction, say the authors. "But too often, struggling readers get interventions that focus on basic skills in isolation, rather than on reading connected text for meaning. This common misuse of intervention time often arises from a grave misinterpretation of what we know about reading difficulties." Struggling readers aren't "wired differently," as some brain research implies. Their brains benefit from high-quality reading instruction with engaging and comprehensible content. The bottom line: more authentic reading develops better readers.

• *Every child writes about something with personal meaning.* "The opportunity to compose continuous text about something meaningful is not just something nice to have when there's free time after a test or at the end of the school year," say Allington and Gabriel. "Writing provides a different modality within which to practice the skills and strategies of reading for an authentic purpose."

• *Every child talks with peers about reading and writing.* Research shows that conversations with classmates improve comprehension and engagement with texts—students analyze, comment, and compare—thinking about what they read. "Time for students to talk about their reading and writing is perhaps one of the most underused, yet easy-to-implement, elements of instruction," say the authors.

• *Every child listens to a fluent adult read aloud.* Listening to a competent adult modeling good reading helps students with vocabulary, background knowledge, sense of the story, awareness of genre and text structure, and comprehension—and yet few teachers above first grade regularly read aloud to their students.

"Most of the classroom instruction we have observed lacks these six research-based elements," conclude Allington and Gabriel. Here are their suggestions:

- Eliminate virtually all worksheets and workbooks and use the money to expand classroom libraries.
- Ban test-prep activities and materials from the school day. There's no evidence that they improve reading or test scores.

"Every Child, Every Day" by Richard Allington and Rachael Gabriel in *Educational Leadership*, March 2012 (Vol. 69, #6, pp. 10–15), summarized in Marshall Memo 428.

---

3. What's Missing in Many Literacy Programs

In this article in *Education Week*, author/consultant Mike Schmoker says that popular, well-regarded commercial literacy programs "often lack a robust evidence base. That's because they are deficient in precisely those aspects most critical to acquiring the ability to read, write, and speak well. Instead, they abound in busywork—worksheets, group activities, and multiple-choice exercises." He urges district leaders and principals to conduct an audit of their literacy programs to see if they have the essential ingredients:

• *Reading* – An intensive phonics component is key, but it must be accompanied by "abundant amounts of reading, speaking, and writing in all disciplines," says Schmoker. "Even before students fully master phonics-based decoding, they should be reading—and listening to—large amounts of fiction and nonfiction." Literacy experts like Timothy Shanahan and Richard Allington are emphatic that students should be reading at least an hour a day, across subject areas. "Without this," says Schmoker, "many students never acquire the knowledge and vocabulary essential to fluency and reading comprehension."

• *Discussion* – Starting in the early grades, there should be frequent, all-class talk about texts, including debates and seminars accompanied by explicit instruction on speaking clearly, audibly, and with civility. "When I do demonstration lessons for teachers," says Schmoker, "it is often apparent that students aren't being taught these vital communication skills." He worries that too much time is spent in unproductive small-group conversations and pseudo-work, including excessive "cut, color, and paste activities" in the elementary grades.

• *Writing* – Almost daily, he says, students need to be writing about what they read—using skills like analysis, comparison, explaining, making arguments, and justifying interpretations. "This daily written work," says Schmoker, "which need not always be collected and scored—should be the basis for longer, more formal papers," and those need to be scheduled at regular intervals.

• *Text level acceleration* – Students should be reading increasing amounts of grade-level texts across subject areas, scaffolded by explicit instruction in vocabulary, background knowledge, annotating, and note-taking—with frequent checks for understanding and on-the-spot adjustment of teaching to reach all students.

"The Problem with Literacy Programs" by Mike Schmoker in *Education Week*, February 20, 2019), summarized in Marshall Memo 776.

Maximizing Reading Success

4   What We Need to Know About the Reading Brain

In this article in *Phi Delta Kappan*, Maryanne Wolf (University of California–Los Angeles) says it's a mistake to believe that learning to read "is natural to human beings and that it will simply emerge 'whole cloth' like language when the child is ready." In fact, reading is an "unnatural cultural invention," barely six thousand years old; on the clock of human evolution, that's a second before midnight. That's why, for virtually all people, systematic instruction is necessary to becoming a proficient reader. And for a variety of reasons, reading is more difficult for some people than it is for others.

Recent findings, combined with previous insights, allow schools to immediately assess which of six developmental profiles describes an entering kindergarten student—and exactly what each child needs to become a proficient reader:

- Children in two of the profiles have average or above-average skills and will need only good instruction to excel.
- Other children have difficulty with letters and sounds, probably because they've had little exposure to the alphabet or the English language; they'll respond quickly if instruction targets these deficits. (Some children in this group may have visual-based difficulties and need further testing.)
- Three of the profiles include children who will be diagnosed with some form of reading disability or dyslexia.

"There are few discoveries more important to those of us who study dyslexia," says Wolf, "than to be able to predict it before the child has had to endure ignominious, daily public failures before peers, parents, and teachers …. By assessing struggling young readers early on, we can prevent some of the emotional detritus that often characterizes their reading experiences …. Nothing in reading acquisition is more important than beginning systematic, targeted intervention as early as possible."

"Some children, particularly boys, show no obvious areas of weakness in their profile but are simply not yet ready to learn to read," Wolf continues. "Understanding this group requires more in-depth evaluation (to ensure that there are no underlying weaknesses) and also more-reasonable expectations for our children than is sometimes the case …. Some children are pushed to read too hard too soon, before they are developmentally ready …. The bottom line is that fears about third-grade state test results should never dictate decisions about when whole kindergarten classes receive instruction for reading." Many children in Europe are taught to read in their equivalent of first grade, and the evidence is that they learn with fewer problems than children who start a year earlier.

Wolf laments that the phonics/whole language reading war ("the debate that never should have been") is still raging in some quarters. It's not either/or, she says; children need systematic instruction on the basics of reading *and* early, deep immersion in stories, authentic literature, word meanings, and creativity. Recently developed assessments allow teachers to see which rungs on the developmental reading ladder a child between ages five and ten might be missing:

- Phonemes and their connections to letters;
- The meanings and functions of words and morphemes in sentences;
- An immersion in stories that require sophisticated deep-reading processes;
- Learning the meanings and grammatical uses of words in increasingly complex sentences;
- Learning about new letter patterns that reappear and help readers figure out word meanings;
- Making basic functions so practiced and automatic that children can focus their attention on increasingly more sophisticated comprehension;
- Expanding background knowledge;
- Regularly eliciting children's own thoughts and imagination in speaking and writing.

"All the rungs are important," says Wolf, "if we are to prepare children to become fluent readers who use both their imagination and their analytical capacities …. Fluent reading involves knowing not only how words work but also how they make us feel. Empathy and perspective taking are part of the complex fabric of feelings and thoughts, whose convergence propels greater understanding …. Deep reading is always about connection: connecting what we know to what we read, what we read to what we feel, what we feel to what we think, and how we think to how we live out our lives in a connected world."

"The Science and Poetry in Learning (and Teaching) to Read" by Maryanne Wolf in *Phi Delta Kappan*, December 2018/January 2019 (Vol. 100, #4, pp. 13-17).

EFFECTIVE PEDAGOGY

5. Reading Recovery's Lessons for Regular Classrooms

In this article in *The Reading Teacher*, Kayla Lewis (Missouri State University) says she was not thrilled when her district made her to go through Reading Recovery training as she took on the role of literacy coach. She had ten years of classroom experience, a master's degree in reading, and had taught literacy at the university level. What could Reading Recovery add? Lewis was familiar with Marie Clay's pioneering work in New Zealand, Reading Recovery's track record with struggling readers, and its spreading implementation in the US beginning in the 1980s. But the training just didn't seem relevant to the coaching she would do with K–5 teachers.

"I am not ashamed to admit that I was wrong," says Lewis. "Reading Recovery training and the teachings of Clay had a profound effect on my teaching and forever changed the way I view students who struggle." Lewis believes that Reading Recovery, while it focuses on individual instruction for at-risk first graders, contains a number of instructional insights that can be helpful to all elementary teachers:

• *Observing well* – "It is essential for us to put aside our own agendas and really notice what students are able to do," says Lewis. One of the most helpful tools is video—teachers watching themselves after a lesson and thinking through all the teaching moves they made and their students' responses.

• *Focusing on what students* can *do* – "Struggling students would come to me needing assistance, and all I saw were the holes and the tangles," says Lewis. She learned how to zero in on the competencies and knowledge students brought to the table ("roaming around in the known" is a Reading Recovery routine in early lessons). When students are overwhelmed by all the standards they have to master, frustrated, and feeling like failures—finding areas of competence is the key to building confidence and ultimately skillful reading and writing.

• *Working in the zone of proximal development* – Vygotsky famously defined the optimal learning zone as what students can do with assistance—what they can *almost* do. It's impractical for teachers to apply this principle to a whole class, says Lewis, but in small groups, teachers can use assessments and observation to tune in on each child's Goldilocks level of difficulty and scaffold their progress with just the right amount of support, not wasting time on things they can already do and not frustrating them with tasks that are too difficult. Children's zones move up as they become more proficient, which prompts the teacher to make constant adjustments.

• *Knowing the difference between scaffolding and rescuing* – During her Reading Recovery training,

Lewis asked for her coach's help with a particularly challenging student. The coach watched a lesson video and said, "You're hovering." A little defensive, Lewis replied that she was *helping* the student. "No," said the coach. "You are making him dependent on you. Every time he struggles, you jump in and help him." Again, Lewis pushed back, saying she was doing her job, teaching the student. The coach corrected her: what she was doing was *rescuing* the boy, teaching him to wait for her support every time he got stuck, instead of having him struggle a little and learn something new. Lewis says this was a pivotal moment in her development as a teacher. Going forward, she always kept Clay's principle in mind: "The teacher never does anything for the child that he could do himself." Lewis suggests three questions for classroom teachers: *Do your prompts promote independence or dependence? Are you scaffolding or rescuing?* and *Who's doing the work here?*

• *Taking responsibility when a student isn't progressing* – "As a classroom teacher, I used to say, 'All students can learn,' but I am not sure that I truly believed it," says Lewis. "I cannot tell you how many students I unnecessarily referred to our special education testing team. Most of the students I referred did not qualify. Why? Because they did not need special education; they needed me to do a better job of teaching them." Most struggling readers have a *difference*, she says, not a disability. Another Clay mantra: "If the child is a struggling reader or writer, the conclusion must be that we have not yet discovered the way to help him learn." Through observations and assessment, the teacher needs to figure out what's going on, reflect on which teaching moves aren't working, and make the appropriate adjustment.

• *Less teacher talk* – "As a teacher, I talk a lot," says Lewis. "We all talk a lot. It is part of our job." But during Reading Recovery training, she realized that what she was saying was often getting in students' way. "Once I realized the power of my words," she says, "I did less talking and made the talking that I did do more precise. I learned to listen and observe, and in those quiet moments, I was able to see what my students could do without my support and constant interrupting. I will not say it was easy. I often had a hard time biting my tongue, but as I became quieter and more deliberate in what I chose to say, my students became more untangled."

• *Seeing that no two readers are the same* – Lewis has learned that one-size-fits-all book introductions and all-purpose lesson plans don't connect with many students. She suggests that classroom teachers systematically cycle through their students—observing two or three a day, taking running records, and learning the type of prompting and support each one needs. "Over time," she says, "you will have gathered information on each student in your class, and another cycle of observation can begin. The time and effort will pay off when your students have one of those lightbulb moments that we teachers live for."

• *The importance of teacher teamwork* – After she completed Reading Recovery training, Lewis served as a literacy coach in her school, working closely with a colleague who taught Reading Recovery to build bridges among Reading Recovery, regular education, Title I, and special education teachers. This meant that students heard "the same language, the same prompting, and the same type of instruction in all places," says Lewis. "Hearing one voice allowed many of our students to make more accelerated progress than any one of us could have achieved alone."

• *Being a lifelong learner* – "I have learned that there are so many people who know so much more about reading than I ever will," concludes Lewis, "and in that, I have learned to listen." She urges all teachers to take this stance. "Soak in the knowledge of those around you. Read often. Keep up with the latest research. Reflect on your own teaching practices. Ensure that your knowledge never remains stagnant and that you continue to grow in your learning."

"Lessons Learned: Applying Principles of Reading Recovery in the Classroom" by Kayla Lewis in *The Reading Teacher*, May/June 2018 (Vol. 71, #6, pp. 727–734), summarized in Marshall Memo 735.

---

6 A Balanced Approach to Challenge

In this *Reading Today* article, literacy consultants Jan Burkins and Kim Yaris describe a common scenario: a student reading below level has guided reading every day, using books at her instructional level. Because she's so far behind, she gets a "double dose" of reading—she's pulled out for a second guided reading lesson, missing a lesson with a more-difficult text in her classroom. "Due to the lack of exposure to texts that stretch her," say Burkins and Yaris, "her reading progress plateaus, which earns her even more time with instructional-level texts and targeted practice in word work."

Exposing students to challenging texts can be taken too far, say Burkins and Yaris. They describe a boy entering a New York State fifth grade as an avid, above-level reader who was asked to read the Universal Declaration of Human Rights, a dense text at the post-graduate level. No amount of scaffolding could make it comprehensible to this student and his classmates, and the eight weeks they spent on this unit sapped their enthusiasm and proficiency.

PROFICIENCY IN READING, WRITING, AND ORAL LANGUAGE

The answer, say Burkins and Yaris, is teachers using good judgment to orchestrate a mix of reading experiences based on an accurate diagnosis of each student. "Students need consistent interactions with texts of varying levels to develop reading proficiency," they say. Here's how they see four kinds of reading instruction contributing to all students' growth:

- *Read-aloud* – The teacher reads to students.
    - Text level – Substantially above grade level.
    - Accessibility – Probably frustration level for most students.
    - Who does the work – The teacher does all the print work; the teacher and students work together to make meaning.
- *Shared reading* – Teacher and students read a text together.
    - Text level – On or a little above grade level.
    - Accessibility – Probably frustration level for many students.
    - Who does the work - The teacher and students do the print and meaning work together.
- *Guided reading* – Students read from a common text with support from the teacher.
    - Text level – On readers' individual level.
    - Accessibility – Instructional level for each student.
    - Who does the work – The student does most of the print and meaning work.
- *Independent reading* – Students read from different texts on their own.
    - Text level – From below grade level through above grade level.
    - Accessibility – Multiple texts for each reader, varying from independent to frustration level depending on the amount of productive effort and students' stamina.
    - Who does the work – The student does all the print and meaning, but intentionally varies the text selections to increase the amount of effort required to solve problems.

"Break Through the Frustration: Balance vs. All-or-Nothing Thinking" by Jan Burkins and Kim Yaris in *Reading Today*, September/October 2014 (Vol. 32, #2, pp. 26–27), summarized in Marshall Memo 553.

7. "Restorative" Literacy Practices That Close the Achievement Gap

"Too often, when children struggle to read, educators assume the problem lies within the children themselves," says Michigan literacy consultant Deborah Wolter in this article in *Phi*

Delta Kappan. "But in fact, decades of research have shown that whatever children's innate skills, strengths, and abilities may be, what really matters are the beliefs, attitudes, and actions of the teachers and other adults in their lives." Wolter believes schools need to ask three key questions:

- *What is it that proficient and fluent readers do when they encounter texts?*
- *How different is that from what our most vulnerable students are asked to do?*
- *What would it take for educators to close the gap?*

In other words, says Wolter, "Rather than holding lower expectations for children who are struggling to read, and rather than giving them lesser experiences with text and language, shouldn't we seek to provide them with the very same kinds of resources, supports, and encouragement that the most fortunate children receive? Shouldn't all students have opportunities to make connections between what they read and what's going on in their own lives? Shouldn't all students be encouraged to take ownership over their reading growth and development?"

Here are Wolter's suggestions for replicating the advantages that good readers have versus pigeonholing struggling readers with low-level materials, highly structured reading formats, and expectations that limit their potential for growth:

• *Access to plenty of books and other reading matter* – Schools can set up Little Free Libraries; maintain a book swap table in the lobby; seek donations of quality multicultural books to share; invite the local librarian in to help families get library cards; and host regular storytelling events, book clubs, and free book fairs in their neighborhoods or apartment complexes. It's helpful if shared books have a sticker explaining their shared status.

• *An army of adult support* – Schools can enlist community volunteers and staff members to read books aloud to students, either individually or in small groups. "Reading aloud increases vocabulary, imagination, understanding of third-party narration, critical thinking skills, and comprehension," says Wolter. "Abundant opportunities for reading aloud set all children on a path toward a lifetime of reading."

• *Choice* – Struggling students need to have a wide selection of reading matter—not just at their presumed readability level—all geared to empowering them to choose texts and expand their background knowledge, interests, motivation, and reading proficiency.

• *Scoping-out skills* – Teachers need to give struggling students tricks they can use to size up a book: checking out the front cover, reading the back cover, skimming a few pages, and reading the introduction.

PROFICIENCY IN READING, WRITING, AND ORAL LANGUAGE

- *Settling in to read* – All students need to be able to read in cozy corners with bean bag chairs, soft moveable furniture, an area rug, and soft lighting.
- *Reading deeply and thoughtfully* – All students need plenty of independent silent reading time and encouragement to read for meaning and for fun, not always having their errors corrected if the errors aren't interfering with meaning. Students should be able to read ahead and go back to check on their miscues and have time to read books that seem easy, or even ones they've already memorized.
- *Effective strategies to get unstuck* – When students come across unknown words and phrases, it's important that they have a repertoire of cognitive and linguistic tricks, including: covering the tricky word with their finger, reading ahead, going back to look for context clues, thinking about another word that makes sense, asking a peer or an adult, or looking up the word in a dictionary. Students should be taught to use phonetic strategies within a text, not just in isolated worksheets or computer programs.
- *Owning their language* – Teachers need to recognize and respect differences in students' accents, pronunciation, and syntax and not talk negatively about students' diction, implying that the way they speak is inferior. "Teachers can let go of the phonemes or syntax that are different," ways Wolter, "and instead, foster and listen for meaning and understanding."
- *Using tools to zero in on the information in a text* – Struggling readers need to do more than answer simple multiple-choice questions. They should be comfortable using highlighters, colored pencils, sticky notes, index cards, graphic organizers, and notebooks to unpack the meaning of complex passages.
- *Honing critical thinking and analytical skills* – Rather than thinking about what the teacher wants to hear, students should be encouraged to discuss content with peers; develop their critical thinking, analytical, and problem-solving skills; and think about how what they're reading is relevant to their lives. Student need to feel free to express their views, even if those views are controversial. "At the same time," says Wolter, "teachers can assure emotional safety by not allowing bullying, claims without evidence, or racist language."

"Moving Readers from Struggling to Proficient" by Deborah Wolter in *Phi Delta Kappan*, September 2017 (Vol. 99, #1, pp. 37–39), summarized in Marshall Memo 703.

Teaching and Assessing Writing

8 Five Principles of Good Writing

This article in *The American Scholar* is from a talk that author William Zinsser gave to incoming international students at the Columbia Graduate School of Journalism on how to write effectively in English. Our language, says Zinsser, is not "as musical as Spanish, or Italian, or French, or as ornamental as Arabic, or as vibrant as some of your native languages. But I'm hopelessly in love with English because it's plain and it's strong. It has a huge vocabulary of words that have precise shades of meaning; there's no subject, however technical or complex, that can't be made clear to any reader in good English—if it's used right."

English comes from two sources, he continues: Latin, "the florid language of ancient Rome," and Anglo-Saxon, from the plain languages of England and northern Europe. "The words derived from Latin are the enemy," says Zinsser. "They will strangle and suffocate everything you write. The Anglo-Saxon words will set you free." Latin words tend to be long, pompous nouns like *implementation, maximization, communication, development, fulfillment*, he says—words that are frequently used by people in authority in American government, business, education, social work, and health care. "They think those long Latin words make them sound important," says Zinsser, and cites a letter he received from a private New York club:

> Dear Member:
> The board of governors has spent the past year considering proactive efforts that will continue to professionalize the club and to introduce efficiencies that we will be implementing throughout 2009.

(Translation: They're going to try to make the club run better.)

In contrast to the Latin-derived nouns, says Zinsser, are straightforward Anglo-Saxon nouns: *house, home, child, chair, bread, milk, sea, sky, earth, field, grass, road*. "When you use those words, you make contact—consciously and also *sub*consciously—with the deepest emotions and memories of your readers."

Even better than these nouns, says Zinsser, are short, plain, *active* Anglo-Saxon verbs: "Active verbs give momentum to a sentence and push it forward. So fall in love with active verbs. They are your best friends."

He then shares his five principles for writing good English: clarity, simplicity, brevity, humanity, and logic:

• *Clarity* – "If it's not clear, you might as well not write it," he says. "You might as well stay in bed." And no more than one thought per sentence. "Readers only process one thought at a time. So give them time to digest the first set of facts you want them to know. Then give them the next piece of information they need to know, which further explains the first fact. Be grateful for the period. Writing is so hard that all of us, once launched, tend to ramble. Instead of a period we use a comma, followed by a transitional word (*and, while*), and soon we have strayed into a wilderness that seems to have no road back out. Let the humble period be your savior."

• *Simplicity* – "Simple is good," says Zinsser. "Writing is not something you have to embroider with fancy stitches to make yourself look smart." This isn't appreciated by many foreigners trying to impress people with their English. One Nigerian woman said that if she wrote simple sentences, people would think she was stupid. Stupid like Thoreau, was Zinsser's retort. Or like E. B. White. Or Abraham Lincoln. Or Barack Obama. "There's no sentence too short to be acceptable in the eyes of God," he says.

• *Brevity* – "Short sentences are better than long sentences," he continues. "Short words are better than long words. Don't say *currently* if you can say *now*. Don't say *assistance* if you can say *help*. Don't say *numerous* if you can say *many*. Don't say *facilitate* if you can say *ease*. Don't call someone an *individual* [five syllables!]; that's a person, or a man or a woman. Don't implement or prioritize. Don't say anything in writing that you wouldn't comfortably say in conversation. Writing is talking to someone else on paper or on a screen."

• *Humanity* – "Be yourself," advises Zinsser. "Never try in your writing to be someone you're not. Your product, finally, is you. Don't lose that person by putting on airs, trying to sound superior." To become a better writer, look for models of good writing. Find writers who are direct and authentic and read their prose (*the New Yorker* is an excellent place to start, he says). "Study their articles clinically," he urges. "Try to figure out how they put their words and sentences together. That's how I learned to write, not from a writing course."

Does this advice apply in the new age of digital media? Absolutely, says Zinsser: video scripts and audio scripts and websites and all the prose for the new media must be "lean and tight and coherent, plain nouns and verbs pushing your story forward so that the rest of us always know what's happening."

• *Logic* – "Sentence B must follow from Sentence A," says Zinsser, "and Sentence C must follow Sentence B, and eventually you get to Sentence Z. The hard part of writing isn't the writing; it's the thinking. You can solve most of your writing problems if you stop after every sentence and ask: What does the reader need to know next?"

"Writing English as a Second Language" by William Zinsser in *The American Scholar*, Winter 2010, summarized in Marshall Memo 395.

---

9. Keys to Effective Writing Instruction

"The ability to express ideas in writing is one of the most important of all skills," say Robert Slavin, Cynthia Lake, and Amanda Inns (John Hopkins University), Ariane Baye and Dylan Dachet (University of Liège, Belgium), and Jonathan Haslam (Institute for Effective Education, England) in this Education Endowment Foundation paper. "Good writing is a mark of an educated person and perhaps for that reason it is one of the most important skills sought by employers and higher education institutions." The researchers reviewed high-quality research on programs that teach writing from second through twelfth grade and synthesized the key characteristics:

- Use of cooperative learning;
- Structured approaches giving students step-by-step guides to writing in various genres, focused squarely on writing outcomes;
- Teaching students to assess their own and others' drafts, providing students more feedback and insight into effective writing strategies;
- Balancing writing with reading;
- Building students' motivation to write and enjoy self-expression;
- Teaching writing conventions (e.g., grammar, punctuation, usage) explicitly, but in the context of creative writing;
- Providing extensive professional development to teachers, in which they themselves experience the writing strategies they will employ.

"In many cases," the researchers conclude, "successful writing approaches will be exciting, social, and noisy, but they should always be intentionally structured to build students' skills, confidence, and motivation. Motivation is particularly important. If students love to write, because their peers as well as their teachers are eager to see what they have to say, then they will write with energy and pleasure. Perhaps more than any other subject, writing demands a supportive environment, in which students want to become better writers because they love the opportunity to express themselves, and to interact in writing with valued peers and teachers."

"Writing Approaches in Years 3 to 13: Evidence Review" by Robert Slavin, Cynthia Lake, Amanda Inns, Ariane Baye, Dylan Dachet, and Jonathan Haslam, Education Endowment Foundation, July 2019, summarized in Marshall Memo 798.

10 Teaching Writing Effectively

"The writing process is a learned skill," say Lucy Calkins and Mary Ehrenworth (Teachers College–Columbia University) in this article in *The Reading Teacher*. "It comes from many hours spent writing a lot. It comes from a mindset that whenever you write, you consider not only what you will write *about* but also how you will write *well*."

There's no question, say Calkins and Ehrenworth, that writing is an essential Twenty-first-century skill—and many schools are not teaching it effectively. Recent complaints from the business world are less about grammar, punctuation, and spelling, and more about "fuzzy thinking," young people not knowing how to bring "focus, energy, and passion" to the points they want to make and not being able to analyze information and write with "a real voice."

"The good news," say the authors, "is that across the nation, thousands of schools are finding that when students participate in a culture that values writing, are given explicit instruction in the skills and strategies of proficient writing, and work toward crystal-clear goals and receive feedback on their progress, their writing skills increase dramatically." They believe these are the key elements:

The enduring essentials of good writing instruction:
• Protected time to write – "Writing, like running or reading, is a skill that develops with use," say Calkins and Ehrenworth. "Writers need time to write. In too many schools, this time is compromised." They suggest that the ideal (daily) writers' workshop should have ten minutes of explicit whole-class instruction, at least half an hour of writing time (with the teacher conferencing with

students), ending with five to ten minutes for students to share what they've done with another writer and set goals.

• Choice – "To write well," say the authors, "writers need to write about topics they know a lot about and care about …. A writer's commitment to his or her subject leads that writer to bring the imprint of his or her own passions to the page, writing with that magical quality we call voice."

• Feedback – The best feedback includes "medals and missions," compliments and next steps. "Feedback is most potent when students don't yet have mastery," say Calkins and Ehrenworth, "and when it is given just in time to learners in the midst of work." The best feedback is frequent, close to the time the writer writes, and followed by opportunities for more practice.

What recent research says:

• Direct instruction – Clear, explicit instruction on specific points takes place in mini-lessons, conferences, and small-group work. "We have found," say Calkins and Ehrenworth, "that when curriculum is organized so all students in a class (or better yet, at a grade level) are working within a shared genre—employing strategies and emulating mentor texts of that genre, teachers have a context within which to explicitly teach the craft and structure of that particular genre."

• Working toward clear goals – "To accelerate achievement, learners need to answer the question, 'Where am I going?'" say the authors. And that means having a crystal-clear vision of what good writing looks like (mentor texts are important) and specific goals for getting there.

• Transfer – Calkins and Ehrenworth quote Grant Wiggins saying that students often don't realize that what they learn in one classroom can help them in another. Sometimes teachers don't realize that either.

The role of school leaders:

• Teachers need a shared vision of good writing. Ideally this is developed collaboratively (the principal as the key orchestrator) and has buy-in across a school. Student exemplars are important to showing and tracking good work over time. "One of the most potent ways for a school or a district to lift the quality of good writing," say Calkins and Ehrenworth, "is for teachers across a grade level to meet together to norm their expectations of student writing, learning to look at student writing with shared lenses."

• Teachers need a shared vision of good writing instruction. Teachers benefit enormously "from observing teaching together, talking afterward about what worked and what could have been better," say the authors. "Raising the level of writing in a school or district takes a collaborative mind-set."

• Teachers need to teach within a strategic cross-grade curriculum. "In too many schools, kids need to luck out to get a teacher who teaches writing," say Calkins and Ehrenworth. Teachers need to develop a grade-to-grade progression of skills, so instruction builds each year on a solid foundation. The Common Core standards provide a good template for this (although poetry needs to be added).

• Teachers need shared expectations and ways to track growth. It's essential, say the authors, to track student progress by looking at regular on-demand writing, where students write from start to finish without help from others. "When teachers study students' on-demand writing from the start of the year until the most recent assessment," they say, "what they see is the effect of their instruction over the year. This requires a mindset wherein teachers study student work not only as a reflection of students' progress but also as a reflection of the teachers' teaching…. Shared assessments, exemplars, and tools for self-assessment and goal setting can make an important contribution toward helping a school move from an individualistic culture to a collaborative culture—one in which teachers think not about 'my kids' but about 'our kids.'"

• Teachers need serious professional development. "Professional development will be the heartbeat of your school," conclude Calkins and Ehrenworth. "It should be intense, collaborative, collegial, and practical. It should be focused on strengthening teachers' methods and spirits. It should be varied in form, flexible, and responsive. Good professional development creates lasting communities of practice."

"Growing Extraordinary Writers: Leadership Decisions to Raise the Level of Writing Across a School and a District" by Lucy Calkins and Mary Ehrenworth in *The Reading Teacher*, July/ August 2016 (Vol. 70, #1, pp. 7–18), summarized in Marshall Memo 645.

---

11. Making Optimal Use of the Six-Trait Writing Rubrics

Writing consultant Ruth Culham is known as the "trait lady" because she's been giving workshops on the six-trait writing rubric for years. The traits are:
- Ideas
- Organization

- Voice
- Word choice
- Sentence fluency
- Conventions
- (Presentation is sometimes added in the six-plus-one model)

In this article in *Educational Leadership*, Culham draws on her work in schools to identify some common myths about this widely-used rubric:

• *Myth 1—The traits are a writing program.* Not so, she says. There are no scripted lessons, no scope and sequence, no packaged materials. "Use the traits to assess student writing to understand what students know and can do," she advises. "Then focus your writing lessons and activities so that students can improve their writing within the curriculum you're expected to teach …. The traits tell writers what they are doing well and what they still need to work on. And they give teachers an effective instructional road map …. The traits bring the writing curriculum to life. But they are *not* the curriculum.

"Use all the traits all the time," Culham advises. "Students need all the traits at every grade level every time they write …. We use the traits for assessment and as a shared vocabulary to describe what good writing looks like at every age …. Using the same terminology from year to year is crucial for building deep understanding. Just as math teachers continue to use the terms *addition* and *subtraction*—instead of inventing new ones at different grade levels, like *plusing* and *minusing*—so should teachers of writing consistently use the same terms."

• *Myth 2—The writing process and the traits are different things.* "Actually, they're two sides of the same coin," says Culham. "The writing traits are a fine assessment tool and a kind of language to communicate about writing. Writing workshop is a structure to encourage writers to write often and for a variety of purposes. And writing process is just that: a series of reflective stages that writers go through as they figure out what to say and how best to convey it in writing …. When these three powerful ideas coexist in writing classrooms, both students and teachers win." The first five traits—ideas, organization, voice, word choice, and sentence fluency—are what a writer bears in mind while drafting, refining, and revising a piece for clarity. For final polishing, conventions (and presentation) come into play.

• *Myth 3—You adopt the traits program.* The traits are a model, not a program, says Culham. "A model is highly flexible; teachers can use it in a variety of ways within a writing program." Ideally, writing programs promote the writing process and are built around "books, magazines, texts, and other rich models that help students aspire to write clearly and effectively." The traits are a helpful adjunct to demystify the revision and editing process. "Use the traits as the language of writers who are desperate to figure out how to be clearer, more powerful, and more interesting," she urges.

• *Myth 4—You teach the traits and the writing takes care of itself.* No, no, no! says Culham. "The traits are not a replacement for teaching …. Traits won't solve all your instructional woes …. They won't make students love to revise. They won't help you find time in your busy schedule to talk to students one-on-one about their writing. But they will give students the opportunity to write more, better, and more widely because they reveal much of the mystery of writing …. To be sure, there is a little magic in writing. But writing is mostly difficult work. Why don't we tell students so?"

• *Myth 5—The traits are not part of writing workshop.* In fact, says Culham, the traits are the *language* of writing workshop. "Managing and coordinating the writing workshop can be a challenge," she admits. "The traits are helpful here because they provide teachers with a built-in model for ensuring that students learn the craft. They offer a common language for assessing and talking about writing, which becomes the core of writing workshop lessons and exposes the 'inside-ness' of writing—how texts are formed and how and why they work."

Culham concludes with some advice on conferencing with students. "As many writers discover—adults and student alike—often the first draft isn't patently wonderful or awful. It's usually somewhere in between, which can make clear communication a challenge as you confer with the author about the piece." Traits give you a convenient way of talking about strong points in the draft and focusing on a few areas that need work. "Don't swamp student writers with every last thing in the world they can do to improve a particular piece of writing," advises Culham. She quotes Ralph Fletcher: "Squeeze it once, and let it go."

"The Trait Lady Speaks Up" by Ruth Culham in *Educational Leadership*, October 2006 (Vol. 64, #2, pp. 53–57), summarized in Marshall Memo 158.

EFFECTIVE PEDAGOGY

12) Advice on Nurturing Student Writers

In this *Journal of Staff Development* article, Vicki Spandel (who helped develop the widely-used six-trait rubric) advises teachers on the most effective ways to develop students' writing to high levels of proficiency.

For starters, she says, it's essential to show students the rubrics that will be used to evaluate their writing—along with samples of proficient writing. "Students have a right to see samples of what we want from them as writers," says Spandel.

Second, student writers need to learn how to self-assess. "Whereas we assess to grade and to coach," says Spandel, "they assess to understand and to revise …. They will be skilled assessors if, like us, they are avid readers and practiced listeners. They will be skilled assessors if, like us, they write every day so that thinking like a writer becomes a habit. They will be skilled assessors if, like us, they continually think about what it is they value in writing." Spandel says teachers can help students assess their own writing by:

- Creating checklists with students and constantly revising them.
- Talking about literature as the work of writers and using every book, article, story, or essay as a lesson about how to write well.
- Treating each piece of problematic writing "as a lesson specially packaged just for you and your students," says Spandel, "asking them, 'If this were your piece, what would you do to make it stronger?'"
- Having students read their writing aloud, more than once, asking, "Does this make sense? Is this text pulling me in or pushing me away?" Hearing one's own writing is essential to self-assessment, says Spandel.

Third, our feedback to students should be *useful*. "I do not mean useful to data gatherers eager to report on perceived growth, decline, or stagnation," says Spandel. "Rather, I am talking about its usefulness to the people assessment should be designed to serve first and foremost: *student writers*. In this spirit, we must ensure that assessment at every level helps students to identify not only the needs to be addressed but, even more important, strengths to build on."

Fourth, it's important to go beyond rubric scores and give students authentic, encouraging feedback on their writing. Grades and numbers are not what students want, says Spandel. "They need our voices and our hearts. They need to know their writing has touched us in some way …. In the end, what matters most in the world of writing is immeasurable. So student writers have a right to assessment that is not just about numbers, but also includes room for a smile, a laugh, a sigh, applause, and the honest and passionate response that all writers hunger to hear."

In other words, says Spandel, our feedback to students should be "not only passionate, but compassionate as well. Anyone can be a critic. Good teachers do something much harder: They look for the precise moment at which a writer stumbles onto her true topic. They listen for that first whisper of the writer's voice, no matter how faint. They listen for the word or phrase too good to replace, for the rhythm of sentences that falls just right on the ear. Teachers hear the deer in the forest."

The whole point of assessment is to uplift writers, says Spandel. "So much of assessment is about identifying problems. But courage is what writers need most. Therefore, encouragement, or the bolstering of that courage, is what we as teachers and writing coaches ought to provide. If I am trying to push a large rock up a hill, the last thing I need is for someone to tell me I probably won't make it—or by how many feet I will miss the mark. For many student writers, the hill feels steep, and the rock is growing heavier by the minute. In that situation, courage is all that stands between that student and giving up."

Finally, teachers should remember that no matter how sure they feel about their own assessment of a piece of writing, another teacher may have a different opinion. "No single assessment can ever be regarded as 'the truth,'" says Spandel. "Assessment at its best offers support and insight, not judgment."

"Assessing with Heart" by Vicki Spandel in *Journal of Staff Development* (currently *The Learning Professional*), Summer 2006 (Vol. 27, #3, pp. 14–18), summarized in Marshall Memo 140.

Building Strong Vocabularies

13 Vocabulary Development as an Essential Leverage Point

"To grow up as the child of well-educated parents in an affluent American home is to hit the verbal lottery," says Robert Pondiscio in this *Education Gadfly* article. "In sharp contrast, early disadvantages in language among low-income children— both the low volume of words they hear and the way in which they are employed—establish a verbal inertia that is immensely difficult to address or reverse …. When it comes to vocabulary, size matters." A robust vocabulary, he says, correlates strongly with school achievement, SAT scores, college attendance and graduation, and higher adult earnings even among those who don't attend college.

So how do less-fortunate students build vocabulary? *Not* through studying and memorizing decontextualized word lists, says Pondiscio, but through repeated exposure to unfamiliar words in context—especially Tier 2 words like *verify, superior,* and *negligent.* These middle-tier words "are essential to reading comprehension," he says, "and undergird more subtle and precise use of language, both receptive (reading, hearing) and expressive (writing, speaking) …. There is a language of upward mobility in America. It has an expansive and nuanced vocabulary that it employs to nimbly navigate the world of organizations, institutions, and opportunities."

Consider the word *durable*. Here's how a student might gradually master the word and add it to long-term memory by encountering it in four content-area texts:

- The Egyptians learned how to make durable sheets of parchment from the papyrus plant.
- With this lightweight and durable telescope, young scientists can explore the natural wonders of the earth or the craters of the moon and beyond.
- Many durable Roman concrete buildings are still in use after more than two thousand years.
- Instead of having to find caves to create makeshift shelters for protection from the weather, early humans started to look for more durable materials with which to build long-lasting dwellings.

In each case, context is vital to figuring out the meaning of *durable* and gradually solidifying it in long-term memory. So is background knowledge. "This is the Matthew Effect in action," says Pondiscio. "Those who have the broadest general knowledge, whether acquired at home, school, or elsewhere in their lives, are most likely to possess the 'schema' necessary to intuit the meaning of the word in context and ultimately incorporate the new words into their vocabulary; those who do not fall further behind. The language-rich grow richer; the poor get poorer."

Students' knowledge base is the "context-creating engine of language growth," he continues. "In short, schools that hope to educate for upward mobility should be doing all they can to make children as rich as possible in knowledge and language—so that they can grow richer still …. Low-income children most specifically need more science, social studies, art, and music to build the necessary 'schema' that drive comprehension and language growth."

"Without a common body of knowledge and its associated gains in vocabulary and language proficiency as a first purpose of American education," Pondiscio concludes, "the achievement gap will remain a permanent fixture of American society, and the odds of upward mobility—already depressingly long—will become nearly insurmountable."

"It Pays to Increase Your Word Power" by Robert Pondiscio in *The Education Gadfly*, December 10, 2014 (Vol. 14, #50), summarized in Marshall Memo 565.

---

14. Myths About Teaching Vocabulary and How to Get Past Them

In this article in *American Educator*, Susan Neuman (New York University) and Tanya Wright (Michigan State University) cite the well-known vocabulary gap—entering first graders from high-income families know twice as many words as their low-income peers. But Neuman and Wright believe the even worse news is the belief that the gap can't be closed. "Luckily," they say, "there is now a rich and accumulated new knowledge base that suggests a far different scenario." Specifically:

- Children learn words most rapidly in the preschool years, giving educators an ideal window to intervene.
- Effective vocabulary instruction can ameliorate reading difficulties later on, allowing children who started school way behind to be on grade level by fourth grade.
- The quality, quantity, and responsiveness of teachers and family members can effectively mediate socioeconomic status.
- Early gains in oral vocabulary can predict growth in reading comprehension and later reading performance.

EFFECTIVE PEDAGOGY

"This means that, in contrast to dire prognostications, there is much we can do to enable children to read and read well," say Neuman and Wright. The news is especially timely because the Common Core standards represent a markedly more rigorous and demanding set of expectations for students.

Before presenting their principles for content-rich oral vocabulary instruction, Neuman and Wright puncture several myths:

• *Myth 1: Children are word sponges.* Earlier research suggested that young children can learn words from a single exposure ("fast mapping"). This turns out to be inaccurate. Instead, kids learn words incrementally by predicting relationships between objects and sounds and getting a more accurate fix on a word every time they see or hear it. "With each additional exposure, the word may become incrementally closer to being fully learned," say Neuman and Wright.

• *Myth 2: Children have an early vocabulary spurt.* The latest evidence is that children absorb words at a steady, cumulative rate, and what accelerates over time is the integration and use of words after repeated exposures. "The high-performing student who knows many thousands of words has learned them not by having received a jolt of oral language early on, but by accruing bits of word knowledge for each of the thousands of words encountered every day," say Neuman and Wright. This suggests that we need to continuously immerse children in oral and written vocabulary experiences.

• *Myth 3: Storybook reading is enough.* Children listening to and interacting with storybooks is certainly helpful, but recent studies have shown that it's not enough to compensate for the deficits of disadvantaged children. Teachers need to supplement oral reading with intentional strategies that get students processing words at deeper levels of understanding.

• *Myth 4: Teachable moments teach plenty of words.* Parents and teachers pause and explain an unfamiliar word, "*Celebrate* means we do something fun," but in busy classrooms, this happens only about eight times a day, and that's not nearly enough to boost the vocabulary of students who are behind. Teachers need to be "proactive in selecting words that have great application to academic texts with increasingly complex concepts," say Neuman and Wright.

• *Myth 5: Just follow the basal reader's vocabulary scope and sequence.* Studies of commercial reading programs reveal wide disparities in the number of words introduced, how they are taught, and their appropriateness to the grade level. Teachers need to supplement basal readers with a much more systematic approach to teaching grade-appropriate academic vocabulary.

Neuman and Wright follow up with these five principles for vocabulary instruction for young children:

- Be both explicit and implicit. It's not enough for children to hear new words in a story or for the teacher to mention them in passing.
- Be intentional about word selection. Teachers can explicitly teach only about four hundred words a year. These need to be words that will take students to a higher level of vocabulary proficiency—words like *habitat, organism, protection,* and *compare, contrast, and observe.*
- Build word meaning through knowledge networks that make sense to students. "It's fair to say that words represent the tip of the iceberg," say Neuman and Wright. "Underlying them is a set of emerging interconnections and concepts that these words represent." And those links are what drive students' comprehension—for example, *abdomen, lungs, heart, brain.*
- Children need repeated exposure to gain vocabulary. Frequency is the key to vocabulary development, with repetition happening in varied, meaningful contexts.
- Ongoing professional development is essential. A proven routine for teaching new vocabulary: (a) Identify words that need to be taught; (b) define the words in a child-friendly way; (c) contextualize words in varied and meaningful formats; (d) review words to ensure they're retained; (e) monitor children's progress and reteach if necessary.

"The Magic of Words: Teaching Vocabulary in the Early Childhood Classroom" by Susan Neuman and Tanya Wright in *American Educator*, Summer 2014 (Vol. 38, #2, pp. 4–13), summarized in Marshall Memo 542.

---

15 Early Systematic Teaching of Sophisticated Vocabulary

In this article in *Elementary School Journal*, University of Pittsburgh professors Isabel Beck and Margaret McKeown argue that systematically and skillfully expanding vocabulary is key to improving reading achievement in high-poverty schools. By learning around four hundred words a year, they say, disadvantaged students could add thousands of words to their vocabularies throughout their school years and become much stronger readers.

The authors begin with the brutal facts about the widening vocabulary achievement gap: In first grade, economically advantaged students know twice as many words as their less-advantaged peers. A child who enters school with a small vocabulary finds it difficult to understand many reading materials and falls further and further behind. By twelfth grade, high-performing students know *four* times as many words as their low-performing peers. Curiously, elementary schools don't emphasize teaching new words, say Beck and McKeown: teachers "do much mentioning and assigning and little actual teaching of new vocabulary." For students who enter school knowing a lot of words, this teaching approach works just fine; for those who don't, it's a significant reason that the achievement gap widens every year.

So how are vocabulary-poor students going to learn the sophisticated words that they need to become mature, literate language users? Four approaches that work for vocabulary-rich students don't work for students who enter school with deficits: (a) Everyday conversations are not very helpful, because this kind of discourse uses everyday words and not the rich vocabulary these children need to acquire. (b) Reading primary-grade storybooks also isn't much help because these books contain grade-level vocabulary and not high-value words. (c) Independent reading is a good way for students to learn new words, but students who know fewer words do much less reading on their own, and when they do read, they are less able to infer the meaning of unfamiliar words from context clues because they know fewer of the surrounding words in the text. (d) Teacher readalouds from more sophisticated trade books have little impact because students hear the more advanced words, but there isn't enough context and repetition for them to sink in.

Beck and McKeown thought there might be teaching potential in the rich vocabulary in some readaloud books and designed two experiments to test their hypothesis—that *systematic* teaching of these words in the context of engaging readalouds would expand students' vocabularies. They chose children's books that were conceptually challenging, contained complex events and subtle expression of ideas, presented unfamiliar ideas and topics, had a flow of events (rather than a series of situations), contained rich vocabulary, and didn't have too many pictures. From each book, the researchers selected a few sophisticated, "second-tier" words that students wouldn't encounter in their everyday conversations and reading, and would have high utility for them down the road (see the lists below).

The researchers then set up control groups in each school (classes that proceeded with the regular literacy curriculum) and trained the experimental-class kindergarten and first-grade teachers to go through specific steps with the second-tier words. Here's an example, using *The Bremen Town Musicians*, whose second-tier words were *feast, exhausted,* and *cautiously*:

- The teacher reads the book aloud, briefly explaining any words that might prevent students from understanding the meaning but not interrupting the flow.
- After completing the story and discussing it with the class, the teacher takes the first target

word, *feast*, and reminds students of its context within the book: "In the story, it said that the animals found the robbers' table full of good things to eat, and so they had a *feast*."
- The teacher defines the word: "A *feast* is a big special meal with lots of delicious food."
- Students are asked to say the word: "Say the word with me: *feast*."
- The teacher gives examples in contexts different from that of the story: "People usually have a *feast* on a holiday or to celebrate something special. We all have a *feast* on Thanksgiving Day."
- Students are asked to judge examples and nonexamples: "Which would be a *feast*: eating an ice-cream cone or eating at a big table full of all kinds of food? Why?"
- Students are asked to come up with their own examples: "If you wanted to eat a feast, what kinds of food would you want?"
- The teacher reinforces the word's sound and meaning: "What's a word that means a big special meal?"
- The teacher repeats these steps with the other second-tier words in the story.
- The teacher reinforces the words over the next few days, keeping second-tier words on a chart, putting a tally mark by each when it is used in class, and using the words whenever possible in class—for example, in a morning message, writing "Today is Monday. Jamal wants a *feast* for his birthday."

Teachers were surprised by how receptive their students were to this rather laborious process, and they were very positive about the experiment. "Kids love words," said one teacher who had been a skeptic. Rigorous follow-up testing showed that students who were taught this way learned significantly more words than students in the control groups.

But Beck and McKeown were not satisfied with the number of words students had learned, and they designed a second experiment in which students were taught second-tier words the same way, but then did more systematic, carefully spaced follow-up teaching in subsequent weeks with a subset of the words. Teachers spent five days on each book:
- On the first day, students heard and discussed the story.
- On the second day, the teacher systematically taught the first three words.
- On the third day, the teacher taught the remaining three words (the target words).
- On the fourth and fifth days, students received more instruction on those three words.
- Four weeks later, the target words were reviewed.
- Three weeks after that, the target words were reviewed again.

Here is the review cycle used for each set of words:

Day	Review Week 1	Review Week 2
1	Words from weeks 1, 2	Words from weeks 6, 7
2	Words from weeks 3, 4	Words from weeks 5, 6
3	Words from weeks 1, 3	Words from weeks 5, 7
4	Words from weeks 2, 4	Words from weeks 5–7
5	Words from weeks 1–4	

Follow-up testing showed that both kindergarten and first-grade students learned the target words at twice the rate they learned the first set of words. The more systematic, spaced instruction really made a difference.

Beck and McKeown conclude that learning sophisticated words as early as possible will give students a significant boost in the years ahead: "The earlier word meanings are learned, the more readily they are accessed later in life," they write. "More specifically, accessing word-meaning information is more efficient and robust for words acquired early. More efficient retrieval in turn promotes comprehension, whereas effortful retrieval jeopardizes it."

The authors note that not all words need to be taught this systematically; many words can be learned with less elaborate procedures in the course of everyday classroom instruction. But their big point is that without very systematic, skilled teaching of sophisticated words, the achievement gap will get wider every year students are in school.

"Increasing Young Low-Income Children's Oral Vocabulary Repertoires Through Rich and Focused Instruction" by Isabel Beck and Margaret McKeown in *Elementary School Journal*, January 2007 (Vol. 107, #3, pp. 251–271), summarized in Marshall Memo 167.

Professional Learning Suggestions for Chapter Seven: Proficiency in Reading, Writing, and Oral Language

Getting Your School on the Same Page with Literacy

Why a chapter on literacy in a book for school leaders? Aside from the fact that literacy is the most foundational skill and sets the stage for student success in almost every other arena, it is the school leader who can ensure that the most effective literacy practices don't simply live in the classrooms of our strongest teachers. As Calkins and Ehrenworth write, the principal is the "key orchestrator" to ensure best literacy practices are implemented consistently throughout the school. Note that these activities are for your *entire* faculty. If you want excellent reading, writing, and vocabulary instruction across the school, you need to involve more than just your English or ELA teachers.

I. Get on the Same Page About *Beliefs*

While you may think you don't need to get buy-in to implement school-wide literacy practices, it's a key ingredient in building everyone's sense of urgency for strengthening literacy throughout the school.

A. Build buy-in for effective literacy practices with research, readings, and surveys.
To begin to build buy-in, try the three activities that follow.

1. Draw staff attention to some of the research on literacy. Here is one example: Research points to a simple conclusion—the more time students read, the more they improve their reading proficiency, that is, the key to improving reading skills is to read! Fountas and Pinnell (article-summary 1) cite research that says students should read two thousand texts by middle school. Pondiscio (article-summary 13) also emphasizes the importance of quantity: "When it comes to vocabulary, size matters.…The language-rich grow richer; the poor get poorer." Share the following with your staff and discuss reactions. This is from a study of fifth graders (Anderson, Wilson, & Fielding, 1988):

The Effects of Adding Just Ten Minutes a Day of Reading		
When students read this number of minutes a day…	**… Increasing that by just ten minutes a day…**	**Leads to these results!**
1.8 minutes of reading per day means reading 106,000 words per year.	🕮🕮🕮🕮🕮🕮🕮🕮	They end up reading 694,889 words per year, or a 556% increase in word exposure.
3.2 minutes of reading per day means reading 200,000 words per year.	🕮🕮🕮🕮🕮🕮🕮🕮	They end up reading 825,000 words per year, or a 313% increase in word exposure.
9.6 minutes of reading per day means reading 622,000 words per year.	🕮🕮🕮🕮🕮🕮🕮🕮	They end up reading 1,269,917 words per year, or a 104% increase in word exposure.
21.1 minutes of reading per day means reading 1,823,000 words per year.	🕮🕮🕮🕮🕮🕮🕮🕮	They end up reading 2,686,981 words per year, or a 47% increase in word exposure.
65 minutes of reading per day means reading 4,358,000 words per year.	🕮🕮🕮🕮🕮🕮🕮🕮	They end up reading 5,028,462 words per year, or a 15% increase in word exposure.

https://bit.ly/32GUmLi

2. Have staff learn more about effective literacy instruction by reading the article-summaries in the first section of this chapter. This section provides a helpful overview of some elements of implementing effective literacy instruction. Have teachers read all three article-summaries in this section (it's only four and half pages!) – "Four Key Elements in Effective Literacy Instruction" (article-summary 1), "The Literacy Experiences Children Should Have Every Day" (article-summary 2), and "What's Missing in Many Literacy Programs" (article-summary 3).

As a large group, discuss:

- What aspects of effective literacy instruction were mentioned in the three article-summaries?
- Which of these do we *already* implement in our school?
- Which aspects would we like to emphasize, learn more about, or improve?

3. Survey students and staff about literacy at your school. In addition to sharing research and having teachers read article-summaries, you can conduct a survey about literacy practices at

PROFESSIONAL LEARNING SUGGESTIONS FOR CHAPTER SEVEN

your school. You can do this anonymously through an online survey like Survey Monkey or Google Forms, or you can conduct informal in-person chats with groups of students or teachers. After reading the article-summaries in this section, decide *what* you would like to know more about and craft appropriate questions. Below are some suggestions (these are written for teachers but can be rephrased for students):

- How many minutes a day do your students read for school (both in school and for assignments)?
- How often do you include the following types of reading in your class: read aloud, shared reading, guided reading, and independent reading?
- How many pages of writing do your students do in a week across all of their classes for school (both in school and for at-home assignments)?
- How frequently do you have students complete on-demand writing pieces?
- Do you actively teach vocabulary, and if so, how?
- What type of choice do students have about the reading or writing they do in your class?
- Is there a common understanding at your school of what "good writing" and "good reading" look like?

These are just a few suggestions; ask the questions that delve into the literacy issues you are most concerned about. After the survey, compile the results to share with teachers so they can understand the most pressing literacy needs at your school. Discuss these results.

B. Create your own literacy manifesto.

Fountas and Pinnell (article-summary 1) share what they believe to be the four most important elements of an effective literacy program. Bring together your leadership team or organize a literacy team (be sure to include some math and science teachers!) to create a literacy manifesto for *your school* after reading through the article-summaries in this chapter. Try to keep it broad enough so it is about *beliefs* not *practices*. There will be time to focus on literacy practices in the next section.

For example, if the team were to base their manifesto entirely on the Fountas and Pinnell article-summary, it might look like this:

EFFECTIVE PEDAGOGY

> We believe that an effective literacy program must have a shared vision of success.
>
> We believe that an effective literacy program must have common goals, common language, and collective responsibility.
>
> We believe that an effective literacy program must have teachers with expertise in research-based literacy instructional strategies.
>
> We believe that an effective literacy program must exist within a culture of continuous professional learning.

II. Get on the Same Page About Literacy *Practices*

The goal of this section is to end up with a set of reading, writing, and vocabulary practices that all teachers use—regardless of grade level or subject taught—across the entire school. The article-summaries in this section emphasize the importance of a shared vision for literacy instruction and consistency across the school. This is the opportunity to create that shared vision.

A. Identify powerful practices in reading, writing, and vocabulary instruction.
Bring your teachers together to read the twelve article-summaries on reading, writing, and vocabulary instruction. Divide up the work by using a jigsaw to have a third of the teachers read the article-summaries on *reading* (4, 5, 6, and 7), a third read the article-summaries on *writing* (8, 9, 10, 11, and 12), and a third read the article-summaries on *vocabulary* (13, 14, and 15).

1. Let teachers choose which topic they are most interested in (reading, writing, or vocabulary), and then read the articles on that topic.

2. Next, have all teachers who read article-summaries on the same topic discuss and create a list of the skills or the points that are most important from each article.

Article Title	Key Takeaways

3. Bring the whole group back together and organize triads of teachers with one teacher who read the reading article-summaries, one who read the writing article-summaries, and one who

PROFESSIONAL LEARNING SUGGESTIONS FOR CHAPTER SEVEN

read the vocabulary article-summaries. Provide time for each person to present key takeaways from the article-summaries they read.

B. Translate literacy ideas into classroom practices.

The article-summaries in this chapter contain a number of important ideas about literacy instruction. Teachers need to translate these ideas into actual practices to understand what these ideas might look like in the classroom. Send your teachers back to the three groups from the previous exercise (the reading, writing, and vocabulary groups) and have each group focus on their own third of the article-summaries in this chapter.

Have them examine the key takeaways they already identified and any other lessons learned. Next, the small groups should discuss what practices might embody these ideas using a chart like the one below. This chart is just an example—you can give them a blank chart *or* include one or two of the ideas below. Note, this isn't a time to decide which ideas or practices are best; it is simply an exercise to *gather* all of the ideas into one place and infer the types of practices that are suggested by these ideas. Examples are below:

Effective Literacy Instruction *Lessons Learned*	*Effective Literacy Instruction* *Possible Practices*
Good Reading Instruction	
Teachers should help students read within their zone of proximal development. (Lewis)	• Include small-group instruction. • Formatively assess students frequently so we know what level students are on and when to change their groups.
Students should have choices in what they read. (Allington, Wolter, Calkins/Ehrenworth)	• Require that students read an independent book in addition to the shared class reading. • Provide a range of reading materials in class from novels and nonfiction books to magazines and newspapers.

EFFECTIVE PEDAGOGY

Readers need effective strategies to get unstuck. (Wolter)	• The school provides PD on the skills successful readers use. • Every classroom (including math and science) posts a poster with a list of effective strategies when reading gets tough. • Teachers deliver mini-lessons to explicitly teach students the effective strategies students use when stuck in their reading.
Etc.	
Good Writing Instruction	
Students need time to write.	• Teachers will include time to write every day (explanations in math, hypotheses in science, free-writes in ELA, etc.)
Good feedback is necessary to improve writing. (Calkins/Ehrenworth, Spandel)	• Feedback on student writing will be given before the final draft so students have opportunities to improve their work. • Feedback on student writing will clearly identify what needs to be improved and the strengths to build on—grades and numbers are not feedback.
Etc.	
Good Vocabulary Instruction	
Vocabulary needs to be explicitly taught. (Neuman/Wright, Beck/McKeown)	• Teachers of all subjects need to come up with a list of Tier 2 words to teach. • Teachers need to set up a Word Wall in their classrooms and repeatedly refer to and assess the words on that wall.
Etc.	

PROFESSIONAL LEARNING SUGGESTIONS FOR CHAPTER SEVEN

C. Come to consensus on six literacy practices across the school—every teacher, every subject.

Now that you have one long list of all of the suggested practices from the article-summaries that contribute to good reading, writing, or vocabulary instruction, it's time to prioritize. What are the six literacy practices that your entire school will commit to implementing regardless of grade level or discipline?

Buy-in is essential in making this happen. To do this, create large posters with all of the possible practices listed above. Give each teacher six Post-it notes and have them vote for the top six literacy practices they would like to see implemented across the school by placing their sticky notes on those practices. You can certainly do this electronically, but it helps to have teachers walking around the room and seeing each other physically place their votes.

Once votes have been counted, have the group discuss the top three to four practices for reading, writing and vocabulary. Conduct a large-group discussion so teachers can think through the feasibility of enacting these practices in the different subject areas and grade levels they teach. Use this discussion to come to consensus around two practices for each of these three areas and record them below:

\multicolumn{2}{c}{**Six Across-the-School Literacy Practices – Every Teacher, Every Subject**}	
Reading	1.
	2.
Writing	3.
	4.
Vocabulary	5.
	6.

Chapter Eight:
Differentiation and Personalization

In a normal classroom discussion, power often rests with the quickest minds. The ability to quickly respond with a well-constructed verbal retort dominates conversation from debate halls to playground walls.
—Jason Hilton

Teachers want all students to succeed, but given the myriad differences that exist in any classroom, it's difficult to meet all their needs. Differentiation, individualization, and personalization are three closely related ways to address this perennial challenge, and digital technology opens up new possibilities for customizing instruction to engage students at different levels of motivation and achievement.

But while almost everyone agrees on moving away from stale lecture-and-worksheet instruction, there's been pushback on how far to go with differentiation, individualization, and personalization. Should students decide *what* as well as *how* they learn? Will differentiation lower standards for some students and balkanize classrooms? Will trying to cater to so many individual needs result in teacher burnout? The articles in this chapter address these and other concerns; the way mastery learning addresses the challenge; and low-tech and high-tech ways to engage students and boost learning.

Why Differentiate and Personalize? Donna de la Cruz opens up a world of possible ideas for differentiation by asking students what they wish their teacher knew about them. Kim Marshall disagrees with the traditional content-process-product approach to differentiation, suggesting

DIFFERENTIATION AND PERSONALIZATION

instead three sequential steps: building in success up front with unit and lesson planning; nimble teaching with continuous checks for understanding; and following up with students who aren't yet successful. Paul France corrects three misconceptions about differentiation, saying there should be small- and large-group work; students' horizons can be expanded through all-class instruction; and in the long run differentiation doesn't have to burn teachers out. Benjamin Herold asks what personalization is, what are its aspirational goals and philosophical roots, who's pushing it, and whether it's effective. Carol Ann Tomlinson wonders if personalization is ready for prime time.

Differentiation by Pushing for Mastery – Thomas Guskey summarizes Benjamin Bloom's powerful theory, in which there's immediate intervention with students who might otherwise slide along with sub-mastery performance. Jonathan Bergmann and Aaron Sams describe their "flipped mastery" model for high-school chemistry, with students watching short lesson videos at home and engaging in classroom discussions, experiments, and assessments tuned to their questions and needs. Kristina Doubet tells how several middle-school teacher teams used formative assessments to differentiate instruction and continuously improve their teaching.

Low-Tech Differentiation – Kathleen McClaskey describes how Universal Design for Learning (UDL) personalizes student access, engagement, and expression. Marian Small says that asking open-ended math questions elicits a variety of student answers and posing parallel tasks challenges students at different achievement levels. Cathy Vatterott reports several elementary teachers' successful experiments with having students choose from a list of creative, open-ended homework assignments.

High-Tech Differentiation – Jason Hilton tells how his eighth-grade students spent the first fifteen minutes of class silently "conversing" in an online discussion forum about a question he'd posed. Stacy Kitsis describes how her high-school English students follow up on in-person literature circles by blogging about their reading after class. Joe Terantino, Karen Graf, and Nicole Naditz report on their successful use of Facebook pages with their high-school world language classes and clubs. Ryan Becker and Penny Bishop use Twitter to get their middle-school science students interacting with content, classmates, and outside resources. And Jeffrey Carpenter describes several ways to broaden engagement by having students use digital "backchannels" to chime in and interact during classes.

EFFECTIVE PEDAGOGY

Questions to Consider:

- What is the problem to which differentiation is the solution?
- Can teachers differentiate successfully without burning out?
- How can teachers cater to students' individual needs while also building self-reliance?

Why Differentiate and Personalize?

1. I Wish My Teacher Knew …

In this *New York Times* article, Donna de la Cruz describes a get-to-know-you strategy some teachers use at the beginning of the school year: they ask students to complete the sentence, "I wish my teacher knew …" Here are some responses:

- I wish my teacher knew I don't have pencils at home to do my homework.
- I wish my teacher knew I love my family.
- I wish my teacher knew that my family and I live in a shelter.
- I wish my teacher knew I am smarter than she thinks I am.
- I wish my teacher knew that sometimes my reading log is not signed because my mom isn't around a lot.
- I wish my teacher knew that my little brother gets scared and I get worried about getting up every night.
- I wish my teacher knew I love animals and I would do anything for my animals. I would love to work at the MSPCA so I could help animals get adopted.
- I wish my teacher knew that my mom and dad are divorced and that I am the middle of seven kids. Five out of that seven are boys.
- I wish my teacher knew I want to learn more about history.
- I wish my teacher knew that my mom might get diagnosed with cancer this week and I've been without a home three different times this year alone.
- I wish my teacher knew that my dad works two jobs and I don't see him much.
- I wish my teacher knew how much I miss my dad because he got deported to Mexico when I was three years old, and I haven't seen him in six years.

These and other thoughts from students are available in a book by Kyle Schwartz, *I Wish My Teacher Knew: How One Question Can Change Everything for Our Kids* (Cambridge, MA: Da Capo Press, 2016). Twitter hashtag: #iwishmyteacherknew.

"What Kids Wish Their Teachers Knew" by Donna de la Cruz in the *New York Times*, August 31, 2016, summarized in Marshall Memo 651.

EFFECTIVE PEDAGOGY

2 | Framing Differentiation in Terms of Intentions and Outcomes

In this article in *Phi Delta Kappan*, Kim Marshall states the obvious reasons for differentiation: "Students walk into school with a wide range of differences in prior knowledge, vocabulary, reading proficiency, fluency in English, attitudes toward school, mindset about learning, tolerance of frustration and failure, learning-style preferences, special needs, and distracting things on their minds." In a classroom with even a few of these differences, whole-group instruction is likely to leave many kids bored or confused. So differentiation would seem to be a moral imperative.

Carol Ann Tomlinson, a leading expert in this area, makes a compelling case for "effective attention to the learning needs of each student, … getting to know each student and orchestrating the learning environment, assessments, and instruction so all students learn what's being taught." Tomlinson and other proponents suggest that teachers differentiate by content (what is taught), process (how it's taught), and product (how students are asked to demonstrate their learning).

For all its obvious appeal, differentiation is not without its critics, and they've raised the following concerns:

- Can a teacher realistically tailor instruction to twenty to thirty different students?
- Is differentiation inherently exhausting, leading to teacher burnout and attrition?
- Will differentiation result in lowered expectations for students who are behind?
- Does it spoon-feed students, undermining self-reliance and initiative?
- Does it balkanize classrooms, sacrificing group experiences and cohesion?
- Is it effective?

On the last question, in 2010 author/consultant Mike Schmoker said there was no evidence that differentiation works. It's based "largely on enthusiasm and a certain superficial logic," he said and described what he had seen in classrooms around the country: teachers trying to match each student's or group's "presumed ability level, interest, preferred 'modality,' and learning style …. In English, creative students made things or drew pictures. Analytic students got to read and write …. With so many groups to teach, instructors found it almost impossible to provide sustained, properly executed lessons for every child or group."

In response to Schmoker's critique, in the same year Tomlinson and David Sousa conceded that trying to customize worksheets and coloring exercises to students' supposed learning styles is "regrettable and damaging." They also agreed on the importance of clear objectives, high standards, and frequent checks for understanding. But they stoutly defended differentiation's track record:

students learn better, they said, when the work is at the right level of difficulty, personally relevant, and appropriately engaging.

This hardly settled the issue, and three other experts have weighed in. John Hattie's comprehensive meta-analysis, *Visible Learning* (2008), ranked individualization 100th out of 138 classroom methods, with an effect size of only 0.23. In 2005 cognitive psychologist Daniel Willingham debunked the idea of catering instruction to students' individual learning styles. And in 2015, PD guru Jon Saphier said that differentiation is a "low-impact strategy" that's not the best target for professional development if other fundamentals aren't in place. The debate continues, leaving many educators scratching their heads about the best approach to the day-to-day challenge of teaching students with many different needs.

Marshall suggests stepping back and analyzing the differentiation challenge from a broader perspective. Consider the following classroom scenarios with two questions in mind: Which is the most, and which is the least, differentiated? And in which is the most learning taking place?

- A college professor gives a lecture to seven hundred students.
- First graders sprawl on a rug engrossed in books they individually chose.
- Eighth graders watch a film about the Holocaust.
- Seventh graders read an article on climate change at five different reading levels.
- Fifth graders use a computer program that uses their responses to adjust difficulty.
- A Reading Recovery teacher tutors a struggling first grader for thirty minutes a day.
- A middle-school physical education class does jumping-jacks in unison.
- Kindergarteners paint with watercolors with individual feedback from the teacher.

On the first question, differentiation would seem to range from very low in the college lecture hall to very high with one-on-one tutoring and a personalized computer program.

On the question of where the most learning is taking place—well, it depends. "Even one-on-one tutoring can be off-track on curriculum standards and produce bored, confused, and alienated students," says Marshall. "But handled skillfully, each scenario has the potential for high levels of appropriate learning"; even the college lecture (in the hands of a brilliant and charismatic professor) and the phys. ed. class (aerobic exercise has an especially beneficial impact on ADHD and overweight students, so an element of differentiation is built in). The conclusion: trying to assess a teacher's work by asking *is it differentiated* runs the risk of missing the forest for the trees. Better, says Marshall, to ask two broader questions (tip of the hat to Rick DuFour):

- *What are students supposed to be learning?*
- *Are all students mastering it?*

"Embedded in these questions," says Marshall, "are all the variables that research tells us will produce high levels of student learning: appropriate cognitive and noncognitive goals for the year, the curriculum unit, and the lesson; a positive classroom culture; instructional strategies that will best convey the content; the right balance of whole-class, small-group, individual, and digital experiences; frequent checking for understanding; a clear standard of mastery (usually 80 percent); effective use of assessment data to fine-tune teaching; and follow-up with students below mastery."

With those two questions in mind, teachers' work (and principals' support and evaluation of that work) falls logically into three phases: (a) planning units and lessons, (b) delivering instruction, and (c) following up with students who are not yet successful. These are more in synch with the day-to-day work of teachers than the content/process/product approach.

• *Phase 1: Planning units and lessons* – Unit plans map the learning destination and lesson plans the day-by-day strategy. "All students learn more," says Willingham, "when content drives the choice of modalities." Teachers also need to put well-chosen visuals on the classroom wall—essential questions, examples of student work, rubrics, worked problems, word walls, anchor charts, graphic organizers, and mnemonics.

Critical success factors in Phase I are teachers avoiding overthinking, overworking, and burning out. It's helpful for teachers to co-create and share unit and lesson plans; tap into Internet resources; and know when enough is enough—not letting the perfect be the enemy of the good.

• *Phase 2: Delivering instruction* – "Lessons are where the rubber meets the road," says Marshall, "and a major factor in student success is a set of in-the-moment moves that effective teachers have always used, among them: knowing students well; being culturally sensitive; good classroom management; making the subject matter exciting, relevant, and clear; making good use of visuals and props; involving students and getting them involved with each other; having a sense of humor; and nimbly using teachable moments." Equally important is checking for understanding (with dry-erase boards, clickers, probing questions, looking over students' shoulders) and using students' responses to continuously fine-tune teaching.

Critical success factors in Phase 2 are: being sharp and fresh every day for energetic and sensitive lesson execution (another reason for not working too long on lesson planning the night before); managing student behavior so the teacher is able to move around the room delivering appropriate support and help; a classroom culture in which students are comfortable asking for help and helping each other; ways of checking the whole class's understanding and following up; and resisting the urge to do too much for students.

• *Phase 3: Following up after instruction* – "No matter how well teachers plan and execute," says Marshall, "some students won't achieve mastery by the end of the lesson or unit. This is the moment of truth; if the class moves on, unsuccessful students will be that much more confused and discouraged and fall further and further behind, widening the achievement gap." Timely follow-up with these students is crucial—pullout, small-group after-school help, tutoring, Saturday school, and other venues to help them catch up.

Critical success factors in Phase 3 are: time for same-grade/same-subject teacher teams to meet and look at student work; having prompt access to data from well-crafted common assessments; analyzing what material students had problems with and why; organizing effective help for struggling students; and honestly assessing teaching techniques in light of the results. If these factors aren't in place, teacher team time can result in a cycle of repeated failure.

In all three phases, another priority is building students' self-reliance and not doing too much for them. "Among the most important life skills that students should take away from their K–12 years," says Marshall, "is the ability to self-assess, know their strengths and weaknesses, deal with difficulty and failure, and build a growth mindset. Student self-efficacy and independence should be prime considerations in planning, lesson execution, and follow-up so that students move through the grades becoming increasingly motivated, confident, and autonomous learners prepared to succeed in the wider world."

"Rethinking Differentiation—Using Teachers' Time Most Effectively" by Kim Marshall in *Phi Delta Kappan*, September 2016 (Vol. 98, #1, pp. 8–13), summarized in Marshall Memo 652.

3. Three Myths About Personalization

In this *Edutopia* article, San Francisco educator Paul France addresses common beliefs that he says prevent many teachers from meeting individual student needs. Each has a grain of truth, but there are strong counterarguments:

• *Myth 1: All students should be working on their own projects with unique products.* Not only is this impossible to manage, says France, but it's not the best full-time structure for teaching and learning. "Yes," he says, "we want to differentiate content for our students in order to help them access it in ways that work for them, but we also don't want them working in silos, void of interaction and deprived of shared experiences." France advocates mixing individualized "passion projects" with whole-class and small-group experiences where students interact around common content through discussions, observing peer models, and participating in a learning community. Of course, shared curriculum experiences shouldn't be one-size-fits-all, he says: "Instead, these activities and lessons will have multiple entry points allowing for varied paces without having to plan twenty to thirty unique activities."

• *Myth 2: Students should be working only on what interests them.* Since students' self-identified interests may initially be quite narrow, this approach risks selling students short, says France. When he taught Westward Expansion, for example, it wasn't on the short list of topics that fascinated his students. But they became engaged because he used methods and materials that aroused interest and kicked involvement into high gear. "What's more," he says, "this series of lessons was another way to debunk Myth 1, showing that if students are able to be active prosumers of information, a well-planned shared experience will personalize itself."

• *Myth 3: Personalization is too much work for teachers.* True, it may entail extra work at first, says France. But if it's done well, there should be no net increase in teacher workload. The same amount of prep time shifts from reading the teacher's manual, making copies, and grading "benign" assignments to planning and orchestrating a student-driven, teacher-curated curriculum. "In a personalized curriculum," he says, "teachers spend time building soft skills, finding authentic materials that can be used for future students, and conducting authentic formative assessments that build momentum. Students slowly become more autonomous—more reflective—and we start to see a return on investment …. This ends up actually saving us time in the classroom, as our practice becomes less reactive and more embedded into natural routines of inquiry, disequilibrium, and student-driven problem-solving."

"Three Personalization Myths" by Paul France, *Edutopia*, June 19, 2015, summarized in Marshall Memo 602.

DIFFERENTIATION AND PERSONALIZATION

4. What is Personalized Learning, and Does It Work?

In this *Education Week* article, Benjamin Herold explores whether personalized learning is a transformational development in K–12 education or a "billionaire-backed boondoggle, aimed primarily at replacing teachers and extracting data from children." His questions:

• *What exactly is personalized learning?* The term is being used to mean "just about anything," Herold reports. To some, it's adaptive software that adjusts computer instruction to each student's current level of proficiency. To others, it's a way of using digital data to group students and make instructional decisions. To still others, it's a philosophy of giving students more voice and choice in what and how they learn and demonstrate mastery. It can also be a way to push schools to nurture each child's social, emotional, and physical development.

• *What are the aspirational goals?* The big-picture aim is to customize learning experiences to each student's skills, abilities, preferences, background, and experiences. Many educators have always wanted to do this, and recent developments in digital technology have made it possible to use student data to cater more precisely to individual skills and preferences.

• *What are the philosophical roots?* One strand is the "engineering" model (think B. F. Skinner), with experts defining what children need to learn, diagnosing their current status, and creating an efficient (often self-paced) pathway to mastery. A competing model comes from the progressive tradition (think John Dewey and project-based learning) with students' interests, questions, and explorations driving the curriculum. "In both cases," says Herold, "what is new is the way in which technology—from big data to online collaboration tools to social media—is being used to amplify methods educators have been using more or less forever."

• *Who's pushing it?* In the last decade, personalized learning (in its many forms) has been promoted by the Obama-era Race to the Top legislation, the Gates Foundation, the Chan/Zuckerberg Initiative, and many states, nonprofits, and advocacy groups.

• *What has been the reaction in US schools?* A 2018 survey of principals found that more than half saw personalized learning as promising or potentially transformational, and 97 percent said they were using technology to personalize learning to some degree.

• *Is personalized learning effective?* We can't get a clear answer to this question, says Herold, because of the myriad ways the concept is being implemented. To the extent that personalized learning involves rapid, accurate feedback to students and meaningful differentiation, there's solid research support, but on other aspects, results are mixed. "The evidence base is very weak at this point," says John Pane of the RAND Corporation. And the Summit Public Schools, a California-based charter network designed by Dianne Tavenner to implement the personalized learning philosophy (and supported by the Chan/Zuckerberg Initiative), have declined to undergo independent third-party evaluation.

"The PL Explainer" by Benjamin Herold in *Education Week*, November 6, 2019 (Vol. 39, #12, pp. 10–11), summarized in Marshall Memo 811.

5. Ten Questions About Personalization

In this *Educational Leadership* article, differentiation guru Carol Ann Tomlinson (University of Virginia–Charlottesville) applauds the ideals of personalized learning. "Personalization is a kind of differentiation—or perhaps multiple kinds," she says. "The dialogue about personalization gives me hope. On the other hand, it also gives me pause…. We don't yet have much evidence that 'personalization' works—or for whom, or under what circumstances." To get it right, she believes ten questions need to be addressed:

• *Why personalized learning?* "If your school focused significantly on personalized learning for several months," she asks, "what would an observer see after that time that he or she wouldn't see now?"

• *How much of the curriculum will be learned?* Do the mechanisms of personalized learning (perhaps self-paced computer programs) convey a standard curriculum at a different pace for different students? Do students have choices of individualized projects or independent study within a general curriculum framework? Or is it "anything, anywhere, anytime learning," with students determining what, when, and how they learn?

• *When is personalization most effective?* Is it more appropriate for some K–12 grades than others? For some subjects? At certain times in the school day? How much is too much?

• *Is personalization suitable for all students?* For students learning English for the first time? Students struggling with reading? Students who lack background knowledge? Students with weak attention spans? Students who are academically advanced? Will those students get the resources, guidance, and personal attention they need?

• *How will old and new paradigms coexist?* Imposing personalization by fiat is unwise, but how will the shift be handled? "If teachers can opt in or out," asks Tomlinson, "is it acceptable for all second grade teachers to volunteer but only half of the third grade teachers? Will it work if the math department signs on but the science department doesn't?"

• *What supports do teachers need?* Many teachers will require extensive training and support. "Educators may need guidance on logistical issues," says Tomlinson, "like how to orchestrate a classroom in which multiple things are happening simultaneously, give more than one set of directions, or monitor student progress. Imagine, for instance, trying to move from teaching mathematical algorithms to the whole class to serving as an effective coach for thirty students who receive their mathematical input from adaptive technologies, but still need teacher involvement in their learning."

• *Who will help teachers retool?* Principals will need to provide sustained, high-quality PD to support these shifts in beliefs, thinking, and practice—and it will need to be personalized because teachers are all over the learning curve.

• *What will be demanded of principals?* Can they move from a compliance mode to being coaches of semiautonomous teachers with lots of autonomous students? "How can a school leader handle inevitable discouragement with and overt resistance to personalized practices?" asks Tomlinson. "And if personalization suggests that the individual is at the center of all decisions, how does the building leader consistently model personalization for *teachers*?"

• *How about parents?* Even those who choose a school that embraces personalization will need to be brought up to speed on the exact details for their children: What are the standards for quality work? How should parents support their children's learning? How will teachers communicate with them on progress? And what about state standards?

• *What are the implications for the school environment?* This includes scheduling classes, class assignments for students, grading, discipline, class rankings, teacher evaluation, the use of classroom and library/media space—and the role of technology, materials, and support personnel.

We will fulfill the hopeful promise of personalization, Tomlinson concludes, "by deep thinking, informed planning, and wise leadership exercised reflectively and persistently, site by site, classroom by classroom. I hope we have that in us."

"Let's Celebrate Personalization: But Not Too Fast" by Carol Ann Tomlinson in *Educational Leadership*, March 2017 (Vol. 74, #6, pp. 10–15), summarized in Marshall Memo 676.

Differentiation by Pushing for Mastery

6 Benjamin Bloom's Mastery Learning

In this *NASSP Bulletin* article, Thomas Guskey (University of Kentucky) argues that one of the most powerful strategies for closing the achievement gap was developed by Benjamin Bloom in the 1970s: mastery learning. Extensive research over the decades has shown that mastery learning can have exceptionally positive effects on student learning. A research meta-analysis in 1990 concluded: "Few educational treatments of any sort were consistently associated with achievement effects as large as those produced by mastery learning" (Kulik, Kulik, and Bangert-Drowns). It has also been suggested that the impressive math achievement of Japanese students in recent decades is largely explained by classroom practices that strongly resemble mastery learning. In addition, researchers have found that mastery learning can improve students' confidence, attendance, engagement, and attitudes toward learning (Guskey and Pigott, 1988).

What *is* mastery learning? Here's a capsule summary. University of Chicago professor Benjamin Bloom is best known for his taxonomy of learning, but in the 1960s, he had another powerful insight. Most teachers, he observed, taught all of their students pretty much the same stuff within the same blocks of time. This worked just fine for some students, and they learned a lot. Others who were exposed to the same instruction learned somewhat less. And a third group of students learned very little. In other words, the same teaching delivered in the same amount of time produced major variations in student learning—the familiar bell-shaped curve of achievement. Over time, Bloom noted, this pattern produces an ever-widening achievement gap.

Bloom also noticed that when teachers gave tests at the end of a curriculum unit, they usually recorded the grades and moved on to the next unit, rarely following up with feedback and guidance that helped struggling students improve. These summative unit tests did little more than catalogue the typical pattern of unequal learning in most classrooms: some students got it, some sort of got it, and some didn't get it at all.

Bloom was troubled by these gap-widening classroom practices and compared them to two situations where learning goes well:

• One-on-one tutoring (perhaps the ideal setting for learning) – When the student makes an error, the tutor immediately points it out (feedback) and follows up by explaining and clarifying (correctives) until the student reaches mastery.

• Academically successful students – When these students make a mistake on a quiz or a test, they do not sulk or blame it on bad luck. They ask the teacher for help, look up the answer in the textbook or encyclopedia, or go back to the problem and figure out what they did wrong. This is every teacher's dream student.

Bloom took these insights, figured out a way to apply them to regular classrooms of twenty-five to thirty students, and dubbed it mastery learning. This was his plan:

- At the end of each curriculum unit, the teacher gives a brief *formative* assessment and uses the results to give students immediate feedback on their learning so far.
- Students who show mastery on this test (80 percent or above) go into an enrichment or extension loop involving special projects, reports, academic games, or complex problem-solving tasks.
- Students who are below mastery get individualized corrective instruction and/or are directed to textbook pages, learning kits, and other forms of correctives to straighten out their misconceptions and confusion.
- After one or two class periods working on these correctives, the below-mastery students take another formative test (different questions) to see if they have mastered the concepts or skills.

Bloom argued that this tailored, "just-in-time" approach would bring the advantages of the one-on-one tutorial and the good habits of high-achieving students into regular classrooms, allowing teachers to nip learning problems in the bud and prevent minor difficulties from accumulating and developing into chronic low achievement. Mastery learning, Guskey explains, "gives teachers a practical means to vary and differentiate their instruction to better meet students' individual learning needs. As a result, many more students learn well, master the important learning goals in each unit, and gain the necessary prerequisites for success in subsequent units …. This, in turn, would drastically reduce the variation in students' achievement levels [and] eliminate achievement gaps," squeezing the bell-shaped curve higher and to the right.

During the 1970s and 80s, mastery learning was widely adopted in the US and other countries and produced impressive results. Guskey believes that programs that were true to Bloom's ideas had four essential ingredients:

• *Feedback* – Mastery learning requires regular, formative classroom assessments that give students diagnostic, prescriptive feedback on what they have learned well and what they need to learn better. These assessments can be short pencil-and-paper quizzes, essays, compositions, projects, reports, performance tasks, skill demonstrations, or oral presentations.

• *Correctives* – Since no single method of instruction works best for all students, it's essential that teachers follow up on formative assessments with differentiated instruction. "To be optimally effective," Guskey writes, "correctives must be qualitatively different from the initial teaching. They must provide students who need it with an alternative approach and additional time to learn." This is challenging for teachers, but it's possible if schools provide time and encourage teacher teams to share ideas, materials, and expertise. The good news is that there are many more options now than there were thirty years ago: CDs, computer games, web-based activities, etc.

• *Enrichment* – Students who master the initial formative assessment should be challenged to go further in enrichment and extension activities. As with correctives, there are rich resources available to today's teachers. The correctives and enrichment phase of mastery learning pose classroom management challenges. Some suggestions: The two groups can pursue their different learning agendas in the same classroom, or two teachers can divide the groups between two classrooms. A third approach is to divide students into heterogeneous groups and have them work cooperatively until all students master the material.

• *Instructional alignment* – Guskey argues that for mastery learning to be effective, there must be a tight alignment between standards and learning goals, instruction, and assessment. If standards call for higher-order thinking and fluent writing and the teacher covers only lower-order skills and assesses with a multiple-choice test, even the best application of mastery learning will fail to produce high achievement. "Every time they administer an assessment, grade a paper, or evaluate students' learning," says Guskey, "teachers communicate to students what is most important to learn. Using mastery learning simply compels teachers to make these decisions more thoughtfully, intentionally, and purposefully."

Guskey says a frequent objection to mastery learning is that the corrective/enrichment phase takes too much time and teachers will not be able to cover the curriculum. Guskey agrees that teachers using mastery learning will move more slowly through the first few units. Students need to be introduced to the process and the correctives/enrichment loop takes additional time. But once students are familiar with the process, mastery learning classrooms typically move along at a brisker pace than other classes: students do better on formative assessments, less time is required for feedback and correctives, and all students move into subsequent units with stronger foundational skills and can therefore learn more quickly and efficiently.

"A Historical Perspective on Closing Achievement Gaps" by Thomas Guskey in *NASSP Bulletin*, September 2005 (Vol. 89, #644, pp. 76–89), summarized in Marshall Memo 105.

7. Combining Flipped Classrooms with Mastery Learning

In this article in *Educational Leadership*, Jonathan Bergmann and Aaron Sams (high-school chemistry teachers and early advocates of flipping) note that Benjamin Bloom's mastery learning theory is difficult to implement because of two challenges:
- How can teachers deliver direct instruction on new material when students are all over the place in terms of prior knowledge and achievement?
- How can teachers have the time to create multiple versions of assessments so that students can take them on subsequent attempts to achieve mastery?

Bergmann and Sams believe both problems can be solved by using new technological advances and a "flipped-mastery" model. Online videos make it possible for students to learn new content outside the classroom at their own pace (even catching up with months of missed work if they enter a classroom at midyear). And learning management systems and online quizzing (such as Moodle, BlackBoard, Canvas, My Big Campus, Schoology, Pathwright, Quia, and Haiku Learning) make it much easier for teachers to create multiple iterations of assessments.

Here is how Bergmann and Sams recommend planning and implementing a curriculum unit:
- Break the unit into learning objectives (for example, being able to calculate using the combined gas law).
- Create the videos and problem sets or decide on the textbook segments needed to learn each chunk of material.
- Decide on required activities that students need to complete—for example, hands-on experiments, inquiry-based labs, teacher demonstrations, and online simulations.

Bergmann and Sams created short videos (about fifteen minutes long for their tenth graders) for most objectives, required students to watch the videos outside of class, and then followed up in class with worksheets, hands-on activities, and lots of interaction.

Is this too much work for teachers? Bergmann and Sams say they already had most of the worksheets and activities from years of conventional chemistry teaching, and they don't recommend creating a video for every objective—for example, atomic theory was too abstract to be explained in a video. But they believe there's value in teachers making their own videos, because "students recognize that their teacher is taking the time to 'teach' them."

How does this continuous-progress approach deal with the tyranny of pacing guides and marking periods? At first Bergmann and Sams set up a curriculum calendar, telling students what they needed to accomplish each week, but students who learned at a slower pace weren't mastering content and fell behind. "We almost gave up because of this," say the authors. Then they hit upon a solution: they reorganized objectives to front-load the most essential material, and saved the nice-to-know material for the end of each grading period. That way, students who fell behind missed only the material that was less essential.

On the issue of assessments and grading, Bergmann and Sams decided on two layers to meet their school's requirements and still remain true to their model:

• Real-time checks for understanding – "The most important part of our assessment system was simple conversations we had with our students," they say. "When students felt they had mastered an objective, they approached us with their evidence, which usually included their worksheets, experiment write-ups, and notes from their interaction with an instructional video." The teachers quizzed students and were able to judge their mastery quite quickly and redirect them if they weren't there yet.

• Summative tests – Students were able to take unit assessments as many times as necessary to demonstrate mastery. Using Moodle as their learning-management system, Bergmann and Sams generated multiple versions of each assessment, with the computer randomly pulling from item banks so that each test was unique. Teachers followed up with students individually after tests and discussed items they got wrong. "We realized that these face-to-face interactions take a lot of time," they say. "But we were able to take the time by shifting all the low-level content delivery out of the classroom."

Bergmann and Sams feel strongly that flipped classrooms should not be used to reduce the number of teachers by replacing them with videos. "In the flipped-mastery model, teachers are even *more* valuable," they say. "Their time in the class is maximized. The teacher's main role is not to be a disseminator of knowledge, but rather a facilitator of learning."

DIFFERENTIATION AND PERSONALIZATION

"Flipping for Mastery" by Jonathan Bergmann and Aaron Sams in *Educational Leadership*, December 2013/January 2014 (Vol. 71, #4, pp. 24–29), summarized in Marshall Memo 515.

8. A Middle School Uses On-the-Spot Assessments to Differentiate

In this *Middle School Journal* article, Kristina Doubet (James Madison University) describes a rural middle school that was not making adequate progress despite a heavy training focus on differentiation. Teachers were pushing back, says Doubet: "It seemed daunting—even impossible—to regularly accommodate the wide range of readiness needs exhibited by their diverse student body. Some faculty members believed that weaving differentiation into daily lesson plans was simply not a realistic possibility because they feared pigeonholing students, were confused about how to incorporate additional scaffolding and challenges, and were frustrated with the ever-present pressures of time constraints."

The principal and instructional coach decided to make a tactical shift to focusing on formative (aka on-the-spot) assessments—checking on students' learning in bite-sized chunks during instruction. Teachers had previously been trained to plan lessons around KUD—know, understand, and be able to do—so when this was presented in an end-of-summer PD session, teachers saw it as a logical next step. However, while they had no problem coming up with assessment questions on K and D—factual knowledge and skills—they struggled with formulating good assessment questions on U—understanding the big ideas and essential concepts of a lesson.

What to do now? The leadership team asked teachers to practice crafting all three types of on-the-spot assessment questions and then, at the next grade-level meeting time, bring an assessment they'd used and discuss how it had gone. Trial and error crafting questions turned out to be an excellent "coach." What was most valuable was looking at actual student responses to the various exit tickets, quick quizzes, and short written responses teachers had used. "I loved seeing everyone else's examples," said one teacher. Teams zeroed in on glitches in some of the assessments as revealed by students' less-than-perfect responses. "The need to choose questions carefully is critical in order to get the information you need," said another teacher.

The instructional coach was pleased with how these teacher discussions went: "They asked genuine, trying-to-figure-it-all-out questions, took notes, and shared a lot of information and tips among themselves."

The leadership team's next step was asking teachers to give another quick assessment and bring the instrument and the results to a grade-level team meeting. Teachers arrived with a wide variety of assessments, and in the conversations that ensued, helped each other improve the prompts so they focused specifically on what they wanted to measure. For example, this three-two-one exit ticket:

- three ways to prevent global warming
- two possible effects of global warming
- one question you still have

was revised to more accurately measure the intended learning outcomes:

- three *causes* of global warming
- two things you can do to *prevent* global warming
- one possible *negative effect* global warming may have on your health

"At the same time," says Doubet, "teachers were realizing the importance of articulating the know (K), understand (U), and be-able-to-do (D) objectives before designing assessments." An eighth-grade teacher said, "Using the KUDs really helps me stay focused in my planning."

Teachers were impressed by the wealth of information they got from short assessments—how quickly and clearly they identified student misunderstanding and confusion and how much more timely and efficient these assessments were than traditional twenty-five-question unit tests. The team meetings devoted to constructing and reviewing these assessments was time well spent.

Up to this point, however, teachers were using on-the-spot assessment data to make decisions about *whole-class* instruction—not to differentiate according to the varying needs of their students. "It was time for teachers to start looking at assessment results in terms of the patterns they saw emerging within each class," says Doubet, "and then to use these patterns to determine groups and tasks to address learning gaps and strides revealed in these patterns." The instructional coach asked teachers to give another formative assessment and come to team meetings prepared to discuss how they had used the results to form groups and provide different tasks for those groups.

To the coach's delight, teachers immediately made the leap of connecting quick assessments to differentiation. "In essence," says Doubet, "the faculty had reintroduced themselves to differentiation, and they seemed quite pleased with the connection …. Differentiation was no longer a nebulous and hypothetical concept; rather, it was a natural response to actual student needs as revealed by nonthreatening assessment measures …. These teachers had inductively and independently come to adopt and even embrace the philosophy of assessment that is held by teachers in regularly differentiated classrooms." At the end of the year, teachers were eager to expand their repertoire of on-the-spot assessment techniques and learn more about how to scaffold instruction and follow up with subgroups of students.

"For a faculty that was 'differentiation weary,'" concludes Doubet, "this year of staff development had provided growth, motivation, and direction. Through focusing on formative assessment, they had come to see that differentiation is not a big, scary monster; rather, it naturally occurs when teachers set goals, see where students are in relationship to those goals, and respond accordingly. This realization opened teachers' eyes to the possibility that differentiation could, indeed, be part of their daily instruction rather than a strategy reserved for large, cumulative projects. It helped them know their students better and made them want to respond to their students' needs appropriately. It also helped them know themselves better as teachers and see themselves as learners."

This initiative seems to have been a contributing factor in significant gains in student achievement at the school that year.

"Formative Assessment Jump-Starts a Middle-Grades Differentiation Initiative" by Kristina Doubet in *Middle School Journal*, January 2012 (Vol. 43, #3, pp. 32–38), summarized in Marshall Memo 422.

Low-Tech Differentiation

9. Using Universal Design for Learning to Personalize Instruction

In this article in *Educational Leadership*, Kathleen McClaskey (Personalize Learning) touts the power of Universal Design for Learning (UDL) to reduce barriers to student learning and personalize instruction. Her simplified formula for UDL lesson planning—Access, Engage, Express—maximizes learning by taking into account how students:

- Access and process information;
- Engage with content;
- Express what they know and understand.

McClaskey suggests having students develop a learner profile to get insights about their own strengths, challenges, and other traits. Here's sample profile by a seventh-grade boy:

- *Access*: I'm an excellent reader with an extensive vocabulary. I have a hard time visualizing what I read or hear. I find it difficult to read online. I prefer to read hard copy and need a quiet place.
- *Engage*: I am good at organizing information and planning my time and like to research and investigate issues. I don't always understand what others say to me, and I get overwhelmed when trying to listen to multiple people at once. I prefer to work with a partner rather than a group, and I need a quiet place to stay focused.
- *Express*: I enjoy writing and illustrating nonfiction stories and reflecting on and measuring progress on projects. I don't like to speak in front of groups. I have a hard time presenting with technology. I sometimes stutter when I'm presenting. I prefer to write my ideas, and I need to have a script if I present.
- I am independent, quiet, funny, shy, reflective, focused, self-reliant.
- I like World War II history, geography, reading daily, organizing, writing, baseball, and drawing cartoons. I want to be a writer, cartoonist, or librarian.

This student discusses his profile with his teacher and decides to tackle his biggest challenges—presenting to a group and using technology—by working on an iMovie presentation for his class. He also plans outreach to librarians and writers to explore career ideas. The profile helps build the student's relationship with his teacher and shape the kind of environment in which he learns best.

DIFFERENTIATION AND PERSONALIZATION

McClaskey suggests that teachers look at a representative sample of four student profiles and plan lessons that present content and skills in ways that will maximize students' ability to access the material, engage in the lesson, and express their skills and understanding.

"Personalization and UDL: A Perfect Match" by Kathleen McClaskey in *Educational Leadership*, March 2017 (Vol. 74, #6, online only), summarized in Marshall Memo 678.

9. Differentiating Math with Open Questions and Parallel Tasks

In this *Educational Leadership* article, Canadian educator Marian Small bemoans the fact that so many elementary and middle-school math teachers believe that:
- All students should work on the same problem at the same time.
- Each math question should have one right answer.

"We need to find a way to meet the needs of a broader range of students with richer activities," says Small. How? With open questions and parallel tasks. Using this approach, she has found, "More students experience success with meaningful tasks, more students are engaged, more students see themselves as competent in math, and more students enjoy learning math." Here's how:

• *Open questions* – These are questions broad enough to challenge and involve a wide range of students—for example:
- The answer is 10. What might the question be?
- Create a sentence using the words and numbers: product, 8, almost, and 50.
- How are the formulas for the circumference and the area of a circle alike? How are they different?

As students grapple with open questions in class, they have choice (a key feature of differentiation), they're challenged at different levels, and they learn from each other's answers. Small suggests four strategies for creating open questions:
- Start with the answer—for example, *the tenth term in a pattern is 36. What might the eighth and ninth terms be? Describe the pattern.*
- Ask for similarities and differences—for example: *4, 8, 12, 16, 20—4, 7, 10, 13, 16. How are these two patterns alike? How are they different?*

- Allow choice in the data provided—for example, *Choose a value for the fourth number in the series that follows and calculate the mean: 4, 5, 6, __.*
- Ask students to create a sentence—for example, *Use the words increasing, decreasing, pattern, and the number 18 in a sentence.*

If students consistently choose not-very-challenging questions, the teacher should prompt them to step it up.

• *Parallel tasks* – This consists of assigning work that can be challenging to students of varying levels of achievement. Small suggests two steps:
- Let students choose between two problems, one harder than the other—for example, Choice 1: *There are 427 students in a school; 99 leave for a field trip. How many are in the school now?* Choice 2: *There are 61 students in third grade; 19 of them are in the library. How many are in classrooms?*
- Pose common questions for all students to answer—for example, *Before you calculated, could you tell if the number of students in classrooms was more or less than one-half of the total? What operation did you use and why? Would it be easier to solve if one student had left the classroom? How could you use mental math? How did you solve your problem? What was the answer?*

"Beyond One Right Answer" by Marian Small in *Educational Leadership*, September 2010 (Vol. 68, #1, pp. 28–32), summarized in Marshall Memo 351.

---

10. Personalizing Homework

In this *Educational Leadership* article, Cathy Vatterott (University of Missouri–Saint Louis) describes how five teachers in a suburban Massachusetts elementary school experimented with customized homework. Teachers generated topics based on their curriculum expectations, standards, unit big ideas, and individual needs. Some examples:
- Creating a song with lyrics on multiplication facts;
- Writing detailed descriptions of characters and plotlines in books read;
- Writing word problems based on real-world situations;
- Preparing a class presentation to build self-confidence and speaking skills;
- Writing reports on airplanes, snakes, 3-D structures, and other interests.

Then students decided on weekly projects and were responsible for monitoring their own progress.

Some students had difficulty with the responsibility of choosing a topic or project, staying on track, and completing the week's homework by the deadline (usually Monday). "They didn't know what to do when given a voice in directing their own learning," says Vatterott, "and most of them had no experience with self-assessing their strengths and weaknesses." Teachers found it took a lot of modeling and "gentle guidance" to bring these students up to speed—including a sheet with suggestions and weekly all-class discussions to generate ideas. Some students struggled with procrastination—Sunday night syndrome—and learned (with varying degrees of teacher support) how to pace themselves through the week. "The experience provided students with helpful insights into their work habits," says Vatterott. "Without this opportunity, they may not have learned these lessons until much later in their education."

Overall, how did this experiment go? Teachers told Vatterott that the element of choice and the wide range of options changed the hum-drum homework routine. "The assignments were generally longer, had more depth, and were much more creative when compared to traditional homework I had assigned," said one. "In my twenty-three years of teaching, I have never seen a group of students get this excited about homework," said another. There was definitely more work for teachers monitoring and evaluating multiple projects, but they said the payoff in student engagement made it worthwhile. Some parents were skeptical at first, but became converts when they saw their children's engagement and motivation.

And how about homework compliance compared to the traditional model? On balance, more students did their homework. "They are motivated and interested to complete what is assigned," said one teacher. "It is meaningful to them, so they do it—it's as simple as that!"

"One-Size-Doesn't-Fit-All Homework" by Cathy Vatterott in *Educational Leadership*, March 2017 (Vol. 74, #6, pp. 34–39), summarized in Marshall Memo 677.

High-Tech Differentiation

11 Silent Fifteen-Minute Online Dialogues among Students

"In a normal classroom discussion, power often rests with the quickest minds," says Jason Hilton (Slippery Rock University, PA) in this *AMLE Magazine* article. "The ability to quickly respond with a well-constructed verbal retort dominates conversation from debate halls to playground walls."

That's why, when he was teaching the Bill of Rights and related Supreme Court decisions to eighth graders, he had students spend the first fifteen minutes of each class in complete silence "conversing" with each other in an online discussion forum. "All discussion had to be online," says Hilton, "even if they were engaged in a discussion with someone sitting right next to them." When Hilton called time-out and closed the discussion forum so students could return to their wiki projects, the silence was broken by moans and complaints, and he had to promise to open the forum again at the end of class.

Reflecting on the experience, Hilton sees several advantages. First, the discussion board and wiki projects, which were student-centered, problem-based learning, "place every step, from content knowledge to argument synthesis, in the hands of the students." Second, "Even though the students were sitting in the same classroom, the digital medium through which the students were asked to participate presented an opportunity for students to overcome traditional barriers to classroom conversation. It no longer mattered what students looked like, who their friends were, or where they might be sitting. Instead, the more thoughtful students who may have been shut out of a traditional classroom dialogue by its rapid pace were able to take their time to craft a more powerful commentary." Finally, the online discussion seemed to energize students who were normally passive and silent.

Hilton acknowledges that without several key elements, this discussion would not have been as successful:
- A meaty and intriguing topic that would engage students at a high level;
- Being able to put a computer in front of every student;
- Requiring that all contributions and dialogue take place through silent keyboarding;

DIFFERENTIATION AND PERSONALIZATION

- Careful monitoring by the teacher during class and after hours to ensure appropriate, respectful exchanges;
- Knowing when to bring closure.

"The Power of Silent Discussion" by Jason Hilton in *AMLE Magazine*, February 2015 (Vol. 2, #6, pp. 29–31), summarized in Marshall Memo 573.

12. Enhancing Literature Circles with Blogging

In this *Educational Leadership* article, Massachusetts teacher Stacy Kitsis describes how she improved her high-school literature circles with online discussion groups. Previously, she had students choose books from a list of titles thematically related to the curriculum, assigned them to small groups, and had students read their books in literature circles about once a week, taking three to four weeks on each book. The downside, she says, was that conversations within the groups frequently stalled, even when students liked their books.

In her new approach, literature circles continued to meet once a week, with students posting comments on a class blog in between. Kitsis provided prompts (for example, *Talk about a moment that stood out for you*), quickly approved entries, and added comments. At first, she required that every student contribute one comment a week, limited to two hundred words, and provided a rubric on ideas and topic development, evidence from the text, style and voice, mechanics, and contributions to the group. Themes emerged from exchanges and students incorporated them into final products presented to the whole class.

Kitsis reports that blogging increased the level of student involvement inside and outside class and provided rapid responses to comments without putting undue strain on her. "In my classes," she says, "I saw students who almost never turned in traditional homework regularly contribute to the blog." Blog entries helped students get past the stilted silence to substantive discussions. Comments ranged from simple clarifications (openly admitting confusion), predictions, connections, evaluations, and challenges of others' ideas. Students who had been superficial before were forced to expand their contributions, and students who had never interacted with each other found themselves engaging in give-and-take online. Some groups got so involved in a book that they continued blogging after final assignments were handed in.

The system helped the teacher, too. "The virtual environment enabled me to listen in on multiple conversations without missing a word and without changing the dynamic with my presence," says Kitsis. "Because students interacted and got feedback from their peers throughout the discussion, they needed less feedback from me." Her role was supplying prompts, monitoring the online discussion, and visiting groups when they met during class time to share reactions, point out significant comments, give background information, and prod students to dig deeper.

The system was also paper-free. "I happily abandoned the messy stacks of spiral-bound reading journals, often containing weeks of assignments that students completed in one furious sprint the night before they were collected," says Kitsis. At first, she printed out posts and used the rubric to comment, but eventually she just gave a "check," "check-plus," or "check-minus" in her grade book.

Assessing the new system and looking at the final blog, Kitsis learned several practical lessons:

- Which prompts worked best, which books needed to be removed from the book list, and where students most often got confused;
- How to pace the work to accommodate students with limited Internet access;
- Deciding on alternative assignments for students who preferred not to share their ideas online;
- Deciding whether people outside the class could read the blog and contribute;
- Deciding whether to preapprove every post (which slows interaction) or monitor from a distance, intervening when necessary;
- Setting ground rules—first names only, no identifying information, and using separate accounts for school work and their personal lives.

"The Virtual Circle" by Stacy Kitsis in *Educational Leadership*, September 2010 (Vol. 68, #1, pp. 50–54), summarized in Marshall Memo 351.

13. Facebook Pages Engage Students in World Languages

In this article in *The Language Educator*, Joe Terantino and Karen Graf of Kennesaw State University (GA) and California French teacher Nicole Naditz discuss the use of Facebook in high-school world language classes. Like many teachers, Naditz had decided not to "friend" students on Facebook, but she was finding that e-mail and her website were not effective ways to communicate with many of her students. So she created a Facebook group page for each of her classes, her French Club, and the French Honor Society, all separate from her personal Friends page. (To set up the page, Facebook policy required that she include one "friend", so she enlisted another French teacher.) Students requested membership in the French pages (as did some parents), Naditz approved them, and they were off and running.

Naditz has found the Facebook pages were amazingly effective for rapidly getting the word out to all her students about club events, French-language resources, class news, francophone world news, her video tutorials, announcements, and helpful Internet links. Students loved using the pages to ask questions about homework or any of the content and to share resources with their classmates. Spontaneously, almost all communication on the pages was in French.

Terantino and Graf are equally enthusiastic, listing four benefits to using Facebook in world language classes. First, it gets students engaged in informal communication with peers in the target language in a familiar format. Second, it allows easy sharing of culturally relevant photos, videos, and music, promoting social and language learning. Third, "the nature of student-to-student and student-to-instructor interactions is more multidimensional than in traditional writing assignments," they say. Feedback is more rapid and comes from teachers and peers.

Finally, they say, "we have never encountered such genuine excitement on behalf of the students when participating in an activity using the target language. We could not have predicted the sheer amount of linguistic production from the students, especially that which emerged outside of the formal writing assignments. The students seemed to enjoy lurking, checking, reading, and writing—completely in Spanish. Even students who were typically reserved and nonparticipatory in class quickly emerged as highly productive students in this environment."

"Like all Internet resources, Facebook is merely a tool," Naditz concludes. "In and of itself, it will not improve instruction, nor will it ensure that all students more actively engage in the curriculum or automatically become more proficient. It is the way in which teachers employ all the tools at their disposal that will determine whether or not we achieve those goals."

Terantino and Graf add three cautionary notes: It's important to protect students' and instructors' privacy, so access to classroom pages must be restricted. Clear guidelines are needed on appropriate communication on classroom Facebook pages. And finally, they recommend not correcting errors in language usage on Facebook for fear of discouraging the free flow of ideas and content. Students are graded on those aspects of the curriculum in formal papers and tests.

EFFECTIVE PEDAGOGY

"Using Facebook in the Language Classroom as Part of the Net Generation Curriculum" by Joe Terantino and Karen Graf, and sidebar, "'Friend' or Foe: Facebook in a High-School Language Class" by Nicole Naditz, in *The Language Educator*, November 2011 (Vol. 6, #6, pp. 44–47), summarized in Marshall Memo 411.

14. Using Twitter in a Science Classroom

In this article in *Middle School Journal*, Ryan Becker (Woodstock, Vermont, teacher) and Penny Bishop (University of Vermont–Burlington) describe Becker's use of Twitter in his middle-school science classroom:

• Personalized and relevant curriculum – Connecting students to reputable, relevant scientific people and organizations in real time—Neil de Grasse Tyson, Bill Nye, PBS's Nova, Discovery Channel's MythBusters, NPR's Science Friday, and more.

• Formative assessment – Becker's classes have mini-discussions using tweets, he can display responses on his interactive whiteboard, and he uses Twtpoll to check for understanding and immediately discuss errors and misconceptions.

• An authentic audience – Students constantly tweet ideas, assignments, projects, suggestions, and photographs to each other, broadening the reach of their thinking.

• Embedded literacy – Students get plenty of practice with succinct writing as they share analyses and observations.

"Like any new initiative, especially one involving technology, the path to implementing Twitter in a middle school is not without challenges," say Becker and Bishop. These included:

- Getting students set up with Twitter accounts; it turned out that significant guidance was necessary to overcome technical glitches.
- Finding time within classes to guide students in how to use Twitter; this included setting norms and expectations on personal conduct, overcoming technical problems, and gathering feedback on how it was going.
- Managing students' encounters with objectionable material from the outside world, including occasional use of profanity and sexually suggestive follower requests.

Despite these challenges, say Becker and Bishop, "the benefits of Twitter outweigh the drawbacks. In an age where media is constantly competing for students' attention, and where messages in popular media are often at odds with in-school norms and expectations, opportunities to model, discuss, and practice the appropriate use of Web 2.0 technologies are critical."

"'Think Bigger About Science': Using Twitter for Learning in the Middle Grades" by Ryan Becker and Penny Bishop in *Middle School Journal*, April 2016 (Vol. 47, #3, pp. 4–16), summarized in Marshall Memo 634.

15. Frontchannel and Backchannel Digital Discussions

In this *Educational Leadership* article, Jeffrey Carpenter (Elon University) says that as a young teacher, he believed whole-class conversations with his high-school students went well. "A few extroverted or extra-motivated students could be counted on to contribute," he remembers, "and discussions would pass by pleasantly enough. A decent quantity and quality of ideas were shared, and awkward silences were rare."

But over time, Carpenter realized that only a handful of students were taking part while the majority tuned out or engaged in an illicit "backchannel," whispering, note-passing, flirting. "When teachers ask, 'Any questions?'" he says, "they often encounter silence, even though the questions are lurking out there."

The solution? Allowing students to use mobile devices to create a legitimate "backchannel" that engages all students in the discussion. "In the backchannel," says Carpenter, "students can offer opinions, answer questions, analyze frontchannel content, or share supplementary information." Here are four scenarios:

• *Collaborative conversations* – A US history teacher asks what students found confusing in their Civil War homework. Several students speak while others use the class's Todaysmeet.com chat room to chime in. The teacher skims the backchannel content, sees confusion about the economic differences between the North and South, and verbally clarifies the point.

• *Parallel discussions* – A small group of ninth graders debates who was to blame for the tragedy in *Romeo and Juliet*, while students in a fishbowl use digital devices to summarize, comment on, and add to the conversation. The teacher monitors frontchannel and backchannel discussions, and when there's a lull says, "I see here in the doc that Kaitlyn thinks that if Friar Lawrence hadn't gotten involved, then nothing would have happened. Any thoughts on that?" A student blurts out, "But he had good intentions!" and both channels light up.

- *Interactive notes* – Eighth-grade science students conduct a lab on using citrus fruits to build batteries; they tweet their predictions, questions, or pictures of collected data on the class-specific hashtag. "Will the size of the fruit matter?" asks one student. "Some fruits will be better batteries than others," tweets another. After a few minutes, the teacher displays all the tweets and leads a frontchannel discussion while students continue to tweet their suggestions.

- *Formative assessment* – Toward the end of a world-history class on the spread of global capitalism, the teacher asks students to summarize the day's most-important idea in Socrative, then displays responses and invites students to vote on the best. This sparks further discussion, and the teacher makes a mental note to clarify a misconception in the next lesson and create a Do Now on labor unions.

Carpenter believes digital backchannels can involve far more students, enhance student-to-student interaction, and improve the breadth and depth of discussions. He offers these suggestions:

- Make sure all students have access to devices (sometimes working in pairs).
- Establish norms for helpful and unhelpful backchannel comments.
- Monitor the backchannel and keep comments focused on the topic.
- Have agreed-upon "devices off" signals to return to an all-class discussion.

"Digital Backchannels" by Jeffrey Carpenter in *Educational Leadership*, May 2015 (Vol. 72, #8, pp. 54–58), summarized in Marshall Memo 588.

Professional Learning Suggestions for Chapter Eight: Differentiation and Personalization

Examining the Many Faces of Differentiation and Personalization

Adapting instruction to meet the needs of diverse learners is not new. Back when we had one-room schoolhouses, teachers had to find ways to teach students of widely varying ages with vastly different readiness levels. However, schools are far from having mastered this skill. Despite the emergence of theories about differentiation and personalization and the hope that technology would help educators turbo-charge their ability to tailor instruction to individual student needs, we still have a long way to go. Below are exercises to help educators grapple with this challenging task.

I. Understanding Differentiation and Personalization

Below are three exercises to help teachers think about and discuss the ideas behind differentiation and personalization and consider what is the problem for which individualization is the answer.

A. Have teachers read and discuss "I Wish My Teacher Knew…"(Donna de la Cruz article-summary 1). This is a very short piece that will help teachers understand the rationale for differentiating and personalizing learning. Have teachers read it silently and then discuss in pairs the implications of this article-summary for teaching and learning. If you have time before this meeting, ask teachers to have their students complete the prompt, "I wish my teacher knew…" and bring those responses to the meeting to discuss as well.

B. Have your school come up with a common definition of "differentiation" and "personalization."
It's hard for your teachers to adopt principles of differentiation or personalization if everyone is using a different definition. Have your teachers read through the articles in the first section (article-summaries 2, 3, 4, and 5) as a start, and then also look online to find some common definitions. Below are some sample definitions or explanations of these terms:

EFFECTIVE PEDAGOGY

> "Effective attention to the learning needs of each student … getting to know each student and orchestrating the learning environment, assessments, and instruction so all students learn what's being taught" and to be sure to differentiate by content (what is taught), process (how it's taught), and product (how students are asked to demonstrate their learning). (Carol Ann Tomlinson in summary 2)

> "Personalized learning is a process and series of decisions schools and districts make to create learning environments more aligned to the interests, identities, and abilities of all students as they achieve mastery of skills and standards at their own pace." (Shawn C. Rubin and Cathy Sanford in *Pathways to Personalization*, p. 1)[1]

> Personalized learning defined as "prioritizing a clear understanding of the needs and goals of each individual student and the tailoring of instruction to address those needs and goals." From a Gates Foundation study quoted on p.xiv in *Deeper Learning* by Michael Fullan, Joanne Quinn, and Joanne McEachen.[2]

    1. After reading article-summaries and searching online, have teachers put their favorite definition (or create one based on what they've read) in large print on a piece of paper and post that definition on a wall (this works virtually, as well, with an online collaborative board like in Padlet or Nearpod).

    2. Have all teachers do a gallery walk to read the posted definitions they each found or created. They should put their initials next to any *terms* in the definitions they liked.

    3. The facilitator should pull out the terms from all of the definitions that have the most initials. From those terms, either a subcommittee or the whole group should create a common definition of differentiation and personalization that the school will plan to use.

C. Have teachers engage in a debate: "Does it work to weave differentiation into daily lesson plans? Should we focus on mastery learning instead?"

    1. Divide teachers into two groups and assign one to be *pro* (yes, it works to weave differentiation into daily plans) and the other to be *con* (no, it doesn't, and the focus should be on mastery learning) and have them sit in these two groups.

---

[1] Shawn C. Rubin and Cathy Sanford, *Pathways to Personalization: A Framework for School Change* (Cambridge, MA: Harvard Education Press, 2018) 1.

[2] Michael Fullan, Joanne Quinn, and Joanne McEachen, *Deeper Learning: Engage the World Change the World* (Thousand Oaks, CA: Corwin Press, 2017) xiv.

PROFESSIONAL LEARNING SUGGESTIONS FOR CHAPTER EIGHT

2. Ask all teachers to silently read "Framing Differentiation in Terms of Intentions and Outcomes" (Kim Marshall article-summary 2), "Three Myths About Personalization" (Paul France article-summary 3), and "Benjamin Bloom's Mastery Learning" (Thomas Guskey article-summary 6).

3. Give each group a piece of chart paper and ask the *pro* group to write down all of the reasons they can argue for differentiation while the *con* group writes down reasons we should shift the focus to mastery learning.

4. Once each group has prepared their thoughts on the chart paper, you can do a simple debate or just have everyone discuss the ideas in the articles. The goal is to have an in-depth discussion about mastery learning and differentiation. Be sure to weave this question into the debate, *"What is the problem for which differentiation is the solution?"*

II. Let's Explore Examples of Differentiation and Personalization and Take Action

There are many ideas in the articles for ways teachers can differentiate and personalize learning. In fact, teachers might already be doing some of these things without even knowing it. This section exposes teachers to a variety of ways to meet the needs of their learners and gets them to take some action steps to do so.

A. Have teachers explore what a cycle of mastery learning might actually look like.

1. Have teachers read "Benjamin Bloom's Mastery Learning" (Guskey article-summary 6) and discuss the implications of these ideas for their own teaching.

2. Next, have teachers work in pairs with someone who teaches a grade or subject as close to theirs as possible. Have them plan an actual upcoming unit by taking Bloom's ideas about a cycle for mastery learning (starting with teachers giving a brief *formative assessment*) and mapping out how and when they would use Bloom's ideas (formative assessment, enrichment, individualized corrective instruction, and another formative assessment).

B. Have teachers learn about high-tech or low-tech examples of differentiation and personalization. Meeting the needs of individual students is often described as making learning more aligned to students' readiness, interests, and learning profiles. The article-summaries in the third and fourth sections of this chapter—Low-Tech Differentiation and High-Tech Differentiation—share different examples of ways teachers have attempted to do this by differentiating instruction.

1. To use a jigsaw approach to introduce all of the low- and high-tech ideas for differentiation to teachers, start by asking teachers to choose two of the following article-summaries: "Combining Flipped Classrooms with Mastery Learning" (7), "Using Universal Design for Learning to Personalize Instruction" (9), "Differentiating Math with Open Questions and Parallel Tasks" (10), "Silent Fifteen-Minute Online Dialogues Among Students" (12), "Enhancing Literature Circles with Blogging" (13), "Facebook Pages Engage Students in World Languages" (14), and "Frontchannel and Backchannel Digital Discussions" (16).

2. Have teachers read the two articles they chose silently and note whether the technique being used helps to differentiate by readiness, interest, learner profile, or several of these. They should enter their notes into the handout on the next page that they will then bring with them when they circulate to do the jigsaw.

PROFESSIONAL LEARNING SUGGESTIONS FOR CHAPTER EIGHT

Article-Summary	What's the Low- or High-Tech Idea?	Does This Differentiate by Readiness, Interest, Learner Profile, or Several?
"Combining Flipped Classrooms with Mastery Learning" (summary 7)		
"Using Universal Design for Learning to Personalize Instruction" (summary 9)		
"Differentiating Math with Open Questions and Parallel Tasks" (summary 10)		
"Silent Fifteen-Minute Online Dialogues among Students" (summary 12)		
Enhancing Literature Circles with Blogging" (summary 13)		
"Facebook Pages Engage Students in World Languages" (summary 14)		
"Frontchannel and Backchannel Digital Discussions" (summary 16)		

3. Then have teachers walk around the room and find someone who has read a different article-summary. Teachers will share a description of one of the two techniques they learned about, how it serves to differentiate, and whether they've ever tried anything like this. The listener can take notes on the handout above. Do this for several rounds until teachers have learned about the ideas in three different article-summaries.

4. Finally, of all of the techniques they've read about or learned about, have them choose one to implement within the next two weeks. Ask them to create a plan, and then find an accountability partner with whom to share their plan and choose dates to observe each other trying

these techniques. They should also choose a date to share their observations and feedback with each other.

C. Brainstorm ways to personalize something almost all teachers do—give homework.
A number of the article-summaries in this chapter describe a larger and more in-depth process of ensuring that instruction meets the needs of individual students. But it is also possible for teachers to make smaller changes to weave personalization into their daily lesson plans.

1. Ask teachers to bring their homework assignment for the next day to this meeting.

2. Next, have all teachers read "Personalizing Homework" (the Cathy Vatterott article-summary 11) and come up with one way they might personalize the homework assignment they brought to this meeting.

3. Have teachers sit in groups of four. One teacher at a time starts by presenting the homework assignment and then shares his/her idea to personalize that assignment. The three other teachers brainstorm *other* ways to personalize the assignment and the presenting teacher writes these down. Continue this activity with each of the other three teachers presenting.

4. Teachers will now have a list of different ways to personalize their next homework assignment. They should choose one or several ways to do so and report out about the results either at the next meeting, by email, or face-to-face with the three teachers in their group.

III. Responding to Pushback About Differentiation and Personalization

There has been pushback to the idea of differentiating or personalizing instruction from teachers, leaders, and researchers. Some researchers state there is little evidence of its impact on student learning and some teachers believe it's a fool's errand when they have thirty students in the classroom and far too many standards to teach already. In this section, the leadership team will think more deeply about differentiation and personalization and explore ways to make it more effective so they can address this pushback.

A. Have the leadership team discuss the school's current state of affairs when it comes to differentiation and personalization.
Gather the leaders at your school to discuss the following questions:

PROFESSIONAL LEARNING SUGGESTIONS FOR CHAPTER EIGHT

1. In what ways does our school currently create a learning community that addresses the needs, interests, identities, and abilities of individual students?

2. In what ways do we still need to grow in this area?

3. What are the obstacles we currently face or we imagine we will face in differentiating and personalizing learning for all students?

4. What questions do we have about tailoring learning to the needs of individual students? What more information do we need?

B. Have the leadership team rethink what differentiation and personalization could be.

To help the school leaders rethink what it could mean to meet the needs of individual students, have them read a few article-summaries with the four questions from Part A in mind:

1. Have the school leaders silently read "Framing Differentiation in Terms of Intentions and Outcomes" (Kim Marshall article-summary 2), "Benjamin Bloom's Mastery Learning" (Thomas Guskey article-summary 6), and "A Middle School Uses On-the-Spot Assessments to Differentiate" (Kristina Doubet article-summary 8).

2. As leaders read, ask them to mark up the article-summaries as follows: a check mark next to those things the school already does (see Question 1 above); a leaf for areas the school still needs to grow in (see Question 2 above); an exclamation point for any obstacles the school faces or might face (see Question 3 above); and a question mark for any questions they have or information they need (see Question 4 above).

3. After reading and marking up these three article-summaries, have the school leaders discuss what aspects of differentiation and personalization they would like to strengthen or initiate at their school. Note that you may want to hold off on this step and assign everyone to do more research as there is no complete soup-to-nuts plan among the articles for implementing full personalization in your school. But once research and discussions have occurred, create an action plan with your leadership team for addressing the needs of all of your students as individuals at your school with a fresh approach.

C. EDUCATORS CONTINUOUSLY IMPROVING

Chapter Nine: **Results-Focused Teacher Teams**

Research Insights on Teamwork   315
Collaboratively Analyzing Assessments   321
Overcoming What Can Go Wrong   329
Singletons and Scheduling   338
Professional Learning Suggestions   344

Chapter Ten: **Professional Learning That Works**

Past and Present PD Shortcomings   355
Characteristics of Effective Professional Learning   361
Practical Applications   368
Innovative Practices and Cautionary Notes   373
Professional Learning Suggestions   381

Chapter Eleven: **Teacher Leadership**

Addressing the Barriers to Teacher Leadership   390
Distributing Leadership   395
Tips for Teacher Leaders   403
Other Pathways for Teacher Leadership   407
Professional Learning Suggestions   416

Chapter Nine: Results-Focused Teacher Teams

If the goal is to increase student learning, one of the biggest mistakes education leaders can make is allowing teachers to work in isolation.
—Greg Kushnir

Many schools say they have "professional learning communities," but what exactly is a PLC? The basic concept is collective ownership of student achievement, but it's been implemented in multiple ways, including what Richard DuFour and Douglas Reeves dubbed "PLC lite." The articles in this chapter look at the fundamentals of teamwork, teachers collaboratively analyzing assessments, overcoming what can go wrong, and how to deal with "lonely singleton" teachers and scheduling.

Research Insights on Teamwork – Atul Gawande tells how doctors have shifted from a "cowboy" ethos—lots of autonomy—to working closely with colleagues to solve problems and prevent errors. Julia Rozovsky reports what Google identified as the keys to successful teamwork: psychological safety, dependability, structure and clarity, meaning, and impact. Ronald Gallimore and three colleagues describe what happens when teamwork is skillfully orchestrated in schools: teachers attributing success to their own efforts; increased willingness to try new methods; and accepting accountability for results. Karin Chenoweth describes how teamwork operates in schools that beat the socioeconomic odds.

Collaboratively Analyzing Assessments – Richard DuFour describes grade-level teacher teams analyzing the results of common assessments, following up with students, and improving teaching practices. Jan Matthews, Susan Trimble, and Anne Gay share detailed recommendations for teacher data meetings, including premeeting preparation and structured agendas. Lissa Pijanowski recommends that schools orchestrate three layers of conversation about interim assessment results: individual teachers, grade-level teams, and the full faculty. Jen Munson and Tamyka Morant describe teacher teams looking at students' math work, identifying misconceptions and trends, and improving curriculum, assessments, and instruction.

Overcoming What Can Go Wrong – Susan Trimble, Anne Gay, and Jan Matthews describe five stages of teachers moving from confusion and distrust to accepting and using student data to improve teaching and learning. Richard DuFour and Douglas Reeves bemoan "PLC lite" and list the key elements of successful teacher teamwork. Michael Wasta says the missing element in many teacher data meetings is taking a hard look at which instructional practices are working and which aren't. Greg Kushnir reminds us of ten elements that can't be overlooked in establishing a strong collaborative culture.

Singletons and Scheduling – Casey Reason describes how four "lonely singleton" teachers of German met every week on Google Hangouts to discuss curriculum and assessments. Breez Longwell Daniels reports how a small middle school, where every teacher was a singleton, used vertical and horizontal teams to accomplish the same goals as larger schools with grade-level teams. Anne Jolly presents a wide range of ways to create blocks of time for teacher team meetings, ranging from better use of existing time to radical rescheduling.

Questions to Consider

- What makes some teams especially effective?
- What is the role of principals and facilitators in teacher teams?
- What are some barriers to teacher teams getting results?

Research Insights on Teamwork

① Does a Paradigm Shift in Medicine Apply to Schools?

In this *New Yorker* article, Boston surgeon/writer Atul Gawande describes the sea change that's occurred in medical practice over the last two generations. Doctors can no longer be "cowboys," he says—independent entrepreneurs who handle almost everything and hold all the important information in their heads. In the old days, "One needed only an ethic of hard work, a prescription pad, a secretary, and a hospital willing to serve as one's workshop …. The nature of knowledge lent itself to prizing autonomy, independence, and self-sufficiency among our highest values …." Now, says Gawande, "… medicine's complexity has exceeded our individual capabilities as doctors."

The secret of the most successful hospitals and health-care organizations is that they function like a *system*. "By a system," says Gawande, "I mean that the diverse people actually work together to direct their specialized capabilities toward common goals for patients. They are coordinated by design. They are pit crews. To function this way, however, you must cultivate certain values that are uncommon in practice and not often taught." In fact, the key values are a radical departure from the old cowboy mentality. They include:

• *Data about results* – It's essential to know when you've succeeded and when you've failed. People in the most-effective systems put considerable effort into collecting information, refining it, and understanding the implications for their work.

• *Systematic solutions to recurring glitches* – Successful practitioners identify recurring problems and implement fixes. In aviation, engineering, and medicine, one of the most successful innovations has been the checklist. "Checklists seem lowly and simplistic," says Gawande, "but they help fill in for the gaps in our brains and between our brains. They emphasize group precision in execution."

• *Coordination so the system approaches zero errors* – The challenge is getting colleagues along the entire chain executing at a level that produces very high-quality results. This requires humility (no matter how experienced or smart you are, you'll occasionally fail), standardization (following best practices every time will reduce failures), teamwork (others can save you from failure), and discipline.

"These values are the opposite of autonomy, independence, self-sufficiency," says Gawande. "Many doctors fear the future will end daring, creativity, and the joys of thinking that medicine has had. But nothing says teams cannot be daring or creative or that your work with others will not require hard thinking and wise judgment. Success under conditions of complexity still demands these qualities." Fewer cowboys. More pit crews.

Researching this article, Gawande interviewed an actual cowboy: "He described to me how cowboys do their jobs today, herding thousands of cattle. They have tightly organized teams, with everyone assigned specific positions and communicating with each other constantly. They have protocols and checklists for bad weather, emergencies, the inoculations they must dispense. Even the cowboys, it turns out, function like pit crews now. It may be time for us to join them."

"Cowboys and Pit Crews" by Atul Gawande in the *New Yorker*, May 26, 2011, summarized in Marshall Memo 596.

② What Google Learned About Its Most Successful Teams

In this article in *re:Work*, Julia Rozovsky reports on what Google found in a two-year study of why some of its teams were more effective than others. After conducting two hundred-plus interviews, they gleaned hundreds of attributes and thought they could crunch the perfect mix of individual traits and skills—perhaps one Rhodes scholar, two extroverts, one expert engineer, and a PhD.

"We were dead wrong," says Rozovsky. "*Who* is on a team matters less than how the team members interact, structure their work, and view their contributions. So much for that magical algorithm."

The conclusion of all their work boiled down to the following dynamics shared by highly successful teams:

- *Psychological safety* – Team members feel comfortable taking risks and being vulnerable in front of each other (this was by far the most important).
- *Dependability* – Team members get things done on time and meet a high standard of excellence.
- *Structure and clarity* – Roles, plans, and goals are clear.
- *Meaning* – The work is personally important to each member.

- *Impact* – People fundamentally believe that what they are doing matters.

Rozovsky says that any team can do a quick analysis of its internal workings by taking a close look at performance on each of these factors.

"The Five Keys to a Successful Google Team" by Julia Rozovsky in *re:Work*, November 17, 2015, summarized in Marshall Memo 701.

③ Byproducts of Effective Teacher Teamwork

In this *Elementary School Journal* article, researchers Ronald Gallimore, Bradley Ermeling, William Saunders, and Claude Goldenberg report on their successful work planning instruction and using assessment data with grade-level teams in Title I schools. The result was that teachers were more aware of students' needs, planned better lessons, and used better instructional practices. The researchers noticed these shifts:

• *Changes in attribution* – As teachers tried new practices learned from team discussions, they began to attribute student gains to their own teaching—in contrast with teachers in schools not implementing these practices, who tended to attribute student achievement to external factors such as socioeconomic conditions, students' poor proficiency in English, lack of ability, or low levels of parent involvement.

• *A sense of efficacy* – The work of teacher teams changed what had previously been an *I taught it and they didn't learn it* approach. Instead, when a classroom strategy didn't work, teachers took responsibility for trying different approaches until they saw progress. "We hypothesize," write the authors, "that critical learning opportunities arise when teachers focus on a specific student need over a period of time and shift to an emphasis on *figuring out* an instructional solution that produces a detectable improvement in learning, not just *trying out* a variety of instructional activities or strategies."

• *Administrators balancing support and pressure* – The changes in these schools wouldn't have happened without principals supporting teacher teams and holding them accountable for keeping up the inquiry/improvement process until they saw tangible results. Teachers said it mattered that the principal built trust, and wasn't critical or evaluative, keeping students' interests front and center. It was also important that the principal remained "firm," teachers said, pushing back against statements like, "Well, I don't know if I can do this" and "I don't know if my children can do this." One teacher remembered the principal saying, "Look, this is what you need to do. So like it or not, do it."

The researchers identified a number of key prerequisites to getting this dynamic operating in a school:

• *Job-alike teams* – Ideally, these would be three to seven teachers who teach the same subject or course to students at the same grade level (for example—third grade, seventh-grade pre-algebra, or ninth-grade English). "Absent a common task immediately relevant to each teacher's own classroom, it is difficult to create and sustain the kind of inquiry cycle observed in the scale-up schools and others in which we now work," say the researchers.

• *Clear goals* – "To be successful," they write, "teams need to set and share goals to work on that are immediately applicable to their classrooms. Without such goals, teams will drift toward superficial discussions and truncated efforts to test alternative instruction."

• *Trained peer-facilitators* – Skillful facilitation is vital to sustaining teams to the point where they begin showing results. Peer leadership is preferable to administrators leading meetings, say the authors. "Peer-facilitators are uniquely positioned to model 'a leap of faith,' frame the work as an investigation, help the group 'stick with it,' and guide protocol use as a full participant in the inquiry process. Teacher-facilitators are trying out in their classrooms the same lessons as everyone else in the group." Another advantage is that peer leaders free up literacy and math coaches and administrators to move from team to team and provide support where it's most needed.

• *Inquiry-focused protocols* – Each team followed these steps: identify appropriate and worthwhile student learning goals; find or develop appropriate means to assess student progress; bring to the table expertise from colleagues and others to accomplish the goals; plan, prepare, and deliver lessons; use evidence from classrooms to evaluate results; and reflect on the process to decide what to do next. This structured approach increased teachers' focus on cause-effect planning, getting them to pay close attention to students' needs, gather helpful classroom artifacts and observations, constantly question existing instructional practices, look carefully at alternative approaches, and use evidence to make decisions.

• *Stable settings* – "For teams to stick with the protocol long enough to see and attribute improved student learning to their teaching," say the researchers, "there must be a stable, protected setting in which the work of inquiry can get done." Administrative vision and support were crucial to keeping the process going—time for meetings, consistent membership, facilitation, and support.

"Moving the Learning of Teaching Closer to Practice: Teacher Education Implications of School-Based Inquiry Teams" by Ronald Gallimore, Bradley Ermeling, William Saunders, and Claude Goldenberg in *Elementary School Journal*, May 2009 (Vol. 109, #5, pp. 537–553), summarized in Marshall Memo 307.

④ Key Characteristics of Highly Effective Schools

In this article in *American Educator*, Karin Chenoweth (Education Trust) describes the variables she has observed in her research on beat-the-odds schools:

• *Teacher collaboration* – "No one teacher can be an expert in all aspects of the curriculum, all possible ways to teach it, and every child who sits in his or her class," says Chenoweth. "But every teacher should have expertise that can be tapped by other teachers to improve their knowledge of their subject, their teaching skill, and their knowledge of their students." Effective schools carve out regular common planning time for same-grade and same-subject teacher teams and set cultural norms for those meetings, including:

- If you don't say it in the meeting, don't say it in the parking lot.
- Talk about the things the school can control.
- Focus on teaching and learning, not administrative matters that are more efficiently handled in bulletins or e-mails.

Chenoweth found that principals in highly effective schools often sat in on meetings at the beginning of the year to make sure the norms were well-established, then visited from time to time and received reports from group members. Principals made a point of hiring highly competent, collaborative teachers and made the school's cultural expectations explicit to applicants up front. They were also quick to counsel out or remove teachers who were not willing or able to abide by collaborative norms.

• *A laserlike focus on what students need to learn* – The previous generation of school reform had things exactly backwards, says Chenoweth: considerable teacher freedom on *what* to teach but lots of top-down control on *how* to teach it, including one teaching fad after another. "Teachers should be the experts in *how* to teach," she says, "but on their own, they should not be deciding *what* to teach …. That doesn't mean that there shouldn't always be room in a school day or year for teachers to share their passion for the more obscure plays of Wiliam Shakespeare. But the bulk of the curriculum should be devoted to the knowledge and skills that we as a society have decided are essential for students to become educated citizens."

Fortunately, there is a growing consensus on a common set of expectations for high-school graduation that will launch an adolescent into college success and a decent job. The hard part is teasing those expectations back from twelfth grade to kindergarten and coming up with a *manageable* list of knowledge and skills for each grade. Teachers then need to create curriculum calendars and unit and lesson plans to execute the curriculum—something that's best done by teams of teachers collaborating in their common planning time. Chenoweth reports that some of the effective schools she's visited give new teachers a full set of lesson plans to help them get through their rookie year.

• *Interim assessments* – To check how well students are learning the curriculum, teachers in Chenoweth's exemplary schools give frequent, common assessments and follow up relentlessly, analyzing, reteaching, tutoring, and fine-tuning their units and lessons, always asking what led to the wrong answer. "Sometimes it is just inattention," she writes. "Sometimes it is a misunderstanding of a word or a lack of background knowledge. In this way, teachers catch small problems before they grow."

• *Collaborative data-driven instruction* – Beyond using interim assessments to help struggling students, teacher teams in highly effective schools use data to see patterns that aren't visible to teachers on a day-to-day basis. For example, in one school teachers noticed that vocabulary was the weakest area for all groups of students, not just English language learners, and launched a schoolwide initiative in vocabulary development.

"Piece by Piece: How Schools Solved the Achievement Puzzle and Soared" by Karin Chenoweth in *American Educator*, Fall 2009 (Vol. 33, #3, pp. 15–23), summarized in Marshall Memo 305.

Collaboratively Analyzing Assessments

5 A Teacher Learns How to Work with His Colleagues

In this article in *Educational Leadership*, the late Richard DuFour looks back with sorrow on his early teaching years in the 1970s. He remembers giving tests on Friday, spending hours marking them over the weekend, and returning students' work on Monday. "I had a sense of smug self-satisfaction," he says, "because I believed that my challenging assessments, my willingness to devote hours to grading papers, and my commitment to returning tests promptly was proof positive that I was a great teacher."

As students looked over their tests, DuFour would go over items that had caused problems. He then gathered up the tests, signaling that the unit was over, grades were final, and they were moving on. "It never even occurred to me to review the results with colleagues, to use this evidence of student learning to inform and improve my teaching, or to provide students with additional time and support to master the content." The bell-shaped curve of grades was what it was. Students who performed well were a testament to successful teaching, and students who didn't do well either lacked ability or hadn't worked hard enough.

DuFour believes that in recent decades, US educators have made a significant shift. We've moved "from an era in which what was taught, how learning was assessed, what instructional materials were used, and how grades were assigned were all determined by the individual teacher to whom a student was randomly assigned. Now we're asking teachers to work in collaborative teams to achieve common goals for which they are mutually accountable." At the heart of the new process is teams analyzing the results of common interim assessments and asking themselves four questions:

• *Which students were unable to demonstrate proficiency on this assessment?* The team identifies these students by name and gets them into a "system of intervention" that is timely (immediately after the assessment), directive (students don't have a choice), diagnostic (e.g., unable to subtract two-digit integers), and systematic (the school has a plan for additional time and help until all students reach proficiency).

• *Which students are highly proficient and would benefit from extended or accelerated learning?* Research has shown that these opportunities (as opposed to tracking) greatly improve learning.

During the intervention/enrichment block in one school in Illinois, three to five additional teachers flood into the grade level to provide additional support and keep group sizes small.

• *What can I learn from colleagues who got excellent results in an area where my students struggled?* Transparency and candor are important at this point, making it possible for teachers to admit instructional failures and ask for help. The transfer of successful practices can take place through meetings, viewing videos, sharing lesson plans, or observing classes.

• *What are we going to do about areas where none of us achieved the results we expected?* Effective teams take a hard look at the data, reach out for ideas, set goals, and check back with subsequent assessments to see what's working best.

DuFour is encouraged by the way this kind of teamwork is taking hold, but he's concerned about one missing element. Many schools agree on appropriate curriculum goals, give common assessments, and give students additional time and support. "What they fail to do, however, is to use the evidence of student learning to improve instruction," he says. "They are more prone to attribute students' difficulties to the students themselves." (They need to study harder, do a better job on homework, or ask for help.) "Rather than listing what students need to do to correct the problem," says DuFour, "educators need to address what *they* can do better collectively."

"How PLCs Do Data Right" by Richard DuFour in *Educational Leadership*, November 2015 (Vol. 73, #3, pp. 22–26), summarized in Marshall Memo 610.

6. Teacher Leaders Supporting Interim Data Analysis

In this *Principal Leadership* article, Jan Matthews, Susan Trimble, and Anne Gay describe the process used by the Camden County, Georgia, schools after each quarterly assessment. "Data from benchmark tests are only useful if teachers and principals know how to use them to modify instruction," they write, and suggest the following steps:

• *Rapid turnaround and dedicated meeting time* – Matthews, Trimble, and Gay stress the importance of teachers having access to interim assessment data *immediately* after students take the assessments, so they can revise their instruction in real time. It's critical to convene the teachers who share the same subject and grade, give teachers uninterrupted time to study their results, allow more time (perhaps a half day) the first time teachers get interim assessment results, and not schedule data sessions on days when school pictures are being taken or pep rallies are being held.

• *Thorough preparation for data meetings* – Teachers can be resistant to changing their instructional strategies, say the authors, so it's vital for the principal and lead teachers to present interim assessment data with a plan in mind. Their suggestions—

- Start with data reports for the whole school, then for each grade, then by teacher, then by student. This helps put teachers' results in the context of whole-school areas of strength and weakness.
- Examine team-level data, zeroing in on "intensive care" objectives—areas where students in a particular grade or subject need lots of improvement—and seeing if those areas were also weak in the grade above and below (for example, if seventh graders were weak in the elements of plot in literature, were sixth and eighth graders also weak in that area?).
- Look at actual test items. For the "intensive care" areas, see if individual test items were confusing or poorly worded.
- For the areas in which students struggled, come prepared with suggested classroom strategies, websites, and other resources.
- Keep all testing materials, including data reports, tests and answer sheets, each teachers' results, and resource materials.

• *A structured agenda for data meetings* – Matthews, Trimble, and Gay have attended many data sessions since the district began giving interim assessments, and have this advice for administrators and lead teachers—accentuate the positive, give teachers time to vent without interjecting comments, and then work to keep the meeting on track, following an agenda like the one below. The authors also recommend that administrators not schedule teacher performance evaluations when data meetings are going on, as teachers may be in a somewhat fragile state of mind. "Teachers will need support and encouragement as they try to reach students in new ways," they write. "They will also need reassurance that they won't be penalized for attempting new strategies." Matthews, Trimble, and Gay suggest the following protocol for meetings—

- Scrutinize the test (ten minutes). Begin data meetings by looking at the actual test students took, with correct answers and objectives added. This gives teachers a chance to look for problematic test items and plunge into the specifics of the assessment. In this segment, teachers are often critical of individual test items and make comments like: "That last question seems vague to me; I bet they missed that one," or "I didn't use those terms when I taught," or "We don't use that word," or "I didn't teach that yet."

- Review the data (forty minutes). Teachers should get data for their own class and the whole grade level (but not other teachers' class reports) so they can compare their own students' performance with the bigger picture without invidious comparisons. It's helpful to have students' performance charted with bar graphs so teachers can look at the areas in which students did best and worst. Teachers can also look at the item analysis of their students' incorrect answers to get insights into their misconceptions and errors. In this phase, teachers might look at each other's graphs and the specific test items on which their colleagues did better and ask what higher-performing teachers did to get better results. "This interaction marks the beginning of true collaboration," write Matthews, Trimble, and Gay. It's the turning point—the moment when teachers begin to consider specific interventions to improve their students' performance.

- Learn a new strategy (twenty minutes). At this point, the lead teacher or administrator presents ideas—a classroom strategy, graphic organizer, game, website, etc.—that might improve students' understanding on one of the "intensive care" objectives. It's important for teachers to have time to discuss and become comfortable with the ideas before using them with students.

- Develop an action plan (twenty minutes). Having identified students with common areas of weakness, teachers can divide students and share the job of reteaching (for example, one teacher going over map skills while another reteaches the economics of a region). Teachers might also meet to review student work from a specific lesson to get insights into students' thinking and the effectiveness of the lesson.

"But What Do You Do with the Data?" by Jan Matthews, Susan Trimble, and Anne Gay in *Principal Leadership*, May 2007 (Vol. 7, #9, pp. 31–33), summarized in Marshall Memo 185.

⑦ Three Layers of Interim Assessment Data Analysis

In this *Journal of Staff Development* article, Lissa Pijanowski, then associate superintendent in the Forsyth County Schools in Georgia, reports on her district's impressive student-achievement gains, which she attributes to "focused, collegial conversations" about interim assessment results. Pijanowski says the key was organizing three levels of reflection on interim assessment results, with teacher leaders involved at every stage of the process.

- *Level 1—Individual teachers* – Classroom teachers look at their interim assessment item analyses and ask themselves:
    - Which items did my students miss most frequently?
    - Which standards were each of these items assessing?
    - How did my students' results compare to school performance on each item?
    - Why did most of my students choose the incorrect responses they did?
    - What will I do now to reteach the most problematic missed standards?
    - Which students need additional help based on these results?

"These questions lead teachers to delve deeply into the standards they teach and to reflect on their instructional practice in a low-risk environment," says Pijanowski. "Teacher understanding of their own performance data must precede conversations within a professional learning community."

- *Level 2—Grade-level or content teams* – Having done their individual reflections, teachers meet in same-grade or same-subject teams and ask:
    - What are our team strengths based on these results?
    - What are our team challenges?
    - What factors in our curriculum and instruction do we feel influenced these results?
    - How can we collaboratively modify instruction and reteach standards that our students had the most difficulty learning?
    - How will we know if our students have mastered each standard?
    - What remediation and intervention will be most effective for individual students with low performance?
    - Is there additional professional development and learning support that we need as a team to help us achieve our goals for student learning?

"The team sessions continued the learning of the individual teacher reflections," says Pijanowski. "Teachers analyzed their results even more intensely and took actions they may not have otherwise considered in isolation."

- *Level 3—Schoolwide dialogue* – Finally, school leaders got the whole staff together to focus on interim assessment results and other schoolwide data, asking:
    - Do the results show we are making progress toward meeting our school improvement goals?

- How did we perform on the reading/English language arts and math target areas we identified for improvement this year?
- How did our subgroups and at-risk students perform?
- Are there strategies and actions in our school improvement plan that need to be modified based on these results?
- Are our remediation and intervention strategies closing the achievement gap?
- Do we need to modify our professional learning plan to provide additional support?
- What resources do we need to accomplish the curriculum and instructional changes we have identified?

"Striking a Balance: Georgia District Adds Assessments and Transforms Classroom Practice" by Lissa Pijanowski in *Journal of Staff Development* (currently *The Learning Professional*), Fall 2008 (Vol. 29, #4, pp. 43–46), summarized in Marshall Memo 249.

8. Third-Grade Teachers Use Math Interim Assessments

In this article in *Teaching Children Mathematics*, consultant Jen Munson and professional developer Tamyka Morant describe a yearlong process of working with third-grade teacher teams around curriculum and assessments. Here are the steps they followed:

• *Defining the big math ideas* – These came down to twelve to fifteen deep, conceptual math foci for each grade level, much broader than what Munson and Morant call the "atomized curriculum of isolated skills."

• *Developing high-quality assessment tasks* – Teacher teams found items that would tap into students' thinking and were formatted to allow children to show their work. Here's a third-grade example: *Eight children have been invited to a cookie party. Mrs. Johnson has thirty-two cookies for the children to share equally. How many cookies will each child get? (a) Draw a picture to represent the problem; (b) Write a number sentence that goes with your picture; (c) Explain why your picture goes with the number sentence.*

• *Unpacking the assessment* – Grade-level teams met five times a year to look at each assessment item and ask: What does it ask students to do? What can we learn about students' conceptual understanding, strategies, ability to organize space efficiently, understanding, ability to communicate their understanding in pictures and words, and use of mathematical language.

- *Looking at one student's work together* – The teacher team randomly chose one student response, projected it with a document camera, and thought aloud about evidence of what the student understood, nearly understood, and misunderstood.
- *Analyzing student work* – Teachers then dove into examining their own students' responses and created a one-page Mastery-at-a-Glance checklist of their class's current mathematical reasoning. As they analyzed their students' work, teachers came across responses that raised questions about students' reasoning, and the whole team looked at these papers on the document camera to share ideas. "These difficult cases added depth to teacher content knowledge and fine-tuned our lens for the nuances in student work," say Munson and Morant.
- *Identifying classroom trends* – Teachers then scanned vertically on their own checklists asking:
  - What have nearly all students mastered?
  - What are some students struggling with, and who are they?
  - What are most students struggling with?

Teachers collected these findings on a template. "Taking the time to identify the classroom trends first made this collaborative work on instruction relevant, urgent, and authentic for teachers," say Munson and Morant.

- *Naming instructional implications* – As teachers debriefed their analyses, several common trends emerged and the team brainstormed pedagogical moves and mathematical experiences that would help students bridge the gaps. These were the key questions:
  - To grow this skill, what do students need from us?
  - If we want students to do math in this way, what does that mean for instruction?
  - Where must we meet these students on the concrete-pictorial-abstract continuum?

"Identifying the instructional moves our students needed was the greatest area of growth for our teachers," say Munson and Morant. "One of our key realizations was that when teachers taught the content the first time, they were giving students their best instruction; so, when students needed something more or different for proficiency, teachers were left with few tools to rely on. We quickly recognized that our task as professional developers is to grow teacher content knowledge and improve their toolkits for constructivist pedagogies to fill that gap in capacity." Working with a number of teacher teams, they identified these strategies:

- *Think aloud and model.* Students need to see how to think through tasks and express reasoning, and teacher modeling helps.

- *Build student math talk.* Teachers need to show students authentic, consistent structures for math talk.
- *Develop math writing and representation.* Students need help getting their oral understanding into writing.
- *Build conceptual content knowledge.* Students need lots of help moving along the concrete-pictorial-abstract continuum.

"A Vehicle for Instructional Improvement" by Jen Munson and Tamyka Morant in *Teaching Children Mathematics*, October 2011 (Vol. 18, #3, pp. 170–181), summarized in Marshall Memo 411.

Overcoming What Can Go Wrong

9 **Five Phases of Teacher Reactions to Interim Assessments**

In an article in *Middle School Journal*, Susan Trimble, Anne Gay, and Jan Matthews describe how grade-level teacher teams in the Camden County, Georgia, schools used interim assessments to improve teaching and learning. Over a period of five years, the district, whose per-pupil spending was among the lowest in the state (171st out of 180), raised its English language arts and math achievement into the top thirty. But the process didn't go smoothly at first. Here are the five phases, each lasting two to three months:

 • *Phase 1—Confusion and overload* – At first, almost all teachers were overwhelmed and frustrated by the flood of numbers, columns, graphs, and percentages from the interim tests. "This is too much!" was a common reaction. "I can't understand any of it. I have enough to do. I was hired to teach, not do statistics." Teachers had a point: the reporting format for the interim assessments (designed by a consulting firm under contract to the district) used a completely different format from statewide tests. Lead teachers listened sympathetically to these concerns, helped simplify the reporting format, and walked teachers through the reports one subject at a time.

 • *Phase 2—Feeling inadequate and distrustful* – As teachers analyzed the test results in the early part of the year, they were alarmed at how poorly their students performed on material they had taught. Their first impulse was to blame the test: "How can two questions on a test possibly establish mastery of an objective? These questions are terrible! We don't use this format, vocabulary, terminology, etc. in our classes. I don't teach it that way! These scores can't be right. I taught this concept for a whole week …. Something is wrong." The lead teachers, sometimes feeling they needed to wear a suit of armor, listened as teachers vented—and began to see the glimmerings of a desire to investigate the cause of the low scores.

 • *Phase 3—Challenging the test* – Teachers insisted on looking at copies of the actual tests, indicating "a need to avoid personal responsibility and to identify the test as the cause of the low scores." Sitting with their lead teachers, teams looked at items that most students had answered incorrectly, identifying the wording and "tricks" that had thrown their students. One English teacher said, "No wonder those items about business letters scored low; look at this test question. We don't use this word in class—'editing the letter for *publication*'—publication? There's the reason right there for those low scores." The intrepid lead teachers asked, "Is this a problem with the test question or the instruction?" Teachers continued to blame the test but said that maybe they would start using the word "publication" in their lessons.

With other test items, it was a different story. Looking at an item where the correct answer was *ears* and 30 percent of students picked *ear's*, teachers groaned, "But we've taught plurals and possessives." When the lead teacher asked, "Is this a test question problem?" teachers had to agree that it wasn't. In Phase 3, the lead teachers continued to listen, offer suggestions, and guide the discussion toward scrutinizing the data for insights about students' progress and confusions. It was clear that teachers had never before looked at test scores, test items, and their own teaching in such a detailed way.

- *Phase 4—Examining the results objectively and looking for causes* – At this point in the year, teachers looked at their classes' test reports without the skepticism and resistance of the earlier phases. They searched for patterns in students' responses, examined similarities among the high-scoring items, and brainstormed possible causes for low-scoring items. "They looked at all the variables, such as the types of students in their classes, the time of day, the time of the week, the sports schedules, the number of attempts to reach parents, sibling rivalry, and their own teaching strategies." Teachers began to compare notes ("What are you doing with symmetry that gets those results?") and sharing teaching techniques that seemed to be working in some classrooms (e.g., using geomirrors or having students write in a daily math journal).

The threat level of the tests diminished as teachers stopped assuming that low scores reflected on their competence. Teachers used the tests to answer two questions:

- Which students need extra help and in what topic?
- Which topics do I need to reteach in different ways?

Lead teachers kept the focus on data analysis by persistently asking, "What do these scores tell us?" In this phase, teachers accepted the value of the data for improving their teaching and realized that if students were not understanding, perhaps their teaching strategies needed to be improved. They began asking the questions: Did the test measure the learning objective? If the test item was clear, how was my teaching? Did I teach the objectives in a manner that showed connections among the concepts and had relevance for these students? Did I give them enough opportunity, enough variety, to allow them to master the content? Was the content interesting to them?

- *Phase 5—Accepting data as useful information, seeking solutions, and modifying instruction* – By this point, teachers fully accepted the usefulness of the interim tests and spent almost all their time searching for more effective teaching strategies. Some teachers conferred with individual students and set SMART goals for the next benchmark test (Specific, Measurable, Achievable, Results-oriented, Time-bound), for example, raising a score from 50 percent to 70 percent. Some put together customized study packets. Others encouraged students to analyze their errors and examine their learning style. Teachers also wrote shorter interim tests and quizzes to keep track of students' learning between benchmarks.

Summing up the transformation that the interim assessments brought about, one lead teacher said, "Prior to implementation of formative assessments … teachers were shooting in the dark. They were standing at the goal line in a dark gymnasium taking aim at a hoop they could not see. Now, we can see the goal and have a much better chance of ringing the basket!"

"Using Test Score Data to Focus Instruction" by Susan Trimble, Anne Gay, and Jan Matthews in *Middle School Journal,* March 2005 (Vol. 36, #4, pp. 26–32), summarized in Marshall Memo 78.

10. How Some PLCs Are Going Off the Rails

In this article in *Phi Delta Kappan*, Richard DuFour and author/consultant Douglas Reeves say that, unfortunately, "PLC Lite" is the most accurate way to describe the current state of professional learning communities around the country. "Educators rename their traditional faculty or department meetings as PLC meetings," say DuFour and Reeves, "engage in book studies that result in no action, or devote collaborative time to topics that have no effect on student achievement—all in the name of the PLC process. These activities fail to embrace the central tenets of the PLC process and won't lead to higher levels of learning for students or adults." Here are what the authors believe are the characteristics of a true professional learning community:

- A teacher team takes collective responsibility for students' learning;
- A guaranteed and viable curriculum is established, specifying the knowledge, skills, and dispositions students are expected to acquire, unit by unit.
- Frequent, common, team-developed interim assessments measure students' mastery of the curriculum.
- These assessments identify (a) the students who need additional time and support; (b) students who would benefit from enriched or extended learning; (c) teachers' individual

strengths and weaknesses based on what their students learned; and (d) areas where none of the team members were able to bring students to proficiency.
- A system of interventions guarantees that struggling students get additional time and support in ways that don't remove them from new instruction.

All this flows from the four questions school staff are continuously asking themselves:
- What do we want students to learn?
- How will we know if they have learned it?
- What will we do if they haven't learned it?
- How will we provide extended learning opportunities for students who have mastered the content?

"We recommend that faculty members keep a very simple one-page protocol that helps them focus on these questions," say DuFour and Reeves. "Meetings that only address standards, that focus entirely on disciplinary issues and parent complaints, or that center on employee issues may be very interesting, but they do not represent the work of high-performing PLCs."

The authors go on to discuss three areas that are particularly important in productive professional learning communities:

• *Assessments* – DuFour and Reeves draw a distinction between on-the-spot checking for understanding and periodic interim assessments, two equally important but quite distinct success factors. With on-the-spot assessments, teachers direct questions at randomly selected students; move around the room checking students' work; and use whiteboards, clickers, and exit slips to see how well students are grasping the material—following up appropriately. Students are also involved in assessing their own understanding and taking increasing responsibility for improving their work.

With interim assessments, team members give students a test or performance-based assessment and use the results to identify struggling students, provide timely, systematic support, give students another chance to demonstrate their proficiency, and use the data to improve their classroom skills. DuFour and Reeves are scathing in their assessment of the "uninformative" interim assessment process they see in many schools. It often amounts to little more than shallow test prep, with very brief team conversations concluding with, "Thank goodness that's over—now we can go back to what we were doing." Even if state tests consist largely of multiple-choice questions, say DuFour and Reeves, a teacher's job "is not to mimic state tests but to challenge students to show what they know in ways that exceed traditional tests."

• *Data analysis* – "Many PLC Lite schools have no process for collective analysis of student learning," say the authors. Without that structure, teacher teams may spend time discussing their policy about student use of cell phones or sharing preferences about how to teach a skill ("I've always taught it this way."). All too many teams fall into the time-honored rut of teach, test, hope for the best, assign students to remediation, and move on. "Perhaps the worst examples of faux data analysis are the unfortunately named 'war rooms' in which district leaders display data from the previous year's state tests and use this as a vehicle to publicly praise and humiliate principals and faculty members," say the authors. "This is what military veterans call 'fighting the last war'.... The best examples of data analysis lead to specific actions by teachers and administrators so that an examination of the data leads to interventions and changes in instruction, feedback, and support."

- *Interventions* – The key question is, "What happens in your school when students don't learn what you have deemed is essential?" say DuFour and Reeves. "The least effective response to this question is that students must repeat a grade or a course.... The research is overwhelmingly against retention, but facts are merely an annoyance to those with strongly held opinions." What does work? Systematic, intensive, focused, immediate follow-up instruction at the individual or small-group level. "These interventions do more than improve student success," say DuFour and Reeves. "They also dramatically improve faculty morale. Imagine what next year would be like if we had fewer repeaters and more elective classes. It might begin to restore the joy of teaching and the reason most teachers entered the profession: to make a positive difference in the lives of students."

"The Futility of PLC Lite" by Rick DuFour and Douglas Reeves in *Phi Delta Kappan*, March 2016 (Vol. 97, #6, pp. 69–71), summarized in Marshall Memo 628.

11. The Missing Piece in Many PLCs

In this article in *Phi Delta Kappan*, consultant Michael Wasta says many teacher teams are looking at student work and assessments, identifying areas where kids are having difficulty, and defining specific goals for improvement and criteria for progress. But after observing more than one hundred PLCs in action, Wasta and his colleagues noticed that a crucial part of the data process is often missing: "how team members would have to change their teaching practices to reach those goals." This, he says, squanders a "tremendous opportunity to help teachers find out precisely what is and is not working in their classrooms." All too often, teacher teams are looking at effects without investigating the causes—their day-to-day instructional practices.

To fill this gap, Wasta recommends that when teams analyze student results, they go beyond vaguely defined follow-up strategies—for example, *We will increase the amount and quality of feedback to students*—and get much more specific, drawing on research-based practices, for example:

- Deliver feedback within the class period as close as possible to task completion;
- Indicate errors students made and specific corrections that are needed;
- Link corrections to a clear criterion;
- Encourage students to keep working until a problematic item is correct.

"The key to this process lies in identifying precisely what counts as exemplary performance," says Wasta. Then it's possible to tell whether it was the strategy that was flawed or the fact that it was poorly implemented. Teams should aim for a "sweet spot, ensuring some consistency of implementation while still letting individual teachers bring their own style and creativity to the classroom."

Outlining the details of a follow-up classroom strategy is the first step. Next, team members should monitor how they're doing by observing each other's classrooms or viewing ten- to fifteen-minute classroom videos. In one school implementing the four-part student feedback strategy outlined above, a team concluded that: (a) overall, the strategy wasn't being implemented very well at all; (b) one teacher was doing much better than the others, making her the go-to person for the team; and (c) the second practice (indicating student errors in real time) wasn't being implemented by any of the teachers.

This spurred them to set a measurable goal for improvement and redouble their efforts to implement the strategies. Some approaches they considered:

- Observe the most proficient teacher;
- Prepare and deliver mock lessons to the team;
- Research video examples of exemplary implementation;
- Bring in an outside expert;
- Video classroom samples and review and critique them as a team.

"In effect," says Wasta, "these teachers are designing and implementing their own professional development, focusing on an issue that they have identified as important to them. Over time, they will monitor both data streams—the change in their practice and the change in student performance—and these sources of information will guide the direction of their work." Wasta believes these are the key conditions for the PLC process to work really well in a school:

- Active leadership by the principal;
- Teacher commitment;
- Trust between leaders and teachers, and among teachers;
- Time—a minimum of two forty-five-minute team meeting blocks a month;
- Patience—a recognition that progress will take weeks or months;
- Some structures—roles, agendas, notes.

"PLCs on Steroids: Moving Teacher Practice to the Center of Data Teams" by Michael Wasta in *Phi Delta Kappan*, February 2017 (Vol. 98, #5, pp. 67–71), summarized in Marshall Memo 674.

12. How Principals Can Orchestrate Effective Teamwork

"If the goal is to increase student learning, one of the biggest mistakes education leaders can make is allowing teachers to work in isolation," says Greg Kushnir in this *All Things PLC* article. "Traditional school cultures that leave a single teacher responsible for addressing all of the learning needs present in his or her classroom are a recipe for disaster." Kushnir believes professional learning communities are the antidote, and he describes ten "cultural building blocks" that leaders must put in place for teams to be optimally effective:

• *Clear communication* – "Clarity precedes competence," he says. "Too often school leaders make the mistake of organizing teachers into teams without spending the time to ensure that teachers understand the why, the how, and the what of a PLC culture." *Why professional learning communities?* Because effective teacher teamwork is the key to getting all students to achieve at high levels. *How do they work best?* Teams with autonomy to make decisions about curriculum, assessment, intervention, and instruction develop intrinsic motivation because they have all of Daniel Pink's key components—belonging, purpose, autonomy, and mastery. *What does this look like?* "All students," says Kushnir, "not just the ones we like, the ones who are easy to teach, or the group of students who are currently successful. This has to be the driving force of the school's work." Some commitments that PLCs need to make for real impact are:

- to collaborate at least an hour every week;
- to clarify the most important student learning outcomes;
- to create common interim and summative assessments;

- to collectively inquire and do action research;
- to create systemic interventions that ensure extra time and support for all students;
- to use assessment data to guide next steps in instruction and intervention.

How these commitments are expressed is important, says Kushnir: "The language of *I* and *try* must be replaced with *we* and *will*. The word *try* states an intention, not an action. The road to PLC failure is paved with good intentions. The word *will* is a commitment to action, and *we* means no one person is responsible for accomplishing our goals. Only through making collective commitments to actually change behavior will a culture develop in your school that actually increases student learning."

• *Commitment to the PLC process* – Only by implementing the full professional learning community process will teams immerse themselves in "the difficult work of tackling the behaviors and practices that are getting in the way of continuous sustained improvement," says Kushnir. "This is by no means easy work, and all schools that engage in the process can expect to encounter conflicts between what they are currently doing and what we know to be best practice."

• *Participation and shared responsibility* – "Each member of your school community must understand how his or her work connects to the work of others and how important that work is to the success of the whole," says Kushnir. That includes singleton teachers, educational assistants, office staff, custodians, and part-time employees. At the same time, school leaders need to refrain from micromanaging PLCs, giving them autonomy for day-to-day decisions. A leadership team should monitor the overall process and provide support and guidance as needed.

• *Reciprocal accountability* – "A team must develop a belief that if we are to accomplish our mission of learning for all, then we all have to work together," says Kushnir. "In other words, I am counting on you and you are counting on me." For this to happen, there must be a shared goal that serves as a constant reminder of the work in process and a way of checking in on whether the chosen approaches are working. Goals should include the specific area for improvement; the target date for completion; the desired level of student performance; and an assessment to see if the goal was accomplished.

• *Relationships based on mutual respect* – Some school leaders believe PLC members must like each other, but that's unrealistic given the inevitable pushback and dissension that arise when educators confront long-established practices that aren't producing results. "What matters," says Kushnir, "is that each member of the team commits to achieving high levels of learning for all students, treats the other members with respect, and acts in a professional manner …. One of the challenges to becoming a highly effective team is to develop a process for respectful disagreement, discussion, and decision making …. Having a culture of respectful relationships means that each team member feels safe in acknowledging his or her weaknesses and mistakes and seeks the team's help to improve."

• *Solution orientation* – In an effective PLC, teachers "move past identifying the problem to relentlessly pursuing the solution," says Kushnir. "Collectively finding solutions that help previously unsuccessful students is highly motivating and inspiring for teachers …. Successfully working together to solve problems develops a belief that their work is making a difference and dramatically changes a staff's outlook and attitude toward the art of the possible." PLCs escape the frequent downside of teachers working in isolation—not being able to solve students' learning problems, becoming frustrated, and blaming external factors for their students' poor performance.

• *Honesty* – "Since the first step to solving any problem is to admit we have one, becoming a PLC means that schools must develop the capacity to find fault without blame," says Kushnir. "Identifying areas for improvement must be embraced by teams as opportunities to learn how to improve their practice and help more students learn at high levels." This is cushioned by making improvement, not perfection, the goal.

• *Support* – Teacher evaluation is not a high-value strategy for improving performance, says Kushnir. Carrot-and-stick, punish-and-reward management was developed for the low-level tasks of nineteenth-century factories, but it's not well suited to the complex, creative work of classrooms. Teachers and PLCs will make mistakes, and "the path to improved student achievement will have peaks and valleys and a few bumps along the way," he continues. What teachers need from their supervisors is understanding and support.

• *Equity* – Every day, teachers make decisions about instruction, assessment, and follow-up. When those decisions are made in isolation, a lot is left to chance variations in skill, knowledge, and repertoire. "While teachers are well meaning," says Kushnir, "the result is an inequitable classroom experience for students from one classroom to the next within the same school." High-functioning PLCs level the playing field for students by spreading effective practices and helping to eliminate pedagogy and materials that aren't working.

• *Celebration* – "A gain, no matter how small, is still a gain," concludes Kushnir. "PLCs recognize this fact, and as a result, they celebrate each success that moves them one step closer to accomplishing their shared goals. They understand that success breeds more success!"

"10 Steps to Creating a PLC Culture" by Greg Kushnir in *All Things PLC*, Summer 2017, summarized in Marshall Memo 696.

Singletons and Scheduling

13 Addressing the Challenge of "Lonely Singleton" Teachers

In this article in *All Things PLC*, consultant Casey Reason addresses the frustration of teachers who want to attend data analysis meetings but don't have colleagues in their school who teach the same content. Reason gives the example of Rogene, a high-school world language teacher in a rural district who was eager to collaborate on the content and assessments of her German courses, but the nearest teacher of German was one hundred miles away. This teacher:

- Lacked a peer group to examine the curriculum and identify essential learning;
- Was working with the Spanish teacher in her school to improve their respective interim assessments but didn't have a colleague with whom to share the student results on the specific assessments she was using;
- Didn't have a discipline-specific colleague to challenge her with new perspectives or sensibilities because she was working alone;
- Therefore couldn't explore the deepest elements of collaboration and immerse herself in the process of reciprocal accountability—leading and being led.

What are singleton teachers like this to do? The answer, says Reason, is virtual collaboration. Here's how it worked for Rogene:

• *Establishing a virtual team* – She found three other German teachers in her state and got support from all four districts to carve out professional time to collaborate online. By banking PD time, the districts allowed the four teachers to have an in-person meeting at the beginning of the school year and set up the protocols and norms for their team, as well as deciding on their weekly time for virtual meetings.

• *Curriculum focus* – The teachers decided to collaborate only on German 1 and master the unfamiliar process of collaborating at a distance with this one course. Although each district had its own graded courses of study, their curriculum goals were based on state and national standards, so expectations were quite similar.

• *Virtual meetings* – The teachers used Google Hangout for their weekly get-togethers. In Rogene's school, she was able to use a digital course room (a "shell") for the meetings and the other three teachers were given access. Teachers were able to post meeting notes, ask each other questions in discussion spaces, share data, and see each other's faces live as they met.

• *Broadening collaboration* – As the weeks went by, teachers flooded the course room with links to articles, videos, and other teaching tools. Weekly logins increased, and the teachers began to rely on each other as important contributors to their work. Rogene was active on Twitter and found twenty other German 1 teachers from other states who, although they didn't join the weekly Google Hangout meetings, began sharing ideas and materials with the team.

• *Spreading the word* – At the end of the school year, the virtual German 1 team got the green light from their districts to design and present their own PD webinar in the fall, highlighting what they had learned in their PLC. With help from a retired international headmaster who was teaching German in North Florida, they arranged to bring in a guest speaker from Switzerland for their webinar.

Reason sums up the ways this virtual team was able to capture all the key elements of a conventional in-person teacher data team:

- Communication – The electronic course room gave the team virtual office space to store and share key items and communicate asynchronously.
- Collegial horizon – Rogene remained friendly with the Spanish teacher in her school but greatly expanded her professional scope.
- Innovation – Ideas flowed among the teachers in the regular meetings and the resources accumulated in the course room, both from the core group of four teachers and from others who joined informally in the course of the year.
- Access to professional expertise – Contributions from around the US and abroad greatly expanded Rogene's teaching repertoire.
- Best practices – "Interestingly," says Reason, "Rogene found that there were some rather significant differences of opinion emerging both from within her team and from the outside perspectives that were shared as others made contributions along the way. What her team learned was that their differences made them stronger. Debate was encouraged, and as always, it came down to examining their own measurable results."
- Acceleration – By committing ideas to writing in the course room, these teachers found they had to be more precise than if they were making comments in an in-person meeting. Their ideas "congealed and improved," says Reason, and dialogues "became deeper and, in many cases, more stimulating."

Reason concludes with a few cautions for virtual teams: (a) Don't cut corners on the fundamentals of the data analysis process. (b) Tempting as it may be to get caught up with a remote team, stay grounded in your own school's mission and values. (c) It's important to meet in person at least once, preferably at the beginning of the collaboration. (d) Use a format that allows team members to see each other's faces live. (e) Establish a space that allows materials to be shared asynchronously. (f) Allow ideas, best practices, and materials to be shared on an open source basis.

"Crossing the Chasm: Singleton Teachers and Virtual Teams" by Casey Reason in *All Things PLC*, Winter 2017, summarized in Marshall Memo 675.

14. A Small School Figures Out PLCs

In this article in *All Things PLC*, Wyoming principal Breez Longwell Daniels explains why implementing teacher data meetings was challenging in her 220-student middle school:

- All sixteen teachers in the school were singletons (no same-grade/same-subject colleagues), and they tended to work in isolation.
- Because there were only two or three teachers in each department, students often saw teachers several times as they moved from fifth to eighth grade.
- In a school this size, says Daniels, "there is truly no place to hide a teacher who gets consistently poor results …. Student data are teacher data."
- But when state test-score results were reported each year, the culture of the school was to avoid discussing them "for fear of embarrassing a single teacher in a small town."

How could effective teacher data teams function in this environment?

The school started by setting up vertical subject-area teams in math, ELA, science, social studies, and other subjects and having them meet at least weekly. Each team tackled the first two questions posed by Richard DuFour: *What do we want our students to know and be able to do? How will we know when they are successful?* Content teams identified essential learnings for each grade, created a grade five to eight vertical pacing plan, agreed on common vocabulary and procedures, and crafted end-of-grade and interim assessments of student learning.

Then, after each interim assessment, teams began looking at each teacher's data, student by student and skill by skill. The school adopted a football field metaphor for student progress: "Every student needs to gain yardage, or measurable growth, from fall to spring," says Daniels. "The overarching goal is 100 percent academic growth." A SMART goal was established: 0 percent of students below the 20th percentile, 80 percent above the 50th percentile, and 40 percent of those students at or above the 80th percentile in reading, math, and science.

This focus on the 20th, 50th, and 80th percentiles "allows teachers to monitor student growth from three perspectives," says Daniels. "By looking at three distinct data points within the content area and grade level, we can clearly see trends and analyze cohort growth as a whole." Because the school is so small, changes in performance by one or two students can have a major impact on the data—which is a good thing for transparency and follow-up.

"This extra push toward academic excellence at the 80th percentile," says Daniels, "is directly linked to success on the ACT in high school and is a game-changer in a small rural community where students may not be pushed to the highest levels of academic achievement."

The dynamic in the vertical team meetings was powerful, she says, since teachers "know each other's students because they either taught them a year or two before or they will be teaching them in the next year or two." From the start, teachers realized that "all students are our students" and began sharing effective strategies and fixing what wasn't working. Students realized that their content teachers were talking to each other all the time. They might hear a teacher say, "I know Mrs. Smith showed you how to solve the problem this way" and draw the same illustration on the board that students had seen the year before. Teachers created "memory loops for students through spiraling and scaffolding skills."

Daniels wondered how the school would focus on the third and fourth DuFour questions: *What do we do when students struggle with new learning? What do we do when students are ready for a challenge?* This was tackled by horizontal grade-level teams who often shared the same daily schedule and were in touch with the same corps of parents. "The grade-level content teacher," says Daniels, "is the core specialist and provides the time, structure, and differentiation necessary to support student learning." They "build fluid and flexible schedules for students to get the support they need in each content area at that grade level." Content teachers took full responsibility for their students' progress, seldom outsourcing responsibility to math or reading specialists outside their classrooms.

"It is imperative that small schools create a culture where data transparency is the norm," Daniels concludes. "Accountability specific to systems of support for student learning must hinge on teachers consistently being considered the essential factor in student success. In this no-excuses environment, some teachers will choose to walk away, while others will purposefully choose to be part of a winning team."

How did the school do? Students made dramatic progress and the school won several awards, including being named a Model PLC School by Solution Tree in 2017. And Daniels was named National Distinguished Principal and Wyoming Principal of the Year in 2017.

"Growing a PLC from Rural Roots" by Breez Longwell Daniels in *All Things PLC*, Fall 2018 (pp. 10–15), summarized in Marshall Memo 761.

15 Ideas for Carving Out Time for Teacher Team Meetings

In this article in *The Learning Professional*, Anne Jolly lays out an extensive menu of ways to give teams time to meet during and after the school day.

- *Use existing time more effectively:*
  - Put routine announcements in newsletters and/or e-mails to staff and reserve faculty meetings for professional learning.
  - Provide shorter, more-frequent meetings by spreading time from existing planning days across the calendar.
- *Use common time:*
  - Schedule common planning time for same-grade/same-subject teachers to meet.
  - Organize special subjects into blocks to create common time for teams to meet.
  - Schedule planning periods immediately before or after lunch to allow for double-period meeting time.
  - Create double planning periods in the schedule.
- *Use resource personnel for student learning activities:*
  - Get administrators teaching some classes to free up teachers for meetings.
  - Allow teaching assistants and/or college interns to monitor classes.
  - Pair teachers so one teaches while the other meets with colleagues.
  - Plan off-site student field trips and use the time for meetings.
  - Ask parent volunteers to monitor classes for an hour while teams meet.

- Have professionals from local colleges, businesses, government agencies, and community agencies lead student activities and use the time for teacher meetings.

- *Free teachers from noninstructional requirements:*
  - Use non-homeroom teachers to occasionally perform homeroom duties to give teachers a block of before-school and homeroom time.
  - Reassign school personnel to allow teachers to meet during pep rallies and assemblies.
  - Reassign noninstructional clerical and management tasks so teachers have more time to focus on instruction and collaboration.

- *Bank time:*
  - Lengthen the regular school day and save the extra minutes to create larger blocks of time for team meetings.
  - Start school thirty minutes earlier Monday through Thursday and dismiss two hours early on Friday to create a weekly block of time for meetings.
  - Schedule regular early-dismissal or late-start days.
  - Shave minutes off lunch and bank the time for team meetings.
  - Total the hours teachers meet after school and don't require teachers to report to school for that amount of time on regularly scheduled teacher workdays (when practical).

- *Buy time:*
  - Use paraprofessionals to release teachers during the school day for meetings.
  - Hire a team of rotating substitute teachers to release teachers for meetings.
  - Hire one or two permanent substitute teachers to regularly free teachers to meet.
  - Schedule a team of substitute teachers for a day a week to release teachers on a rotating basis.
  - Hire more teachers, clerks, and support staff to expand or add teacher meeting time.

- *Add professional days to the school year:*
  - Create multiday summer learning institutes for in-depth PD.
  - Create a midyear break for students and use those days for teacher learning.

"Team Basics" by Anne Jolly in *The Learning Professional*, December 2017 (Vol. 38, #6, pp. 63–68), drawn from Jolly's book, *Team to Teach: A Facilitator's Guide to Professional Learning Teams* (Oxford, OH: National Staff Development Council, 2008), summarized in Marshall Memo 719.

Professional Learning Suggestions for Chapter Nine: Results-Focused Teacher Teams

Maximizing the Effectiveness of Your Teacher Teams

Having effective teacher teams that focus on results is one of the most powerful ways to improve teaching and learning at your school. However, it is not enough to simply put teachers into groups and wait for the improvements to come rolling in. The activities in the first two sections below help teachers better understand the attributes of a successful team, assess the effectiveness of their own team, and do some planning to improve their own team. The third section addresses an often-overlooked ingredient needed to create effective teams—the leader's supervision and support of teams. You'll find four useful activities to ensure you don't omit this crucial element. Finally, the last section includes an activity to help brainstorm ways to address two obstacles to collaborative teams—lack of time and singleton teachers who don't have grade-level or subject-area colleagues.

I. What Makes a Teacher Team Successful?

Below are a few exercises to help teachers think through the attributes of an effective team and assess their own team's functioning.

A. Discuss the paradigm shift from "cowboys" to "pit crews."
Atul Gawande (article-summary 1) and Richard DuFour (article-summary 5) examine the change that has occurred in education from teachers working in isolation to teachers working in teams. Even if you already have teams in your school, it's worth it to go back to the basics and have leaders or teachers read these two article-summaries and discuss:

- What has changed over the past few decades in terms of teachers collaborating in teams?
- How complete is this change, or do you still see teachers working on their own in certain areas?
- What have been the benefits of this change, and what are some of the obstacles involved in this change?

PROFESSIONAL LEARNING SUGGESTIONS FOR CHAPTER NINE

B. Compile a list of attributes of a successful team.

While schools may have teachers meet together in groups, this does not mean these are successfully functioning *teams*. Have teachers or leaders read Rozovsky article-summary 2; Kushnir article-summary 12; and Gallimore, Ermeling, Saunders, and Goldenberg article-summary 3; and use the chart below to record attributes of what makes a group into a successful team. Then have them add their own ideas, as well, on the right-hand side.

Attributes of a Successful Team (from article-summaries 2, 3, and 12)	Attributes of a Successful Team (Our own ideas)

C. Self-assess: Are we a group or are we a team?

Have your teacher teams assess whether they are functioning more like a group or a team based on the attributes from the three article-summaries in the previous exercise. Let them individually fill out a self-assessment like the one below and then compare results. Note that there will be a self-assessment later that focuses more specifically on whether teams are actual PLCs (Professional Learning Communities).

Are We a Group or Are We a Team? *Rate your team on a scale of 0 (not at all) to 5 (always)*	
Team members feel comfortable taking risks and being vulnerable.	
Team members are dependable: they get things done on time with a high level of quality.	
The team operates with clear structures: clear goals, clear meeting agendas, clear action plans, and clear roles.	
The team focuses on the work that is most essential to the school: improving teaching and learning.	
The team is results-oriented and its work has an impact on teaching and learning.	
The team focuses on a common task that is relevant to all teachers on the team.	
The teachers leading the teams are skilled facilitators.	
The team follows a cycle of identifying student learning issues, setting goals, improving instruction and providing interventions, assessing student progress, and reflecting on evidence of results.	
The team can rely on stable settings to do its work: protected time during the day to meet, consistent membership, and support from the administration.	

II. How to Improve the Effectiveness of Our Own Teacher Teams?

This section includes activities to help teachers dive more deeply into what they need to do to improve their teacher teams. It includes activities that range from how to develop team norms to how to create an agenda for collaboratively analyzing student work and data.

A. Have each team create or revisit team norms.

There are many specific skills and structures teams need to function effectively. This activity helps to strengthen just one of those structures. Have teams read article-summary 4 by Karin Chenoweth to understand (and be inspired by) the importance of teacher collaboration to the success of a school. In her research on highly effective schools, she found that one structure effective teams had was developing norms for meetings. Next, have teams go through the following structured process to create or revisit team norms:

PROFESSIONAL LEARNING SUGGESTIONS FOR CHAPTER NINE

Process to Create or Revisit Team Norms
1. On index cards, have team members write one thing that frustrates them about working in a team on one side ("I hate when people arrive late ….") and one thing about how they work best in a group on the other side ("I like to withhold my ideas until I've heard what everyone else has to say first ….")
2. Have individuals share what they've written, out loud, with the team.
3. Based on what everyone has shared, distribute blank index cards and have team members propose ideas for meeting *norms*, writing one on each card.
4. As a team, organize the proposed norms on cards into related groups on the floor. Have people propose to eliminate any norm, and if another person agrees, eliminate it. Continue doing this, along with discussing the norms, until fewer than five norms remain to be adopted by the team.

B. Have teachers examine the four essential questions of a Professional Learning Community (PLC).
The goal of any PLC is to address four essential questions key to teaching and learning:

What do we want students to learn?
How will we know if they have learned it?
What will we do if they haven't learned it?
How will we provide extended learning opportunities for those who have learned it?

Two of the article-summaries address those questions—DuFour article-summary 5 and DuFour-Reeves article-summary 10. If your school currently has PLCs or hopes to put them in place, it's helpful to go back to the heart of what makes a PLC a PLC.

- Have everyone read article-summaries 5 and 10 silently.
- Divide the staff into four groups, assigning one of the four PLC questions to each group.
- Give each group chart paper and have them discuss what their question *really* means and what *tasks* a team might do to address this question. Then have them put their answers on chart paper like this:

PLC Question 1: *What do we want our students to learn?*	
What does this *really* mean?	What tasks might a team engage in to address this question?

- Hang the completed chart papers on the wall and conduct a gallery walk by having everyone view what each group has written. Finally, discuss the four questions as a larger group to create a more shared understanding of what they mean and what they might look like in action.

C. Have teachers develop a team agenda for analyzing student data and student work.

Three of the article-summaries provide suggestions for what might go into an agenda for team data meetings: Matthews, Trimble, and Gay article-summary 6; Pijanowski article-summary 7; and Munson and Morant article-summary 8. Have teachers read these three article-summaries and come up with their own structured agenda or protocol to use for meetings when they analyze student data or work.

D. Reflect on two common problems in teacher teams.

The article-summaries by DuFour (10) and Wasta (11) focus on two common problems with teacher teams—they don't fully operate as a true PLC (article-summary 10), and they don't get teachers to actually change their teaching practices (article-summary 11). If the teams at your school are experiencing either of these issues, have those teams read the appropriate article-summary and do the following:

- Have everyone read article-summary 10 or 11 silently and underline any parts that resonate with them.
- Go around and ask each person to share what they think are the implications of what they've underlined for their *own work* as part of this team.
- Go around and ask each person to share what they think are the implications of what they've underlined for the *team as a whole*.
- The article-summaries introduce crucial tasks PLCs should be doing: implementing common formative assessments, conducting data analysis, providing interventions, and changing teacher practice. Have the team do an informal self-assessment of how

effectively they are implementing these tasks by using a "fist-to-five" vote (for each task, raise a fist to represent zero to show it isn't being implemented at all, or any number of fingers up to five, which represents full implementation).
- Based on the fist-to-five vote above, have the team choose the PLC task they most need to improve and set aside the next meeting to bring ideas to improve this task.

III. The Principal's Role Supervising and Supporting Teams

While most school leaders see it as their responsibility to supervise and support *individual* teachers, and do so by observing teaching and giving feedback, it is less common to find principals actively involved in providing guidelines for, observing, and giving feedback to *teams*. Below are some exercises for the principal to reflect on alone or with a leadership team about how best to support and supervise teams.

A. Plan to observe a team meeting and give feedback.

Before observing a team meeting, it helps to know what to look for in a successful team. Take some time to read Rozovsky article-summary 2 and Gallimore, Ermeling, and Saunders article-summary 3—and make a list of the attributes of a successful team you plan to look for. Below is a suggestion based on ideas from article-summary 2. Once you've chosen items to look for, be sure to ask the team for time at the end of the meeting to share your feedback.

Possible Items to Look for When Observing a Team Meeting
- **Psychological safety:** Do team members feel comfortable taking risks and being vulnerable in front of each other?
- **Dependability:** Do team members get things done on time and hold each other accountable?
- **Structure and clarity:** Is there a clear goal? Does everyone have a clear role? Does the meeting have a clear agenda? Does the meeting end with a clear plan of action?
- **Impact**: Is there a results-orientation? Do conversations focus on impact on teaching and learning?

B. Plan to stay apprised of the work happening in teams.

As the school leader, you can't attend every team meeting. But you need an overview of the work that is being done at these meetings so you will know when they need support. Brainstorm a list of ideas for doing this. What follows are four ideas, but brainstorm ones that work for you.

1. You might create a biweekly leadership team meeting with the teachers leading these meetings to ask for an update and provide an opportunity for these teacher leaders to share concerns.

2. You might ask for a short, four-line email at the end of each team meeting asking teacher leaders to email you one sentence addressing each of the four essential questions of a PLC (this idea is from Douglas Reeves and Richard DuFour):

What do we want students to learn?

How will we know if they have learned it?

What will we do if they haven't learned it?

How will we provide extended learning opportunities for those who have learned it?

3. Michael Wasta (article-summary 11) says that teams often lose sight of the fact that the goal is to *change teacher practice*. Read this article-summary, and then you might ask teacher teams to send you an email with the dates and times when they will be trying the new teaching strategies so you can observe teachers specifically for those strategies.

4. Greg Kushnir (article-summary 12) lists ten important building blocks needed to build a team *culture*. Read this article-summary and then ask teams to create a self-assessment with some of the items on this list and periodically use it to take a temperature read on the culture of the team. You can ask to see the results as a way to stay apprised of the successes and challenges each of your teams is facing. It is particularly important to review whether the team feels it is getting *support* and is being *celebrated*, both of which you, as the school leader, can and should address.

C. Model leading a team in collaboratively analyzing assessments.

Three of the article-summaries focus on analyzing student work and data, but teams do not always feel confident with these skills. Read these three article-summaries—Matthews, Trimble, and Gay (6); Pijanowski (7); and Munson and Morant (8)—and create an agenda for a meeting *you will lead* to model how to analyze student data or work.

IV. Handling the S's: Singletons, Small Schools, and Scheduling

Some leaders are hesitant to implement collaborative teacher teams because of significant obstacles, two of which are addressed in the last section of this chapter: no time in the schedule for

PROFESSIONAL LEARNING SUGGESTIONS FOR CHAPTER NINE

meetings; or too many (or all teachers) who do are singletons (no same-grade, same-subject colleagues). Below is an activity to help brainstorm solutions.

With a leadership team, or with teachers—brainstorm solutions to singletons and scheduling using this process:

- Before anyone has read any of the article-summaries, give people time to do a quick-write on their own: What are all of the ways you can think of that we can address the issue of singletons/scheduling so our teachers can benefit from collaborative team work?
- Next, have people read the article-summar(y/ies) appropriate to their topic and underline any *new* ideas for tackling their problem: If the concern is singletons, have them read Reason article-summary 13 and Longwell Daniels article-summary 14. If the concern is no time for collaboration, have them read Jolly article-summary 15.
- Now have people look through their quick-writes and their notes in the article-summaries and choose their top three ideas for addressing the issue. They should put each idea on a sticky note.
- Gather the sticky notes, organize them by topic, and have a full group discussion about the ideas that are most promising (those ideas that have the greater number of sticky notes) for your school.

Chapter Ten:
Professional Learning That Works

Regrettably, professional development leaders too often fall into the same trap in planning that teachers do when they plan their lessons. They plan what they are going to do rather than what they want their students to know and be able to do.
—Thomas Guskey

Over the years, professional development has been heavily criticized, especially "sit and git" workshops that many teachers consider a waste of their time. Other chapters in *The Best of the Marshall Memo* books describe approaches that can, if done well, improve teaching practices. *The Best of the Marshall Memo: Book One* includes approaches such as: instructional coaching (Chapter Five); evaluation (Chapter Six); and positive classroom discipline (Chapter Eight). *Book Two* explores: articulating the key elements of good teaching (Chapter Five); differentiation and personalization (Chapter Eight); and results-focused teacher teams (Chapter Nine). The chapter you are reading focuses more narrowly on whether direct efforts to educate teachers can be effective. The articles fall into four categories: past and present shortcomings of PD; the characteristics of effective professional learning; practical applications of new ideas; and innovative practices (with cautionary notes).

Past and Present PD Shortcomings – Joan Richardson is saddened that outstanding teachers work in isolation and colleagues seldom learn from effective practices in the classroom next door. Mary Kennedy says PD strives to improve teachers, but they have their own ideas on what works and may learn more from each other than from packaged programs. Dina Hasiotis and colleagues share the findings of a TNTP study of professional development: it's expensive, ineffective, and school districts need to do better.

Characteristics of Effective Professional Learning – James Surowiecki describes the revolution that has taken place in athletic training in recent years and how the process of continuous improvement can be applied to schools. Thomas Guskey lists five ways we evaluate PD, starting with whether it's enjoyable, and says schools should design backwards from the ultimate goal: student learning. Denise Morgan and Celeste Bates point to key factors in professional learning, including active learning, collaboration, models, coaching, feedback, and duration. Paul Bambrick-Santoyo says that to be effective, PD must focus on specific teacher actions, come in bite-size chunks, and get teachers practicing with immediate feedback.

Practical Applications – *Journal of Staff Development* editors suggest thirty-five ways teachers can boost their effectiveness through individual learning experiences, learning with colleagues, collaborating with colleagues, and having an impact beyond their classrooms. Lauren Porosoff describes how schools can tap resources within their own faculties to develop and spread effective teaching practices. Michael McNeff describes how his North Dakota district opens school later every Wednesday and gives teacher teams time to work on curriculum, look at student work, read research, plan classroom and school visits, and write about what they've learned.

Innovative Practices and Cautionary Notes – Catherine Lewis and three colleagues explain why a California elementary school's implementation of lesson study succeeded, while the model has failed in other settings in the US. Erin Axelsen, Lorie Cristofaro, and Jill Geocaris describe how they organized asynchronous book study groups using the Voxer app, with five to six educators reading a book chapter by chapter, chiming in with their reactions, and listening to the conversational thread at their convenience. Meg Bates, Lena Phalen, and Cheryl Moran list five situations where online professional learning can be very helpful but stress the importance of teachers bringing insights and ideas back to their own schools. William Ferriter and Nicholas Provenzano say that educators who pursue professional learning through blogs, Twitter, and "unconferences" need to be sure the information is balanced and accurate, and need to document the value of this kind of PD to skeptical superiors.

EDUCATORS CONTINUOUSLY IMPROVING

Questions to Consider

- Why has "professional development" had such a bad reputation in schools?
- How can we bridge the gulf between educational theory and teacher practice?
- What kind of professional experiences actually improve teaching?

Past and Present PD Shortcomings

① Opening Classroom Doors

In her editor's note in *Phi Delta Kappan*, Joan Richardson recalls visiting the classroom of a highly regarded fourth-grade teacher named Katie. "As she taught," says Richardson, "she seemed to be tapping into multiple brains simultaneously, quickly analyzing what different students needed and responding in the moment to meet those needs. Add to that her warmth and humor, and her classroom was alive with learning."

As Richardson left this classroom, two other teachers accosted her and shyly asked what made this teacher so effective. It turned out they had never watched Katie teach. "I was dumbstruck," says Richardson. "This trio had been colleagues for years. One teacher had worked in the classroom next to Katie's for seven years; the other teacher had worked on the other side of Katie for nine years and in two different schools. Not once had either of them ever been in Katie's classroom while she was teaching …. As I drove away from Katie's school, I thought about how demoralized her colleagues must have felt about being excluded from the knowledge that Katie could have shared and that might have helped make them better teachers. So near and yet so far." And what about all the other students in that school and district who could have benefited from sharing the specific techniques of that classroom?

"Keeping an exemplary teacher's knowledge isolated inside a classroom isn't just poor practice," Richardson concludes, "it's almost malpractice."

"Getting Better at Learning" by Joan Richardson in *Phi Delta Kappan*, November 2016 (Vol. 98, #3, p. 4), summarized in Marshall Memo 662.

② The Dubious Impact of Professional Development

"Human beings have taught one another for centuries," says Mary Kennedy (Michigan State University) in this *Review of Research in Education* article, "and for most of that time everyone invented their own approaches to teaching, without the guidance of mentors, administrators, teacher educators, or professional development. Today, teachers receive guidance from almost every corner."

Kennedy is particularly interested in PD, and says studying it is tricky because three issues are involved: what teachers need to learn, how they learn, and how we will know when they've learned enough. Any study of professional development can be off the mark, she says, if it gets even one of these hypotheses wrong. "Furthermore," Kennedy continues, "teachers themselves may learn about teaching independently, in ways we don't see. They take formal courses, they read things, they ruminate about their own experiences, and they seek advice from colleagues. They may even get a brainstorm about their teaching while watching a movie."

Kennedy offers five observations about researchers' and laypeople's often incomplete understanding of teaching:

• *The child's-eye perspective* – Teaching is like no other profession because, as children, we've all spent about twelve thousand hours observing teachers and coming to conclusions about what they do in their classrooms and what makes some better than others. But these conclusions about teaching are naïve and can be wrong, says Kennedy: we might believe that "teaching practice comes naturally, or is effortless, because teachers always appear to know what to do …. We see their actions but not their thoughts, their goals, their motives, their frustrations. Moreover, we don't see *what they see*, from their vantage point at the front of the classroom …." In fact, Kennedy's research has found that a lot of what teachers do is based on in-the-moment information—for example, "I could see that Billy was about to jump out of his seat."

• *Idealized models of teaching* – Theorists have developed a number of teaching paradigms: Piagetian, behaviorist, open classroom, and others. These are interesting, says Kennedy, but they "embrace the naïve view of the teacher as always in full control of the classroom, still failing to recognize the contingent nature of teaching."

• *The attribution error* – "Since we tend to assume teaching comes naturally," she says, "and that teachers are entirely in control of events in their classrooms, we also assume that whatever behaviors we see are purposeful, rather than spurious responses to events." For example, an observer might conclude that an elementary teacher didn't accept a student's clever suggestion because she didn't understand the mathematical thinking behind it, when in fact the teacher got it but quickly concluded it would be too difficult and time-consuming for the rest of the class to understand.

• *Hopes for professional development* – PD has proliferated, says Kennedy, taking up many hours each year, and people expect it to solve all the classroom problems in sight. PD has standards, goals, and models of good practice, consumes a lot of teachers' time—and is expensive.

• *The bootstrap approach* – PD can be ineffective if it's based on the wrong model or if its pedagogy isn't successful with teachers—and both occur with regularity. An alternative is encouraging teachers to help each other with the day-to-day challenges of their jobs. This kind of informal peer mentoring has "no cost, no formal schedule, and no uniform curriculum," says Kennedy, yet it might have more impact on teaching and learning than formal (and much more expensive) professional development.

Kennedy then asks how we can measure the benefits of the many professional development programs out there. The starting point, she says, is what teachers actually need to learn: "The central premise underlying all PD is that there is something the researcher knows about teaching that teachers do not know." She lists three categories:

- Procedures—discrete practices teachers use to maximize student learning;
- Content knowledge—in-depth understanding of the material being taught;
- Strategies and insights—dealing effectively with in-the-moment decisions, which involves seeing what might facilitate or interfere with the lesson objective.

Comparing PD initiatives in these three areas, Kennedy found the most positive effects were with strategies and insights. These programs had more artifacts—videos of classroom events, interviews with children, and student work—and they were often taught by people who had lots of classroom experience.

There have been many attempts to "package" effective PD programs and take them to scale. "But what if program effectiveness depends on the PD provider's own personal knowledge of classroom life," asks Kennedy, "or on his or her ability to spontaneously generate examples or to spontaneously notice things while visiting teachers' classrooms? If the quality of the message depends on the provider's intimate knowledge of classroom life, other providers, even when trained in the PD approach, might not be able to achieve the same outcomes."

Kennedy's major conclusion is that packaged programs don't work. She also says that most PD studies are seriously flawed because they look at only one year of intervention and end-of-year test scores. This assumes that teachers rapidly adopt new practices and student learning is affected within that school year. In addition, what if teachers privately disagree with the suggestions being made, says Kennedy, "but comply with them only to be polite or to get their coaches to leave them alone. If this occurred, we might see a gain during the program year, but the gain would reflect compliance rather than genuine learning, and it would go away the following year." The conclusion: studies of PD should extend over at least two years.

This, along with a fundamental rethinking of professional development, is essential, says Kennedy, because "teachers are essentially tinkerers. They are accustomed to working in isolation, they depend heavily on their own personal innovations, and they depend on automated habits and routines."

The bottom line: "We have reached a situation in which our knowledge about how to conduct productive PD is increasing but our ability to spread that knowledge is not. Meantime, teachers are being 'treated' with ever-increasing volumes of packaged PD, at great expense to school districts and with almost no benefit for themselves or their students." This brings us back to the power of informal peer-to-peer sharing and support, which can have much more impact than elaborate and expensive PD programs.

"How We Learn About Teacher Learning" by Mary Kennedy in *Review of Research in Education*, March 2019 (Vol. 43, pp. 138–162), summarized in Marshall Memo 791.

3. A Troubling Report on Professional Development

In this report from TNTP (formerly The New Teacher Project), Dina Hasiotis et al. issue a stinging critique of professional development in US schools. Hasiotis and her team spent two years investigating how three large school districts and one charter network try to develop their teachers, including efforts by the districts, schools, and teachers themselves. Here are the conclusions:

• *Schools are making a massive investment in teacher improvement.* These nationally representative districts spent an average of almost $18,000 per teacher per year on professional development, broadly defined. Extrapolated for the fifty-largest districts in the US, this comes to at least $8 billion. Teachers reported that they spent nineteen full school days a year on PD activities. "This represents an extraordinary and generally unrecognized commitment to supporting teachers' professional growth as the primary strategy for accelerating student learning," says the TNTP report.

• *Despite these efforts, most teachers don't improve from year to year.* The evaluation scores of seven out of ten teachers in the study remained constant or declined over the last two to three years. The improvement curve was especially disappointing after teachers' first few years on the job, with many teachers plateauing while still having lots of room for improvement. "As many as half of teachers in their tenth year or beyond were rated below 'effective' in core instructional practices, such as developing students' critical thinking skills," says the report.

• *Even when teachers do improve, it's not clear why.* Some teachers do get dramatically better, say the researchers, especially in their first few years in the classroom, but "No type, amount, or combination of development activities appears more likely than any other to help teachers improve substantially, including the 'job-embedded,' 'differentiated' variety that we and many others believed to be the most promising …. Every development strategy, no matter how intensive, seems to be the equivalent of a coin flip: Some teachers will get better and about the same number won't…. Teacher development appears to be a highly individualized process, one that has been dramatically oversimplified. The absence of common threads challenges us to confront the true nature of the problem—that as much as we wish we knew how to help all teachers improve, we do not." This was true in the charter school management organization scrutinized by TNTP as well as the three regular public-school districts; even though the charter schools had more-impressive teacher growth and impact, there were no clear findings about the kinds of PD that helped and didn't help.

• *School systems are not helping teachers understand how to improve.* "Teachers need clear information about their strengths and weaknesses to improve their instruction," says the report, "but many don't seem to be getting that information …. Currently, most teachers are told in innumerable ways that their level of performance is good enough. The resulting culture is an enormous drag on growth." The TNTP team found a mixture of grade inflation on teacher-evaluation scores, inflated self-assessments by teachers, teachers rejecting critical assessments, low expectations for teacher development and performance, and a widespread feeling that PD activities were not a good use of teachers' time. One interesting finding: there was more teacher improvement in schools where teachers' self-assessment was close to their formal evaluations. Frequency of administrators' classroom visits also showed some correlation with improvement. Charter school teachers were strikingly more humble in their self-assessments (only 4 percent rated themselves 5 on a 5-point scale, compared to 30 percent of teachers in the districts) and much more likely to say they had instructional weaknesses (81 percent of charter teachers said this, versus 47 percent of district teachers).

"In short," concludes the report, "we bombard teachers with help, but most of it is not helpful to teachers as professionals or to schools seeking better instruction. In spite of this, the notion persists that we know how to help teachers improve and could achieve our goal of great teaching in far more classrooms if we just applied that knowledge more widely. It's a hopeful and alluring vision, but our findings force us to conclude that it is a mirage. Like a mirage, it is not a hallucination but a refraction of reality: Growth is possible, but our goal of widespread teaching excellence is further out of reach than it seems …. Our research suggests that, while understandable and well-intentioned, layering on more support is not the solution. Instead, we believe school systems need to make a more fundamental shift in mindset and define 'helping teachers improve' not just in terms of providing them with a package of discrete experiences and treatments, but with information, conditions, and a culture that facilitate growth and normalize continuous improvement."

Here's a summary of the report's recommendations.

Redefine what it means to help teachers improve:
- Clearly define "development" as observable, measurable progress toward an ambitious standard for teacher and student learning.
- Give teachers a clear, deep understanding of their own performance and progress.
- Encourage improvement with meaningful rewards and consequences.
- Reevaluate existing professional learning supports and programs:
- Inventory current efforts.
- Start evaluating the effectiveness of all PD activities against the new definition of "development."
- Explore and test alternative approaches to development.
- Reallocate funding for particular activities based on their impact.

Reinvent how we support effective teaching at scale:
- Balance investments in development with investments in recruitment, compensation, and smart retention.
- Reconstruct the teacher's job.
- Redesign schools to extend the reach of great teachers.
- Reimagine how we train and certify teachers for the job.

"The Mirage: Confronting the Hard Truth About Our Quest for Teacher Development" by Dina Hasiotis, Andy Jacobs, Kate McGovern, and a number of other TNTP researchers, leaders, designers, and editors, published by TNTP, August 4, 2015, summarized in Marshall Memo 598.

Characteristics of Effective Professional Learning

④ What Educators Can Learn from Athletic Training

In this *New Yorker* article, James Surowiecki reviews the advances that have been made in athletic coaching since the 1970s and how they can be applied to improving classroom instruction. Professional athletes used to work out and get in shape but didn't do much weight and skill training. "Most of the guys had this mental attitude that if you're not good enough the way you are, then you'll never be good enough," said Bob Petrich, a defensive end with the San Diego Chargers in the 1960s. Either you have it or you don't.

Kermit Washington changed that mindset. Recruited by the Los Angeles Lakers based on his American University record of twenty points and twenty rebounds a game, he was a major disappointment in his first three years in the NBA. His skills didn't match those of professional players and he spent more and more time on the bench and thought his pro basketball career was coming to an end.

But Washington didn't accept that his skills were finite, and spent the next summer working with Pete Newell, a Lakers special assistant, getting schooled in the basics of footwork, positioning, and shooting. The following season, Washington improved in all aspects of the game, and after another summer working with Newell, he got even better. By the end of the 1970s, he was an All-Star. The word got out, and more and more professional athletes began to engage in the same kind of intensive skill training.

"Today, in sports, what you are is what you make yourself into," says Surowiecki. "Innate athletic ability matters, but it's taken to be the base from which you have to ascend. Training efforts that forty years ago would have seemed unimaginably sophisticated and obsessive are now what it takes to stay in the game …. What we're seeing is, in part, the mainstreaming of excellent habits." Athletes work harder—and smarter.

The same continuous-improvement process has happened among chess players, classical musicians, and in US manufacturing. The quality revolution that began in Japan in the 1970s spread to US industry, and the rate of defective automobiles, televisions, and other products has gone down dramatically. "The ethos that underlies all these performance revolutions is captured by the

EDUCATORS CONTINUOUSLY IMPROVING

Japanese term *kaizen*, or continuous improvement," says Surowiecki. "In a *kaizen* world, skill is not a static, fixed quality but the subject of ceaseless labor."

This led him to examine what's been happening in the world of K–12 schooling, where progress has been agonizingly slow. The problem, Surowiecki believes, is similar to the one other field he had to confront: a belief in the "natural-born teacher"; either you can teach or you can't. "As a result, we do little to help ordinary teachers become good and good teachers become great," he says. "What we need to embrace instead is the idea of teaching as a set of skills that can be taught and learned and constantly improved on."

The fact that most Americans don't buy this idea has resulted in weak teacher preparation and training. "If American teachers—unlike athletes or manufacturing workers—haven't got much better over the past three decades," says Surowiecki, "it's largely because their training hasn't, either." Countries whose students far outperform the US—Japan, Finland, Canada—"all take teacher training extremely seriously. They train teachers rigorously before they get in the classroom, and they make sure that the training continues throughout their work lives." Here are some specifics:

- Teachers observing each other at work and discussing what they see;
- Using videos of lessons for close scrutiny of effective and ineffective practices;
- Teachers reviewing curriculum materials and designing lessons together;
- Developing specific classroom techniques that work, like the Japanese *bansho*, the art of writing out a math problem with possible solutions on the board;
- A relentless focus on small details and constant feedback;
- Refining sets of specific practices that work (the Japanese term is *jugyokenkyu*);
- Deploying a staff of full-time trainers and coaches.

Will this cost money? Of course, says Surowiecki – but probably not as much as the cost of continuously replacing failing, discouraged teachers, or the societal costs of churning out mediocre students year after year.

"And there will be some teachers who will find all the feedback intrusive," he says. "But what's happened in sports over the past forty years teaches that the way to improve the way you perform is to improve the way you train. High performance isn't ultimately about running faster, throwing harder, or leaping farther. It's about something much simpler: getting better at getting better."

"Better All the Time" by James Surowiecki in the *New Yorker*, November 10, 2014 (pp. 81–85), summarized in Marshall Memo 560.

---

5 Planning Professional Learning with the End in Mind

In two *Journal of Staff Development* articles, Thomas Guskey lists the ways educators might evaluate the effectiveness of professional development activities.

• *Level 1: Participants' reactions* – Did they like the workshop? Did they believe their time was well spent? Did the content and material make sense to them? Were the activities well-planned and meaningful? Was the leader knowledgeable, credible, and helpful? Did they find the information useful? Were the amenities satisfactory? To gather data on this dimension, questionnaires are the best approach.

• *Level 2: Participants' learning* – Did they learn what they came to learn? What new knowledge, skills, attitudes, and dispositions were acquired? Gathering information on this is a little more difficult than the "happiness quotient" at Level 1; self-reports aren't always reliable.

• *Level 3: Organizational support and change* – Are key elements in place "back home" to make implementation of the PD content possible? For example, teachers might attend a workshop on cooperative learning, master the key principles and practices, and return to their school full of enthusiasm, only to find that their students will be graded on a curve in a highly competitive environment. In such cases, even high-quality PD will not bear fruit.

• *Level 4: Participants' use of what they learned* – Did teachers actually carry out what the PD recommended? Did the new knowledge and skills make a difference in their professional practice? Data on this question can be gathered only by thoughtful classroom observations.

• *Level 5: Student learning outcomes* – This is the true bottom line: Did the professional learning affect students in specific, measurable ways? It's important to look at a broad range of possible outcomes, measured in valid and reliable ways that are linked to the intervention—for example, student test scores, performance tasks, grades, student surveys, staff questionnaires, and other measures. Suppose, for example, that students' test scores went up as a result of changed professional practices but more students dropped out.

Guskey says that a professional development program can fall apart at any of the five levels. For example, teachers might enjoy a workshop but never apply the new ideas—resulting in zero impact on student learning. Guskey says that school leaders need to keep an eye on all five levels, since each provides important information during the school year and at year's end. He quotes a nice definition of formative versus summative evaluation: "When the cook tastes the soup, that's formative; when the guests taste the soup, that's summative" (Robert Stake).

Guskey then argues that *planning* professional development in this sequence is a mistake. "Regrettably," he writes, "professional development leaders too often fall into the same trap in planning that teachers do when they plan their lessons. They plan what they are going to do rather than what they want their students to know and be able to do. Their planning tends to be event-based or process-based, not results-based."

The antidote to this tendency is to plan professional development *backwards*, starting with the last step listed above and proceeding to d, c, b, and then a. Each step has direct implications for the next, and all are driven by whether student learning will improve as a result.

First, school leaders should identify the student learning outcomes they are seeking (e.g., improved reading comprehension, math problem-solving skills, behavior in class, collaboration with peers, persistence in school) and plan the assessments that will be used to judge the success of the professional development program (e.g., test scores, rubrics, portfolios, projects, performance tasks, survey data).

Second, school leaders should decide what classroom practices and school policies are most likely to produce these student learning outcomes. Leaders should look carefully at the research evidence for any new program, ask how reliable the evidence is, and find out whether it was gathered in contexts similar to theirs. "Be particularly mindful of innovations that are more opinion-based than research-based," cautions Guskey, "promoted by people more concerned with what sells than with what works. Before jumping on any educational bandwagon, always make sure that trustworthy evidence validates the selected approach."

Third, leaders should look at whether support, resources, time, instructional materials, technology, etc., are in place so the PD has a good chance of succeeding.

Fourth, leaders should decide what knowledge and skills teachers need to acquire to successfully implement the new program. "What must they know and be able to do," asks Guskey, "to successfully adapt the innovation to their specific situation and bring about the sought-after change?"

Finally, leaders should focus on the adult learning experiences that will most effectively get the new skills and knowledge into teachers' heads. Workshops? Seminars? Study groups? Action projects?

"Taking a Second Look at Accountability" by Thomas Guskey in *Journal of Staff Development* (currently *The Learning Professional*), Winter 2005 (Vol. 26, #1, pp. 10–18), summarized in Marshall Memo 69.

---

6. How to Get Traction with Professional Development

In this article in *The Reading Teacher*, Denise Morgan (Kent State University) and Celeste Bates (Clemson University) summarize the findings of a 2017 report on the ideal design elements of professional development:

• *Focused on content* – "Content anchors everything," say Morgan and Bates. "It is ultimately what allows teachers to connect theory to practice." Of course, content has to be coupled to the best instructional strategies for the students that teachers are working with. PD leaders need to do their homework and guide colleagues in book and article study groups and viewing relevant classroom videos.

• *Active learning* – Professional development sessions should minimize lectures and maximize hands-on activities, including looking at student artifacts, exploring materials that teachers will use in their classrooms, participating in and modeling lessons, watching lesson videos, grappling with questions, and reflecting on local problems of practice.

• *Support for collaboration* – This can be one-on-one, in small groups, or with the whole faculty, the key being sufficient time to nurture a "togetherness mindset" and develop collective knowledge and relational trust. "Contrived collegiality can look collaborative," say Bates and Morgan, "but is really a superficial relationship in which members will often meet but are not afforded the time to dig deeply into the issues." True collaboration involves unit and lesson planning, classroom observations, collective analysis of student work, and tweaking plans and strategies in an ongoing effort to meet the needs of all students.

• *Models of effective practice* – Teachers need to see instructional practices in action through videos, demonstration lessons, peer observations, case studies, and samples of student work—giving instructors a sense of how lessons will unfold in their own classrooms. Seeing a variety of models, say Bates and Morgan, "allows teachers to understand that no two students follow the same path and shows the importance of teacher expertise in instruction."

• *Coaching and expert support* – This can come from instructional leaders, literacy coaches, university faculty, or expert peers and should include classroom visits and debriefs, video analysis, co-planning, and looking at student work. "Coaches who view their role as tentative and adopt a co-learner stance," say Bates and Morgan, "assist teachers in seeing multiple possibilities when making decisions."

• *Feedback and reflection* – There needs to be enough time built into PD "for teachers to think about, receive input on, and make changes to their practice," say the authors. "For feedback to be helpful, it must be viewed as constructive and not critical." Trust and a sense of common purpose are essential to teachers hearing and acting on feedback.

• *Sustained duration* – "A one-shot, sit-and-get approach to professional learning, no matter how dynamic, is not sufficient," say Bates and Morgan. Teachers need ongoing support over weeks, months, and even years as they identify issues in their classrooms, study them, implement changes, reflect on results, and continuously improve their practices.

"Seven Elements of Effective Professional Development" by Celeste Bates and Denise Morgan in *The Reading Teacher*, March/April 2018 (Vol. 71, #5, pp. 623–626), summarized in Marshall Memo 729. The full report is "Effective Teacher Professional Development" from Learning Policy Institute by Linda Darling-Hammond, Maria Hyler, and Madelyn Gardner, June 2017.

---

7. Three Keys to Effective Professional Learning

In this article in *Phi Delta Kappan*, Paul Bambrick-Santoyo (Uncommon Schools) shares three lessons he's learned about effective professional learning:

• *Be concrete*. The first step with a professional learning session is to define the objective in terms of concrete actions teachers will take in their classrooms. "Until you name an outcome, your workshop doesn't have teeth," says Bambrick-Santoyo. For example, planning a workshop on diversity, here are three possible objectives:

- Really abstract: Be aware of the diversity of our students and the experiences they've had.
- Still too abstract: Understand the current political and social challenges of our community and how they affect our students.
- Actionable: Redirect a noncompliant student with one of the three nonbiased strategies presented in the workshop.

Actionable objectives should also be observable in classrooms so administrators can keep track of whether they are implemented effectively.

• *Bite-sized is best*. "Once you start breaking down your PD topic into actionable objectives, you'll soon realize that there are far too many to teach all at once," says Bambrick-Santoyo. "A PD session should never have more objectives than you can accomplish in the amount of time allotted."

Better to take one manageable objective for each session and accomplish the broader goal over time. Here's an illustration:
- Very broad—Teachers being Common Core ready.
- Narrower—Effectively teaching more-complex texts.
- Narrower still—Using a "ladder" of texts within a specific topic, teachers select a set of increasingly complex texts on the same topic so that students will evolve more quickly as readers by staying within a topic and applying their new learning to more-complex texts on the same material.
- Optimal—Teachers find three informational texts on a topic in the novel they are reading with students, each passage at a higher Lexile level. Teachers then work in grade-level teams to exchange feedback on their text choices and begin to design a lesson plan.

Bambrick-Santoyo also suggests some common-sense strategies for improving the quality of professional development: (a) Make PD routine—weekly or bi-weekly is best. (b) Make PD sessions longer; this is possible only if students are dismissed early on PD days. (c) Make hard choices. "Because you can't address everything," he says, "always select your PD objectives with an eye to what's most urgent and what actions will have the biggest effect."

• *To see change, practice.* Teachers need high-quality practice opportunities if they are going to have the skill and confidence to implement new skills. Bambrick-Santoyo recommends:
- Repetition – "The more 'at bats' and opportunities teachers have, the more deeply they can learn a skill," he says.
- Feedback – As teachers practice, peers and administrators should say how they are doing.
- Immediacy – Practice should take place right in the PD session; it's unrealistic to expect teachers to go off and practice on their own. In the diversity PD example above, teachers get a series of written classroom scenarios in which a student acts out and the teacher responds inappropriately; then teachers rewrite the responses and role-play to see how their ideas work.

"Leading Effective PD: From Abstraction to Action" by Paul Bambrick-Santoyo in *Phi Delta Kappan*, April 2013 (Vol. 94, #7, pp. 70–71), summarized in Marshall Memo 482.

Practical Applications

8. Thirty-Five Ideas for Improving Professional Development

In this sidebar in a *Journal of Staff Development* article, the editors share a list of suggestions for going beyond standard PD workshops. They suggest using these ideas to build educators' learning leadership, advocate within schools and districts for more-effective use of professional learning time, and communicate with parents and community members about how educators develop themselves. [The JSD items are grouped here into four categories.]

Personal learning:
- Read journals, magazines, blogs, and books.
- Video your own teaching.
- Keep a reflective blog or journal.
- Maintain a professional portfolio.
- Consult an expert.
- Study content standards for your state.
- Attend an in-depth institute in a content area.
- Enroll in a university course.
- Pursue additional certifications or degrees.

Learning with colleagues:
- Observe a model lesson.
- Do a classroom or school walk-through.
- Shadow a student, a teacher, or another professional.
- Learn with the support of a coach or mentor.
- Participate in a Critical Friends Group.
- Participate in a Twitter chat.
- Join an online or face-to-face network.
- Attend or lead webinars.

Collaborating with colleagues:
- Plan lessons and units.
- Participate in lesson study.

- Write assessments.
- Engage in a cycle of inquiry.
- Examine student data.
- Conduct action research.
- Develop team facilitation skills.

Having an impact beyond one's classroom:
- Lead a book study.
- Invite colleagues to observe you.
- Coach a colleague.
- Be a mentor.
- Join a cadre of in-school or in-district trainers.
- Participate in school-improvement planning.
- Write an article about your work.
- Create new teaching resources.
- Give presentations at conferences.
- Share teaching successes with board and community members.
- Advocate for your profession.

"Beyond the Workshop" in *Journal of Staff Development* (currently *The Learning Professional*), June 2016 (Vol. 37, #3, pp. 54–55), summarized in Marshall Memo 643.

9. Four Ways to Use a School's Internal Expertise

In this article in *Independent School*, teacher/author Lauren Porosoff suggests ways to use resources within a school for professional learning:

• *The Bring-Back* – Teachers who have been to conferences share ideas they found particularly helpful. For example, a teacher went to a technology conference and attended a workshop on how game-making helps students be creative and understand how ideas interconnect. Back in her school, she showed slides from the workshop and led a discussion on how her colleagues might use the ideas in their classes. A science teacher thought about how to make games to learn the parts of a plant, and a history teacher considered modifying a board game about the US Constitution that he once used. "In a bring-back," says Porosoff, "everyone explores and experiments together—in much the same way as we aim for our students to do."

- *The Workshop* – A faculty member presents an idea that's had a positive impact on students. Then, with the presenter's guidance, colleagues try doing it themselves. For example, a math teacher at Porosoff's school showed how he was making short, explanatory videos for students to watch at home—opening up more class time for working with groups of students on challenging problems. This teacher showed colleagues how to make videos in their subject areas and deal with the inevitable challenges—students who don't watch the video or don't understand fundamental aspects of the content—and how to help students work together to solve problems. In Porosoff's school, there's been no shortage of teachers with useful ideas to share in workshops.

- *The Toolbox Share* – A school leader or department chair poses a question to colleagues and everyone contributes ideas. Some examples—
    - How do we incorporate movement into our sixth-grade classes?
    - How do we communicate with parents when a kid gets a bad grade?
    - How do we examine math resources for bias?
    - How do we use historical fiction in our classes?

On the last question, members of the history department might ponder this question before the meeting and bring books from their classroom libraries and historical fiction writing assignments they've given. "Rather than having one expert share a 'best' practice," says Porosoff, "and narrowing the faculty's repertoire to include only that practice—teachers can expand and diversify their collective repertoire to include more ways to help students learn."

- *The Council* – Several teachers describe a classroom challenge or dilemma and ask colleagues for ideas. Some examples—
    - How can I teach grammar in a way that improves student writing?
    - How can I make algebra fun?
    - How can I incorporate discussions of current events?
    - Instead of an essay on the Civil War, what creative project can I assign?
    - Why did so many of my students fail this test when they seemed to understand?
    - How can I include service learning in my classroom?
    - How can I make best use of new technology without letting it use me?
    - How can I teach compassionate behaviors?
    - How can I give students brain and body breaks?

- How can I get Donny Crawford to talk in my class?

Once several questions have been posed, teachers form groups of four to seven and serve as a "council" for each question. The presenter describes exactly what is happening in the classroom, states the desired outcome, answers clarifying questions, and then is silent while the group discusses the issue and offers insights.

Tackling the question of how to get Donny Crawford participating in class, a colleague who knows the student might tell about his interest in current events, another teacher might suggest partner discussions and writing prompts, yet another might suggest rethinking what participation looks like. "By presenting," says Porosoff, "teachers benefit from the collective expertise of their colleagues, who in turn benefit from hearing and wrestling with a colleague's dilemma. Even if the groups don't solve every problem, presenters might leave feeling surprised by successes they hadn't noticed, inspired by their colleagues' insights, aware of new resources, and ready to try new methods …. And the whole group becomes stronger by working together toward the success of one of its members."

Porosoff suggests asking a few accomplished veteran staff members to take the lead in presenting problems to overcome the fear others might have admitting classroom weaknesses and failures.

School leaders—principals, department chairs, deans, directors—can use all four of these formats to orchestrate high-quality professional development meetings. In classroom visits, team meetings, and conversations with colleagues, leaders need to keep their eyes open toward: spotting expertise within the faculty; listening for common concerns; noticing teaching strengths and weaknesses; keeping track of conferences teachers are attending and books they're reading; carving out time for PD; and observing whether ideas are being used in classrooms and are making a difference.

"Closer Than You Think" by Lauren Porosoff in *Independent School*, Fall 2017 (Vol. 77, #1, pp. 30–36), summarized in Marshall Memo 705.

---

10. Weekly Before-School Professional Learning in North Dakota

Giving the same PD to an entire school faculty is the easiest but "least effective way to address professional development," says North Dakota superintendent Michael McNeff in this article in *The Learning Professional*. "If the learning does not apply, then how will teachers change their practices for the better?" In his district, the school day begins later every Wednesday morning, giving schools sixty minutes of fresh-energy PD time that is almost never interrupted by vacations or extracurricular activities. (Families can still drop off their children at the regular time; in one school, about one hundred students read and chat in the library under the supervision of paraprofessionals.)

For teachers, most of the Wednesday PD time is devoted to unpacking standards, developing assessments, defining mastery, mapping out units, planning interventions and enrichment, and looking at student learning results. Each PLC is responsible for setting a learning goal (for example, improving student engagement), reading a book and several articles, deciding between two options—visiting another school or taking part in their school's peer observation program—and reflecting in writing on what they learned and implemented.

"Teachers need autonomy and personalized learning to grow," says McNeff. "We believe we have found the right combination of freedom and accountability within our professional learning plan …. When teams of teachers are given time to research best practices, observe other teachers, and reflect on what they've learned, they grow professionally."

"Let's Focus on Quality of Instruction Rather Than Quantity" by Michael McNeff in *The Learning Professional*, April 2017 (Vol. 38, #2, pp. 12–14), summarized in Marshall Memo 682.

Innovative Practices and Cautionary Notes

11 Lesson Study Thrives in a California Elementary School

In this *Phi Delta Kappan* article, Catherine Lewis, Rebecca Perry, Jacqueline Hurd, and Mary Pat O'Connell describe the implementation of Japanese lesson study in a California school. They show how the school overcame three hurdles that many US schools have encountered trying to import this idea: lack of time, many teachers' "Lone Ranger" syndrome, and limited access to content knowledge.

Inspired by the description of lesson study in *The Teaching Gap* (1999), teachers at Highlands Elementary School in San Mateo gradually implemented lesson study until it was an integral part of the school's practices, structures, and identity. Each year the faculty decides on a schoolwide theme (e.g., reducing the achievement gap) to provide a common focus. Teams of three to six teachers at the same or adjacent grades loop through two lesson study cycles a year, following these steps:

- Each team decides on a specific instructional challenge (for example, multistep math problems).
- Teachers study relevant background materials (research, articles, books, and insights from district math specialists).
- They collect data from classrooms (student work on multistep problems that reveals students' difficulties).
- They collaboratively plan a "research lesson" to address the challenge.
- One team member teaches the lesson while others observe. (Teachers noticed that the strategies students had been taught, including underlining information in the problem and looking for question marks, did not help many students solve the problems.)
- The team gathers data on students (assessment results or student work).
- Teachers discuss the lesson, sharing information and discussing implications. (In this case, teachers decided to teach students a five-step problem-solving model that had students ask themselves *What do I know?* and *What do I want to know?* as they approached problems.).
- They follow up in their classrooms. (In this case, all teachers used the same five-step process

across subject areas, prompting one student to exclaim when his teacher pulled out the telltale sheet, "Oh no. You have it too!".)

The principal provides two hours a month within the school day by reducing the number of faculty meetings and handling routine faculty business in other ways.

Lewis, Perry, Hurd, and O'Connell share four insights about lesson study that the Highlands staff have articulated over the years:

- *It's not just about the lesson.* When they first began, teachers saw lesson study as a process of developing and polishing wonderful lessons and sharing them with others. After a few cycles, they began to see lesson study differently—more as an opportunity for teachers to conduct action research, test their own knowledge of how students think, and understand what they are teaching and why it's important. They dropped their initial idea of sharing "canned" lessons on the district's intranet, deciding instead to spread their work in open houses in which colleagues could see actual lessons and hear teachers talk face-to-face about what they had learned.

- *Lesson observations need to get below the surface.* At first, Highland teachers watched for whether students were engaged, on-task, behaving, and treating their peers with respect. With experience, they moved to a higher level, asking themselves—what were students' solution strategies? How were they organizing information? What types of errors were they making? Teachers who were being observed also posed more specific "look-fors" for their colleagues to focus on when they observed a lesson.

- *Lesson study is enhanced by reaching out to the knowledge base.* After a parochial beginning in which Highlands teachers consulted mostly with each other and worked only with their adopted textbooks, they began to bring in content experts from outside their school, compare the way different textbooks treated the topic, and read articles and books for insights into their lesson.

- *Implications need to go beyond the immediate lesson.* Highlands teachers initially saw the lesson they taught as a final performance. Over time, they made a point of applying the learning derived from each lesson to their future teaching, and began each new cycle by reviewing what they had learned from previous data. They were also less perfectionistic about the lessons they taught, sometimes having a team member teach an initial, imperfect lesson before moving into their planning.

Why was lesson study successful at Highlands when it had foundered in some other US schools? The authors point to several factors:

- *Flexibility* – Highlands teachers adapted Japanese lesson study to their unique setting.
- *Humility* – Teachers learned not to consider themselves experts after one or two lesson

study cycles and instead adopted the posture that there is always more to learn about teaching. "Premature expertise may pose a substantial threat to lesson study," say the authors. "The appropriate attitude for those who would help others adopt lesson study is captured in the proverb, *The road is made by walking.*"

- *Depth* – At first, teachers "tinkered around the edges" of mathematics and language arts; over time, they have delved into the core problems of teaching and learning each subject.
- *Teachers as students* – Before diving into a lesson or assignment, teachers do the work themselves; they have found this very helpful toward understanding students' misconceptions and confusions.
- *Data-driven* – They use formative assessments to check on whether students are learning what was taught in lessons and use the data to modify their strategies.
- *Inside-outside* – Highlands teachers maintain control and ownership for the lesson study process but constantly broaden their horizons by pulling in outside experts and readings.
- *Micro/macro* – The school's lesson study cycles focus on specific learning challenges at each grade level but are also part of a schoolwide effort to make sense of California standards and prepare students for high-stakes tests. The principal conveys the idea that lesson study is not "one more demand on teachers but the primary means of addressing the many demands they face."
- *Short-term/long-term* – Teachers address immediate classroom issues and also track long-range data.

Lewis, Perry, Hurd, and O'Connell close with four recommendations for helping lesson study "scale up" in U.S. schools:

- First, they suggest that teachers reach out to those who are using lesson study in other schools. There are some mistakes that don't need to be made again and again. For example, hearing from another school might speed up the evolution of a school's math lesson observations from focusing on student behavior to looking at core mathematical issues.
- Second, they suggest that instructional coaches and principals meet across schools to share larger-scale observations and strategies about lesson study.
- Third, the authors urge lesson study groups to look critically at textbooks and other instructional materials. "US teachers," they write, "often face textbooks that include untested or ill-conceived instructional ideas and omit important ones." Lesson study is an ideal forum

for teachers to combine their on-the-ground experience with a broader view of what students need to learn effectively.

- Finally, they suggest that we see lesson study as a grass-roots strategy for improving American education—and a way of building demand for better teaching and learning. This can happen when teachers invent ingenious solutions to stubborn learning problems, but also when lessons bomb. "The desire to improve is also stimulated by seeing what's *not* working," they write. "When you realize that the fourth-grader you just observed showed no understanding of concepts supposedly 'mastered' in your third-grade class, you want to improve your practice for the sake of your current and future students."

"Lesson Study Comes of Age in North America" by Catherine Lewis, Rebecca Perry, Jacqueline Hurd, and Mary Pat O'Connell in *Phi Delta Kappan*, December 2006 (Vol. 88, #4, pp. 273–281), summarized in Marshall Memo 164.

12. Using a Voicemail App to Run Cross-District Book Discussions

In this article in *The Learning Professional*, Illinois district leaders Erin Axelsen, Lorie Cristofaro, and Jill Geocaris describe how an app made it possible for them to use commuting or exercise time to take part in book studies with several colleagues. Voxer is a free mobile app that allows people to leave voice messages with other members of a group, and it notifies members when someone chimes in. Recipients have the choice of clicking on the message and listening to it live (as if on a walkie-talkie) and joining the discussion, or waiting until later to click on it and participate.

Axelsen, Cristofaro, and Geocaris say there's no way that interested educators in different districts could have managed in-person book discussions, but using the app came pretty close. "Voxer allowed us to hold a discussion at times that are convenient for each individual," they say, "yet still facilitate a conversation that builds on one another's ideas."

The authors, who had been involved in coaching pairs the previous year, recruited a number of colleagues and organized them into groups of five or six. Each group appointed a facilitator, decided on a book, set up a chapter schedule, and established a few norms, including confidentiality so people would feel free to speak candidly. Discussions often began with one person citing a quote or idea from the assigned chapter that was particularly striking, then others chimed in with reactions, new ideas, or questions.

A big advantage of this asynchronous dynamic, say Axelsen, Cristofaro, and Geocaris, "is that participants don't need to wait for an upcoming meeting to share an idea. As you read the book and something comes to mind, you can quickly grab your phone and share your idea or ask your question immediately." When some participants are too busy to take part, the facilitator can jump in and move the discussion forward.

One interesting feature of the free version of Voxer is that voice messages can't be edited or deleted (for a fee, this feature can be added). Not being able to make deletions makes discussions more like an actual conversational stream of consciousness, leading members to adopt the kind of etiquette a group would use in a face-to-face discussion.

"Your Voice Mailbox Is Full—of Learning" by Erin Axelsen, Lorie Cristofaro, and Jill Geocaris in *The Learning Professional*, October 2019 (Vol. 40, #5, pp. 36–38), summarized in Marshall Memo 808.

---

13. Online versus In-Person Professional Learning Experiences

In this article in *Kappan*, Meg Bates and Cheryl Moran ((University of Chicago) and Lena Phalen (IPG Media Lab) offer advice on how teachers can make best use of the mind-boggling array of online professional learning opportunities. For starters, they suggest thinking about online learning in three categories:

- Synchronous – These PD experiences happen in real time—for example, webinars, distance education courses, virtual coaching, and opportunities to collaborate with other teachers. Basically, these are traditional in-person PD experiences in a virtual setting.
- Asynchronous – These happen at different times for different participants—for example, teacher social networks, discussion boards, self-paced online courses (including MOOCs), and resource-sharing websites. Teachers decide when, how, and what they learn.
- Hybrid – Online activities take place as part of a larger bricks-and-mortar learning opportunity—for example, an in-person workshop or course that requires virtual collaboration off-site or online completion of tasks between sessions.

Which category teachers choose depends on the time they have available, their preferred learning style, and what they're looking for—certification, salary-step credits, resources, ideas from similarly situated colleagues. Although most teachers initially request synchronous online experiences, the authors have found that the majority end up using asynchronous channels.

When is online professional learning a better choice for teachers than in-person experiences? The authors believe there are five scenarios where online is the way to go:

- *To study a topic that's not offered within the district in a particular year.* Professional development is typically planned around new initiatives (e.g., Common Core), new curriculum materials, or external mandates. For teachers who are looking for something beyond the district's offerings, online learning is perfect.

- *A particular expert is not available in the school or district.* There are only so many consultants that a district can bring in to support teachers with curriculum and pedagogy, and external helpers can only stay for so long. Online seminars, courses, and collaborative arrangements can give teachers experiences that aren't available locally.

- *Singleton teachers can reach out to similarly isolated teachers in other locations.* A common example is the lone physics teacher in a small- or medium-size high school who would benefit greatly from taking part in a weekly Google Hangouts meeting with singleton physics teachers around the state or nation.

- *Online resources can fill immediate needs, facilitating higher-quality in-person work.* For example, teacher leaders can suggest websites to teachers that can provide a plethora of lesson plans, assessments, videos, and other tools. "Doing so can allow teachers (and professional developers) to focus less on meeting needs and more on the true work of improving instructional practice—work that is best done in person," say the authors. In addition, pulling in resources from the Web is far more efficient than trying to create them from scratch.

- *Online PD can be significantly less expensive and more feasible than in-person PD.* Online learning can be as good as, if not better than, in-person courses, say Bates, Phalen, and Moran, "but educators must research the quality of online opportunity and not make a decision based on cost or convenience alone." Teachers also need to look into sustainability—will a particular online resource continue to be available long-term?

The authors close with two caveats. The first: "Learning of any kind is best done collaboratively with supportive colleagues and facilitators who can push thinking, provide accountability structures, and ensure a quality learning experience. Relying on online professional development becomes dangerous when the learning is too independent and isolated." For example, taking part in a webinar with one hundred other educators may be stimulating, but if there's little interaction online and no follow-up afterward, it may add little value in teachers' classrooms.

Second—Bates, Phalen, and Moran point to studies showing that when teachers go online for resources, they often gravitate to those that are immediately useful rather than looking at material that challenges them and helps them grow professionally. "School-based collaboration is still necessary," conclude the authors, "maybe even more necessary, in an environment where teachers are participating in independent online learning activities." The best scenario may be teachers sharing a variety of online resources with their immediate colleagues—for example, looking over materials to see how they fit with the school's goals for student learning, taking part in a webinar as part of a school-based group, or viewing a classroom video together and pushing each other to discuss key aspects of the pedagogy.

The authors' parting words for teachers: "Use online learning to meet your personal needs, but find ways to take that learning back to your school."

"Online Professional Development: A Primer" by Meg Bates, Lena Phalen, and Cheryl Moran in *Phi Delta Kappan*, February 2016 (Vol. 97, #5, pp. 70–73), summarized in Marshall Memo 625.

14. Using Blogs and Twitter to Improve Teaching and Learning

In this article in *Phi Delta Kappan*, William Ferriter (a North Carolina sixth-grade teacher) and Nicholas Provenzano (a Michigan high-school English teacher) sing the praises of using blogs and Twitter to have two-way conversation with fellow teachers around the world and of broadening their professional horizons in "unconferences." (Provenzano's *The Nerdy Teacher* has almost thirty thousand Twitter followers.) However, they add, educators who embrace new learning spaces need to be aware of three cautionary notes:

- *Balance* – Having a customized stream of information tuned to one's own vision can result in professional blind spots. "Avoiding these self-created intellectual echo chambers depends on educators who intentionally seek out dissenting voices to learn with," say Ferriter and Provenzano. "The primary goal of social spaces should be to challenge, instead of to simply confirm, what we already know and believe."
- *Accuracy* – No one is actively policing the content of the Internet, say the authors. We all need to be critical consumers of information from the Web.

- *Recognition* – Few educators view social spaces and unconferences as valid forms of professional development. "If connected educators want this to change," say Ferriter and Provenzano, "they must systematically document the effect that nontraditional learning opportunities are having on their practice." And district leaders should partner with innovative PD providers and create additional opportunities for teachers to explore new ideas.

"Today's Lesson: Self-Directed Learning … for Teachers" by William Ferriter and Nicholas Provenzano in *Phi Delta Kappan*, November 2013 (Vol. 95, #3, pp. 16–21), summarized in Marshall Memo 509.

Professional Learning Suggestions for Chapter Ten: Professional Learning That Works

Learning How to Improve Professional Learning

This chapter introduces some of the shortcomings of present approaches to professional learning, outlines a few key characteristics of effective professional learning, and provides some suggestions for improvement. Below are activities to help both leaders and teachers learn more about and think through ways to improve professional learning at their own school.

I. Building on the Expertise in the Building

There are many shortcomings of traditional PD, but one of the most significant and unfortunate ones is that schools fail to maximize the expertise in their own buildings. These two activities help educators think about this dilemma and come up with new ways to share best practices.

A. Spark a discussion about sharing teacher expertise with a quotation from the first article-summary.
Post the following quotation from "Opening Classroom Doors" (Richardson article-summary 1) for all to see: "Keeping an exemplary teacher's knowledge isolated inside a classroom isn't just poor practice, it's almost malpractice."

    1. In pairs, ask teachers to discuss what this quotation means to them.

    2. Next, have everyone read "Opening Classroom Doors."

    3. Now have a large-group discussion about the article-summary and the implications of the quotation for professional learning at your school.

    4. Finally, do a whip around the room and have everyone share one word they would use to describe the current state of professional learning at your school.

B. Have a more in-depth conversation about peer-to-peer sharing at your school.
Ask everyone to read "Opening Classroom Doors" (Richardson article-summary 1) and "The Dubious Impact of Professional Development" (Kennedy article-summary 2) during a meeting.

1. In small groups, have teachers discuss the following three questions:
   - In what ways does your school already share best teaching and learning practices?
   - What other ways might your school share best practices if there were no limitations?
   - What obstacles might get in the way of these ideas? (Think about time, resources, scheduling, culture, teacher experience level, etc.)

2. Back together as a large group, pool ideas that were discussed in the small groups above. You could use newsprint with three columns or share ideas virtually with a program like Padlet:

Ways We Currently Share Best Practices	New Ideas for Sharing Best Practices Among Teachers	Obstacles That Might Impede New Ways of Sharing

3. Take a vote on which ideas are most exciting to the group. Ask for volunteers to create a committee to explore ways to increase the sharing of professional knowledge and skills within the school.

II. Explore the Characteristics of Effective PD

The activities below help educators dive into what really makes PD effective. The second activity helps the leadership team directly apply new ideas as they collaboratively plan a single PD session based on the characteristics of effective PD.

A. Help teachers embrace the idea that teaching is a skill that can be learned.

Have the entire faculty do a "live" read (that is, read during an actual meeting) and underline key passages in "What Educators Can Learn from Athletic Training" (James Surowiecki article-summary 4), a perfect choice for a full-faculty read because it applies to all grades and subjects. Then have groups of three do the following protocol:

PROFESSIONAL LEARNING SUGGESTIONS FOR CHAPTER TEN

- One person shares a passage he or she underlined and why this resonates with them. (One minute.)
- The same person shares reactions to the following quotation from the article-summary, "What we need to embrace instead is the idea of teaching as a set of skills that can be taught and learned and constantly improved on." (One minute.)
- Finally, that person shares one of the seven specific ideas at the end of the article-summary for what teacher "training" might involve that most resonates with them. (One minute.)
- The group discusses the first person's reactions to the article-summary. (Two minutes.)
- Each person in the small group takes a turn sharing, using the five-minute protocol above until all have gone.

B. Have the leadership team collaboratively design a PD session using backward planning.

Have your leadership team or school leaders (principal, assistant principal, department chairs, teacher leaders, etc.) meet and read "Planning Professional Learning with the End in Mind" (Thomas Guskey article-summary 5).

1. Have the group discuss the process and benefits of planning PD backwards and compare this process to how people in the school typically plan PD.

2. Then in smaller groups, have each team think of one upcoming professional learning session they would like to plan. Have them follow Guskey's approach, using the chart below to collaboratively map out this one PD session. Start at the top of the chart.

Guskey Level	What to Do	Your Plan
5: Student learning outcomes	• Identify the student learning outcomes for the PD (math skills, class behavior, etc.). • Plan the assessments to measure learning outcomes (test scores, survey data, portfolios, etc.).	
4: Participants' *use* of what was learned	• Plan classroom observations to determine if the PD impacted professional practice.	
3: Organizational support and change	• Determine what school policies, practices, time, technology, instructional materials and other resources need to be in place to support the PD.	
2: Participants' learning	• Outline the knowledge, skills, attitudes, and dispositions participants are to gain.	
1: Participants' reactions	• Choose PD activities that will most engage participants by taking adult learning into account.	

3. After everyone conducts their PD session, hold a future meeting in which the leaders go through the five levels and evaluate how successful their PD sessions were at each of the five levels.

C. Have school leaders (leadership team, admin team, department chairs, grade-team leaders, anyone who might plan PD) read the article-summaries in the section: Characteristics of Effective Professional Learning.

1. Have half of the leaders read these two article-summaries; "What Educators Can Learn from Athletic Training" (4) and "Three Keys to Effective Professional Learning" (7). Have the other half read the other two article-summaries: "Planning Professional Learning with the End in Mind" (5) and "How to Get Traction with Professional Development" (6). Ask everyone to think about ideas for improving *single* PD sessions and professional learning *overall* as they read.

2. Pair up each school leader with someone who read the other two article-summaries. Ask each person in the pair to share the *content* of each of the two article-summaries they read and

PROFESSIONAL LEARNING SUGGESTIONS FOR CHAPTER TEN

their own ideas about the *implications* for the school. While listening, the other person should take notes in a chart like the one below. Then switch roles.

Ideas to Improve a *Single* PD Session	Ideas to Improve Professional Learning *Overall* at Our School

3. Come back as a large group and share ideas from the paired discussions. Decide which ideas, if any, the leadership team would like to pursue to improve professional learning at the school.

III. Some Practical Applications to Improve PD at Your School

The following activities get teachers to think beyond the single sit-n-git PD session to add other forms of professional learning to their repertoires.

A. Have faculty expand their view of ways to improve professional practice.
When asked what professional development is, teachers often struggle to think of structures other than the single PD workshop session. We need to expand their ideas of what it means to engage in professional learning that changes practice.

1. Do a large-group brainstorm of all of the ways that teachers can improve their professional practice.

2. Next, share "Thirty-Five Ideas for Improving Professional Development" (article-summary 8) and have teachers read through this list.

3. Next, designate the four corners of the room for the four categories of professional learning mentioned in the article: professional learning, learning with colleagues, collaborating with colleagues, and having an impact beyond one's classroom. Have teachers choose the category they are most interested in and go to that corner.

4. Ask each of the four groups to discuss the topics in their category and why they are interested in these topics.

5. Finally, have each group come up with an action plan for implementing some new idea in

this category. It doesn't need to be a complicated plan; teachers could simply fill out a form like the one below:

Simple Action Plan Template				
WHY are we doing this	WHAT will we do	WHO is doing what	HOW will we implement this	WHEN will we do each part

B. Have teachers try one method of sharing internal expertise.

Have the full faculty read "Four Ways to Use a School's Internal Expertise" (article-summary 9) and focus closely on the section about *The Council*.

1. Introduce teachers to the structure of the Consultancy Protocol (go to schoolreforminitiative.org or use the modified version below) as a technique for teachers to share a teaching dilemma and get advice and strategies from colleagues. Discuss and get feedback for any modifications to this protocol that teachers might want to make. Add appropriate times for each step as well.

Modified Consultancy Protocol	
Time	Steps
	1. Presenter gives overview of the dilemma.
	2. Others ask clarifying questions (just brief factual questions).
	3. The group asks probing questions to expand the presenter's thinking and ideas.
	4. The presenter responds to the group's questions and ideas.
	5. Repeat so each person has a turn to present.

2. Ask teachers to come to this meeting with an instructional dilemma in mind and perhaps even with some initial writing and thinking about their problem. Put them in small groups with others who have similarly-themed dilemmas and have them use the protocol above so each person gets to present a dilemma.

C. Have teachers explore the ways PLCs (professional learning communities) meet the criteria for effective professional learning.

If you are thinking of implementing or improving the use of PLCs at your school, ask teachers to

PROFESSIONAL LEARNING SUGGESTIONS FOR CHAPTER TEN

read "Weekly Before-School Professional Learning in North Dakota" (article-summary 10) and "How to Get Traction with Professional Development" (article-summary 6). Then have them discuss the ways that PLCs might meet the criteria for effective PD in article-summary 6.

IV. Find Ways to Innovate the Way You Do PD

The final four article-summaries present innovative methods for approaching PD that your school may or may not have tried before: lesson study, asynchronous book studies, online professional learning opportunities, and blogs and Twitter. The activity below asks teachers to explore one of these innovative approaches.

Have teachers read one article on an innovative PD approach and explore how they might use it.

1. Ask teachers to choose and read one of the following four article-summaries: "Lesson Study Thrives in a California Elementary School" (11), "Using a Voicemail App to Run Cross-District Book Discussions" (12), "Online versus In-Person Professional Learning Experiences" (13), or "Using Blogs and Twitter to Improve Teaching and Learning" (14).

2. Organize the teachers into four groups based on the article-summaries they read. All teachers who read article-summary 11 go in one group, all who read article-summary 12 go in another—etc.

3. Some of the article-summaries mention more than one idea for PD. Have each of the four groups choose one idea and brainstorm answers to the four questions in the chart that follows. In the spirit of innovation, consider using a program like Padlet to organize answers to these questions into columns and to let teachers comment on each other's ideas.

Name of the PD Idea/Technique/Approach:			
What is it? How does it work?	Advantages of using this for PD?	Potential obstacles to using this for PD?	What might teachers need to start using this (resources, support, etc.)?

Chapter Eleven: Teacher Leadership

As servant leaders, teacher leaders understand that their belief in others' capabilities and conveying that belief in words and actions will result in ordinary people accomplishing extraordinary things.
—Joellen Killion et al.

Deeply entrenched in many US public-school faculties are three norms: autonomy (my classroom, my castle); egalitarianism (we're all the same here, and we're nice to each other); and seniority (the best teaching assignments go to those who've served longest). In schools where these beliefs pervade, it's hard for teacher leaders to be agents of change. The articles in this chapter examine the barriers to teachers taking on leadership roles, describe attempts to distribute leadership, give practical tips to teacher leaders, and describe other pathways to teacher leadership.

Addressing the Barriers to Teacher Leadership – Roland Barth says strong cultural headwinds have worked against teacher leadership in the past, but he believes conditions now favor the idea. Melinda Mangin and Sara Ray Stoelinga say if teacher leaders are to have an impact, they must challenge the norms of egalitarianism, autonomy, and privacy; accept the role of expert; and have difficult conversations with colleagues. Elisa MacDonald says teacher leaders need to recognize and confront the "culture of nice" by taking the initiative in team meetings, responding in the moment, and following up with colleagues.

Distributing Leadership – Sarah Fiarman describes how she, as a principal, built teachers' leadership skills and got out of the way so teams could do meaningful work. Chris Bierly, Betsy Doyle, and Abigail Smith say that many of the "soft roles" teacher leaders can play in schools don't have the mandate, time, and authority to be effective—and suggest five steps to empower colleagues and distribute the key functions of coaching and teamwork. Rebecca Cheung, Elisa Stone, Judith Warren Little, and Thomas Reinhardt describe how science lead teachers provided their colleagues with resources, coordination, modeling, and advocacy.

Tips for Teacher Leaders – Marsha Ratzel lists telltale signs that a teacher might be ready to take on an expanded role. Joellen Killion and five colleagues list the key considerations for maximizing the impact of a wide variety of teacher leaders. Jason Margolis has practical suggestions for teacher leaders, including using humor, building on existing classroom work, and not overloading teachers with too many strategies.

Other Pathways for Teacher Leadership – Teacher leaders Gayle Davis and Margaret Metzger report the key features of their program to onboard and support new teachers in their Massachusetts high school. Julia Koppich and Daniel Humphrey describe the Peer Assistance and Review (PAR) program, in which experienced teachers coach and evaluate novice and underperforming colleagues. Susan Moore Johnson and John Papay propose a career ladder for teachers with these steps: probationary, tenured, master teacher, and outstanding teachers released from classrooms to assume broader responsibilities. Frederick Hess suggests how teacher leaders can be effective speaking truth to power in the political arena.

Questions to Consider

- What are the inherent challenges of being a teacher leader?
- How can teacher leaders be trusted by colleagues *and* be a force for school improvement?
- What does successful teacher leadership look like?

Addressing the Barriers to Teacher Leadership

① Dealing with Headwinds

In this article in *Educational Leadership*, author/consultant (and former principal) Roland Barth says there are five reasons the idea of teacher leadership has been slow to take off. First, principals want to be in control. "If I, as a principal, delegate or accept a teacher's leadership of something and it goes badly," says Barth, "… the superintendent isn't going to call that teacher. He or she is going to call me." Second, some teachers resent a colleague with special responsibilities: "Who the heck do you think you are?!" Third, teachers' plates are full; with increasing accountability for student achievement, most teachers can't find time for schoolwide matters. Fourth, in schools with an us-versus-them dynamic, teacher leadership can be seen as siding with the enemy. Finally, the traditional business model in schools hasn't supported teacher leadership; the usual message to line workers is, *Do your job*.

These challenges notwithstanding, Barth believes teacher leadership has huge potential because:

• *School leadership is too big a job for one person*. "For a long time, people have realized that the principal alone can't run something as complex and enormous as a school," says Barth. "But now I think *principals* realize that." When he was a school leader, Barth asked teachers every September what piece of the school they wanted to take responsibility for: the parent committee, professional development, a curriculum innovation, etc. "If all teachers are expected to be leaders," he says, "no one is breaking the taboo about standing higher than the others because everyone is on the same higher level."

• *The Common Core is a golden opportunity for teacher leadership*. It spells out *what* students should know but not *how* it should be taught. The road is wide open for teachers to shape the classroom details.

• *New models of leadership are emerging*. A number of schools are experimenting with different roles for teachers. Colleges and universities are a good model here—professors are involved in decisions about curriculum, graduation requirements, scheduling, hiring of colleagues and administrators, finance, and use of space.

• *Teacher leadership can unlock teachers' secret passions*. "Teachers tend to keep two sets of books," says Barth. "One lists what they have to do to comply; the other lists what they believe is best for their students." As principal, he got everyone involved in a weekly two-hour elective where they could teach something they really cared about, and the energy and enthusiasm filtered into the rest of the week.

Barth flinches when he hears an educator say, "I'm just a teacher." All teachers are significant leaders of their students, he says. "The shift comes when you also take a piece of leading the school. There's tremendous satisfaction that comes from making that jump, to being an owner rather than a renter here." That's when everyone's learning curve—teachers, students, principals—gets a lot steeper.

"The Time Is Ripe (Again)" by Roland Barth in *Educational Leadership*, October 2013 (Vol. 71, #2, pp. 10–16), summarized in Marshall Memo 504.

2. Core Dilemmas in the Teacher Leader Role

In this *Journal of Staff Development* article, Melinda Mangin (Rutgers University) and Sara Ray Stoelinga (University of Chicago) highlight the dilemma faced by teacher leaders: if they come across as "experts," they risk alienating teachers, but if they present themselves as colleagues, they risk not being taken seriously. "How can the teacher leader be both a trusted colleague and a resource for instructional improvement?" ask Mangin and Stoelinga. "Making teacher leadership an effective tool for improving instructional practice depends on resolving this paradox."

Teacher leaders often try to earn teachers' trust and acceptance by downplaying the credentials they bring to the job. This conforms to the norm of egalitarianism that is pervasive in American schools—we're all co-learners here. But being "just one of the gang" undercuts the teacher leader's impact. "If teachers view the teacher leader as lacking expert knowledge," say Mangin and Stoelinga, "there is little incentive to seek the teacher leader's advice or guidance …. By describing themselves as nonexperts, teacher leaders unintentionally devalue their work and become a less desirable resource."

There's another problem with teacher leaders presenting themselves as co-equal: they are less likely to give critical feedback that might make a colleague uncomfortable. Rather than violating the norms of egalitarianism and autonomy, teacher leaders tend to provide less-intrusive assistance to teachers—getting them materials and resources, teaching demonstration lessons, sitting in on team meetings. All this may be seen as a necessary step to gaining enough trust to have difficult conversations about instruction, but many teacher leaders never take the next step. A further reason for not providing hard feedback is that few teacher leaders have training and experience in this area.

Mangin and Stoelinga believe that teacher leaders can solve this dilemma by taking three steps:

• *Accept the role of expert.* "Peer relationships must be reconceptualized to make room for teachers to lead in areas where they have strengths," they say. "As such, formal structures must be put in place in schools to allow a broad base of classroom teachers to lead professional development, provide advice to peers, and share aspects of their practice that are exemplary."

• *Have difficult conversations.* Classroom instruction won't improve unless teachers receive honest feedback about ineffective and mediocre practices, and it has to be understood that providing this kind of feedback is part of the teacher leader's job. "While such conversations are inherently evaluative in nature," say Mangin and Stoelinga, "they should also be free from stigma, presenting all teachers with an opportunity to learn with and from one another." Teacher leaders (as well as many principals and other school administrators) need training in and practice with these difficult conversations.

• *Redefine school norms.* Teachers must let go of the dysfunctional norms of egalitarianism, autonomy, and privacy—and embrace collaboration, dialogue, and deprivatized practice. One of the biggest jobs faced by teacher leaders is developing the trust needed for this to occur. "Schools must become places where the norms of teaching reflect an expectation that peers have the capacity and ability to engage in the joint work of effectively critiquing one another's instructional practice," say Mangin and Stoelinga. It's also essential, they say, to provide time in the schedule for these interactions, get teachers observing each other's classrooms, use videotape and assessment evidence to examine practice, and use rubrics to guide instructional practice.

"Peer? Expert? Teacher Leaders Struggle to Gain Trust While Establishing Their Expertise" by Melinda Mangin and Sara Ray Stoelinga in *Journal of Staff Development* (currently *The Learning Professional*), June 2011 (Vol. 32, #3, pp. 48–51), summarized in Marshall Memo 388.

3 Dealing with the "Culture of Nice"

"Teachers must be willing to expose their struggles and failures with their colleagues," says Massachusetts-based consultant Elisa MacDonald in this *Journal of Staff Development* article, "or teams will go through the motions of collaborative inquiry but never see results." She believes teacher leaders need to do four things to move beyond what is often called "the culture of nice":

- *Recognize the signs.* MacDonald identifies the following symptoms of a too-congenial team culture—
    - Teachers rarely question their practices, assumptions, and beliefs. They compliment each other a lot and don't look for classroom improvements that might boost student learning.
    - Teachers share only exemplary student work for fear that their colleagues will judge them. As a result, the team doesn't discuss strategies for getting better work from failing students.
    - Teachers make excuses for why some students aren't successful. They blame the assessment or the student rather than looking at instruction.
    - Teachers recommend strategies to colleagues but don't look in the mirror and consider improvements they themselves need to make.
- *Take the initiative in team meetings.* Here are MacDonald's suggestions for nipping the culture of nice in the bud—
    - Articulate norms and make sure they're followed—for example, *We question our assumptions, beliefs, and actions. We go beyond the surface. We respectfully challenge viewpoints. We agree to disagree without being disagreeable. We zoom in on the real issue.*
    - Create common assessments and lessons so that looking at results won't foster defensiveness on the part of individual teachers.
    - Set an example by going first or raising a concern based on student work and asking for suggestions on how to teach differently.
- *Respond in the moment.* Teacher leaders can act in ways that short-circuit the culture of nice and lead to deeper discussion—
    - When the team is making positive comments, go deeper—for example, "*What specifically worked? How do we know? Why do we think it worked?*
    - Focus on the dilemma, not the teacher. Teachers sometimes hold back presenting less-than-proficient student work because they are afraid their colleagues will think less highly of them. The team leader can reduce this fear by analyzing student work and asking

questions like, *What next steps does this student need?* "Focusing the discussion on students reduces any concerns of blame or judgment," says MacDonald, "and encourages the team to look more analytically, discuss more openly, and problem-solve collaboratively."

- Model curiosity, observation, and honesty. Teacher leaders can foster productive dialogue by constantly wondering about what's going on in students' minds and what can be done to improve their performance. "The wondering brings the discussion to a safe but more critical level," says MacDonald, "allowing for others to build on the teacher leader's observation or feel comfortable expressing their own observations."
- Redirect. Sometimes the teacher leader needs to confront the culture of nice directly, saying, for example, "I've heard a lot of positives about the student work and teacher's instruction. With the time remaining, let's look to see if there are specific areas in which the students can improve. For example, I notice in paragraph two of the student essay …"

• *Follow up.* If a team hasn't moved beyond congeniality, there may be not-so-nice comments in the parking lot afterward. To prevent this, the team leader needs to—

- Debrief at the end of each meeting, getting frank opinions on the rigor of the discussion (based on a clear definition of what a rigorous discussion looks like).
- Ask colleagues to fill out exit tickets—perhaps, *What new thinking do you have? How might you apply it? How can the team and teacher leader support you?*
- Check in individually with colleagues to get their candid opinions on how the meeting went.

"When Nice Won't Suffice: Honest Discourse Is Key to Shifting School Culture" by Elisa MacDonald in *Journal of Staff Development* (currently *The Learning Professional*), June 2011 (Vol. 32, #3, pp. 45–47, 51); summarized in Marshall Memo 388.

Distributing Leadership

④ Fostering a Leadership Mindset in Teachers

In this article in *Educational Leadership*, former principal Sarah Fiarman remembers the critique she once received from a retired principal on the way she'd conducted a beginning-of-year faculty meeting. Her agenda had many good elements – a trust-building exercise, discussion of a new instructional improvement plan, teacher-generated goals, and team breakouts—and Fiarman expected praise. But her mentor took her to task for being too much at the center of everything: "Instead of focusing on what you need to cover," he said, "you should be thinking about the leadership skills you want to develop in teachers."

The comment stung, but Fiarman knew her mentor was right. Although she'd run an interactive meeting, solicited teachers' input on the professional development plan, and gotten teachers working in teams, it was still her plan and her meeting. She set about building a schoolwide leadership mindset and creating "a culture in which each professional feels an urgent responsibility to influence the achievement of *all* students." Here are the steps she discovered:

• *Building leadership skills* – "For a teacher, leading peers requires acting in ways that may feel uncomfortable," says Fiarman. That's because it butts up against longstanding norms of autonomy, egalitarianism, and seniority (as catalogued in Dan Lortie's classic 1975 book, *Schoolteacher*). Fiarman used instructional leadership team meetings to build team leaders' confidence and skills in getting their grade-level peers to think beyond their silo, used tools like the "Five Whys" to get full-staff meetings drilling down to the root causes of schoolwide problems, and formalized schoolwide values and expectations that empowered any staff member to advocate for improvement.

• *Sharing responsibility for meaningful work* – "When teachers see that their leadership has improved something they care about, it brings a satisfaction that fuels them to continue," says Fiarman. She made a point of getting out of the way so teacher teams could grapple with key issues. The literacy team worked on which aspect of writing instruction most needed improvement. The math team aligned math practice standards across the grades and presented a plan to the staff. Another team worked with the assistant principal and special education director to craft a schedule that would maximize time for interventions. When the district mandated Response to Intervention, a large group of teachers met several times to develop a plan for the school. "In the end," says Fiarman, "the plan was more thoughtful than what I would have proposed. And equally important, teachers were invested in it." Of course, not every meeting went smoothly and some teams needed her intervention and support, but Fiarman is convinced that the end results were better as a result of her radical decentralization.

• *Setting clear expectations* – Teachers get discouraged when they commit time and expertise, only to have their work nixed by the principal. That's why it's crucial for teacher teams to know up front if their input is advisory, if it's subject to the approval of the principal, or if they'll have the final say. Fiarman learned to clarify the locus of decision-making, spell out standards of quality, and then stand back and let teams do their work.

• *Adopting two-track thinking* – "Every staff interaction holds an opportunity to either reinforce the existing egg-crate model of teacher isolation or actively develop an improvement-oriented culture of whole-school responsibility," says Fiarman. "Because most teachers aren't used to thinking from a whole-school perspective, they'll need reminders. Over and over again." She learned to listen while simultaneously planning how to empower teachers, asking questions like: *What might be the root cause of the problem? What support will teachers need to roll out the new math assessments? How can we ensure that we are considering multiple perspectives?*

There are times when top-down decisions are necessary, but Fiarman worked to move responsibility to teachers as much as possible and foster a climate in which teachers:

- Identified and engaged with teaching and learning issues across grades and subjects;
- Went to their colleagues first with problems and solutions;
- Collaborated more than was formally expected;
- Expected to participate in significant design decisions;
- Took responsibility for identifying and addressing problems outside their classrooms.

With this approach, Fiarman believes, "we should expect to see more innovation and a greater sense of professional success among teachers as they lead the way to improving student learning."

"Building a Schoolwide Leadership Mindset" by Sarah Fiarman in *Educational Leadership*, May 2017 (Vol. 74, #8, pp. 22–27), summarized in Marshall Memo 685.

5 How to Implement Distributed Instructional Leadership

In this Bain & Company study, Chris Bierly, Betsy Doyle, and Abigail Smith bemoan the fact that (a) most principals have an unmanageable number of teachers and other staff reporting to them, (b) many principals make very little difference to the growth and development of their colleagues, and (c) few schools have figured out how to boost principals' effectiveness by getting assistant principals, deans, department heads, grade-level and PLC (Professional Learning Community) chairs, teacher leaders, mentor teachers, and instructional coaches working as a cohesive, coordinated team to help teachers improve their craft and get better results from students.

"While many districts are investing heavily in new leadership roles," say Bierly, Doyle, and Smith, "—upwards of 25 percent of teachers have taken on a 'teacher leader' title, for example—our research shows that very few of these additional leaders feel responsible for the performance and growth of the teachers they lead …. All too often we are investing in one-off roles and a broad menu of professional development efforts without a clear vision for how schools should be led or how that model will improve teaching and learning. Simply put, we aren't expecting the right things from our leaders and we aren't setting them up for success."

The Bain team surveyed, observed, and interviewed more than forty-two hundred educators in twelve US school districts and charter management organizations to better understand the instructional leadership challenge. A major conclusion: many of the instructional support roles that have been added to schools in recent years are too "soft" to make a difference in classrooms. "Teacher-leader roles can be a valuable way to give teachers opportunities to grow outside the classroom," say Bierly, Doyle, and Smith. "They expose teachers to new responsibilities and give them a chance to use their skills to help peers succeed. But more often than not, teacher leaders aren't given specific responsibility for leading and developing other teachers in the building. And most don't feel accountable for the performance of those they are working with." A teacher leader in a large urban district put it this way: "I am not responsible for the learning and development of the students taught by these teachers, nor do I feel empowered to impact the learning and development of these students."

In addition to the problem of mandate and authority, there's the problem of time—time to observe classrooms, meet with teacher teams, analyze student performance data, and confer one-on-one with colleagues in ways that produce real change. Professional Learning Communities (PLCs) have a similar problem. According to the Bain researchers, "they usually fall short of plugging the leadership gap. That's because they aren't typically led by an empowered leader with the responsibility, time, and authority to help those within the community materially improve their instructional practice. They rely on meetings and group discussion rather than empowering the PLC leader to work closely with team members through observation, coaching, and feedback."

The good news, say Bierly, Doyle, and Smith, is that some districts and CMOs are successfully addressing these leadership dilemmas. Here are the key steps they recommend to harness the potential of the instructional support roles within each school and provide cohesive, authoritative instructional support and direction to teachers:

• *First, decide on a district-wide leadership model.* In setting up school leadership teams that make more effective use of administrators, teacher leaders, and other instructional support roles, districts need to answer four key questions.

- What will the core leadership roles be and what responsibilities will those leaders have?
- How will leaders be deployed to support teams of teachers?
- How will classroom observations and teacher feedback and coaching work?
- Who will be responsible for teacher evaluations and who will have input?

The Bain team recommends that districts decide on one model for all schools. "We don't ask principals to design the IT system from scratch or write their own textbooks," they say. "The school leadership model is no different—it is a tool that is best designed, with plenty of principal and teacher input, to serve the system as a whole with latitude for school-level customization." The Denver Public School district is an example of this approach, with 80 percent "tight" (centrally mandated) and 20 percent "loose" (school-decided).

• *Second, empower and develop leaders working with a manageable number of teachers.* One approach is to empower teacher leaders and boost their leadership capacity. Denver took this route, creating Team Leads who are released from classroom duties up to 50 percent of the week so they can coach eight to twelve teachers and work closely with one grade-level or subject-area teacher team. The Team Leads observe and support team members, have input on their evaluations, and share responsibility for their performance. "Denver chose to focus on teacher leaders," say Bierly, Doyle, and Smith, "because it believed that current teachers would have the most credibility among their peers and would bring to the process the most relevant and up-to-date content expertise.

"Denver also believed that empowering such a group of 'player coaches' promotes a healthy culture of teacher collaboration." Charlotte–Mecklenburg (CM) is using a similar approach. "We very deliberately designed our model to keep our best teachers in the classroom but also to allow them to expand their input," said a CM zone superintendent. "Our great teachers want to impact more than just their own students."

All this is an adjustment for principals, who need to learn how to step back from trying to be the leader of *everyone* to empowering, training, and supervising their leadership team. "When the Team Leads in Denver began to take on more responsibility, for instance, some principals instinctively used their newfound 'extra' time to double down on working with teachers they knew were struggling," say the Bain researchers. "Some had to learn to pull back and get out of the way. Their job in the new model was to coach and develop their Team Leads to handle those problems, not jump in themselves."

- *Third, focus leaders on frequent, high-quality coaching of teachers.* "An effective distributed leadership model starts with an understanding that teaching is an incredibly difficult job—not just technically, but also emotionally," say Bierly, Doyle, and Smith. "Many teachers invest heavily in their students, reveling in their successes and sharing the burden of their failures. But maintaining enthusiasm and energy for the job is a daily challenge. Too often, teachers see the limited guidance they get as punitive—a one-way, arms-length demand for better performance. The most effective school leaders understand this and see their roles as helping to create energy for teaching by ensuring teachers get the support they need."

Leadership team members need to spend serious time in classrooms, understand what's going on, and provide one-on-one support, encouragement, and guidance to each of their teachers. "I am in my teachers' classrooms every week," says a Denver Team Lead. "I think about the big picture and what needs to change and then I think about small actions that will help us move forward and we focus together on those. In some classrooms, kids really aren't clear on what they are supposed to be learning. I work with those teachers to make their objectives clear to kids and then we work together to plan their lessons to ensure they line up against those objectives."

- *Fourth, support teams in frequent collaborative work.* Grade-level and subject-area teacher teams meet frequently and are guided and supported by their AP or teacher leader. Team meetings are the main vehicle for breaking the historic culture of teacher isolation. Teams are where teachers share challenges and effective practices, look together at student work and assessments, and (with the leader's help) connect the team's work with what is going on in individual classrooms. One California high-school teacher said, "If you are a new teacher you are immediately led to your PLC leader and given all the tools you need along with incredible support. How you deliver is up to you, but you are part of a community. You are part of a family and they won't let you fail."

- *Finally, give leaders the time and authority to continuously improve teaching.* "Having more leaders in our schools with true end-to-end responsibility for the development of our teachers is a key part of addressing the current leadership gaps," say Bierly, Doyle, and Smith, "schools led by thinly-stretched principals; too many isolated teachers who are not growing as instructors; and, ultimately, too many schools with poor student outcomes. But adding more leaders is only part of the answer. Systems must also set those leaders up for success with both the time and authority to effectively lead a team of teachers."

That means a manageable span of control (ideally no more than ten teachers per leader, say Green Dot's leaders)—releasing teacher leaders from classroom duties up to 50 percent of the time; a clear expectation of frequent classroom visits followed by coaching and support for each teacher; a significant voice in teachers' evaluations; and focusing their team meetings on curriculum, pedagogy, and results. For schools that take the approach of increasing the number of assistant principals, a key element is principals making sure that APs aren't loaded down with noninstructional duties. And the role of the principal has to change: "Principals need to be able to step back, delegate authority, and focus on 'leading a team of leaders,'" says the Bain team.

"For some," they conclude, "the threat of distributed leadership is that it creates more bosses and more bureaucracy. But a well-designed model for empowering more leaders actually has the opposite effect. Instead of a top-down system based on cursory evaluations and little individual support, distributed leadership invites collaboration, shared responsibility, and a sense that we are all in this together on behalf of our students…. None of this is easy. It requires a multi-year, system-wide focus on change—restructuring roles, adjusting cultural norms, and creating alignment around major shifts in how schools are organized and run. Yet our research over the past year has left us energized and optimistic. We've seen districts and CMOs making real investments in developing and deploying transformative leadership in their schools, and we've seen tangible evidence of success."

"Transforming Schools: How Distributed Leadership Can Create More High-Performing Schools" by Chris Bierly, Betsy Doyle, and Abigail Smith of Bain & Company, January 14, 2016, summarized in Marshall Memo 623.

---

6 Four Roles for Science Teacher Leaders

In this *Phi Delta Kappan* article, Rebecca Cheung, Elisa Stone, and Judith Warren Little (University of California–Berkeley) and consultant Thomas Reinhardt describe a district's teacher leader model aimed at supporting the implementation of Next Generation Science Standards. The science lead teachers served four major functions:

- Providing resources—
    - Sharing readings, lessons, and ideas;
    - Creating and adapting lessons and units;
    - Suggesting science events, field trips, speakers, free and donated materials;
    - Supporting regular access to district-provided materials and supplies;
    - Keeping abreast of and accessing science-related news, resources, and technology.
- Collaborating—
    - Mentoring and coaching teachers to improve their practices;
    - Facilitating science-focused professional development sessions;
    - Initiating and facilitating peer collaboration;
    - Participating in science PD for the lead teachers' own benefit;
    - Developing productive meeting formats and processes;
    - Improving the skills of mentoring, supporting, and coaching a variety of teachers;
    - Contributing to the science teacher leader community.
- Modeling—
    - Reflecting on and being open to improving one's own teaching practices;
    - Being open to being observed by colleagues and jointly critiquing lessons;
    - Analyzing and discussing the effectiveness of different teaching practices;
    - Making effective science instruction visible;
    - Committing to a deep understanding of Next Generation Science Standards;
    - Balancing and integrating non-science commitments to maximize science instruction.
- Advocating—
    - Identifying and developing common pedagogies across subject areas;
    - Promoting science in schoolwide decision-making;
    - Building alliances to further science instruction;
    - Keeping abreast of science-related policies, expectations, and decisions;

- Regularly communicating and reminding administrators and teachers about science expectations and opportunities;
- Identifying opportunities to integrate science into the core instructional plan;
- Ensuring representation for science instruction in school governance;
- Analyzing the political climate and context of the school to support science instruction.

A two-year study of forty of the science lead teachers affirmed the value of these four roles and confirmed the success of teachers' work on the quality of science instruction in the district.

"Defining Teacher Leadership: A Framework" by Rebecca Cheung, Elisa Stone, Judith Warren Little, and Thomas Reinhardt in *Phi Delta Kappan*, November 2018 (Vol. 100, #2, pp. 38–44), summarized in Marshall Memo 762.

Tips for Teacher Leaders

⑦ How to Spot a Blossoming Teacher Leader

In this *Education Week Quality Counts* article, Kansas middle-school teacher Marsha Ratzel lists five telltale signs of an emerging teacher leader:

• *You wish you had an impact beyond your own classroom.* This might include sharing a lesson plan with a teacher down the hall, unpacking the Common Core standards with your department, offering to lead a workshop on bullying, blogging about how your students are using iPads for letter recognition, sharing ideas in topic-focused Twitter chats, or submitting an article to your favorite professional journal.

• *Colleagues often ask you for advice.* Fellow teachers start to turn to you (yes, YOU!) for ideas on how to handle difficult situations.

• *You "think big" about problems.* "When others are complaining, you're imagining solutions," says Ratzel. "You can see ways that the system can change to help you and your colleagues to better serve students—whether at the school, district, state, or national level." This might manifest itself in talking about ideas with your principal, working through the union, acting as a spokesperson for your grade level at a school board meeting, or working on a district leadership committee.

• *You want to take new teachers under your wing.* This could start with offering a newbie the kind of advice you wish you'd had when you first started and progress to serving on "learning walk" teams, taking on an official mentoring role in which you observe teachers and offer follow-up suggestions, and getting involved in training new teachers.

• *You always want to know more.* You're curious about research and effective pedagogy and read a lot. Perhaps you want to pursue National Board Certification.

Ratzel suggests the Teacher Leader Model Standards as a further reference for teachers who show some of these signs: http://www.teacherleaderstandards.org/

"5 Tell-Tale Signs You're Becoming a Teacher Leader" by Marsha Ratzel in *Education Week Quality Counts 2012*, Feb. 21, 2012, summarized in Marshall Memo 425.

8   A More-Ambitious Agenda for Teacher Leaders

"The work of a teacher leader is often undefined, unsupported, and sometimes unrecognized and undervalued, thus limiting the potential for positive impact," say Joellen Killion and five colleagues in this *Learning Forward* white paper. The authors believe teacher leadership is more than the usual outside-the-classroom roles taken on by teachers: committee member, team leader, curriculum writer, department chair, association leader. These and other roles are important, but they are often narrowly defined, inflexible, and structured to carry out the expectations and desires of higher-ups. Teachers may conclude that to have true leadership power, they need to leave the classroom and become administrators.

Killion and her colleagues make the case for stretching the definition of teacher leadership for real impact on teaching and learning. Because teachers are in daily contact with students, the authors argue, they "are in the best position to make critical decisions about issues related to teaching and learning. Moreover, they are better able to implement changes in a comprehensive and continuous manner. Expanding teacher roles also serves an ongoing need to attract and retain qualified teachers for career-long, rather than temporary, service …. It is a transformation of the way educators work within schools every day to strengthen culture and professional practices and enhance professional learning opportunities leading to student success."

Killion et al. list some key considerations for maximizing the impact of teacher leadership:

• *There is a variety of teacher-leadership roles.* These include mentoring and coaching peers; promoting and facilitating professional learning and collaboration; designing, implementing, and supporting school and district change efforts; contributing to research and policy; and serving as spokespersons for their schools, districts, and the profession.

• *Teacher leadership often operates outside of official structures.* "For teachers, leadership is more about influence than power and authority," say Killion et al. "More often, teacher leaders act without formal designation as leaders …. The most important form of leadership occurs when teachers recognize a need and step in to help address it."

• *District leaders' beliefs really matter.* Most important is accepting the potential of shared/distributed leadership, valuing the expertise of teacher leaders, engaging them in significant and authentic leadership responsibilities, and giving honest, learning-focused feedback.

• *All teachers can lead.* This could take the form of helping to mentor and support novice members of the profession, adding to the body of craft knowledge, or collaborating with peers to influence professional practice. It's helpful when schools and districts provide roles for teacher leaders to contribute.

• *Support for teacher leaders is key.* This can take the form of coaching and mentoring from administrators and more-experienced peers, networking opportunities, and regular feedback from a knowledgeable colleague.

• *Certain competencies are essential for teacher leaders.* These include knowledge about the design, implementation, and evaluation of professional learning; interpersonal skills to build trusting relationships within the organization; engaging peers and administrators in collaborative learning; ensuring that student learning should be the focus of all decisions; and the belief that all students and teachers can grow and succeed. "As servant leaders," say Killion et al., "teacher leaders understand that their belief in others' capabilities and conveying that belief in words and actions will result in ordinary people accomplishing extraordinary things."

• *Teacher leaders need courage and flexibility.* They must be open to criticism from others and "cross back and forth between the boundaries of the teaching arena and the leading arena," say the authors. "For that reason, teacher leaders are called on to embrace ambiguity and to be flexible as their work unfolds and as they and their peers grow comfortable with their new responsibilities and identity as a leader."

• *Teacher leaders take responsibility for their own professional development and the development of others.* They operate from a growth mindset and "have as much vested in the growth of their colleagues as they do in their own growth," say Killion et al.

• *Teacher leaders foster collaborative cultures.* "They catalyze a sense of urgency and efficacy among adults and engender peer-to-peer accountability and collective responsibility for the success of every teacher and student," say Killion et al. They foster a climate of peer support and continuous improvement.

• *Teacher leaders are driven by evidence.* They continuously collect data on their impact on teaching and learning and the factors that make a difference in their schools and districts.

"A Systemic Approach to Elevating Teacher Leadership" by Joellen Killion, Cindy Harrison, Amy Colton, Chris Bryan, Ann Delehant, and Debbie Cooke in *Learning Forward*, November 2016, summarized in Marshall Memo 671.

---

9 Practical Tips for Teacher Leaders

In this *Educational Leadership* article, Washington State University–Vancouver professor Jason Margolis writes about the "subtle dynamics" involved in teacher leaders working successfully to change instructional practices in their schools. Teachers learn best, he says, when they are actively involved, are in a comfortable environment, see theoretical material grounded in classroom examples, and the teacher leader understands that they might feel overworked, overwhelmed, and underappreciated. Margolis suggests that teacher leaders:

• *Use humor.* This reduces tension, alters the power dynamics, and produces a more relaxed atmosphere for adult learning.

• *Work with teachers in all content areas.* Don't limit yourself to your own subject area (e.g., literacy); find ways of applying insights across content areas.

• *Be brief.* Limit direct instruction to five to fifteen minutes and then give colleagues a chance to practice techniques, observe others practicing, and debrief.

• *Stress easy implementation.* Key phrases include: *takes no prep time, actually helps us to go faster, adaptable, flexible.*

• *Build on teachers' existing work.* Start by asking teachers to share approaches they are using, validate their work, and then ask them to consider how the new ideas might complement what they're doing.

• *Model continual learning.* Admit the struggles you've had implementing these ideas with students, while showing a hunger for new approaches to address classroom challenges.

• *Include samples of student work.* You'll be more successful if you show work your own students have produced.

• *Don't talk too much.* Shift the focus to participants.

• *Don't focus solely on your own classroom.* Help teachers find connections to their own classrooms.

• *Don't lecture and then ask, "Any questions?"* This is usually greeted by silence.

• *Don't overload teachers with too many strategies.*

"How Teachers Lead Teachers" by Jason Margolis in *Educational Leadership*, February 2009 (Vol. 66, #5, online only), summarized in Marshall Memo 282.

Other Pathways for Teacher Leadership

⑩ Lead Teachers Onboarding and Mentoring Rookies

In this article in Phi Delta Kappa *EDge*, teacher leaders Gayle Davis and Margaret Metzger describe the program they developed to support new teachers in their large Massachusetts high school. The outcome: only 10 percent of new teachers washed out, compared with as many as 70 percent nationally. Here are the program's main features:

• *Orientation* – When they first started the program, Davis and Metzger made a common mistake in their beginning-of-the-year orientation meeting: they overwhelmed new teachers with too much information at too abstract a level. New teachers needed to know *practical* stuff: How can I get the keys to my room? Where are the supplies? How do I make copies? What is the attendance system? The beginning of orientation is no time for lofty educational goals and philosophy. Davis and Metzger turned the first meeting into a question-and-answer session in which the newbies could get answers to these and countless other questions, as well as a tour of the campus, a handbook with maps, class and lunch schedules, tips from veteran teachers, and sample copies of course syllabi and student learning expectations. Their homework between the first and second day of orientation was to write a first draft of their own course expectations. After all this, the new teachers got more general advice, including how to start the year with clear, firm expectations, assigning homework from the get-go, and so forth.

• *Monthly seminars* – All the new teachers (about twenty-five each year) met once a month with Davis and Metzger and other veteran teachers. The meetings overlapped with professional development meetings for the rest of the staff so there was no above-and-beyond time commitment for the new teachers. Monthly meetings were two hours long to leave enough time for real substance, including presentations by outside speakers, questions and answers, journal writing, and large- and small-group discussions. Topics included lesson planning, maintaining life balance, using school resources, communicating with parents, and classroom management.

• *Mentoring* – Each new teacher was assigned a mentor who met regularly with the mentee; observed classes; and gave counsel on curriculum, classroom management, and teaching in general. Many mentors spent several hours a week with their mentees and were enormously helpful. But mentor-mentee relationships were not always rosy. One new teacher wrote in her year-end evaluation, "Our philosophies and attitudes were quite different. I actually felt a little 'belittled' and had my ideas shot down. It ate away at me all year." Davis and Metzger worked on issues like this as they supervised the mentors.

Over the years, they identified three key elements that helped optimize mentor-mentee relationships:
- Shared office or classroom space, which promoted frequent informal interactions;
- Teaching the same courses, which allowed the mentor to guide the new teacher through curriculum sequence and expectations;
- Shared planning time, which made regular meetings far more likely to occur.

Mentor teachers, who were freed up from a duty and paid a $450 stipend each year, attended an extensive orientation, including standard pointers and lots of role-playing around common scenarios. Confidentiality was a tricky issue, and the sessions dealt with the question of when it was necessary to break confidentiality—for example, when the mentor feels that students are being harmed.

After the initial orientation, teacher leaders Davis and Metzger met with mentor teachers twice more during the year, discussing issues of concern and updating them on topics that new teachers are bringing up in their monthly meetings. One recurring topic was mentors' tendency to give new teachers a quick fix rather than helping them to understand a problem and come up with their own solution. There were also frequent discussions of curriculum coverage and preparation for state tests, and the degree of autonomy new teachers should have on what they taught.

• *Watching veteran teachers in action* – Davis and Metzger believed that observing experienced teachers was one of the most powerful learning experiences for new teachers. They scheduled numerous observations, and the coordinators prodded new teachers to follow through by posting a schedule of all observations. New teachers first observed veterans in the same department, then branched out to observe teachers in other subject areas. "These old teachers have so much energy," exclaimed one newbie. "The ed school said the old teachers were all burnt out, but they're not!" New teachers were much more observant when they observed others than they were in graduate school; now they knew how hard teaching was!

Davis and Metzger counseled new teachers on what to look for during these observations—for example, what students do before class, classroom routines, proactive classroom management strategies, methods of differentiating instruction, formative assessment, etc. They also talked through some typical reactions after an observation ("She just has good kids." "He's a natural.") and helped new teachers realize that what looks easy is in fact the result of experience, strategy, and hard work. They also confronted the misconception that a teacher can't be "hard" and at the same time popular with students by showing them veteran teachers who were strict and demanding but were still beloved.

• *Classroom observation by the coordinators* – Davis and Metzger regularly observed all new teachers' classrooms, and gave them unvarnished but confidential feedback. "The importance of observing new teachers cannot be overstated," they say. "In addition to the support we are able to offer, these experiences also allow us to identify perennial problems and to shape the entire induction program." At the beginning of each year, they divided up the list of new teachers and started their observations immediately, so as not to miss any start-up problems. Post-conferences after each observation often lasted an hour, and advice was dispensed on several key topics: assuming command, teaching all kids, and planning and pacing.

• *Social events and a retreat* – Each monthly meeting began with coffee and conversation, and there were periodic Friday social gatherings during the year, parties at individual teachers' houses, occasional outings to plays, and an end-of-the-year "congratulations" party. But most important, each cohort had an overnight retreat right after first-quarter grades were handed in (a relatively quiet time in teachers' workload). The retreats took place at a local conference center and were funded by a community foundation (at a cost of about $3,000). Everyone arrived Friday afternoon and dropped their stuff in cabins amidst beautiful country surroundings. After dinner, they had an ice-breaker activity and then kicked off general small- and large-group discussions with a question like, *What did you worry about in September?* and *Where are you now with that issue?* New teachers opened up and voiced wide-ranging fears and hopes. Many of them stayed up all night, singing and playing games and talking across grade levels and disciplines.

On Saturday morning, there were workshops led by experts from within the school (no outside consultants) on issues like assessment, power, race, and gender in the classroom; substance abuse among students; English as a second language; and proactive options for discipline. "This was a bonding experience that I needed to stay here," said one teacher. "I made real friends. And I felt far less isolated the next week."

Davis and Metzger were proud of their rookie teacher support program and believe it accomplished four things:

- It decreased teacher isolation. "Teachers need to feel comfortable going into each other's classes, talking about problems, and collaborating on solutions," they say.

- It gave veteran teachers a way to give back. "We have concluded that we, the seasoned teachers, must teach the skills that have helped us survive and thrive to our new colleagues so that they, too, will find lifelong success and satisfaction in the classroom."
- It was a valuable career track experience for veteran teachers short of going into administration.
- It encouraged all teachers to be reflective practitioners. "Strong veteran teachers, even after years of experience, still question their assumptions about students and curriculum. Reflective practice includes the ability to live with ambiguity, to assess situations with critical attention, and to understand one's role in relation to problems and their solutions. The most profound support we can offer new teachers is our willingness to question our successes and to admit our failures."

"Teachers Mentoring Teachers" by Gayle Davis and Margaret Metzger in *EDge*, January/February, 2006 (Vol. 1, #3, pp. 3–19), summarized in Marshall Memo 120.

11. Teachers Evaluating Teachers

In this *Education Week* article, consultant Julia Koppich and Daniel Humphrey of SRI International challenge the widely-held belief that teacher evaluation must be separated from teacher support. "It's an assumption that makes perfect *prima facie* sense," they say, "but as our research shows, the assumption is wrong .... Truly effective evaluation programs combine accountability and support."

Koppich and Humphrey studied two California districts (Poway and San Juan) that implemented Peer Assistance and Review (PAR), in which carefully selected veteran teachers leave their classrooms for a period of time and provide a year of intensive support to beginning or underperforming colleagues. The consulting teachers, as they are called, receive a stipend in addition to their regular salaries and in most cases are responsible for conducting end-of-year evaluations of their teachers. These summative evaluations are reviewed by a joint labor-management board, which then makes recommendations on PAR teachers' employment status to the superintendent and school board. Here are Koppich and Humphrey's observations about how this program is working in the two districts:

• *PAR consulting teachers* – They combine evaluation with support—and the combination seems to work well. Consulting teachers diagnose each participating teacher's strengths and weaknesses vis-à-vis the district's standards, develop a customized year-long improvement program, and work with each teacher to implement it, conducting as many as thirty informal and five formal observations of each teacher. "Many teachers make it out of PAR," report Koppich and Humphrey, "but some don't…. Making tough decisions about individuals' employment status is never easy. But it must be done, and done with care and rigor."

How did consulting teachers' evaluations compare with those of building principals? Koppich and Humphrey found that although principals almost always came to the same bottom-line conclusions about teachers, the difference in the quality of their evaluations was dramatic. "Principals' evaluations were much sketchier than those undertaken by consulting teachers," they say. "Their ratings were based on many fewer observations. Their analyses of teachers' practice tended to focus on one or two areas rather than on the whole picture of teaching. Documentation and evidence were sparse." Principals had about seven pages of documentation on each teacher, compared with 190 pages gathered by consulting teachers. This was because principals were spread thin in terms of the number of teachers they evaluate and their limited subject-area expertise. "Who has the time and the knowledge to do this important work?" The authors believe consulting teachers can do a far better job.

• *The PAR governing board* – Koppich and Humphrey observed meetings and couldn't tell which members represented the district and which represented the union. "Conversations focused on intensive, high-level questioning and probing about serious matters of teaching and learning," they report. "The boards ensured both that consulting teachers focused on improving instruction and that their evaluations of participating teachers were based on solid evidence." Board members were also not shy about criticizing principals' evaluations of teachers, and sometimes asked principals to redo them with more evidence.

• *Labor-management relations* – In these districts, the PAR boards also provided a forum in which district and union officials collaboratively addressed operational and policy issues that might have wound up in grievances or remained unresolved. "Though both Poway and San Juan have in the past experienced rocky union/district relations," report Koppich and Humphrey, "PAR has served as a springboard for building strong connections. More than simple collaborative efforts, through PAR, management and unions are doing the hard work of confronting tough, high-stakes issues and reaching accord on how to proceed when decisions carry real and human consequences."

"Getting Serious About Teacher Evaluation: A Fresh Look at Peer Assistance and Review" by Julia Koppich and Daniel Humphrey in *Education Week*, Oct. 12, 2011 (Vol. 31, #7, pp. 25, 28); summarized in Marshall Memo 407.

12. A Career-Ladder Proposal

In this *Educational Leadership* article, Susan Moore Johnson and John Papay (Harvard Graduate School of Education) say that past attempts to use merit pay to improve instruction and attract higher-caliber teachers have never worked. Johnson and Papay acknowledge that we now have better sources of information on individual teachers' impact, but they predict that renewed attempts to implement merit pay will meet the same fate.

Here is what's been missing, they say: "Policymakers and administrators, responding to short-term demands for better test scores, have often overlooked the importance of making schools places where teachers can succeed with all students and can build professionally rewarding, financially sustainable careers. They have failed to join the potential of pay with the power of teaching's intrinsic rewards—doing meaningful work, watching students learn and grow, and collaborating with others to achieve a greater good."

To fill these perennial gaps, Johnson and Papay propose a tiered pay-and-career structure. Here's how it works.

- *Four tiers of career growth* – The goal is to attract strong candidates to teaching, support their development over time, and offer incentives to outstanding teachers who improve instruction outside their own classrooms. Based on comprehensive evaluations, teachers can progress from one level to the next:
  - Tier I—Probationary teachers;
  - Tier II—Tenured teachers; (Achieving this is not an easy or automatic process.)
  - Tier III—Master teachers (as documented by evaluations, student results, and parent satisfaction) who act as models and mentors to colleagues and serve as grade-level team leaders, department heads, or school data analysts; (Most continue to teach full-time.)
  - Tier IV—Outstanding teachers who are relieved of classroom duties to take on broader responsibilities—including induction of new teachers, peer evaluation, and introducing new curriculum initiatives.

Moving up a tier would bring substantial jumps in pay, and there would be annual step increases within each tier to encourage loyalty and retention.

• *A learning and development fund* – This is designed to get teachers learning new skills and taking on additional responsibilities throughout their careers. "Teaching is a complex craft continually demanding new skills and knowledge," say Johnson and Papay, "yet most districts' professional development is superficial and sporadic. Meanwhile, huge sums of money meant to reward learning are tied up in the lanes of a district's salary scale." The fund would gradually move money from automatic step increases to investing in training immediately relevant to teachers' classrooms. Each year, a committee of teachers and administrators would decide on the highest-impact areas for professional training. This fund would also support tiers III and IV master teachers.

• *Short-term, local incentives for special situations* – For example, attracting special-education teachers to fill a shortage, assembling faculty for a school turnaround, or paying bonuses for special accomplishments.

Johnson and Papay believe their plan would give prospective teachers a clear career pathway, improve support for rookies, assure competent teachers a steady income, and give exceptional teachers an exciting career ladder and the prospect of higher pay. Several factors would need to be in place for the plan to succeed: (a) collaboration among teachers, union leaders, administrators, and school boards; (b) a fair and transparent decision-making process; (c) on-going monitoring and leadership; (d) improved techniques for evaluating teachers; and (e) gathering evidence that it improves student learning.

"Merit Pay for a New Generation" by Susan Moore Johnson and John Papay in *Educational Leadership*, May 2010 (Vol. 67, #8, pp. 48–52), summarized in Marshall Memo 335.

---

13. Some Suggestions for Teachers Speaking Truth to Power

In this article in *Kappa Delta Pi Record*, Frederick Hess (American Enterprise Institute) says that many American teachers are feeling disempowered, disrespected, and ignored by policymakers and legislators. "Believe it or not," says Hess, "teachers have a sympathetic audience. People care what teachers think." According to the 2013 Kappan/Gallup poll on schooling, more than 70 percent of Americans have "trust and confidence" in public school teachers. But educators need to be smart and strategic in how they present their concerns, says Hess: "Put simply, teachers must engage as professionals if they are to change a maddening status quo. Doing so can empower them to take a more assertive role in shaping policy that promotes a more professional culture." Here are his ideas for educator advocates:

• *Teachers need to recognize that they are in an asymmetrical relationship with policymakers.* "These officials can do more for educators than educators can do for them," says Hess. "For better or worse, education is going to be governed by public officials. Those officials determine how money will be spent, performance will be judged, and children will be served."

• *Given that unequal power relationship, winning policymakers' trust is essential.* "It helps enormously to know what policymakers are looking for," says Hess. They want to do good things for their constituents but aren't always sure what's the best way to "do good." They get conflicting advice, have limited resources, and are extremely reluctant to raise taxes. They know that good ideas are sometimes messed up in practice, so they're wary about whom to trust. "That's why they're eager to find people who understand their aims, know what's happening on the ground, and can help boost the chances that policies work as intended," says Hess. "How do you convince them that you're one of the people they can rely on?"

• *Recognize the environment policymakers live in.* "Practitioners can expect policymakers to be busy and scattered," he says, "so they'll pay more attention to 10 people than to one—and to a concrete proposal than a vague suggestion."

• *Trust-building begins with acknowledging weak links and suggesting solutions.* "For example," says Hess, "if police stand by silently when colleagues fail to perform acceptably, or excuse irresponsible colleagues, we question their professionalism. That may be unfair, but the result is a loss of confidence all the same." According to a recent survey in *Education Next,* teachers say that about five percent of those teaching in their local schools deserve an F grade and another eight percent deserve a D. This handful of poor performers will dominate the policy discussion unless the problem is faced squarely and constructive ideas are offered.

• *When addressing policymakers in public forums, don't start by demanding more money.* Everyone wants more money, even school districts spending more than $20,000 per student a year. "If policymakers had more money to give," says Hess, "they would give it."

• *Emphasize shared concerns.* "In other words, presume that they care about the same kids that you do," says Hess, "and explain the idea with a view to how they might see things."

• *Talk about the things that policymakers can change.* "Think beyond your immediate frustration," says Hess. "Make sure you know what change you're asking for and how the policymaker you're talking to might help. Officials can't help people with things they don't control."

• *Bring data*. "Your voice and story matter," he says, "but data supersizes the impact." It's especially compelling when teachers talk about measurable gains in student achievement and how they happened.

• *Articulate what should happen*. Say specifically what needs to change and how that change will solve the problem. "That takes some work," says Hess. "It's not easy, and it will require talking to people and making sense of things. Once you do that, though, you're a huge asset to a policymaker."

"How Professional Educators Can Make Policy Work for Their Profession" by Frederick Hess in *Kappa Delta Pi Record*, October–December 2015 (Vol. 51, #4, pp. 160–162), no e-link available, summarized in Marshall Memo 610.

Professional Learning Suggestions for Chapter Eleven: Teacher Leadership

Maximizing the Role of Teacher Leaders

Done well, teacher leadership can be a powerful force in improving teaching and leading at your school or district. However, Kim and Jenn have seen far too many schools that don't take the time to anticipate obstacles to teacher leadership, map out the precise roles teacher leaders should play, or provide ongoing training and support for teacher leaders. The following exercises will help your school overcome all three of these impediments so you can maximize this invaluable resource.

I. Thinking and Planning for Teacher Leadership

To begin, have your leadership team or even your full faculty think through some of the obstacles to effective teacher leadership.

A. Have the leadership team or your entire staff consider the barriers to teacher leadership.
Whether you want to begin to incorporate teacher leadership into your school or improve your existing model, it is helpful to consider the barriers to overcome.

    1. Do a large-group brainstorm of all of the potential barriers to teacher leadership before reading anything.

    2. Now have people choose to read one of the three article-summaries that discuss some of the barriers—"Dealing with Headwinds" (Barth article-summary 1), "Core Dilemmas in the Teacher Leader Role" (Mangin and Stoelinga article-summary 2), and "Dealing with the 'Culture of Nice'" (MacDonald article-summary 3).

    3. In triads with one person who read each of the three article-summaries, use the ideas from the brainstorm and the three article-summaries to gather all of the possible obstacles to teacher leadership. Then, think of potential ways to address these obstacles. You can distribute charts like the one that follows (paper or virtual) for the small groups to organize ideas:

PROFESSIONAL LEARNING SUGGESTIONS FOR CHAPTER ELEVEN

Obstacles to Teacher Leadership	Possible Ideas to Address Obstacles

4. Come back together as a large group and have people share out their best ideas for addressing obstacles to teacher leadership at your school.

B. Have the leadership team discuss the ideal leadership mindset that would be necessary for teachers to step into teacher leadership roles.

Teacher leadership is not just a role, it's a mindset. Here are some steps to consider the mindset needed to develop teacher leaders at your school.

1. Have your leadership team read "Fostering a Leadership Mindset in Teachers" (Fiarman article-summary 4) and underline what resonates for them.

2. Next, use a simple protocol to discuss this article-summary. Have people take two minutes each to share one part they underlined, why this section resonated for them, and what implications it might have for the work at your school. After each person speaks, give the group two minutes to respond.

3. After this discussion, ask the group what it would take at your school to create a teacher leadership mindset, that is "a culture in which each professional feels an urgent responsibility to influence the achievement of *all* students."

C. Have the leadership team or your full faculty think about ways for teacher leaders to have more authority to improve teaching.

Even when schools do have teacher leaders, this role often does not have the teeth to strongly impact teaching and learning. What structures and expectations would need to be in place to give teacher leaders the *authority* to impact teaching and learning in a deeper way?

1. Post these quotes around the room (or in a virtual space) and ask people to walk around and post their reactions to them:

> "There's another problem with teacher leaders presenting themselves as co-equal: they are less likely to give critical feedback that might make a colleague uncomfortable." (article-summary 2)
>
> "Many of the instructional support roles [like Teacher Leaders] are too 'soft' to make a difference in classrooms." (article-summary 5)
>
> "Teacher leaders aren't given specific responsibility for leading and developing other teachers in the building. And most don't feel accountable for the performance of those they are working with." (article-summary 5)

2. Next, have them read "Core Dilemmas in the Teacher Leader Role" (article-summary 2) and "How to Implement Distributed Instructional Leadership" (article-summary 5).

3. As a large group discuss what authority your current teacher leaders have. Or, if you don't have any teacher leaders yet, what authority do you think they *should* have?

4. If your school wants teacher leaders to have the authority to more deeply influence teaching and learning, what *structures* and *expectations* would have to be in place? Have the group brainstorm ideas based on what they've read and their own ideas (note, if they haven't read article-summary 4 about mindset in the previous activity, you might want them to read that article as well before brainstorming):

If we want our teacher leaders to have the authority to impact teaching and learning…	
Structures	Expectations

D. Is your school or district ready for teacher leadership?

If you are thinking of introducing the role of teacher leader to your school or district, or strengthening that role, consider taking a self-assessment to guide you. The free online self-assessment from the CSTP (the Center for Strengthening the Teaching Profession) can help your leadership team determine if the following factors are in place to support teacher leaders: culture, district support, professional learning opportunities for teacher leaders, and resources.

http://cstp-wa.org/cstp2013/wp-content/uploads/2013/11/CSTP_tool_school_district_capacity.pdf

II. The Role of Teacher Leaders

Part of why the role of teacher leader isn't maximized is that there's often confusion about what this role involves. Why? We haven't *defined* it. This section helps a leadership team or teacher leaders themselves clarify the role of the teacher leader.

A. Collaboratively write a job description for teacher leaders.

Have your leadership team or your teachers outline exactly what teacher leaders at your school are responsible for.

1. Have everyone read "How to Implement Distributed Instructional Leadership" (article-summary 5) and "Four Roles for Science Teacher Leaders" (article-summary 6) and think about what roles teacher leaders in your school/district should play. Capture people's ideas in a simple chart like the one below.

Roles and Responsibilities of Teacher Leaders
(e.g., mentoring new teachers, leading grade-team meetings, etc.)

2. After examining the roles that teacher leaders might play at your school, have the team read "How to Spot a Blossoming Teacher Leader" (article-summary 7) and "A More-Ambitious Agenda for Teacher Leaders" (article-summary 8). With what they've learned from these two article-summaries, the list of roles for teacher leaders in the previous step, and their own ideas—have the team list the knowledge, skills, and dispositions they would want in any teacher leader candidate in the chart that follows:

Teacher Leader Knowledge, Skills, and Dispositions		
Knowledge	Skills	Dispositions

    3. Use the ideas from Steps 1 and 2 to collaboratively write a job description for the role of teacher leader at your school.

B. *Determine who might be interested in serving as a teacher leader.*
Create a survey for teachers (a Google Form, Survey Monkey, etc.) using the statements in "How to Spot a Blossoming Teacher Leader" and the job description from Step 3 above. Send this survey to teachers along with the teacher leader job description to find out who might be interested in taking on more responsibility as a teacher leader.

III. Supporting Existing Teacher Leaders

The key to the initial and ongoing success of teacher leaders is to provide both training and support. Plan ahead with your teacher leaders and your leadership team to ensure that this key piece is in place before launching official teacher leader roles at your school or district.

A. *Help teacher leaders understand the needs of adult learners.*
When teachers move into a teacher leader role, they may have never worked with adults before. It is essential to support them in understanding the needs of adult learners.

    1. Ask teacher leaders to think about how *they* learn. This will give them some insight into the needs of adult learners. Share the following statements that are indicative of some of the ways in which adults learn. Read each statement and ask the teacher leaders to stand up along a continuum with those who feel strongest about the statement standing near one wall of the room and those who feel less decisive standing along the opposite wall, and those who feel somewhat mixed standing in the middle.

PROFESSIONAL LEARNING SUGGESTIONS FOR CHAPTER ELEVEN

- I like learning when it builds on my past experiences and knowledge.
- I like learning that is relevant to my current work.
- I like learning within a group with opportunities for connection.
- I like learning that is autonomous.
- I like to have some degree of choice and control over my learning.
- I like to get feedback when I learn.
- I can learn only when I feel safe.
- I need a clear goal in order to be able to learn.
- I like learning that is hands-on and active.

2. Have the group discuss what they learned from watching where they stood and where others stood in the room. What are some elements that impact adult learning? How diverse were the responses in the room? What role do you think *learning styles* played in where people stood? What role do you think *generation (Baby Boomer, Generation X, Millennial,* and *Generation Z)* played in where people stood?

3. Have teachers read the short article, "Practical Tips for Teacher Leaders" (article-summary 9) as a model of some quick tips to keep in mind for their roles. Based on this model and what they learned in the continuum exercise and discussion above, have each teacher leader create a list: "Top Five Tips for Me to Keep in Mind in Working with Adult Learners." When they are done, have teacher leaders share their tips in pairs and discuss why they chose these five to guide their work.

B. Create a plan for ongoing training and support of teacher leaders.

One of the biggest mistakes is to assign a teacher leader role to staff members and provide no support or training. In a similar way that the mentor teachers in "Lead Teachers Onboarding and Mentoring Rookies" (article-summary 10) provide training and support for new teachers, the leadership team must do the same for teacher leaders.

1. Have the leadership team read "Lead Teachers Onboarding and Mentoring Rookies" (article-summary 10) as a model of training and ongoing support. Ask them to discuss what the team might take from this article-summary that would apply to their work with teacher leaders.

2. If they were not involved in the earlier activity, ask the team to outline the knowledge, skills, and dispositions your school would like its teacher leaders to possess.

Teacher Leader Knowledge, Skills, and Dispositions		
Knowledge	Skills	Dispositions

3. Next, have the team prioritize which of these knowledge, skills, and dispositions should be developed in an "orientation" training before school or early in the year. Ask for volunteers to lead this training.

4. Find a time in the schedule when you will bring all teacher leaders together for *monthly seminars*. As a leadership team, decide which of the remaining knowledge, skills, and dispositions are most important and assign them as the topics for different months. Be sure to leave some months open for issues or topics that arise during the year for which teacher leaders may want more training or practice. Possible skills you may want to include in these monthly seminars:

How to coach and give feedback;

How to facilitate a team meeting;

How to develop important interpersonal skills;

How to handle difficult conversations and conflicts;

How to work with different generations;

How to use quantitative and qualitative data to improve teaching and learning;

How to boost your own emotional intelligence;

How to plan for professional learning.

Appendix A

Marshall Memo Article-Summaries for "Live" All-Faculty Discussions

In this book there are twelve Marshall Memo article-summaries that are uniquely suited to being read and discussed by an elementary-, middle-, or high-school faculty during a meeting. This activity gets educators thinking about important topics, sharing ideas with colleagues, and coming to agreement on effective practices. Here is how this process is handled in some schools:

- The leadership team decides on an article-summary that addresses an issue of importance, choosing from the list below. (There's a longer list in the Marshall Memo archive (log in at www.marshallmemo.com, click *Search Archive*, check the *All-Faculty Discussion* box at the top of the topics list, and click *Search*.)
- In an all-faculty meeting, thirty to forty minutes are blocked out for this activity, with educators sitting with three to four colleagues with whom they don't usually interact.
- After a brief introduction to the activity and its purpose, hard copies of the article-summary are handed out (in remote meetings, a soft copy).
- Everyone reads the piece silently, underlining and highlighting ideas and quotes that seem important. (*Why not ask people to read it beforehand?* Because inevitably, half of the group won't get around to doing so. It's important for the whole group to have the ideas fresh in their minds before discussing them. It also good for people to read the Memo summary rather than the full article, since time is of the essence in faculty meetings.)
- After seven to ten minutes, each group uses a protocol to go around and hear each person's big takeaways, agreements, disagreements, and favorite quotes.
- The faculty comes back together for a facilitated whole-group discussion of the action implications for the school and how the ideas apply to their practice.
- The leadership team follows up appropriately.

APPENDIX A

Here are article-summaries in *Book Two* that lend themselves to this activity:

"What Parents and Teachers Can Do to Teach Self-Regulation," Daniel Willingham—Chapter Two, summary 7

"A Theory About Homework," Bruce Jackson—Chapter Four, summary 12

"Getting Every Student Thinking and Working," Paul Bambrick-Santoyo and Stephen Chiger—Chapter Five, summary 5

"The Elements of Effective Feedback," Grant Wiggins—Chapter Five, summary 10

"Getting Students to Do the Heavy Lifting," Dylan Wiliam—Chapter Five, summary 11

"Teaching Blind People to Use Canes and What It Can Teach Others," Matthew Maurer, Edward Bell, Eric Woods, and Roland Allen—Chapter Five, summary 12

"Not Overloading Working Memory," Andrew Watson, Michael Wirtz, and Lynette Sumpter—Chapter Six, summary 2

"Understanding Two Very Different Kinds of Memory," Clare Sealy—Chapter Six, summary 3

"How Remembering Improves Remembering," Pooja Agarwal, Henry Roediger, Mark McDaniel, and Kathleen McDermott—Chapter Six, summary 4

"Using Pretests to Improve Achievement," Benedict Carey—Chapter Six, summary 5

"What Did You Learn in School Today?" Kathy Ganske—Chapter Six, summary 6

"Five Principles of Good Writing," William Zinsser—Chapter Seven, summary 8

Book One Article-Summaries for "Live" All-Faculty Discussions

In *The Best of the Marshall Memo: Book One*, there are eleven summaries that lend themselves to all-faculty discussions:

"Managing Feelings, Values, and Expectations," Jena Pincott—Chapter Three, summary 9

"Fixed and Growth Mindsets in Teacher Candidates," Carol Dweck—Chapter Four, summary 2

"Predicting and Preventing Classroom Problems," Timothy Landrum, Amy Lingo, and Terrance

MARSHALL MEMO ARTICLE-SUMMARIES FOR "LIVE" ALL-FACULTY DISCUSSIONS

Scott—Chapter Eight, summary 1

"When Educators Act in Ways That Increase Student Misbehavior," Eric Toshalis—Chapter Eight, summary 3

"Teacher-Student Mediation in Action," Ondine Gross—Chapter Eight, summary 11

"A California High School Crafts Schoolwide Essential Questions," Nancy Frey and Douglas Fisher—Chapter Nine, summary 3

"A Teacher Realizes What He Wasn't Doing," Craig Barton—Chapter Ten, summary 5

"Crafting Good 'Hinge' Questions," Dylan Wiliam—Chapter Ten, summary 6

"Misconceptions Get in the Way of Better Grading," Thomas Guskey—Chapter Eleven, summary 2

"Pointed Questions About Grades," Jennifer Gonzalez—Chapter Eleven, summary 3

"Preventing Cheating by Shaping Classroom Motivational Climate," Eric Anderman and Alison Koenka—Chapter Eleven, summary 10

Appendix B

The Years from Which Marshall Memo Summaries Were Drawn

The article-summaries in *The Best of the Marshall Memo* books One and Two were selected from all issues going back to 2003, the year the Marshall Memo was launched. Since then, there have been almost eighty-five hundred article summaries, of which about three hundred were chosen for books One and Two—about one in twenty-eight.

The graphs below show the number of articles in books One and Two chosen from each year. Here are a few thoughts on the distribution:
- It's striking that article-summaries were chosen from every year of Marshall Memo publication.
- There's a clear pattern of an increasing number of summaries from more-recent years.
- This may reflect the steady increase in the number of publications read—and perhaps an improvement in the quality of K–12 research and writing.
- The bulge in certain years reflects increases in writing on certain "hot topics," for example—teacher evaluation, professional learning communities, and research on memory.

THE YEARS FROM WHICH MARSHALL MEMO SUMMARIES WERE DRAWN

Index

acceleration, 112, 118, 239, 244, 252, 260, 321, 339
accountability, 55, 58, 72, 73, 132, 196, 336, 338, 341, 372, 378, 405
achievement gap, 8, 10, 23, 24, 26, 109, 111, 118, 136, 154, 189, 233, 234, 245, 259, 261, 262, 279, 264, 284, 285, 326, 373
acting white, 104, 111
ADHD, 277
adolescents, 18, 20, 25, 26, 32, 47, 61, 75, 95, 320
advisory programs, 63, 70, 72-73, 82, 149,
African American, 5-6, 8, 23, 26, 37, 85-86, 88, 90, 95, 96, 103, 104, 107, 110, 111-12, 117, 121
Agarwal, Pooja, 211
aggression, 64, 75-76,
All Things PLC, 335-7, 338-40, 340-42
Allen, Roland, 195-96
Allensworth, Elaine, 21-23, 39
Allington, Richard, 237-38, 239
American Educational Research Journal, 5-7
American Educator, 29-31, 63-66, 220-22, 259-61, 319-20

American Enterprise Institute, 49-52, 413
American Journal of Education, 73-75
American Scholar, The, 148-50
AMLE Magazine, 296-97
anxiety, 14, 20, 38, 65, 111, 147, 184, 186, 212, 236
arithmetic, 13, 193
Aronson, Joshua, 109-11, 131
ASCA School Counselor, 71-73
ASCD Inservice, 179-80
assessments, summative, 192, 284, 288, 335, 393, 410
Asian American, 90, 100, 110, 112
asynchronous/synchronous learning, 128, 339, 340, 363, 377, 378, 387
athletic training, 361, 382, 384
Atlantic, The (formerly *Atlantic Monthly*), 60-62, 111-13,
attribution error, 356
attribution, 25, 317
Axelsen, Erin, 376-77
Bacon, Francis, 214
Bailey, Rebecca, 67-69, 81
Bain & Company, 397-400
Bambrick-Santoyo, Paul, 181-82, 366-67
Barth, Roland, 390-91

Bates, Celeste, 365-66
Bates, Meg, 377-79
Bay State Banner, 136
Baye, Ariane, 250-51
Bechdel test, 92
Beck, Isabel, 261, 264
Becker, Ryan, 273, 300
beliefs about intelligence, smartness, 3-45
Bell, Edward, 195-96
Benson. Jeffrey, 70-71
Bergmann, Jonathan, 287-89
Bierly, Chris, 397-400
Big Five (OCEAN) traits, 57, 79
Birmingham Sunday, 181
Bishop, Penny, 300-301
Bjork, Elizabeth Ligon, 214
Bjork, Robert, 215, 220
blind people, 195-96
Blodget, Alden, 203, 205, 230
blogs, blogging, 165, 353, 368, 379, 387
Bloom, Benjamin, 284-87, 305, 309
book discussions, 376, 387
Brainology, 9
Brion-Meisels, Gretchen, 67-69
Brookings *Evidence Speaks,* 56-59
Brookings Institution, 217-18
Brooks, David, 31-32

INDEX

Brown decision, 16
Bryan, Chris, 404-05
Burkins, Jan, 244-45
Calkins, Lucy, 251-53
Camden County, GA, 322, 329
Canada, Canadian, 18, 154, 293, 362
cane instruction, 195-96
career ladder, 412-13
Carey, Benedict, 213-15, 218-20
Carpenter, Jeffrey, 301-02
Chan Zuckerberg Initiative, 281, 282
character education, 48-54
Charlotte-Mecklenburg, 398
checking for understanding, 155, 175, 179, 188, 239, 273, 276, 288
Chenoweth, Karin, 319-20, 346
Cheung, Rebecca, 401-02
Chicago Consortium on School Research, 21-23, 57, 61
Chicago Debate League, 73
Chiger, Stephen, 181-82, 199
childcare, 149
China, 29
Choi, Jun-ah, 150-51, 168
civic education, 54
classroom management, 62, 65, 199, 286, 407, 408
Clay, Marie, 242
Cliffe, Sarah, 114-15
close reading, 227
coaching of teachers, 242, 365, 376, 377, 398, 399, 400, 401, 404
Collaborative for Academic, Social, and Emotional Learning (CASEL),
college admissions, 14
colorblind, 117

Colton, Amy, 404-05
Comer, James, 112
Common Core, 204, 224, 225, 232, 253, 260, 367, 378, 390, 403
Cooke, Debbie, 404-05
cool pose culture, 104, 106
cooperative learning, 62, 184, 250, 363
Cristofaro, Lorie, 376-77
Culham, Ruth, 353-55
Cult of Pedagogy, 115-17
cultural capital, 73-75
cultural proficiency/competence, 114-21
culture of nice, 393-94, 416
curiosity, 55, 124, 136, 235, 394
curse of knowledge, 178-79
Dachet, Dylan, 250-51
Dack, Hilary, 118-20
Daniels, Breez Longwell, 340-42
Darvin, Jacqueline, 99-100
data-driven instruction, 320
Davidson, Martin, 90-92
Davis, Gayle, 407-10
de la Cruz, Donna, 275
debate, 73-75
Deci, Edward, 61
deficit language, 11
Delehant, Ann, 404-05
democratic citizenship, 52
Denver, 398-99
desirable difficulty, 220
diagnostic, 14, 286, 321
differentiation, 272-310
difficult conversations, 97, 392, 422
digital discussions, 301, 306, 307
Dionysian trap, 104
direct instruction, 63, 252, 287, 406

disability, 14, 240, 243
discomfort, 74, 87, 98, 128, 225
distributed leadership, 289-92, 309, 400
distributed practice, 222
Doubet, Kristina, 289-92
Doyle, Betsy, 397-400
Duckworth, Angela, 55-56, 80
Dueck, Myron, 154
DuFour questions, 340-41
DuFour, Richard, 277, 321-22, 331-33, 340, 341, 344, 347, 348, 350
Dweck, Carol, 8-10, 25, 28, 34, 38, 40, 70
Dynarski, Susan, 217-18
dyslexia, 240
early childhood, 157, 162, 261
Eberhardt, Jennifer, 103
EDge, 407-10
Education Endowment Foundation, 250-51
Education Gadfly, The, 103, 258-59
Education Next, 143-45, 208-10, 414
Education Update, 149-50, 154-55
Education Week Quality Counts, 403
Education Week Teacher, 120-21
Education Week, 29-29, 120-21, 145-46, 205, 239, 281-82, 403, 410-12
Educational Leadership, 16-18, 70-71, 87-88, 109-11, 118-20, 181-82, 182-84, 188-89, 190-91, 193-94, 191-93, 237-38, 253-55, 282-83, 287-89, 292-93, 294-95, 297-98, 301-02, 321-22, 390-91, 395-96,

406, 412-13
Edutopia, 178-79, 279-80
Edwards, Brian, 117-18
efficacy/self-efficacy, 20-27, 33, 38, 40, 50, 56, 71, 90, 118, 279, 317, 405
Efficacy Institute, The, 136
Ehrenworth, Mary, 251-53, 266, 269, 270
Einstein, Albert, 17
EL Education, 62, 83
Elementary School Journal, 261-64, 317-19
Ely, Robin, 90-92
Emdin, Christopher, 105-07, 132-33
empathy, 46, 50, 53, 57, 58, 63, 64, 68, 88, 93, 124, 178, 226, 241
English Journal, 92-95
enrichment, 285, 286, 305, 322, 372
episodic memory, 208, 210, 229, 230
equity/inequity, 15, 37, 98, 116, 126, 128, 129, 130, 337
Ermeling, Bradley, 188-89, 317-19
Escalante, Jaime, 112
Eskimo, 13
Evans, Robert, 146-48
Facebook, 101, 165, 226, 273, 298-300, 306, 307
Farina, Richard, 181
Farrington, Camille, 21-23, 61-62
Feldman, David, 14-15
Ferguson. Ron, 136
Ferriter, William, 379-80
Fiarman, Sarah, 87-88, 395-96, 417

Fifty Cent, 104
Finland, 362
fishbowl discussions, 94, 180, 301
Flamboyan Foundation, 143, 149
flipped classroom, 287-89, 306, 307
fluency, 213, 214, 215, 225, 229, 230, 236, 239, 254, 276
Flynn, James, 13
food insecurity, 154
forgetting, 178, 204, 214, 219, 220, 221, 228
formative assessments, 191, 285, 286, 290, 291, 300, 302, 305
Fountas, Irene, 235-37
France, Paul, 279-80
Fred Jones Broadsheet, 184-87
Frontchannel/backchannel, 301-02, 306, 307
Gabriel, Rachael, 237-38
Gallimore, Ronald, 317-19, 345, 349
Ganske, Kathy, 215-16, 232
Gardner, Howard, 14-15, 16-18
Gates Foundation, 281, 304
Gates, Arthur, 214
Gawande, Atul, 315-16, 344
Gay, Anne, 322-24, 329-31
Gehlbach, Hunter, 66-67, 81
genetics, 29, 32
Gennetian, Lisa, 146
Geocaris, Jill, 376-77
Ghalambor, Jessica, 144-45
gifted, 14-15
Gilmore, Barry, 92-95
Girls' Leadership Institute, 76-77
global warming, 290
goal orientation, 20, 38, 91, 337, 349, 407

Goldenberg, Claude, 317-19, 346
Goldilocks, 242
Gonzalez, Jennifer, 115-17,
Hammond, Zaretta, 115-17
Goodman, Amy, 151-53
Google, 223-24, 316-17, 378, 420
Google Hangout, 338, 339, 378
Gordon, Molly, 21-23
Gorski, Karlyn, 73-75
governance, 48, 73, 402
GPA, 23, 25, 26
grading, 23, 40, 155, 283, 288, 321, 337-422
Graf, Karen, 298-300
Graff-Ermeling, Genevieve, 188-89
graphic organizers, 94, 247, 278, 324
Green Dot, 400
Greene, Jay, 49-52, 78, 81
grit, 50-51, 55-56, 58, 61, 62
grouping (of students), 71, 82
guided reading, 121, 236, 244, 245, 267
Guskey, Thomas, 284-87, 305, 309, 363-64, 383, 384
Gutierrez, Nancy, 97-98
Hammond, Zaretta, 115-17
Harris, Angel, 139-40
Harrison, Cindy, 404-05
Harvard Business Review, 90-92, 114-15
Hasiotis, Dina, 358-60
Haslam, Jonathan, 250-51
Hatt, Beth, 5-7, 35
Hattie, John, 28-29, 120, 190-91, 201-277
Henderson, Bill, 158-61
Herold, Benjamin, 281-82
Hess, Frederick, 413-15

INDEX

Highlands Elementary School, 373-75
Hilton, Jason, 296-97
Hinueber, Jesse, 117-18
Hirsch-Pasek, Kathy, 138
Hoffman, Jan, 75-77
home influences, 22, 64
home visits, 118, 143-45, 149, 160, 165, 166
Howard, Jeff, 136
humor, 179, 278, 355, 389, 406
Humphrey, Daniel, 410-12
hunger, 53, 257, 406
Hurd, Jacqueline, 373-76
identity abrasions, 90-91
identity charts, 93-94
implicit bias, 87-95, 116, 118, 122, 126
Independent School, 146-48, 206-07, 369-71
inequality, 53
Inns, Amanda, 250-51
Institute of Education Sciences, 211-13
instructional coaches, 375, 397
instructional leadership, 395, 397-400, 418, 419
interim assessments, 193, 320, 321, 323, 326, 329-31, 332, 338, 340
Internet, 167, 176, 223, 224, 278, 298, 299, 379
IQ tests, 14
Jackson, Bruce, 155-58
Jacobs, Andy, 358-60
Japan/Japanese, 29, 188, 284, 361, 362, 373, 374
Johnson, David, 21-23
Johnson, Susan Moore, 412-13
Jolly, Anne, 342-43, 351
Jones, Fred, 184-87

Jones, Stephanie, 67-69
Journal of Staff Development, 356-57, 324-26, 363-64, 368-69, 391-92, 363-64
justice, 53, 98, 101, 115, 116
Kappa Delta Pi Record, 52-54, 413-15
Kennedy, Mary, 355-58, 381
Kenya, 13
keyword, 222
kikan-shido, 188-89
Killion, Joellen, 404-05
kindergarten, 5, 35, 68, 150, 151, 169, 240, 241, 262, 264, 277, 320
KIPP schools, 58, 143
Kitsis, Stacy, 297-98
Klein, Kylie, 21-23
Koppich, Julia, 410-12
Kornell, Nate, 219
Kornhaber, Mindy, 16-18
Kronholz, June, 143-45
Kushnir, Greg, 335-37, 346, 350
Kusuma-Powell, Ochan, 177-78
Lake, Cynthia, 350-51
Language Educator, The, 298-300
laptops, 217-18, 231
Lareau, Annette, 138
Latin, 148
Latino, 5,10, 26, 37, 44, 85, 90, 91, 107, 108, 110, 121
Learning Forward, 404-05
learning management systems, 287
Learning Professional, The, 256-57, 324-26, 342-43, 363-64, 368-69, 371-72, 376-77, 391-92
learning styles, 179, 276, 277, 421
lesson plans, 40, 41, 44, 157, 188, 199, 367, 403
lesson study, 368, 373-76, 387
Levin, Ben, 18-19
Lewis, Catherine, 373-76
Lewis, Kayla, 242-44
Linville, Patricia, 25
Little, Judith Warren, 401-02
Litwack, Scott, 141-42
logic problems, 25
loneliness, culture of, 147
Los Angeles Lakers, 361
MacDonald, Elisa, 393-94
Mahnken, Kevin, 103
Mangin, Melinda, 391-92, 416
Mapp, Karen, 144
Margolis, Jason, 406
Marshall, Kim, 276-79, 305, 309
Marzano, Robert, 175-77, 198
mastery learning, 284-87, 304-06, 307, 309
mathematics, 3, 10, 11, 12, 35, 90, 112, 186, 223, 326, 328, 375, 431
Matthews, Jan, 322-24, 329-31, 348, 350
Maurer, Matthew, 195-96,
McClaskey, Kathleen, 292-93
McDaniel, Bronwyn, 21-23
McDaniel, Mark, 211-13
McDermott, Kathleen, 211-13
McGovern, Kate, 258-60
McIntosh, Peggy, 96-97, 123, 124
McKeown, Margaret, 261-64, 270
McKibben, Sarah, 149-50, 167
McNeff, Michael, 371-72
mean girls, 76
memory, 203-232
mental health, 147
metacognition, 211

Metzger, Margaret, 401-10
Meyerson, Debra, 90-92
microaggressions, 100-102, 128, 130, 131
Middle School Journal, 151-53, 289-91. 300-301, 329-31
mindsets, fixed and growth, 8-10, 10-12, 21-23, 28-29, 33-45, 51, 56, 58, 118, 183, 279, 360, 405
Minkel, Justin, 120-21
misbehavior, 60-61, 87, 103, 151
misconceptions, 12, 104-05, 115-17, 180, 183, 188, 190, 212, 220, 273, 285, 300, 302, 314, 324, 375, 409
misogyny, 105
mission, 28, 57, 71, 72, 82, 91, 340
Mitchell, Derek, 117-18
mnemonics, 221, 278
Molinsky, Andy, 114-15
MOOCs, 377
Moorman, Elizabeth, 141-42
moral education, 48-54
Moran, Cheryl, 377-79
Moran, Seana, 16-18
Morant, Tamyka, 326-28
Morgan, Denise, 365-66
Mozart, 31
multiple intelligences, 16-18
multitasking, 217
Munson, Jen, 326-28, 348, 350
Nadal, Kevin, 101
Naditz, Nicole, 298-300
Nagaoka, Jenny, 21-23
NASSP Bulletin, 284-87
Nation, The, 15-16,
National Mathematics Advisory Panel, 223
Neason, Alexandria, 154-55, 169

Neuman, Susan, 259-61, 270
neural networks, 205, 210, 220, 229, 230
neuroscience, 205, 228, 229, 230
New York City, 8, 9, 25, 62, 97, 108
New York Times Magazine, 213-215
New York Times, 31-32, 55-56, 75-77, 100-102, 104-05, 213-15, 218-20, 223-24, 226-27, 230, 275
New Yorker, 137-39, 249, 315-16, 361-62
New Zealand, 13, 242
Newell, Pete, 361
Ngounou, Gislaine, 97-98
Noguera, Pedro, 107-08
norms and routines, 22, 40
North Dakota, 107, 353, 371, 387
Northern, Amber, 224-25
note-taking, 207, 211, 217, 239
Nuthall, Graham, 191
O'Connell, Mary Pat, 73-76
OCEAN (Big Five) traits, 57, 79
Okonofua, Jason, 103
on-the-spot assessments, 239, 289-91, 309, 332
online PD, 378
open questions, 293, 306, 307
optimism, 20, 38, 46, 49, 55, 56, 60, 120
Pajares, Frank, 4, 20-21, 33, 37, 38, 39
Pandolpho, Beth, 179-80
Pane, John, 282
Papay, John, 412-13
parent involvement, 139-40, 162-63, 317
parent-teacher conferences, 100, 149-53
parenting, 136-42
Patterson, Orlando, 104-05
Peace and Freedom Magazine, 96-97
peer assistance and review (PAR), 410-12
peer pressure, 104-05
Perry, Rebecca, 373-76
perseverance, 20, 42, 49, 61, 62, 200
personalization, 272-310
perspective taking, 66-67, 68, 81, 88, 241, 277, 366
Phalen, Lena, 377-79
Phi Delta Kappan, 18-19, 48-49, 66-67, 67-69, 97-98, 105-07, 107-08, 117-18, 150-51, 177-78, 195-96, 240-41, 245-47, 276-79, 331-33, 333-36, 355, 366-67, 373-76, 377-79, 379-80, 401-02
phonics, 233, 239, 241
Pierce, Chester, 100
Pijanowski, Lissa, 324-26
Pinnell, Gay Su, 235-37, 265, 267
PLC lite, 331-33
PLCs (professional learning communities), 321-22, 324, 331-33, 333-35, 336, 337, 340-42, 345, 347, 348, 386-87, 397
poetry, 17, 226, 232, 240-41, 253
Poliner, Rachel, 70-71, 72
political correctness, 90-92
Pomerantz, Eva, 141-42
Pondiscio, Robert, 258-59, 265
Porosoff, Lauren, 369-71
poverty, 18, 53, 74, 97, 105, 138, 154, 261

INDEX

Powell, William, 177-78
praise, 7, 10, 21, 25, 30, 31, 39, 44, 64, 87, 137, 191, 333
pretests, 213-15, 228-31
Principal Leadership, 8-10, 175-77, 322-24
Principal, 99-100, 158-61,
prior knowledge, 6, 22, 40, 215, 231, 276, 287
protocols, 118, 316, 318, 338
Provenzano, Nicholas, 379-80
Providence Talks, 137-39
psychological safety, 316, 349
puzzle solving, 13, 117
Race to the Top, 281
racism, 96-97, 121, 122-33
Ratzel, Marsha, 403
re:Work, 316-17
read-aloud, 245
reading comprehension, 17, 223, 225, 239, 258, 259, 364
Reading Recovery, 242-44, 277
reading, shared 234, 236, 245, 267
Reading Teacher, The, 215-16, 236-37, 242-44, 251-53, 265-66
Reading Today, 244-45
Reason, Casey, 338-40
Reddy, Christopher, 178-79
Reeves, Douglas, 331-33, 347, 350
Reinhardt, Thomas, 401-02
remediation, 112, 113, 325, 326, 333
Renzulli, Joseph, 14
Republic, The, 49
resilience, 39, 60, 70-71, 73, 74
retreats, 409
retrieval (memory), 210, 211-16, 229, 230, 264

Review of Educational Research, 20-21, 23-27, 141-42
Review of Research in Education, 355-58
Richardson, Joan, 355
rigor, 12, 44, 88, 154, 188, 394, 411
Riquetti, Andrea, 137, 139
Robinson, Keith, 139-40
Roediger, Henry, 211-13, 220
Rogers, Todd, 146
Rohrer, Doug, 219
Rozovsky, Julia, 316-17, 345, 346
rubrics, 190, 192, 253-55, 256, 278, 364, 392
rubric, six-trait, 253-55, 256
rural schools, 6, 289, 338-40, 340-42
Russell Sage Foundation *Journal of the Social Sciences,* 139-40
Ryan, Richard, 61
Sams, Aaron, 287-89
Saphier, Jon, 277
SAT prep, 104
SAT, 14, 104, 109, 258, 319
Saunders, William, 317-19, 345, 349
say/see/do teaching, 184-87, 198, 199
scaffolding, 116, 178, 194, 219, 242, 243, 244, 289, 341
Schanfield, Mara, 71-73
scheduling, 71, 283, 338-40, 350-51, 390
Schmoker, Mike, 239, 278
School Administrator, 13-15
school norms, 301, 392
Schwartz, Kyle, 275
Sealy, Clare, 208-10
Seeley, Cathy, 182-84, 189, 200
segregation, 108, 111, 113

self-efficacy, 20-27, 33, 38, 40, 50, 56, 71, 90, 118, 279, 317, 405
self-management, 50, 56, 59, 68
semantic memory, 208-10, 229, 230
sense-making, 11
Shakespeare, 214, 226, 319
Shanahan, Timothy, 239
Shepherd, Michael, 89-90
Shields, David Light, 48-49, 78, 79
singleton teachers, 336, 338-40, 344, 350-51, 378
Slavin, Robert, 250-51
Small, Marian, 293-94
Smith, Abigail, 397-400
social class, 90, 140
social justice, 53, 98, 101, 115, 116
social-emotional development, 46-83
social-psychological interventions, 23, 24, 26
Socrates, 49
Soderstrom, Nicholas, 214
soft skills, 46, 50, 56-59, 78, 82, 260
Sousa, David, 276
South Korea, 151
Spandel, Vicki, 256-57, 270
Sparks, Sarah, 145-146
Spitzer, Herman, 214
SQ3R, 221
Steele, Claude, 15-16, 37, 109-11, 111-13, 126, 131, 132
stereotype threat, 25, 90, 109-13
Sternberg, Robert, 13-15, 37
Stickle, Laura, 67-69
stigma, 87, 109-11, 292
Stoelinga, Sara Ray, 391-92, 416

433

Stone, Elisa, 401-02
student-led parent conferences, 63, 151-53, 167
study skills, 8, 9, 23, 31, 217-22, 231-32
Sue, Derald Wing, 100
Sumpter, Lynette, 206-07
Sun, Kathy Liu, 10-12, 35, 36
Surowiecki, James, 361-62, 382
synchronous/asynchronous learning, 128, 339, 340, 363, 377, 378, 387
Talbot, Margaret, 137-39
Taveras, Angel, 137
Tavenner, Dianne, 282
Taylor, Kelli, 219
teacher leadership, 390-422
Teaching Children Mathematics, 10-12, 326-28
Teaching Gap, The, 373
Terantino, Joe, 298-90
Thomas B. Fordham Institute, 224-25
Thompson, Michael, 146-48
Tiger Woods, 31
times tables, 224, 224-25
TNTP, 358-60
Tomlinson, Carol Ann, 118-20, 276, 282-83, 304
Tough, Paul, 60-63
toxic stress, 60-63
transfer (of learning), 26, 208, 211, 262, 322
Treisman, Uri, 112
Trimble, Susan, 322-24, 329-31, 346, 350
Turnaround for Children, 82-83
tutoring, 5, 16, 37, 155, 161, 277, 279, 284, 320
Twenty-first-century skills, 56
Twitter, 101, 165, 226, 227, 275, 300-01, 339, 368, 379, 387, 403
Umphrey, Jan, 175-77
unconscious bias, 87-88, 89-90, 122, 123, 128
Unequal Childhoods, 138
union involvement, 403, 411, 413
Universal Design for Learning (UDL), 192-92
upside-down teaching, 182-83
upstanding, 121
Urban Education, 89-90
Usher, Ellen, 20-21, 33, 38
Vatterott, Cathy, 154, 294-95, 308
verbal ability, 31
virtual meetings, 338
voicemail, 376, 387
Walsh, Martin, 136
Walton, Gregory, 23-27
Washington, D.C., 62, 143, 145
Washington, Kermit, 361
Wasta, Michael, 333-35, 348, 350
Watson, Andrew, 206-07
West Point, 217-18
Westheimer, Joel, 52-54, 78, 81, 82
white privilege, 96-97, 121, 122-24, 129
Whitehurst, Grover "Russ", 56-59, 79, 80, 82
whole language, 241
Wiggins, Grant, 191-93, 201, 252
Wiliam, Dylan, 193-94, 201
Willingham, Daniel, 29-31, 38, 41, 63-66, 81, 83, 209, 220-22, 223-24, 277, 278
Wilson, Timothy, 25
Wirtz, Michael, 206-07
Wise, Mark, 179-80
Wolf, Maryanne, 140-41
Wolter, Deborah, 245-47, 269, 270
Wooden, John, 185
Woods, Eric, 195-96
working memory, 64, 206-07, 229, 230
world languages, 298-300, 306, 307
Worthen, Molly, 226-27
Wright, Tanya, 259-61
writing workshop, 254, 266
Xavier University, 112
Yaris, Kim, 244-45
Yeager, David, 23-27
Yoon, Hahna, 100-02, 130
Yoon, Nicola, 92-95
You/We/I teaching, 182-84, 199, 200
zero errors, 315
Zinsser, William, 248-50
zone of proximal development, 242, 269

About the Authors

Kim Marshall was a sixth-grade teacher, central office curriculum director, and elementary principal in the Boston Public Schools for thirty-two years. Since 2002, he has provided one-on-one coaching for principals and offered workshops, consulting, and courses with a special focus on teacher supervision and evaluation, time management, the effective use of student assessments, and curriculum unit design (in collaboration with Jay McTighe and Associates). Kim writes the weekly Marshall Memo and is the author of a number of articles and books, including *Rethinking Teacher Supervision and Evaluation* (Jossey-Bass, second edition, 2013). Kim is married and has two children, both teachers.

Jenn David-Lang has worked in the field of education for over twenty-five years. Currently, she runs THE MAIN IDEA (www.TheMainIdea.org)—a service that develops the professional knowledge of school leaders by connecting them to the latest and most compelling books in education and leadership. Jenn founded THE MAIN IDEA in 2007 because she witnessed that many school leaders who were busy with the day-to-day responsibilities of running their schools had no time for their own professional development.

When Jenn is not up to her ears in books, she facilitates Masterminds (online groups of educational leaders learning together) and offers a variety of consulting services, including: providing workshops for leaders and teachers, coaching teacher leaders, and conducting school evaluations. Prior to this, she received her administrative license and EdM from the Bank Street College of Education, served in a variety of administrative and consulting positions, founded and directed a nonprofit to support urban middle-school students, helped to start a number of New York City schools, served as an adjunct instructor in education, and taught both math and English at the middle- and high school levels.

Jenn's husband is a guidance counselor in the New York City schools, and they have two children—one attending a New York City public school, the other in college.

www.ingramcontent.com/pod-product-compliance
Lightning Source LLC
Chambersburg PA
CBHW080539230426
43663CB00015B/2638